Culture
and Society in
Italy
1290-1420

STUDIES IN CULTURAL HISTORY
SERIES EDITOR:
Professor J. R. Hale

Culture
and Society in
Italy
1290-1420

JOHN LARNER, 1930 –

Charles Scribner's Sons

NEW YORK

for
KIRSTY

A–3-71 (1)

Printed in Great Britain

Library of Congress Catalog Card Number 72–110680

SBN 684–12367–3

Contents

Acknowledgment

The author and publishers wish to thank the following for permission to reproduce illustrations appearing in this book: Aerofilms for plate 12; the Biblioteca Medici-Laurenziana for plate 24, the Bibliothèque nationale for plate 17; the Courtauld Institute of Art for plates 3–5, 9, 18; the Mansell Collection for plates 7–8, 10–11, 15, 19, 21–22; the Museo del Castello Sforzesco, Milan for plates 16 and 23; the Museo dell'Opera del Duomo, Florence for plate 14; the Museo di San Marco for plate 13; the National Gallery of Art, Washington D.C. (Samuel H. Kress Collection) for plate 1; the National Gallery, London for plate 6; and the Uffizi, Florence for plate 2.

Notes on Plates

Plates 1–6 show the development of naturalism in Tuscan art from the symbolic world of Margaritone (1) to the Florentine tradition of Giotto (2) and the Sienese of Simone Martini (3). These styles were modified under the influence of the Black Death (4) and were replaced at the beginning of the fifteenth century by International Gothic (5) and Florentine realism (6)

The next plates illustrate the influence of the commune upon art. For the increasing secularisation of art in the service of the commune, compare the religious motif of Simone Martini's *Maestà* (3) with the combination of neo-Aristotelian allegory and naturalism in Lorenzetti (7–8), and the civic-humanist theme of Taddeo di Bartolo (9). See pages 81–5, 112, 248–9.

Plates 10–18 illustrate other aspects of government patronage: the building of town halls, churches, and cathedrals, town-planning (13), and the symbolic glorification of *signoria* (15–17). Plates 16 and 18 in particular reveal the impulse which governments gave to naturalism through their wish for the representation of specific individuals and historical events.

facing page

Introduction

It was Ambrogio Lorenzetti in his frescoes of *The Rule of Justice and the Common Good*, executed in the Palace of Siena in the late 1330s, who first clearly referred to the relation between culture and society. In this composition the painter showed, amidst the life of his city, the master teaching his students, young girls dancing to music, and citizens going about their work or taking their leisure without fear. In the medallions below appeared symbols of 'the seven liberal studies,' of Philosophy, and of Mercury, the benign planet which rules the arts and sciences. The allegorical meaning of the painting is that the civilisation of the city was dependent upon a particular society and its just and ordered government.

It is this theme which forms the subject of this book: the interaction of literature, art, and their social environment within Italy in the years between 1290 and 1420. The historian cannot explain the creative spirit. Art is produced by individuals, and individuals whose talent is inexplicable. Again, it comes into being through the traditions of style in which or against which the artist is working. But there are certain points in the production of art that a social history can illuminate: the status and education of writers and artists, the character of the patronage offered them, the ways in which society regarded their work, the economic, political, and intellectual pressures upon them. Such a history can help towards a truer understanding of art and literature. It is more difficult than is generally

realised to recapture the authentic flavour of a past culture. It is not
easy to see a painting of the fourteenth century outside the gallery
in which it has been arbitrarily placed, free from the restorations it
has undergone, and free from previous inadequate experience of it
gained from mass reproductions. Our very method of approach
tends to distort its meaning, for we come to it, not as a cult object
designed to excite sacred dread, but as if it were a Renoir or a
Jackson Pollock, to be judged from mainly aesthetic standpoints.
It is equally difficult to see a building of the fourteenth century as it
was in the fourteenth century, when it no longer stands in the context
of other buildings which once surrounded it; and when we enter it,
not as a citizen, proudly coming to the visible symbol of our city,
but as a tourist, fumbling for an entrance-fee at the door. These
works demand of us a knowledge and an imaginative force which,
however strong, can never wholly and satisfactorily recreate the
reality of what existed when they were first made.

It is often as difficult, reading the printed text of a tongue which
must inevitably seem archaic, to appreciate the authentic contemporary emotional force of what was either orally recited or deci-
phered at leisure from the Gothic lettering of a manuscript. Moreover
in both literature and art, our vision of a past work is so much
conditioned by what has come after it. Having read, say (the
example is T. S. Eliot's) Tennyson's *Ulysses*, we can never think of
Dante's again in quite the same way. In these circumstances a
knowledge of the function of art in the society in which it was
produced, a knowledge of the background and conditions in which
it appeared, can help towards the appreciation of the work of art as
it came fresh from its creator; can help us to see it in perspective; as
it really was and is.

There is a very large bibliography indeed for the history, literature,
and art of this period, much larger certainly than any one person
could hope to master. Many aspects of its study are the objects of
acute controversy between scholars and no one, attempting to
bring together these three disciplines, can hope to escape error.
However I would like to thank David Chambers of the Warburg
Institute, Robert Gibbs of the Department of Fine Art at Glasgow

University and John Hale, the general editor of this series, who read the typescript and saved me from many inaccuracies. I would particularly like to express my gratitude to Catherine Ross, who made innumerable suggestions for improvements, and to Phyllis Carr, whose advice on the presentation of my material has been a constant inspiration. I must also thank Mary Brodie who uncomplainingly typed a difficult manuscript, and the Editor of *History* for permission to republish in chapter eleven the substance of an article which first appeared in that periodical.

A Preliminary Note upon Money

At the beginning of the fifteenth century the annual cost of living for a single man in Florence was calculated at 14 gold florins a year. For an unskilled day-labourer a good annual return upon his work might have been the equivalent of 14 florins a year in the first half of the fourteenth century and of 30 florins in the second half. A skilled artisan might expect to earn double these amounts in both periods. In a bank at the end of the fourteenth and beginning of the fifteenth century the office boy might receive 15 florins a year; a branch manager, 100 florins. There was also the possibility of rapid promotion for brilliant men. A clerk receiving 48 florins in 1401, was given 65 florins in 1403, and 100 florins in 1406. In 1407 he became a partner of the bank and his salary was raised to 200 florins. But in such a career business and family connections played an important part. Lawyers, the most prosperous of professional men, might earn from 300 florins at the beginning of their careers to 600 at the end. This was a very high salary indeed. For comparison it can be borne in mind that the average yearly profit of the Florentine branch of the Medici bank between 1397 and 1420 was about 1,100 florins.[1]

There were many systems of coinage in use in Italy apart from that of the Florentine gold florin. In Florence, Siena, and many other towns, there were silver currencies, calculated in pounds, shillings,

and pence, and it was in these coins that small payments, such as
for local purchases and for wages, were normally made. These silver
currencies were being continually devalued in relation to the gold
florin. At Florence, for instance, the florin which had been worth
20 shillings in 1252, was valued at 80 shillings by 1422. Wherever
possible, in citing sums in these other currencies, I append in brackets
their current approximate value in terms of the Florentine gold
florin.

Unless otherwise stated, pounds, shillings, and pence, mentioned
in this work, are normally in the silver money of Florence
(*florentini parvi*).

PART ONE

The Age of Dante and Giotto
(c. 1290–c. 1340)

one

Cultural Change
1290—1340

The age of the maturity of Dante and Giotto (*c.* 1290–
c. 1340) stands out as one of the greatest eras in the history of
Italian culture. The story of literature and the arts in that time is the
more remarkable in that previously the principal traditions of
Italy's civilisation had been found elsewhere. Italians had been
famous for their trade and for their legal and medical studies; but
despite the so-called Tuscan Proto-Renaissance of the twelfth
century and despite the cultivation of the Sicilian court of the early
thirteenth century, Italy had conceded cultural pre-eminence to
others. In music, poetry, and the arts, in classical studies, philosophy,
and theology, Germany and France were her masters. In the twelfth
century Chrétien de Troyes could boast with justice that from
Greece and Rome the highest learning had passed to his own country:
'God grant that it may be maintained here, and that it may be
cherished so that the honour which has come with it may never part
from France; God has bestowed it as another's share, but of Greeks
or Romans no more at all is heard, their fame has passed, and their
living flame extinguished.' Now, suddenly, or so it seemed, this
northern predominance was challenged.

In the arts the first signs of resurgence appear in architecture. It
was in these years that the four great cathedrals of central Italy were
begun: Siena, Arezzo, Orvieto, and Florence. Every town saw the
construction of new churches for the friars; and private and public
palaces acquired a scale of magnificence hitherto unknown. These

buildings, important in their own right, also provided the in-dispensable settings for painting and sculpture, which at this period were much more closely linked to architecture than they are today. The rise of fresco painting in the early fourteenth century, for instance, was in large measure a result of the extraordinary number of churches being built. In Tuscany very few altar-pieces are re-corded before 1300 and there is no record at all of any comprehensive fresco sequences. Their emergence at this time was the result of the new pressure of demand for church decoration. When so many churches were being put up, the old mosaic works were considered too expensive and too slow in the making, and frescoes increasingly took their place.

At the same time a profound change came about in the character of art. The hieratic Romanesque and Italo-Byzantine schools, dedicated to the symbolic expression of a divine truth, were slowly being supplanted by artists who sought a new naturalism and the telling of a human story. In the first place this development can be related to the influence of northern Gothic art. In the sculpture of the twelfth and early thirteenth century at Halberstadt, Freiburg, Amiens, Chartres, and Rheims, can be seen plastic and three-dimensional expression; movement from the abstract and general to the concrete and particular; interest in man; and humanisation of religion. All these appear now, some 50 to 100 years later, in Italian art. Undoubtedly much of this new art was a response to northern work, studied either on visits to France and Germany or through manuscript illuminations and sketchbooks brought to Italy. Gothic influence did not stand alone, however, but combined with what was in many ways a similar stylistic current from the south. In southern Italy, during the first half of the thirteenth century, Frederick II, 'wonder of the world and wondrous innovator' had united in his person the kingship of Sicily and Naples and the dignity of Roman Emperor. Artists at his court had flattered the imperial dreams of their master by the re-evocation of the classical ideals of the early Roman imperial world. Frederick's gold coin-medals, the *Augustales*, had been so called from the representation of the head of Augustus upon them, and the statuary for his Capuan gate had been a conscious attempt to inspire an imperial renaissance. This too stimulated the new art.

From this time artists within Italy began to seek inspiration in the reliques of the classical world which were still found in profusion in its towns. First of these was Nicola Pisano, who had passed his early life in the southern kingdom, and in whose work classical influences were particularly strong. For instance, in sculpting the Adoration of the Magi in his pulpit for the Pisan Baptistery, he drew upon the motifs of a second century Roman sarcophagus decorated with the story of Phaedra and Hippolytus. From sources such as these, Nicola, with his son Giovanni, and his pupil Arnolfo di Cambio, brought to sculpture a new weight and dignity of representation, especially in the portrayal of the human figure. Soon these developments were adapted to other media. With a series of mosaics executed at Rome in or shortly before the 1290s, Pietro Cavallini and Jacopo Torriti introduced a new plasticity into two-dimensional representation. Here the influence of the Pisani was reinforced by the inspiration of the art of early Christianity, the works of the fourth and fifth centuries which Cavallini had studied in the churches of the Lateran and Santa Costanza.

From Rome the style passed a few years later to Assisi. In the upper church of San Francesco, where Cimabue and Torriti worked in fresco, the manner attained a real maturity in the *Legend of St Francis Cycle*. In this work life-sized, volumetric human figures, expressing human emotions, made their first appearance in European painting. Painting took on the plastic qualities of sculpture. The artist here was a man of extraordinary originality, and despite the battles of connoisseurs, it is still tempting to identify him with Giotto. Whether this be so or not, it is Giotto di Bondone who henceforth dominated the art of central Italy. His hold upon 'tactile values', his sense, that is, of a third dimension, his feeling for movement and life, and what Berenson has called 'his dominion over the significant', gave him a preeminent place in the art of the age and in the history of art. In the frescoes of the Scrovegni chapel at Padua and in Santa Croce at Florence, Giotto evoked a whole new range of feeling and expression. It was with justice that by the end of the fourteenth century he should have been acknowledged everywhere as the key figure in the establishment of the new art.

His immediate followers at Florence, Bernardo Daddi, Taddeo Gaddi, and Maso di Banco, for all their narrative invention and human intimacy, were dwarfed by his genius. But at Siena the school of Duccio di Buoninsegna developed its own more lyrical and illustrative style, with jewel-like colouring and linear grace. If Giotto had given painted figures humanity, Duccio established them in recognisable settings, Simoni Martini invested them with poetry, while Ambrogio Lorenzetti set them in their complete physical environment. It was at this time that Florence and Siena produced the first tentative beginnings of portraiture and of landscape in painting. Contemporaneously, outside Tuscany, one finds the beginnings of the Riminese school, the tradition of manuscript illumination at Bologna, and the first modifications of Byzantine influence at Venice with the work of Paolo Veneziano.

Before Giotto, painters had drawn inspiration from sculpture. In Giotto's own generation sculptors were to seek their models in painting. Andrea Pisano executed reliefs for the Campanile of Florence, imbued with the Giottesque sense of the human and three-dimensional, while the Pisan, Giovanni di Balduccio, took the same manner to Milan. Tino di Camaino, after working in Tuscany, passed to Naples, where his tomb-monuments for the Angevin court were clearly influenced by the linear Gothic of Simone Martini. So too was the school of Siennese goldsmiths, which first made its appearance with Guccio di Mannaia. Works in precious metals are more vulnerable to time than those in stone or paint, but from what survives it is easy to understand their Italian and European reputation.

The development of literature in this period parallels to a certain degree the changes in art. Just as before the second half of the thirteenth century Italy had enjoyed no strong native tradition in painting and sculpture, so in literature she had not even formed from the wide variety of her dialects an Italian literary language. In a sense this situation was to endure throughout our period; an Italian prose language was to be the creation of the nineteenth century. Yet what is significant here is that until the 1290s no Italian vernacular dialect was yet considered the equal of non-Italian tongues for literary expression. It is true that at the courts of the Hohenstaufen in southern Italy poets of the 'Sicilian school' had written in their native language, and were followed in this by writers in mid-century Tuscany and in Bologna. But in many places, and in almost all of northern Italy, Italian dialects were still fighting for equal consideration as literary languages with Provençal and northern French. In the feudal courts of the age and at Genoa and Venice, the language of lyric poetry was not Italian but Provençal, and the most powerful Italian poets of the thirteenth century were men who wrote in that language: Ugo di San Circ of Treviso; Bartolomeo Zorzi of Venice; and Sordello of Mantua. Other writers looked to French, or rather to that Franco-Italian hybrid which was accepted as the current literary speech of Lombardy. In this tongue men related anew the epics of the *matière de Bretagne*, the legends around the Tristan story; and the *matière de France*, the tales of Charlemagne. This Franco-Italian was strongly entrenched too as the language of prose. As late as the last years of the century Rustichello da Pisa had employed it to take down the narrative of Marco Polo in the prisons of Genoa. Brunetto Latini delivered his *Livre dou trésor* in that language, he explained, and his words were echoed by many other Italians of the age: *por ce que la parlure est plus délitable et plus commune à toutes gens.*

All this changed with the fourteenth century. The spirit of the new age is expressed by Brunetto's pupil, Dante, who complained of 'those wicked men in Italy who praise the common speech of other nations and despise their own'. Everywhere, in verse if not in prose, the Tuscan dialect came to be accepted as the common literary language of the whole peninsula. The various improbable attempts at sociological explanation of this phenomenon may be set aside. The true causes are first, as Dante argued in the *De vulgari eloquentia*, that it was the best adapted to poetry, and second, that it was Tuscan poets who first made major contributions to Italian vernacular writing. At the same time the use of the vernacular tongue grew in prose. Here again Tuscan was predominant in the quality and quantity of work produced, though it was still only rarely that non-Tuscans wrote in Tuscan for prose as they did for verse. This development did not inhibit the study of Latin, and this era saw the first beginnings of Italian humanism at Padua, Bologna, and Florence: that study of language combined with the passion for antiquity which was to colour all Italian culture in the following generation.

While the turn of the thirteenth and fourteenth centuries saw the first triumphant affirmation of Tuscan and the other Italian dialects as literary languages, so too did it produce a literature of an hitherto unknown richness and variety and a wholly new sense of reality and individuality. Here again French influence was a strong formative force. The worldly lyric refinement of the *langue d'oc* and the naturalistic and vigorous courtly epics and *fabliaux* of the *langue d' oeil* were absorbed slowly, first at the court of Frederick II, and then in the more down to earth world of central Italy, until they had coalesced with a native tradition of formal rhetorical study to produce the first Tuscan poetry. In the works of Lapo Gianni, Cino da Pistoia, Guido Cavalcanti, and their followers, the Florentine *dolce stil nuovo* attained a previously unexplored refinement and psychological insight. In a more robust tradition the realists displayed a powerful directness and raciness of speech, which culminated in Cecco Angiolieri's Oedipal, half-enraged half-humorous sonnets against his father and against life. Midway between these two schools came the worldly romanticism of Folgore di San Gimignano and the burning religious passion of Fra Jacopone of Todi. Above all, spanning these traditions and yet alone in his genius was the 'well-nigh incomprehensible miracle' of Dante Alighieri, the poet of the medieval world.

In both literature and art the styles which emerged at the end of the thirteenth century had a long prehistory which, taken with the individual genius of those who worked in them, can do much to explain, in so far as it can be explained, the character of its leading works. Yet the new enthusiasm for culture, and even, in some respects, the forms that culture took, can be related in a general sense to conditions in society. Why should Italy, a country which had been, comparatively speaking, inferior in the arts, now come to be their principal homeland? Is there anything outside purely stylistic influences which can explain the decline of symbolism and the rise of more naturalistic forms? Any answers to these questions are likely to be partial, oblique, and tentative. But in the hope of discovering them, we shall consider the land, economy, and society in which Giotto, Dante, and their contemporaries lived and worked; the religious and intellectual ideas of their age; and finally, government protection and patronage of the arts.

two

Italy, 1290–1340

Italy in 1300

Trecento Italy was not a political unit but a cultural idea. To the greatest of all Italians, Italy was not a nation but a province of the Roman Empire. Though Dante felt himself in many ways to be an Italian, this emotion was always subordinate, first, to his belief in the need for a world empire, and then to his passionate feeling for his own city-state. Among his contemporaries there was often a deep dislike and even hatred of the foreigner, but there was no sense of nationalism, no common loyalty to the ideals which were slowly helping to create the nation-states of France and England. With the final failure of the Hohenstaufen Emperors in the thirteenth century, Italy had become no more than as assemblage of different and independent cities, lordships, towns, and even villages. Until the nineteenth century there was, properly speaking, no Italian history, but only the history of the various separate communities within the country which today we call Italy.

This triumph of regionalism, the affirmation of local over national patriotism, was emphasized by sharp internal diversities in geography and economic life. To speak of Italy in this period is to evoke a peninsula with a population of between perhaps seven and nine million people, living not only under varying forms of government, but in radically different types of society. There was no Italian language, merely a 'thousand' (the figure is Dante's) different Italian dialects, often so distinct as to be mutually unintelligible. By the end of the fourteenth century this complexity had been partly

simplified. Some of the larger states had swallowed up their neighbours, and men were beginning to visualise the possibility of an
Italian kingdom. But despite these changes, Italy was far from being
a unity.

In the south were the two kingdoms. The kingdom of Sicily, with
its unique blend of Arab, Greek, and Latin strains, had in the past
produced the mosaics of Monreale, the history and translations of
Hugo Falcandus, and the intellectual circle around Frederick II. But
it played a minor role in Italian life and culture. In part this was due
to the perpetual hostility of her northern neighbour, with whom she
was engaged in almost continuous war for a period of more than
fifty years. In part too, it was because she was drawn into the commercial and political interests of her Aragonese rulers. In any event,
until the conquest of Naples by Alfonso v in the second decade of the
fifteenth century, Sicily was to lie upon the periphery of Italian
civilisation.

In the kingdom of Naples, however, some elements of the old
southern culture continued to interact with that of Northern Italy.
In parts of Calabria a curious form of Greek was spoken, as it still is
today, the inheritance, perhaps, of the age of Byzantine control.
Greek memories were strong both here and amidst the ruins of
Paestum, while for centuries Latin civilisation has been preserved in
the monastery of Cassino, dominating the inland road to the north.
In the fourteenth century Naples, compared with the rest of Italy,
was more prosperous than it is today. Though much of the land
suffered from soil erosion and from the sudden intense onset of
summer heat which still devastates its harvests, certain areas such as
Sulmona and Campania, the *felix Campania* of the ancients, were
extremely fertile. In the Capitanata, too, huge flocks of sheep
pastured in winter, and in summer passed along ancient drove roads
into the Abruzzi, to bring rich transit revenues to the crown. In her
ports, Amalfi, Salerno, and Naples itself (with a population of
perhaps 30,000), the merchants of Tuscany, particularly the
Florentines, carried on a prosperous trade. Politically, power was
shared between the king and the upper nobility, the owners of the
great estates or *latifundia*. Under the rule of King Robert I (1309–43)

the system held together. There was an administration of considerable sophistication, a financial machine which gave the king the reputation of being 'monstrously rich', and a foreign policy which extended his influence through north and central Italy. Moreover, with Naples the king had inherited the county of Provence, and his court was the centre of a fruitful interchange of ideas between southern France and the Italian world. With Robert's death, however, there followed the accession of a woman, and the apparent prosperity of the kingdom was broken. With the end of political tranquillity, much of the cultural activity of Naples came to an end.

To the north, the kingdom of Naples bordered on the Papal State, which lay across the middle of central Italy and extended up to Bologna, in the Emilian plain. Here the Popes, despite the resources of a highly developed administrative system, had singularly failed to bring any sense of unity, and the territory was divided up between virtually independent communities and feudatories. The whole area, from the harsh tufa and travertine of Latium to the rich garden-lands of the Romagna, had an overwhelmingly agrarian economy. Even the more important towns and communes, such as Orvieto, Perugia, and Spoleto, acted mainly as market centres for the country-side around. Within the state only two other cities stand out: Bologna, with an estimated population of over 50,000, the seat of a great European university, and Rome, 'head of the world', but soon to be abandoned by the Popes, and to be left semi-deserted, a vast museum of classical ruin.

To turn to Tuscany is to enter another world. In this land of low undulating hills stood the principal centres of Italian civilisation. Within their streets of fortress-towers and wooden houses lived the merchants and bankers whose trade encompassed the known world. To these cities the men of the countryside came to make their fortunes or to swell the numbers of the proletariat. Here, giving or withholding at pleasure a purely nominal allegiance to the emperor across the Alps, flourished the world of the independent republics.

In the heart of the province, on an outcrop of the Chianti hills, stood Siena. In the twelfth and thirteenth centuries the importance of this city had been owed principally to her bankers; by this period, however, Siena had begun to decline in some measure from her former eminence. In the war between the Papacy and the Hohenstaufen, Sienese merchants had supported the losing side and allowed the capitalists of Florence to take over their position as agents of the Holy See. The failure of the *Grande Tavola*, the company of the Buonsignori family, in 1298, was a symbol and warning of the danger to which the city was exposed by ever-increasing Florentine competition. Yet this decline was relative only. Siena still possessed great riches, and a wealthy and leisured class who could enjoy the fruits of civilisation. Under 'The Nine Governors and Defenders of the Commune and People of Siena' the city was ruled prosperously between the years 1287 and 1355 by an oligarchy in which both nobles and merchants played a prominent part.

From Siena the old via Francigena ran through San Gimignano, town of the towers, to Pisa at the mouth of the Arno. The great cathedral and the baptistery already stood here, testifying to the former wealth of the city. The campanile, though as yet unfinished, had already begun to lean from the vertical. But the days of Pisa's greatness had passed. She had withdrawn from the Levant trade, and her commerce with Africa was in decline. The fleet had been annihilated by Genoese rivals in the sea-battle of Meloria in August 1284. With a population of perhaps 38,000 in 1293 some industries were maintained and trade was still carried on with France and Catalonia. Yet in the fourteenth century there was a hard struggle to keep up even this diminished role. In internal politics, Pisa was ruled by a bourgeois-aristocratic oligarchy, which succumbed later to a succession of single rulers or 'tyrants'. Lucca, too, was undergoing a similar political decline, though economically still powerful in the early years of the century. At the centre of silk production in Europe, her bankers were found in prominent positions at the courts of the French and English kings.

To the south-east stood Florence, city of the golden florin. At this period she had a population approaching 95,000, and her third circle of walls were under construction. The Bargello, the Baptistery, and the four bridges spanning the Arno had already been built. The government of Florence was dominated by a group of oligarchs composed of merchants and aristocrats, and led by those men from the plutocratic bourgeoisie who controlled the twelve more prominent guilds. Despite the narrowness of this oligarchy it represented fairly broad interests. Both the *magnates*, the wealthy and powerful who for one reason or another had been excluded from formal participation in decision making, and the lesser bourgeoisie, were linked by common interest to the oligarchy. The *magnates* were often their business partners. The tradesmen and artisans of the city, though hampered by a fiscal system aligned against them in the class interests of their rulers, frequently invested small loans in the companies of the plutocracy, and so had a stake in the prosperity of the government. All these classes were, moreover, drawn together in their mutual fear of the lower orders, upon whose exploitation, whether as workmen in the city, or as peasants leasing land, their prosperity depended. As long as the economic strength of the city continued, this government could be confident of survival. And for the moment Florence, with her cloth industry and, much more important than this, her bankers, was the leading commercial centre of Europe. Florentine merchants found their way into every part of the known world, so that, in the words of Boniface VIII, along with earth, fire, air, and water, they constituted 'the fifth element' in the universe.

From Tuscany, passing north, one comes to the long strip of the Ligurian coast. Here Genoa, with a population in 1300 of nearly 100,000, had risen to be one of the leading ports of Europe. Her merchants traded with Africa and the Levant, Constantinople, and the Crimea; and her trade was still expanding. The value of goods passing through the port had doubled between 1214 and 1274, and more than quadrupled between 1274 and 1293. At the end of the thirteenth century she had triumphed over Pisa, her ancient rival, though still faced in the Levant by the competition of Venice. In the fourteenth century Genoa was to expend her energies externally against the great Adriatic port, while internally she was torn by continual faction conflicts among the merchant nobility who formed her government. As a result she was to fall prey to other powers: first to Milan (1353–6), and then, after a period of independence, to

France (1396). Yet the city was still a great centre of Mediterranean trade. She had not, however—and the fact must warn us against making any superficial equations of economic and cultural development—produced any substantial literature or art as a testimony to her achievements.

Through the Giovi pass were the towns of Piedmont, which by 1300 had largely fallen under the control of local feudatories such as the Count of Savoy. To the east the long Lombard plain was gradually coming under the dominance of Milan. With a population of roughly 100,000, Milan's principal economic importance was as a market centre. Its four annual fairs attracted merchants from all over Italy and the north European world, and their needs were catered for by the great Milanese banking houses. Here too industry flourished: cloth-making, skin and leather production, metal-working and arms manufacture. In the countryside large-scale irrigation works produced rich crops of corn and fruit, while on her farms were bred the *destriers* or heavy war-horses admired throughout Europe. Milan had already largely abandoned that communal government under which she had attained her greatest renown in previous centuries. From 1311 the city fell under the control of the Visconti family, who from then on ruled virtually without internal opposition. Until 1340 they pursued, with alternate success and failure, an expansionist policy aimed at subduing the surrounding communes.

In eastern Lombardy and the Veneto the communes had been able to avoid absorption, but like Milan itself had fallen, or were falling, to the rule of tyrants. In Padua, an important cultural centre, with a population of about 35,000 people, the Carrara family were to seize sole power, and in Verona the della Scala. Venice alone retained a communal or republican form of government. This *miraculosissima civitas Venetia*, with its 100,000 inhabitants, derived its unique character not only from its situation, but also from its contacts with the non-Italian world. It was an eastern town in a strange western setting: the basilica of St Mark, built in the form of a Greek cross, and surmounted by five domes, recalled the world of Constantinople and Alexandria, and was enriched with the spoils of

Byzantium and Islam. In spring and late summer the galleys set out every year for the East, and during the fourteenth century new regular routes were opened to Provence, the Barbary coast, England, and Flanders. Here was the state *Arsenal*, flourishing as a centre of ship-building, and the *Fondaco dei Tedeschi*, the great warehouse of German merchants, marking the importance of the city in the trade of northern Europe. Overseas, Venice had created her own colonial empire, and Venetian communities controlled many of the islands of the Aegean and ports of the Peloponnese. At home she had succeeded, where all other of the great Italian commercial centres had failed, in establishing a really stable constitution. In all other cities, there was conflict between those possessing and those excluded from power. Here in Venice the old merchant-nobility had managed to maintain control. In 1297 the membership of the Great Council was restricted to those 150 to 200 families who already had seats within it. This sovereign body elected for life the Doge, and rigorously controlled his every activity. With this government Venice possessed a sense of unity denied to any other state. The very weakness of her island isolation helped to give the city her greatest strength, a deep sense of cohesion among her citizens which, despite some severe crises, survived throughout the century.

War and Peace

Fortunately it is not necessary to linger on the complex story of inter-communal politics of the age. From the point of view of cultural development, however, it is significant that the years 1290 to 1340 saw the last failure of the German emperors across the Alps to impose their authority on the peninsula. In 1310 the admired and chivalrous Emperor Henry VII marched into Italy in an attempt to restore imperial authority, and bring peace to a divided land. Yet after three years of fruitless war he died at Buonconvento, his cause in ruins. The sole monuments to his struggle were to be in the arts: the great tribute paid to his spirit in the thirtieth canto of the *Paradiso*; and the tomb, erected at Pisa by Tino di Camaino, with its recumbent figure of the youthful emperor, whose lined, tight-lipped face and intense eyes speak of his tragic fate. He had no imitators.

Though Lewis IV crossed the Brenner and marched on Rome in 1327, his expedition was on a smaller scale and had more limited objectives. Later his successor, Charles IV was to visit the peninsula on two occasions. But he, again, came with none of the idealistic aims of Henry VII. More prudently, he sought only to replenish his finances by the sale of high sounding titles and honorary grants. During the fourteenth century Italy was to be free of all imperial control and of any central authority which might have imposed unity and peace. This freedom brought conflict between states and faction within them, the triumph of political anarchy, endless crises and *coups d'état*. There is a paradox here. The function of man, wrote Dante (*De Monarchia*, 1,4), was 'to exercise always his full capacity for intellectual growth', and to achieve this, peace was essential: 'so it was that to the shepherds there rang out from on high the news, not of riches, nor pleasure, nor honours, nor long life, nor health, nor strength, nor beauty, but peace. For the heavenly host proclaimed: "glory to God in the highest, and on earth peace to men of goodwill."' Yet it was precisely in this age of incessant war that Italian culture reached its apogee.

Too much can be made of the ill effects of war upon culture. Dante's own epic, for example, was born of profound meditation upon, and participation in, the conflicts of his own time. On the other hand, war can be so destructive that all cultural life must cease. Fortunately conflict in Italy did not have this character in our period. The use of mercenary soldiers freed the majority of citizens from the burden of militia service and did something to mitigate the savageries of war. Again, a measure of political stability was introduced with the consolidation of the *signorie*: despotisms or single-person governments. In Lombardy, Piedmont, and the communes within the Papal State, the *signori* or tyrants brought a new strength to internal administration and a limit to faction conflict. Only in Venice, Siena, and Florence did the republican commune survive, as only these cities had the confidence to reject this remedy which all others had been compelled to adopt.

The failure of any unitary principle within Italy during the Middle

Ages meant a complex of political confusions and retarded the development of an Italian state until the nineteenth century. On the other hand it brought a proliferation of mutually independent courts and cities, of princely and bourgeois patrons, of variegated themes from different societies at different stages of development, which was to produce the extraordinary richness and variety of Italian civilisation in the fourteenth century.

The Economy

In 1300 the Italians were the principal heirs of a revolution, which, beginning in the eleventh, and reaching its peak in the second half of the thirteenth century, had given to the whole of Europe a new prosperity, and to Italy the supremacy of the medieval world. In later ages she might possess greater wealth or enjoy a higher standard of living, but never again was her economy to expand so fast nor to be so powerful, relative to the rest of Europe, as in those two hundred years. From 1290 to 1340 a comparatively slight recession appears to have set in: competition between states and commercial companies had grown sharper, bankruptcies were more common, plagues and famines more frequent. This was an ominous portent of the full economic crisis which was to hit Italy in the 1340s, but as yet it had only marginal effects upon a country still enjoying a wide prosperity. Contemporaries all agreed that they lived in an age of affluence. They contrasted the rough fare and hard living of the early thirteenth century with their own prosperity, and, according to temperament, either mocked at those who praised 'old times' or, like Dante, lamented that an era of morally bracing, primitive simplicity had passed.[1]

This prosperity rested in the first place upon the Italian cities' empire of international commerce. At north African ports Genoese merchants exchanged European manufactures for gold, carried by camel caravans from the kingdom of Ghana. From Constantinople Genoese and Venetians tapped the end of the Asian caravan routes. In the Black Sea they did business with the Empire of Trebizond on the southern shore, and the Empire of the Mongols to the north. From the Crimean port of Caffa Italians penetrated east to Astrakhan, and from Sinope and Trebizond south along the caravan routes to Persia. At the turn of the thirteenth century, Genoese ships, built in their own colonies, were sailing in the land-locked Caspian and in the Persian Gulf.

The principal goods which the Italians imported from the Levant, and which they then re-exported to the north-European world, were described by contemporaries with the generic term 'spices', a word applied not only to seasoning, but to dyes, medicines, textiles, and all luxury objects. In the East Italians also carried on an extensive passenger trade, impartially taking Christian pilgrims bound for Jerusalem, and Moslems en route for Mecca. From Caffa, and from Tana at the mouth of the Don, they continued that profitable slave trade throughout both the Christian and Mohammedan worlds in which they had been engaged for some two centuries past. It is a curious reflection that the beauty of Venice is owed in no small measure to a vast marketing of human flesh. Westward again, Italian merchants traded in France, in Catalonia, and in Moslem Spain. From 1277 the Genoese, and from 1314 the Venetians, began to sail through the straits of Gibraltar, north to the ports of France, England and Flanders, where such products as Flemish cloth and English wool were exchanged for Chinese silks and Indian peppers.

In addition to this long-distance maritime trade there was also a large amount of local trade in smaller ships between the various ports along the Italian coast. Moreover the merchants of the inland cities joined with those of Pisa, Genoa, and Venice, in the expansion of commerce overland into northern Europe. At the fairs of Champagne up to the 1320s, traders still gathered from all over Italy, and above all from Florence and Siena. Only in Germany were they less successful. German-Italian trade was largely in the hands of German merchants, who brought their metal, timber, and linen through the Brenner and St Gothard passes, and received in return those goods which the Italians had imported from the east.

At the same time the Italian towns began to develop their own industries. The principal merchandise of Italian international commerce was cloth. Until the fourteenth century Italian industry had largely concentrated upon the 'finishing' of cloths imported from the northern world. Generally the soft fabrics of the north were re-sheared and dyed, in order to produce a luxury textile. In these processes the towns of Genoa, Lucca, and Florence attained an early supremacy. In Florence the trade was the monopoly of the capitalist companies organised in the *Arte di Calimala*, a guild which took its name from the narrow street called the Calimala in which they had their shops and warehouses. From this little lane they dominated a commercial empire which extended all over Europe. They bought the northern cloths in England, Flanders, or the fairs of Champagne, and despatched them from there on the long journey to Florence. Here they were processed by dependent craftsmen with dyes and alum that guild-members had purchased in the east. Then the completed and high-grade fabrics were re-exported to ports as distant as Tunis or Caffa.

In addition to this finishing work, the Italian towns had also developed an important industry based on raw wool and the spinning and weaving of primary unfinished cloth. This was presided over by the *Arte della Lana*, or wool guild. At the end of the thirteenth century Flanders, which had been the principal producer of cloth, was disturbed by workers' revolts. To compensate for declining Flemish supplies, Italian wool production increased until it began to rival, and in some places to overtake, the finishing industry in importance. In Lombardy, the Veneto, and Tuscany almost all the larger towns manufactured cloth in considerable quantity by the beginning of the fourteenth century. This industry in its turn gave rise to considerable commerce. Italian wool was generally of poor quality, and so the sheep of North Africa, England, and Scotland were shorn for the raw material to be worked in Italy. However, the merchants of the *Lana*, unlike their colleagues of the *Calimala*, did not themselves engage in this trade. Import of wool and export of cloth they left to those who specialised in such matters. Consequently, the basic cloth manufacturers never attained such importance in the economy as the cloth finishers, who took a full part in the business of foreign markets. None the less, the industry of the *Lana* still played a considerable part in domestic prosperity.

Other industries flourished: Lucca produced silk, Pisa iron-ware, Milan arms. But industry was far surpassed in economic importance by banking and finance. By 1300 Italian financiers dominated the money market from London to Alexandria and Constantinople. In this it was particularly inland towns which took the lead. By the mid-fourteenth century Italian banks were established in all the principal centres of European trade, in Bruges, in Paris (which had 20 houses in 1292), and in London, which had 14 (and a Lombard Street) by 1283. These already carried on most of the operations of modern banking: money-changing between different currencies; the taking of money in deposit; payments by book transfer rather than in specie; the advancing of credit in return for interest payments; and permission to overdraw accounts. A prototype bill of exchange was in existence, and, though not yet in general use, double-entry book-keeping had made its appearance. There was a system of maritime insurance, too; stories like the 'Merchant of Venice', the ruin of a rich man through shipwreck, could now be relegated to the realm of the fairy-tale. Already banking had attained a high level of technical efficiency: detailed accounts were kept, and foreign branches maintained a frequent and regular correspondence with their central offices in Italy. As a result of these services, the more prominent Italian merchants ceased gradually to be wanderers or 'venturers'; henceforth they tended more and more to stick to their central counting houses, and conduct their business by letters to their local factors.

The great banking houses at the end of the thirteenth century were formed by partnerships, whose members were often drawn from the founder's own family. Some of these companies accumulated very large capital, and exercised an extraordinary dominance over the European economy. In 1310, for instance, the Peruzzi of Florence boasted a capital of £149,000 *affiorini*, a sum which in contemporary terms suggests a comparison with the Rothschilds. By 1355, partners in the firm controlled business offices in Florence, Avignon, Bruges, London, Naples, and Palermo, while a staff of 83 factors presided over local banks in every other major economic centre. Yet the Peruzzi were probably second to the Bardi company in the Florentine banking world, and were followed closely by the Acciaiuoli (with 53 factors throughout Europe in 1341). These bankers played a decisive role in the politics of the age. It was the Riccardi of Lucca who financed Edward I of England for the conquest of Wales; the Frescobaldi of Florence who put up the money for Edward II's war with Scotland; the Bardi and Peruzzi who made possible Edward III's attack on France at the beginning of the Hundred Years' War. They seemed amply rewarded. Italian bankers controlled the custom revenues of England, and the entire financial administration of the Plantagenets' continental demesnes. But they were building on unstable foundations, and some of their brilliant careers were to end in disaster. This, however, lay in the future, and throughout the whole of our period the Italians ruled unchallenged the money markets of Western Europe and the Levant. Everywhere the gold coins of their three chief economic centres, the *genovino* of Genoa, the *florin* of Florence and the *ducat* of Venice, were received as the dollars of the medieval world, the principal units of international currency.

This vast expansion of the Italian economy, which lasted, with only slight recession, up to the 1340s, had important social consequences. Italy had still, like the rest of Western Europe, a primarily, agrarian economy in the sense that most men worked on the land, and their main preoccupation was the harvests. Yet a large proportion of the population lived in towns, and the character of all aspects of life was often dictated by them. Within this urbanised society four principal classes may be distinguished. First was the lower class: the peasantry now everywhere almost wholly free from bonds of serfdom, and with them the urban proletariat of the great towns, enjoying a primitive, popular folk culture of song and story, but largely untouched by the higher culture of the age. Second was the lesser bourgeoisie, the artisans and shopkeepers, who, despite a constant struggle to maintain their economic position, could sympathise with some at least of the Italian literature of the day, and who produced from their ranks some of the best-known artists of the time. Third was the upper bourgeoisie, the *popolo grasso*, a phrase which indicates a wide spectrum of status and income. It includes such different ranks as the great merchants of international trade who possessed hereditary wealth, the entrepreneurs enriched in their own lifetime, and the more successful members of the professional classes: doctors, lawyers, and prosperous notaries. The fourth class was the aristocracy: both the ancient feudal families, the descendants of Frankish or Imperial lords; and the more recently ennobled merchants, whose position had been achieved through trade. Often these men had withdrawn from commerce, and sought a more modest prosperity as landowners. In particular, the old feudal nobility, the great and ancient houses of the Guidi, the Ubaldini, the Ubertini, and the Conti da Romena, were often remote from the commercial interests of their communes' rulers. They enjoyed in the castles of their fiefs a virtually independent rule which was not checked until the second half of the fourteenth century. There is some dispute among students of Italian society as to how far in this period this aristocracy had, in the great capitalist centres, merged with the upper bourgeoisie into an urban patriciate with common cultural ideals.[2] Most probably, despite any economic differences, the sentiments and intellectual background of the two classes were the same. There was frequent intermarriage between them, and often a considerable aping of aristocratic modes of life by the bourgeoisie. Great merchant houses, such as the Bardi, bought up the lands and castles of impoverished noblemen, acquired coats of arms, and sought to live a life of feudal splendour. The poems of Folgore da San Gimignano, with their glowing accounts of knightly life, are a bourgeois dream-fulfilment, strictly intended for bourgeois reading. The aristocrats, for their part, could in no circumstances afford to ignore the thoughts and aspirations of their middle-class masters.

For it was the upper bourgeoisie who dominated Italian civilisation at this time. They shaped the most significant aspects of society, and, either individually, or more often collectively, gave the greatest patronage to the arts. In the first place they demanded a high degree of literacy; most of those changes in culture and perception which have been ascribed to the invention of printing are better considered as the result of the economic revolution of the twelfth and thirteenth centuries. Common advice to merchants is '*non si vorebbe mai risparmiare la penna*', 'never stop using your pen.' It is not by chance that spectacles first appear in the Italy of the fourteenth century. By this time the merchant kept elaborate accounts, was a compulsive letter-writer, and was often accustomed to commit his thoughts to private diaries. Behind this literacy, there stood a fairly extensive system of elementary education.

Reading and writing themselves, however, were only one aspect of that more rational ordering of life to which the term *Verbürger-lichung* (*embourgeoisement*) has been given. Since it was the needs of a capitalist and bourgeois society which brought the various aspects of this development, the term can be accepted as having some validity. But it must not be assumed, as it was by Sombart and Von Martin, that 'rationality' was confined to the upper middle classes. And it must be recognised that even a dominating bourgeoisie could still seek to copy the social ideals of the aristocracy. In this rational ordering of life a new emphasis was laid upon everything designed to measure and control the visible world. A new precision emerged: something seen, for instance, in the bill of exchange, double-entry book-keeping, and those detailed and accurate sailing maps called 'portolans'. Significant, too, is the mechanical clock, invented shortly before 1300, and by 1400 found in all Italian towns. When the Milanese chronicler, Galvano Fiamma, wrote of the 24-hour striking clock in the campanile of San Gottardo: 'which marks off the hours from the hours, as is *supremely necessary* for all classes of men',[3] he was heralding a new age in the story of man's ordering of, and subjection to, time. A new numeracy was demanded. In Paolo Gerardi's textbook, written around 1327, arabic numbers were employed exclusively. A Florentine school book of the same period has exercises dealing with such questions as the buying of wool at Pisa and Genoa, and its sale in Florence, working out the disparities of weights, measures, and coinage systems, and the calculation of exchange rates at Tunis in gold florins.

In very much wider spheres 'bourgeois rationality' was to in-fluence religious developments, and to be a major factor in the slow birth of the state. In law, in returning to the Roman ideal of *ratio* (a word which, like the Italian *ragione*, meant both law and reason), bourgeois habits of mind had undoubtedly played a distinctive part. Ideals of authority were no longer drawn from tradition, but from calculations of their everyday efficiency. Ideals of authority were new, because the Italian entrepreneur was a new kind of man.

If 'rationality' was the first aspect of this society, the second was enterprise. It was an enterprise which to the older feudal world of northern Europe could even appear as cowardice. 'By the devil, that's advice worthy of a Lombard!', cried the Count of Artois at the battle of Courtrai, in rejecting the prudent counsel which would have saved his army from heroic annihilation. The courage of the merchant was not recklessness before the known, but willingness to confront the unknown danger. It is the spirit of the Genoese merchant found at Sijilmasa, an oasis of the Sahara, in the early fourteenth century, of Lanzerotto Malacollo, discoverer of the Canary Islands, of the Genoese Vivaldi brothers, who in 1291 sailed through the Straits of Gibraltar in an attempt to reach India from the west. They disappeared, and were heard of no more, but it was perhaps these men who were in the mind of Dante when, in the twenty-sixth canto of the *Inferno*, he came to write of the last voyage of Ulysses, who like them had sailed to gain knowledge of an unpeopled world beyond the sun.

In the east, too, they made their way far past the colonies of the Black Sea ports. 'The road from Tana to Cathay', said Pegolotti, in his merchant's handbook, written in the 1340s, 'is quite safe by day and by night, according to what the merchants report who have used it.' It is a remark which indicates what he expected of his merchant contemporaries. The traveller there, he continued, should let his beard grow long, should acquire a dragoman at Tana, and, if he wanted to be considered of high status, a woman too, preferably one who spoke Cumanic. He should get food in advance at each staging post in the journey, and travel in a caravan of at least 60 men. On reaching China, he should not be surprised by the paper money: 'all the people of the country are bound to accept it, and yet

people do not pay more for merchandise, even though it is paper.'
Pegolotti's account was based on the direct experience of merchants
who had made the journey. In about 1325 there were a large number
of Venetians at the great port of Zaytun, facing the Formosa
Strait. In 1338 the Genoese Andalò di Negro bore gifts of 'horses
and other marvels' to the great Khan in China, who received them
with such pleasure that their praises were sung by the court poet
Chen-long, and were the subject of paintings in the Summer Palace
of Pekin, where they were still recorded in the inventory of 1815.
In 1344 we read of a law-suit in Venice in which a suitor complains
that three years earlier his son-in-law had gone to Cathay with some
money belonging to him.

Other daring spirits made for India. From Tabriz the Genoese
Benedetto Vivaldi and Percival Stancone set out for Malabar in
1315. In the summer of 1338 a Venetian, Giovanni Loredano, left
with his brothers and four partners to trade at Delhi. He and two of
his companions died on the way, but the survivors completed their
journey and returned with 100 percent profit. These men are known
only by accident, the chance survival of some legal document
connected with their affairs. But there were doubtless numerous
others whose records have perished.

Such were the merchants of the upper bourgeoisie. But it must
not be assumed that their spirit was confined to their own class;
it was rapidly diffused throughout the whole of society. *Verbürger-
lichung* was found in any organisations which sought to dominate
the material world: in those associated with government; and, most
noticeably, among the bureaucrats of the Roman *curia*. In the ranks
of the church, eastern missionaries who followed the paths of the
merchant venturers showed the same spirit. In 1245 the Franciscan
John Carpini had been sent by Pope Innocent IV to the capital of the
Mongol Empire at Karakorum in order to spy upon the great Khan
and to report upon the prospects of his conversion. From that year
there began a now largely forgotten attempt to christianise the east,
which ended only in 1368 with the collapse of the Mongol dynasty
in China. In this effort Italian clergy played a major part. In Meso-

potamia and Iran, Italian Dominicans were preaching in the 1290s.
At Cambaluc (Pekin) the Franciscan Giovanni Montecorvino held
the title of Archbishop from 1294 to 1322, and was succeeded by one
Andrea da Perugia, who had with him numerous suffragan bishops,
all Italians. Many of these men were afterwards martyred, and this
was recorded in the art of their distant homeland. For instance,
Lorenzetti's fresco in the chapter house of San Francesco at Siena,
painted around 1326, shows a Tartar lord ordering the beheading
of Franciscan brothers. It was a time of the highest hopes, though
illusory, for missionary Christianity. Odorico da Pordendone,
writing in his convent at Friuli shortly before 1331, told of the
spread of the faith which he had himself witnessed in Canton,
Hangchow, and the other cities of the east, and looked forward in
confidence to the age in which the prophecy of the psalmist
should be fulfilled: 'And all the kings of the earth shall adore Him.'

It is as much within this missionary tradition as those of the
merchant venturers that the book of Marco Polo should be considered. The two elder Polos, Marco's father and uncle, Niccolò and
Maffeo, were merchants, and in search of trade had visited the great
Khan Kublai in his winter palace at Cambaluc as early as 1265. But
when they set out again in 1277, taking with them the young Marco,
they went as ambassadors of Pope Gregory X, almost as lay missionaries rather than merchants. During the next 20 years these men
were not, it would seem, engaged in trade; probably they were
working in the higher ranks of Kublai's civil service. Marco's book,
in contrast to Pegolotti's account of China, was very little concerned with the experiences of a merchant. Nor was it simply a
story of adventure. The reader approaches it looking for a saga, a
tale of heroic individuals. He finds instead only the most laconic
indications of the men who took part in it, the spirit which filled
them, and how they spent their long years in the east. What we are
given is, as its first title indicates, a *Divisament dou Monde*, a description of the world, a geographical and anthropological study. The
book implies a world where heroic undertakings and measureless
travels are commonplace. When his Latin translator, the Dominican

Francesco Pipini, introduces his author, he speaks of Marco, neither as trader nor adventurer, but as one who had given the world knowledge of 'the variety, beauty, and immensity of creation.' It was the desire for this knowledge, the intense curiosity with which Marco and his readers looked at the world, which was the most significant product of the economic revolution, as its effects expanded beyond the purely economic field.

At a more mundane level the economic revolution also produced wealth, large capital surpluses which could be devoted to the patronage of the arts. Some caution, however, is necessary here. By medieval standards the volume of Italian commerce was immense, and its rewards were in proportion. By modern standards it was small, and the risks involved were great; shipwreck, piracy, bandits, dishonest partners, defaulting clients, xenophobic governments, which all menaced the merchant's hopes of gain. Markets and trade routes were liable at any moment to be made inaccessible by war. High transport costs and customs duties reduced profit margins. Much has been made of the steep interest rates charged by Italian bankers. Against this should be set the almost reckless spirit in which money was lent at all, when the creditor was at the mercy of judicial systems which did not look kindly upon the foreigner, and when borrowers might, at the whim of ecclesiastical or political authority, repudiate their debts with ease. Even among the largest and most efficient companies, bankruptcies were frequent.

Some men made vast fortunes, but it need not be assumed that they had any particular interest in the arts. Almost by definition, indeed, it may be taken that the *entrepreneur* or first generation capitalist was a man so highly specialised that he had no time for anything but his business and profits. Any wavering from this central preoccupation in the highly competitive economic life of the time could lead to disaster. The Frescobaldi family became poets shortly before they became bankrupts. The chapels of the Bardi and the Peruzzi, decorated with the frescoes of Giotto, record the names of the two families involved in the most resounding business failures of the fourteenth century. One must avoid, in other words, any over-facile correlation between economic advance and artistic

1 Margaritone of Arezzo, *Madonna and Child* (*c.* 1270?)

2 Giotto, *Maestà* (*c.* 1310–1315)

patronage. Indeed, Robert Lopez,[4] in a stimulating essay, has suggested that periods of artistic development coincide with eras of economic depression. According to this thesis, the business man only puts his money in art when a contracting economy prohibits him from making more profitable investment. This view is extreme, particularly in its assumptions of capitalist rationality, and perhaps deliberately overstated in contradiction to a reigning orthodoxy, but it cannot be entirely dismissed. Certainly, as has been seen in the twelfth and thirteenth centuries, the periods of Italy's most rapid economic expansion, cultural life was still comparatively undeveloped.

However, it is clear that some money came from merchants towards the cultivation of the arts. The second generation, at least, of great capitalists were tempted, often dangerously enough, to divert their thoughts from profit, turning to the arts of civilisation. They built villas in the countryside; and their houses were furnished with French tapestries, elaborately worked mirrors, the large, ornate marriage chests called *cassoni*, and statuettes of the Virgin and saints. The walls were painted with garden scenes, trees, flowers, birds; and, as their social and cultural pretensions grew, with stories of chivalry and coats-of-arms. About 1305, the Dominican Fra Giordano da Rivalto was complaining that the rich were prepared to give £50 to a minstrel, and to spend £300 on having their house painted, but would not give a penny to the poor dying of hunger.

Capital accumulations enabled the rich to form a leisured class. Boccaccio was able to dream away his days at Naples, and return to Florence to pen witty descriptions of avaricious business men, precisely because his father had slaved for a lifetime in the counting-house of the Bardi. The money-lending practices of Dante's uncle and father[5] (by ecclesiastical standards doubtfully orthodox, and in social convention low in esteem) provided the means by which the poet could assert, quite falsely, the nobility of his blood, and the leisure in which he could lament that the spirit of Florence was being corrupted by usurers.

The most significant use of merchant wealth in the patronage of the arts, however, was not individual, but collective. It was through the taxation of bourgeois riches that the governments of the communes were able to raise the buildings and to commission the paintings which might portray the glory, fame, and honour of their cities. And it was often the upper bourgeoisie who were installed as the governing class, and directly awarded that patronage.

three

Intellectual and Religious Life

The Intellectual Background

The styles of art and literature of this period, in their realism, their movement from the transcendental to the human and rational, from the general to the specific, did no more than mirror the intellectual development of Europe in the preceding two centuries. From the early twelfth century the schools of Europe had been deeply influenced by the philosophic and scientific traditions of Greece. At first in versions from the Arabic, then from the original Greek, four generations of translators had restored to the West the writings of Ptolemy, Euclid, Archimedes, and Hippocrates and, most influential of all, of Aristotle. With these texts there came, too, Latin translations of the philosophy and science of the Arab world: the philosophies of Averrhoës and Avicenna, the *Algebra* of Al-Khwarizmi, and the *Astronomy* of Alburnasar. These works were to be a powerful influence in the intellectual life of Europe until the age of Galileo and Descartes.

In philosophy, the thought born of a pagan or infidel world presented an immediate challenge to the traditional authority of the church, which the scholastic thinkers of the thirteenth century had met in one of two ways. The first was that taken by the Franciscan school, noticeably by Alexander of Hales and St Bonaventura (d. 1274), who turned their backs upon the substance of Aristotelianism and tried to refurbish the traditions of Augustinian and neo-platonic thought against its influence. With the distinctions of Duns Scotus between the sacred and profane, between faith and reason, this school ended by virtually separating the disciplines of religion and philosophy, and leaving each autonomous in its own sphere. The Dominicans, on the other hand, notably Albert the Great and St Thomas Aquinas (d. 1274), attempted to integrate traditional Christian theology with the new learning, and thus came inevitably to change the older Augustinian world view. Aquinas took over the Aristotelian mystique of 'the natural', and wedded it to Christianity in the formula: 'grace presupposes nature'. In his scheme of things human reason was seen as a satisfactory instrument for seeking truth in the natural order and for coming to some understanding of the supernatural. The existence of God, for example, was now to be deduced from external reality, from nature; and nature itself, previously condemned, was seen as good. All this, worked out by Aquinas with a lucidity and sense of proportion amounting to genius, brought about a revolution, not only in theology and in thought, but in feeling too. If the Franciscans had left the secular world to its own devices, the Dominicans had in part secularised religion.

The new learning was equally influential outside theology. In the *Ethics*, the *Politics*, and the *Economics*, significantly enough the last works of the Aristotelian canon to be translated into Latin (*c.* 1240–50), Europe was presented with a philosophy of everyday life seen from a wholly human standpoint, a vision of existence without reference to God. Without implying any simple case of cause and effect, it is of some interest that these developments in theology and philosophy, like the increasing naturalism in Gothic art, came first to the northern world, and were received about a generation later in Italy. Though Palermo was an important centre for translation from Greek and Arabic, and though many of the scholastics were, like Aquinas, Italian by birth, during most of the thirteenth century the new philosophy had hardly been studied outside France and the Rhineland. There were no theological faculties in Italian universities at this time, and little interest in theology until the friars began to teach the subject in their own convents at the end of the century.

In the field of science the translations also brought fundamental change, and here Italy played a more important part. Works such as Aristotle's *Animals*, and the pseudo-Aristotelian *Plants* and *Vegetables*, led to a strong interest in the natural world, to the production of encyclopaedias of natural history, and the studies of Albert the Great on animals, plants, and minerals. At the same time, although the character of scientific thought was still mainly inductive, still concerned to define universal forms and 'that which is prior in the order of nature', there were many signs by now of the rejection of traditional beliefs in favour of scientific observation. Albert the Great, for example, declared that: 'it is not enough to know in terms of universals, but we seek to know each object's own peculiar characteristics, for this is the best and perfect kind of science'. Or again (on whales): 'we pass over what the ancients have written on this topic, because their statements do not agree with experience'.[1]

At first sight, the immediate influence of the new science upon art was less than it might have been. In anatomy, for instance, the influence of Galen led to regular public dissections at Bologna from the beginning of the thirteenth century, and in 1316 Mondino produced what was to be a standard text-book with his *Anatomia*. But this work was taken as an authority rather than as a stimulus for future investigations and after his death the science languished. So too with work on optics, based upon translations of Alhazen and Al-Khindi. During the thirteenth century a mathematical theory of sight called *perspectiva* had been developed by such men as Roger Bacon, Grosseteste, and Witelo. Yet this was not to influence artists until the beginning of the fifteenth century. On the other hand the origins of the close studies of animals, birds, and plants made by Lombard painters at the end of the fourteenth century are probably related to the illustration of books of empirical science. And more important than any specific study, the general concern of the new learning for the unique and particular, for personal observation rather than the reproduction of traditional knowledge, provided a real stimulus to the new art. In the first half of the thirteenth century, Frederick II's book on birds had put forward a programme which summarised the new approach to learning. His aim, he wrote, was *manifestare ea quae sunt sicut sunt*: 'to reveal those things which are, as they are.' In this he was echoed by the Mantuan, Vivaldo Belcalzer (*fl.* 1308), in the dedication to his Italian translation of Bartholomew the Englishman's encyclopaedia, *De proprietatibus rerum*. He sought, he says here, 'the understanding of things, which knowledge is no other than truly knowing things as they are, and how, and what, and why, and their causes.'[2] These words foreshadow the rise of the 'Paduan school' of the physical sciences; they place us in the world of realism and the mental climate of Giotto and Dante.

Religious Life

Against this background of intellectual change religion was still the most important shaping factor in *trecento* culture. Although the Church itself was to be no longer the major patron of the arts, the principal function of the artist was still the satisfaction of religious needs. Cathedrals, churches, oratories, and altars had to be built. They had to be decorated with frescoes, panels, statues, stained glass, iron work, carved stalls, and panellings. They had to be furnished with chalices, patens, reliquaries, monstrances, altar frontals, croziers, processional crosses, and eucharistic spoons, and with illuminated missals, breviaries, antiphonaries, and other liturgical books. Outside the visual arts, it was the cathedrals which were the leading centres of musical composition and performance. Even in literature, the most secular branch of culture in the century, the greatest writers, Dante in his 'sacred poem', Petrarch in his attempt to balance the claims of Roman and Christian civilisation, were both preoccupied with religious themes.

This predominance of religion in culture reflected a situation where the organisation and beliefs of the Church pervaded every branch of society. The Papacy itself, with the most efficient bureaucratic and diplomatic administration in Europe, had woven into the fabric of local life in each diocese a complex and variegated network of institutions designed to attract and satisfy the different spiritual and social needs of its adherents. At Florence, for instance, in 1339, there was the cathedral, with its bishop and canons; there were 57 parish and 53 conventual churches, and numerous smaller oratories in the city and suburbs alone. Side by side with the six older monastic houses were the six new and flourishing convents of the friars. In addition to the orders, and often closely linked with them, were the lay fraternities or *Laudesi*. Almost every church had its confraternity of laymen who, under the guidance of a chaplain, would bind themselves to certain moral restrictions (such as not going to taverns or playing at dice) and to regular attendance at prayer meetings in which *laude* or hymns of praise were sung to their patron saints. The membership of these fraternities was predominantly lower middle-class, but the ten largest companies had almost the character of state institutions. The 'Captains' of the *Laudesi* of Or San Michele, for instance, were appointed and supervised by the commune itself. Finally, by the side of all these activities there stood the Florentine inquisitor, with his prisons at S. Maria Novella.

With an establishment which, in this way, encompassed the whole of life, it is difficult to separate religious modes of thought from those of society as a whole. Apart from the adherence of all believers to certain central doctrines, there were as many differences of emphasis and opinion in the ecclesiastical as in the secular world. Everywhere could be found attitudes varying from fanaticism to indifference. On the one hand, there was the hysterical, sado-masochist exaltation of the flagellants, who followed Fra Venturino of Bergamo through Italy in 1335. On the other, there were the half-sceptical enigmatic words of Niccolò Acciaiuoli (Grand Seneschal of the Kingdom of Naples, and cousin of a Bishop of Florence). In a letter to his brother, discussing his plans for the building of a Carthusian monastery at Florence, he wrote: 'the more sumptuous the work shall be, the more I will be pleased. For all other goods that God has given me will go to my posterity and I know not who. The monastery alone with all its enrichments will be mine for all time, and will make my name flourish and last in the city, and if the soul is immortal, as my lord chancellor says, mine will rejoice at that, wherever it is ordained that it shall go.'[3]

Absolute disbelief in Christianity, either the so-called 'philosophic epicureanism' or 'Averroism', was reserved only for a few lonely souls. One such, or so at least it was rumoured, was the friend of

Dante, the high-born poet, Guido Cavalcanti. A certain contempt for Christian ideals was a sentiment not unknown in aristocratic circles. It derived from a tradition first found in Provençal and North French poetry of the twelfth century, and discreetly cultivated in the southern court of Frederick II and his successors. But its literary expression was always cautious and ambiguous, and so difficult to assess. Open heresy, too, which at the beginning of the thirteenth century had posed a grave threat to the church, had diminished considerably. In Italy Catharism and Waldensianism were extinct. What heterodoxy survived was confined to a few cliques inspired by the ideals of apostolic poverty, and found generally within the religious orders themselves, noticeably among the more extreme Franciscans. Preaching at Florence in 1304, Fra Giordano of Pisa could boast that the opponents of Christendom did not dare to show their faces in public and that through God's grace all heresy had ended.

Anti-clericalism, on the other hand, flourished, and found fullest expression, in one way in Boccaccio, in another, in Dante. But this must not be confused with religious dissent, for it partook of the character of quarrels and cruel jokes within a united family. It sprang generally from the inevitable disillusionment felt from time to time at the inadequate human embodiment of cherished ideals. In a society so closely bound up with religion, scandals were unavoidable. It was inevitable, for instance, that the leading families of the lay world should occupy the principal positions in the Church, and that their secular quarrels should be fought out within it; and when there were so many clerics, the number of clerical scandals was likely to be large. However, the overwhelming mass of the Italian people of the fourteenth century believed themselves to be firmly orthodox, though the character of their Christianity might often have been impugned by many of their clergy.

The religious sentiments expressed in the verses of an anonymous Genoese merchant writing in his own dialect at the beginning of the fourteenth century were typical. He knew something of the Bible, and of Bede's commentary on it, and most of his attempts at poetry dealt with religious themes: the Nativity, the Ten Commandments, and individual Saints. Other verses gave pietistic moral counsel, and attacked 'the persecutors of the Church', those 'blaspheming against the Lord Pope', pride, avarice, and the use of cosmetics by women. They recommended alms-giving and good works, and declared that it was 'crazy' to place trust in a world where all are avid for money and gain:

> *Ben a mato chi se fia*
> *en quisto mondo traitor*

Combined with these undoubtedly sincere sentiments there was also the morality of the world in which he was writing: rejoicing at the victories of Genoa over Venice, complaints against priests for their rich clothes and fine horses, and against peasants for rising too quickly in the world. There is also advice on the need to keep accurate scales ('so that you won't be caught out'), on securing a good dowry in marriage, and on how to execute vengeance when injured ('keep quiet until you strike').[4]

What we have here is the typical morality and piety of the conventional Christian in all ages. The saints or Dantes who feel Christian teaching as a challenge to their whole being have always been comparatively rare, and were rare, too, in the fourteenth century. Yet the social-religious context in which these men lived was very different from anything we can easily imagine today. Religion presented much starker extremes of consolation, exaltation or terror than it does now, because society presented a picture of far greater brutality and irrationality than anything we know today, at least in our sheltered corners of the west. In an age when belief in Christianity was universal, the most stolidly unimaginative accepted as a living reality both the most abstruse doctrines of the faith and its most curious accompaniments: visions, miracles, demonic possessions, direct celestial participation in human affairs. To read the pages of the *Acta Sanctorum*, which retail the lives of the canonised and beatified of the period, is for the modern reader a study in depth of extraordinary psychological maladjustments. But for the contemporary these stories were the deepest expression and confirmation of inviolable truth.

One must emphasize this point lest it be swamped by what will be said in the following pages on the theme of 'rationalisation' and the new influence of secular ideals. At this time the clearest minds found no difficulty in accepting as facts the most unaccountable supernatural interventions into mundane events. To the belief that these manifestations still occurred, indeed, many of the greatest works of art owed their existence. In 1264 for example, a German priest celebrating Mass at Bolsena prayed for a sign to remove his doubts upon the reality of Transubstantiation. At this, it was said, the Host had begun to bleed, leaving twenty-five stains of blood upon the *corporale* or mass cloth. On hearing this story, Pope Urban IV proclaimed a new feast, the Corpus Domini, for August 11th, the date of the alleged miracle. The *corporale* was deposited in the old cathedral at Orvieto, and its presence there was the principal stimulus for the laying of the foundations of the new and more splendid cathedral in 1290. Later, in 1337–8, the Sienese goldsmith, Ugolino di Vieri, produced the stupendous gilded silver reliquary, which still stands within the church, in order to house the *corporale*. There was another 'great and manifest miracle', as Giovanni Villani called it (though the friars, as both he and Guido Cavalcanti complained, 'through envy or some other cause' refused to believe in it). This was in July 1292, when the picture of the Madonna in the loggia of the Florentine cornmarket was seen to weep. This manifestation cured blindness, drove out demons, and healed the sick, and to the credit given to these cures we owe today the great building of Or San Michele, and the tabernacle of Orcagna set within it.

Humanisation and Secularisation

Yet religious sentiment was not static; in many ways indeed cultural changes in the *Trecento* corresponded to changing attitudes in religious belief and feeling. These changes, which were rarely sudden or dramatic, but worked slowly and at long remove, can be described as 'humanisation' and 'secularisation'.

Humanisation had become increasingly pronounced in religious sentiment from the eleventh century; religion, moving gradually from being a ritual dedicated to a remote and terrible deity, had come to dwell more and more on the human character of Christ and his mother, and on the human interest attached to his saints. This tendency first appeared in the writings of St Peter Damiani (d. 1072), it was strongly emphasized in the reverence for the Virgin expressed by St Bernard of Clairvaux (d. 1153), and assumed new freshness in the stories that grew up round St Francis of Assisi (d. 1226). Central to this humanisation, this acceptance of man within the sacerdotal cult, was the idea of nature itself as a good. So St Francis, who first created the Christmas crib with all its anecdotal associations with human life, with the kings or Magi as with the shepherds, was also the man who in his *Canticle of the Sun* had praised earth and fire and the heavenly orbs, wind and air and water—

> *la quale è molto utile et humile et pretiosa et casta . . .*

> (which is most useful and humble and precious and chaste)

—as manifestations of the divine beauty and goodness. St Francis did not, as was once believed, create this sentiment, but he was its most impressive exponent.

Latin hagiographies taking up these themes were soon translated into Italian and exercised a powerful hold over the popular mind. Such were the *Golden Legend of the Saints*, written between 1263 and 1268 by the Dominican, Jacopo da Voragine, the *Meditations on the Life of Christ* of the Franciscan, Giovanni di San Gimignano, with its detailed accounts of Christ's childhood, and the *Life of St Francis* by St Bonaventura. From here they passed into the general literature of the age in the writings of the *Laudesi* school. In these works Christ was no longer the Christ in Majesty but a suffering human being supported by his mother, a child helpless in the cradle or filled with child-like gravity as he disputed with the doctors. The aim here was to excite not awe and terror but human sympathy and emotion. Only the austere spirit of Dante resisted this general current of the age. In his work the Romanesque Christ, a Christ seen without tenderness, seen rather as the bearer of an apocalyptic judgement, lived on.

For art the humanisation of religion offered a novel world of feeling and a wide range of themes. It would be wrong to suggest that the new religious feelings directly created the new styles; iconographical innovations, as Millard Meiss has pointed out, can indeed often be considered as the result rather than the cause of stylistic change.[5] None the less, without the new religious sentiment it is difficult to see how the new art could have come into existence. When Simone Martini created the first image of the 'Madonna of Humility', where the Virgin was depicted not as a ruler but as a woman humbly sitting upon the ground, he was only inspired to solve the technical problems of such a representation by that vision of her which had first been formulated by the religious writers of the thirteenth century.

The new thematic material demanded new styles of presentation, since the traditional two-dimensional hieratic art of such as Margaritone of Arezzo and Pacino di Bonaguida was incapable of capturing its spirit. In this sense the work of Cavallini, Cimabue, and Giotto fulfilled an imperative religious need. If Christ's humanity was to be stressed over his divinity, if his human saints were to receive new honours, then art itself had to move to the representation of man. If the 28 frescoes of the life of St Francis painted at Assisi were revolutionary in religious sentiment—as indeed they were, for never before had the Church given such honour to an individual mortal—then it is not surprising that they should also have had a revolutionary character in art. If within ecclesiastical thought there was now an emphasis upon real men in the natural world, it is understandable that art began to lose its symbolic and liturgical quality and started to tell real stories. Narrative in its turn demanded that third dimension in which drama and action could be played out. For this 'Giotto knocks the hole in the wall' and in the frescoes of the Arena chapel seeks that depth without which a story cannot be told. Here, too, there are scenes in which there is a particular emphasis upon the human emotions of human beings, such as that of Joachim's return to his sheepfold and of the marriage of the Virgin.

In Giotto's art there is no search for a predominating naturalism as such. His figures are heroic and idealised and there is no true scenery. Among the first generation of his followers, however, naturalism has become an ideal, and the religious stories are treated with an ever-increasing human familiarity and intimacy. Sometimes, as for instance in Bernardo Daddi's *Nativity*, in the National Gallery of Scotland, where we see the ox, the ass, Joseph asleep on the floor, the shepherds in their workaday clothes, there is an overriding impression of homeliness. The figure of Christ, seen by Giotto as a human and idealised hero, appears now more frequently as the crucified carpenter and demands a much more emotional sympathy. Perhaps an over intense humanisation of religious feeling has diminished the dignity of these works. However this may be, from Tuscany and central Italy these influences spread to other centres, though sometimes at rather a later date. At Venice, for instance, the strength of Byzantine art, which was reinforced by the close trade links of the city with Constantinople, delayed the first appearance of the new style until the second decade of the fourteenth century. It has been suggested indeed that it was only the presence of heresy in the city at that time which brought about the change.[6] According to this thesis the new iconography, with such themes as the Coronation of the Virgin and lives of St Francis and St Dominic, had a particularly anti-heretical character and was introduced in the 1320s as part of a specifically state-directed attack upon unorthodoxy. Yet heresy, and certainly heresy which challenged the position of the Virgin, flourished in the city very much less in the fourteenth than in the thirteenth century. Here the chronology of the change is better explained as the belated cultural transmission of ideas from other centres and the resistance offered by a strong native tradition.

This is not to say that heresy had not played a part in the development of religious feeling. The particular emphasis of this age upon the acceptance of humanity and of nature sprang in part from a profound reaction against Catharism which had threatened the Church at the end of the twelfth and beginning of the thirteenth centuries. The Catharists or Albigensians had professed a complex pseudo-Christian Manichaeism wherein all matter was considered to be evil and where the ideal was the suicide of the body and the extinction of the human race in material form. If in the stories of the early Franciscans St Francis preached to the birds, St Anthony to the fishes, it was because they were seeking in this way to give expression to a respect for that created matter which the Cathar claimed was under the dominion of satanic power.

Too much should not be made of this, for at the same time there was an independent movement towards naturalism in philosophy and theology which sprang from different sources. Humanisation and naturalisation were bound up with changes in the position of Europe since the tenth century. Life had grown sweeter; and the religion of society had acquired a much softer character. If religion was being humanised it was because the lot of human beings was becoming so much more tolerable. Western Europe had once lived on a subsistence economy, without any satisfactory political organisation, and threatened continually by attacks from external enemies: the Slavs, Magyars, Saracens, and Vikings. In three centuries it had become economically supreme in the world, and in the Crusades and the *Drang nach Osten* had expanded against its foes. These developments were owed to two interrelated factors: first, the agricultural and commercial revolutions of the eleventh, twelfth, and thirteenth centuries, of whose effects something has already been said, and second, the slow emergence of the state.

As the role of government loomed larger in the life of western man there was not only a progressive improvement in the everyday conditions of life, but also a new balance in the role played in life by the sacred and secular respectively. Men who still held a profound devotion to Christianity and an implicit acceptance of the idea of the Pope as the Vicar of Christ and custodian of religious truths, had none the less come to reject the papal claim to ultimate power in the lay world and to attack the privileged position of clerics in society. From there they were to go on to assert that laymen, too, had rights within the spiritual order: *sancta mater ecclesia non solum est ex clericis sed etiam ex laicis*: 'Did not Christ die for all men? Our holy mother the Church pertains not only to the clergy, but to the laity as well.' These new secular positions found their fullest

formulation in Marsiglio of Padua's distinction between the provenance of the clergy, confined wholly to the spiritual world, and
that of the laity in which secular government was wholly supreme.
Yet what in fact happened was something rather different. Instead
of lay and clergy becoming distinct in their own spheres, newly
organised lay society was to take over and inspire the direction and
values of religion. Laymen were now wealthy, they were educated;
they sought the satisfaction of their spiritual needs in more sophisticated forms. The effect of this is seen in the arts in such phenomena
as the 'sacred poem' written by the layman Dante, in the humanisation of religion itself, and in the political uses to which the communes
put religious art.

Religious Aesthetic

Little of this new spirit, however, appeared within the official
religious aesthetic of the age. The paintings and sculptures which
were produced for the Church were consciously thought of not as
'art', but rather as cult objects which served a religious purpose.
From the end of the sixth century it had been recognised that the
visual crafts had a firm foundation in the life of the Church. At that
time Pope Gregory the Great had written: 'What writing is to the
learned, painting is to the ignorant, and for the people the image
takes the place of letters. On walls they can read what they cannot
decipher in books'.

In the earlier ages of Christianity the concept of an art which was
solely the handmaid of religion had been used sometimes in a
stern attempt to inhibit artistic individuality. At the time of the
iconoclastic controversy, the second Nicaean council, of 787,
declared that: 'the composition of images is not the invention of
painters, but is based on the tradition and tried legislation of the
Catholic Church. . . . And the composition and this tradition are
not things that concern the painter. To him is entrusted only their
execution. Rather do they depend on the order and disposition of
the holy fathers. . . . And in truth men learn to paint Christ's image
under that appearance in which he was visible'. This curious tradition,

which held that the painter was faithfully reproducing authentic likenesses of Christ and the saints, still had its followers at the beginning of the fourteenth century. In 1306, for instance, Fra Giordano da Rivalto, preaching in S. Maria Novella, and seeking to show that the Magi had been 'great lords' in the East, said this:

> There is another great piece of evidence: the first paintings of them which came from Greece. Paintings are the book of the lay, and indeed of all people, for all paintings are originally from the saints. In order that there should be full knowledge of them, they portrayed the figure of saints as they were, and in their form, condition, and manner. So one finds that Nicodemus paints Christ on the cross in a fine picture in that form and manner that Christ originally had, so that those who saw the picture should be fully aware of the whole event, so well was it executed according to the manner and figure. For Nicodemus was at the cross of Christ when He was placed upon it, and when He was taken down, and his is the picture which brought about that fine miracle which is celebrated on the feast of Holy Saviour. So similarly we find that Saint Luke painted Our Lady in a picture, just as she really was, and the picture is today in Rome, and is held in great veneration. The saints did those paintings to give a clearer impression to people of the facts. Accordingly these paintings, and especially old ones which came long ago from Greece, have a very great authority, since many saints dwelt there who painted these things and gave copies of them to the world—on whose great authority one may draw, as one may from books. So by these paintings that came from Greece we know certainly that the Magi were great lords since they are painted with royal crowns on their heads . . . .[7]

As the century progressed, this idea that the artist gave reliable portraits of past heroes, and that his work was a prop for the ignorant, competed with a tendency to see art as a symbolic language for the educated. This view appears very strongly in the first book of Guillaume Durand's *Rationale Divinorum Officiorum*. Durand, Bishop

3 Simone Martini, *Maestà* (1315)

4 Follower of Ambrogio Lorenzetti, *Maestà* (second half of fourteenth century)

5 Lorenzo Monaco, *Madonna of Humility* (first decade of fifteenth century)

of Mende, was an important administrative figure in the Papal State in the last thirty years of the thirteenth century, and his tomb in S. Maria sopra Minerva shows a lavish, though discriminating visual taste. In the *Rationale* he does indeed bow the knee to Pope Gregory's formula: *pictura et ornamenta in ecclesia sunt laicorum lectiones et scriptura.* Much of his work discussed how art could be used in this way 'to teach how ill is to be avoided and good followed'. For ease of understanding Bishops were to be represented with mitres, abbots with hoods, virgins with lamps or with lilies, doctors with books in their hands. He suggested the themes which might be followed: hell and paradise, religious stories, and so on. Yet along with this material, and tending rather to swamp it, he dwelt on the idea found originally in the *Mystical Mirror of the Church* of the twelfth century theologian, Hugh of St Victor; the idea, that is, of the symbolic meaning of the church and its ornaments. So for instance:

> the material church, wherein the people assemble to set forth God's holy praise, symboliseth that Holy Church which is built in Heaven of living stones ... its height representeth courage; the length, fortitude, which patiently endureth till it attaineth its heavenly home; the breadth is charity, which, with long suffering loveth its friends in God, and its foes for God, and again, its height is the hope of future retribution, which despiseth prosperity and adversity, hoping *to see the goodness of the Lord in the land of the living* [Psalms, xxvii, 13] ... the roof, Charity, *which covereth a multitude of sins* [I Peter, iv, 8] ... the pavement, humility, of which the psalmist saith, *My soul cleaveth to the Pavement* [Psalms, cxix, 25] ....

These comparisons show the frame of mind in which the educated Christian was likely to approach a building or picture. Significantly enough, Durand's book has only one mention of the word 'beauty'. This is where he quotes the Psalms (xxvi, 8): 'Lord, I have loved the beauty of thine house', and at once he characteristically glosses the passage by explaining that it meant a place adorned 'by faith, hope, and charity'. The emphasis given to such symbolic thought was not

confined to the religious culture of the time but could be found in
literature too. So Dante, in his letter to Can Grande della Scala,
explained that the *Divine Comedy* was to be understood in four senses,
literal, allegorical, moral, anagogical. He elucidated these four levels
of meaning by an example from that contemporary biblical study
which had given rise to the concept:

> And for the better illustration of this method of exposition we
> may apply it to the following verses: 'When Israel went out of
> Egypt, the house of Jacob from a people of strange language;
> Judah was his sanctuary and Israel his dominion.' For if we
> consider the letter alone, the thing signified to us is the going
> out of the children of Israel from Egypt in the time of Moses;
> if the allegory, our redemption through Christ is signified; if the
> moral sense, the conversion of the soul from the sorrow and
> misery of sin to a state of grace is signified; if the anagogical, the
> passing of the sanctified soul from the bondage of the corruption
> of this world to the liberty of everlasting glory is signified.[8]

The religious culture of the time, in other words, conceived that
any one statement contained within it a variety of interpretations.
Traces of this attitude are to be discerned throughout the whole of
the fourteenth century. In his *Genealogy of the Gods*, Boccaccio, for
instance, was to stress the value of this method of fourfold interpretation (though in fact he rarely used it). But in secular literature it
was a mode of thought which was to decline sharply after Dante's
death.

In the letter explaining the purpose of the *Divine Comedy*, quoted
above, Dante, like Durand, made no mention of beauty. His poem,
he explained, was a branch of philosophy, though not speculative,
but practical: *gratia operis*, 'for a practical purpose'. 'Leaving aside
any minute examination of this question, it may be briefly stated
that the aim of the whole and of the part is to remove those living
in this life from a state of misery, and to bring them to a state of
happiness.' The primary object was not aesthetic but didactic. This
is an extreme point of view, which does not encompass all of Dante's
own thought on the subject. In fact he prefaced these remarks with

the observation that the aims of a work might be many and various, some immediate, others remote. Moreover, as a description of literary purpose they would have been rejected by most of his lay contemporaries, whose writings were dominated by the simple desire to please, but they summarise concisely the purpose of literature and art as taught by the church.

In the universities, the scholastic philosophers of the thirteenth century never discussed 'art' as such. They did, however, consider the meaning of beauty, and elaborated a well-considered and perhaps influential aesthetic. Treatments of the theme all derived ultimately from a Latin version of the treatise *On the Beautiful* by the early sixth century writer, Dionysius the Pseudo-Areopagite. They are to be found in Albert the Great's *Opusculum de Pulchro*, in the *Summa de Bono* of Ulrich of Strassburg, and in the *Summa Theologica* of St Thomas. The views of Aquinas may be taken as typical; they will in a certain measure be familiar to those who have read Stephen's declaration of aesthetic purpose in James Joyce's *Portrait of the Artist*. The beauty of an object or creature is only a likeness or symbol (*similitudo*) of that divine beauty in which all things participate. Thus in one sense, the beautiful and the good are one. Yet in another sense, 'that of logical priority', they are different, for beauty 'adds to the cognitive faculty by which the good is known as such.' Beauty then is the means by which truth is seen to be truth, and so it is easy to assign to it a didactic role. To achieve it, three things are necessary: *integritas* (wholeness), *proportio sive consonantia* (proportion or harmony), and *claritas* (brightness or illumination).

The canon of St Thomas and his contemporaries, which demanded clear expression, and considered any vagueness as a 'privation of form', did not mirror closely the highest aesthetic practice of the day. (Provençal poetry, for instance, which had a powerful influence on Dante, was often dominated by a tradition of wilful ambiguity.) But it looked forward to the precision and clarity which was to be a leading characteristic of Florentine and Sienese art in the following century. When Ulrich of Strassburg cites Aristotle's *Ethics* (Bk IV) in support of the contention that beauty is found in things 'of full stature', and when he goes on to argue that beauty cannot lie in a form in which the head is disproportionate to the whole body, that 'it is, rather, just measure (*commensuratio*) that makes things beautiful', we think at once of Giotto and those new conventions of realism which were about to emerge in art. It would be too much to claim that the aesthetic produced the art; what could be said, however, is that both philosophers and artists were affected at the same time by the changes in human consciousness and awareness.

Religion as the Patron of Art

In addition, the various institutions of the Church acted as the direct patrons of art. First among these was the papal *curia* itself, which, until its removal to Avignon in 1305, played a major role in Italian cultural development. For the Popes and the Papal court the last decades of the thirteenth century were a time of seeming triumph. They had routed the Hohenstaufen enemy by the mid-1260s, and by the mid-1280s had nothing to fear from the Angevin dynasty imposed on southern Italy in its place. They had suppressed the menacing Cathar and Waldensian heresies of the earlier half of the century. Their interests extended from the court of Karakorum in Outer Mongolia to the shores of Iceland, and they were supported by an unrivalled bureaucratic, financial, and diplomatic machine. The real authority of the popes was only outmatched by the theoretic claims urged in their favour by the canon lawyers of the age, who to the Vicar of Christ and Servant of the Servants of God ascribed not only all spiritual, but all temporal dominion as well. 'The earth is the Lord's and the fullness thereof, the earth and all they that dwell therein'—this was the text which echoed from the halls of the universities to the courts of kings and across the threshold of the papal *curia*.

But these claims could not endure without challenge, once they were seen to be in conflict with the interests of the lay rulers. By the end of the thirteenth century these men administered territories which were now much more firmly knit and had subjects who were sufficiently conscious of their past to be in the grip of a sentiment which can almost be called 'nationalism'. Such men could no longer accept the papal thesis, which canon lawyers were defining with ever-increasing rigour and unreality, that the lay power was subject to the spiritual.

Those of the age who looked deeper could discern the real weakness of the Church behind its impressive façade, the inevitable decline of ecumenical authority when faced with the rise of new national governments in France and England, and the increasing disquiet of those who feared the continual growth of bureaucracy within a spiritual organisation. Symbolic of that unease was the curious moment in July 1294, when the college of cardinals, as if in a painful spasm of self-awareness, elected as pope the hermit who took the title of Celestine v. Here was a man who, in contrast to other pontiffs of the century, was neither a canon lawyer nor an administrator nor a curial, but merely an uncouth illiterate, or semi-literate, saint. Within six months the painful truth emerged that a saint could not rule the Church. In December Celestine made the *gran rifiuto* and resigned the papacy. His successor, Boniface VIII, was a man of different calibre. If he had little interior life he was *audax homo et potenter pontificans*. Yet it was he who was to face disaster.

For the time being, however, Rome's art flourished under papal patronage. It was a great period for those fine tombs and tomb statues, with which pope and cardinals demonstrated their pride as descendants of the apostles. Pietro Oderisi's tomb of Clement IV (constructed 1271–74) set the standard for the movement towards portrait likeness which attained real distinction with Arnolfo di Cambio's monuments, and was imitated by the Cosmati school in numerous works carried out in the 1290s. Statues of people who were still alive were more frequently being commissioned. For Boniface VIII, in whom the instincts of passionate self-assertion ran strong, portrait statues were raised at Rome (in both the Vatican and the Lateran), at Orvieto, Florence, Anagni, and Bologna. For that time this was an unusual display of the cult of personality and it was to give his enemies the chance to accuse him of seeking idolatrous honours.

It was an era of building too. Nicholas III began the curial residence upon the Vatican and the strange, half-Gothic S. Maria sopra

Minerva, the last church to be built at Rome for a century. Nicholas IV initiated a new palace by S. Maria Maggiore, and Boniface VIII the reconstruction of the Senate-house upon the Capitol. Much too was done for the preservation and embellishment of the churches. The restoration of the old St Peter's was begun in the 1280s, and the next decade saw the rebuilding of the apse and façade of the Lateran. Jacopo Torriti executed mosaics in the Lateran and in S. Maria Maggiore, while Pietro Cavallini decisively pointed the way to the future with the realism of his work in S. Maria in Trastevere.

Much of what was done at Rome in these years is probably to be associated with Nicholas IV (1288–92), first of the Franciscan popes. It is likely that he was a principal patron too of the decoration then proceeding in the great Franciscan church at Assisi, where, during his pontificate, painters who already had Roman connections such as Torriti, Cimabue, and the so-called Isaac Master, were at work. A little later one of the curial cardinals commissioned Giotto to execute the *Navicella*, the large mosaic showing the Church as the barque of Peter, which until the seventeenth century dominated the atrium of St Peter's. When this was completed Giotto too probably went on to Assisi. The *curia* did not neglect the other arts. Guccio di Mannaia, first of the great Sienese goldsmiths, executed the splendid chalice of the basilica of Assisi for Nicholas IV, and other Sienese workers in precious metals laboured for the luxury-loving Boniface VIII.

This age of patronage came to an end with the struggle between Boniface VIII and Philip IV of France. By 1303 the king's patience had come to an end and his agents struck. They seized Boniface at Anagni, sacked his palace, and dragged him from his throne. A month later the pope was dead and his power dissolved. It is this dramatic scandal to which Dante referred in the twentieth canto of the *Purgatorio*:

I see the fleur-de-lys enter Anagni, and Christ made captive in his vicar. A second time I see him mocked. I see the vinegar and gall renewed, and him slain among the thieves who live. I see the new Pilate, so cruel that this suffices him not . . . .

Yet it excited little stir among the great of Europe, and none among them were roused to protest against the sacrilege. For the events at Anagni were in many ways merely the symbolic expression of the new relationship between the lay and ecclesiastical forces in Europe, the demonstration of the triumph of secular over ecumenical religious aims. These events merely pointed the obvious, that real papal control was a myth. 'My master's sword', said one of the French king's servants, 'was of steel; the Pope's of words'. This brutal affirmation marked out a future in which real power lay with secular governments, and where they rather than the Church were to represent the values of society.

In the years that followed, succeeding popes, partly in the hope of finding a more secure refuge, partly under pressure from the French monarchy, abandoned Rome. From 1305 to 1378 the Papacy was established at Avignon. The patronage of the popes and cardinals at Rome largely dried up, and goldsmiths like Toro di Siena, painters like Simone Martini, writers like Petrarch, musicians like 'the modern Orpheus', Floriano da Rimini, were drawn north to the new seat of the *curia* in France. From the point of view of the arts, the significance of the crime of Anagni was that what might have been a major centre of patronage and a major centre for the advance of the new ideals of art was now lost to Italy. Did the world of northern Europe correspondingly gain from the change? One would assume so, though most art-historians are particularly emphatic here that 'the Italianisation of European art' in the fourteenth century is not to be ascribed to the papal residence at Avignon but rather to the sensational attractions of the new art itself.[9] However this may be, it is certain that the development of Italian humanism was to benefit considerably from the increased contacts at Avignon between the scholars of Italy and the north.

The bishops, of course, remained in Italy, and had already come to ape the fashions of the *curia* upon which they depended. They, too, had come to feel the need for elaborate tombs; such monuments as that to Tomasso, Bishop of Pistoia, raised by Gano di Fazio at Casola d'Elsa after 1303, and the curious memorial executed by Camaino for Antonio, Bishop of Florence (d. 1321), which seems to show its subject in the first stages of the fit which carried him off. Some of the episcopacy were immensely wealthy and could indulge a passion for art and building on a large scale. The chronicler of Milan, for instance, shows the Archbishop Ottone Visconti (d. 1295) 'adorning his archbishopric with the most beautiful buildings: the castles of Angeria, Travellia, Cassano, Magnano, Legnano, and Abbiategrasso.'[10] But this was exceptional, and episcopal patronage cannot be considered as a major factor in the arts of the time. In the towns the communes had taken over from the Church most of the responsibilities of building the cathedrals and major churches. And in the country the existing pattern of parishes called for no radical building programme; here there were few churches built in the Gothic age, and religious architecture retained, as it still does today, a predominantly Romanesque character.

The monasteries, which were not flourishing in the period, had little influence on art. There were some exceptions: the Abbot of S. Paolo fuori le Mura employed Cavallini and Arnolfo in the mid-1280s; and the order of Monteoliveto, founded in 1319, is said to have placed particular stress on the religious value of art.[11] Yet monastic patronage fades into insignificance beside the cultural influence exercised by the friars. Here the two principal orders were the Dominicans and the Franciscans, who, embodying a new religious ideal, sought therefore new means of religious expression.

Loosely speaking, that ideal can be thought of as the recognition of the need for religion to involve itself with, rather than to withdraw from, the world. In this the two major orders adopted rather different tactics. The Dominicans, taking their name from their founder St. Dominic (d. 1221), had made it their special task to combat heresy through the cultivation of the intellect. So, from the end of the thirteenth century, their principal houses in Italy served as local universities for theological and philosophic studies. It was probably at the Dominican house of Santa Maria Novella in Florence that Dante first attended *le disputazioni de li filosofanti*, and first studied that theological system which he was to interpret in his own way in the Divine Comedy. At a much lower level, the sermons of the Dominicans, with their racy mixture of stories, jokes, and pious exhortations, provided the bulk of the popular culture of the fourteenth century. A preacher like Giordano da Rivalto would lace his moral teachings with a miscellany of stories from Suetonius and Cicero, the epics of Lancelot and Roland, animal stories, anecdotes of the experiences of his brethren in the east, and of his own travels in Italy, France, and England (where he found the inhabitants obsessively concerned with cleanliness). All this, in an age by our standards lacking in public diversions, filled a noticeable gap in the provision of free entertainment. On many planes, therefore, the Dominicans answered to a need in society, and this, together with their avowed pursuit of the ideal of poverty as a way of life, made them immensely popular. As a result they were the beneficiaries of very many grants and wills, and so could erect their large churches [12] and commission for their decoration those numberless cycles of paintings dealing with the mysteries of religion and the glories of the Dominican saints, St Dominic himself, St Peter Martyr and St Thomas Aquinas.

The major cultural rivals of the Dominicans were the Franciscans. Yet St Francis (d. 1226) had himself been indifferent to learning, had forbidden his followers to possess any book, even a psalter, and had reproved the brothers of Bologna for the size of the church they had built. St Dominic had established the ideal of apostolic poverty as a means: as a way of attracting the sympathy of a proletariat alienated from the church of the rich; St Francis, by contrast, held poverty to be a Christ-like state, a virtue in its own right. Hence he asked for humble churches, and would have deprecated the idea of raising expensive monuments on religious themes. His ideal, the meek, joyful pursuit in nakedness of the naked Christ, left behind all culture as an irrelevance. Although he was a poet, a 'troubadour of God', his poetry was merely the expression of heightened religious feeling: poetry and prayer were indivisible. This ideal, however, even during his own lifetime, had been profoundly changed, partly as a result of the expansion and institutionalising of his order, and partly, too, because it seemed to imply a criticism of the papal *curia* in its wealth and power. So the Franciscans, too, had become property-holders, at least by proxy; the wealth of their churches grew; and members of the order were to be found among the leading intellectuals of the century.

Accordingly, by 1300, the Italian Franciscans had, like the Dominicans, become a force for learning, for building, and for patronage of the arts. At the new, splendid church of Santa Croce in Florence (under construction from 1295) the friars taught the doctrines of such eminent university philosophers as St Bonaventura, and observed with pleasure the frescoes by Giotto and Daddi which the rich merchant aristocracy of the commune had commissioned for the walls. Like the Dominicans, they built great churches every-where throughout Italy. Above all at Assisi, over the tomb of St Francis, they erected one of the most lavish temples of Christendom. Within it there were the cycles of paintings by Cimabue, the Isaac Master, and Simone Martini, and, supreme irony because so su-premely opposed to every ideal of Francis himself, the great frescoes by Giotto. These, on a scale unparalleled for any previous saint, exalted the life and deeds of the *poverello* who had taught abnegation of self, absolute poverty, and the humility of the dust.

'The last shall be first'. In this way the Conventuals, or followers of the revised and relaxed rule of St Francis, would have justified the paradox. Again, there was need for compromise with the world: with those hard-headed men of the *curia*, who knew full well that an institution could only preach the virtues of poverty if it were well-endowed with riches. Yet this alienation of the Franciscan ideal had not gone wholly unchallenged within the order. Against the Conventuals, the Spirituals, led by Ubertino da Casale and Pietro Olvi, still preached the need for apostolic poverty, a doctrine so understandably painful to the papacy that in 1322 it was condemned as heretical. They too had developed their culture, whose finest representative is the turbulent poet, Fra Jacapone da Todi, and even after their condemnation their influence was still felt. In these circumstances, it has been easy for certain historians of art to repre-sent the two branches of Franciscan culture as resting on the support of different classes within the communes. They imply that the culture of the Conventuals was subsidised by, and appealed to, the rich and powerful, who could be assumed to welcome an order which had compromised with wealth. This culture was, the argument continues, inspired by the 'rationalising' tendencies of the upper bourgeoisie. By contrast the culture of the Spirituals, addressed to the poor, was essentially conservative. It is not really an argument to be taken seriously. Unfortunately for system-builders, human beings are much more complex than their immediate class interests, and among the patrons and supporters of the Spirituals one finds such wealthy and powerful figures as the Sienese banking families of the Tolomei and Piccolomoni, King Frederick II of Sicily, and that arch-ally of the Florentine plutocracy, King Robert of Naples and his wife Sancia.

The other orders of friars had less influence on the arts. The Carmelites were largely indifferent to them. The Augustinians, though they had criticised the foundation of the Arena chapel as being 'rather for pomp and self-seeking vainglory than for the honour and glory of God,' had some influence in the sphere of literary culture. Michele da Massa Marritima (d. 1337) wrote scriptural commentaries which (almost alone among those of contemporary Italy) showed considerable interest in the Latin classics. Dionigi di Borga San Sepolcro (d. 1342), the author of a commentary on Valerius Maximus, was the friend of Boccaccio and Petrarch, and a principal associate of the Neapolitan school of humanist studies. Later in the century, Luigi Marsigli from the convent of Santo Spirito was a leader in the development of humanist thought at Florence.[13]

Turning to the lay world, the principal organizations were the societies of Laudesi, composed of those who, without taking vows or living communally, gathered regularly to worship together and to organise charitable works. These too contributed to the culture of the age. Their chants before the image of their patron saint were sometimes, as with the Laudesi of Or San Michele, accompanied by viol and hand organ, and were often prepared for by regular choir practice. The lyrics of their songs were often pure poetry; the Laudesi of S. Spirito at Florence, for instance, sang the verses of Fra Jacopone. Again, the Laudesi played some part in the evolution of religious drama. The singing of their hymns could be broken up into dramatic cantatas. So, in a performance by a confraternity of penance at Siena, various members of the fraternity took the parts of the Madonna, Jesus, the crowd, the Magdalen, the two Marys, St John, and the Cross itself, in an interesting chanted dialogue. Perhaps in evolution from this type of performance, the societies began also to put on plays proper. At Orvieto, the Fraternity of St. Francis re-enacted *The Miracle of Bolsena*. The titles of some of these works suggest the use of quite elaborate stage machinery, and doubtless surprising effects were aimed at. In one of his short stories, Sacchetti, writing later in the century, describes a performance at S. Maria del Carmine in Florence, illustrating the Ascension, in which the player of the Saviour was drawn up from the stage on a bell-rope towards the roof, where he disappeared. Besides all this, the *Laudesi* patronised the visual arts, both by commissioning the images before which they prayed and by the erection of oratories or hospitals and other buildings designed for the refuge of the poor and sick. The company of S. Maria della Misericordia, for instance, commissioned Duccio in 1285 to paint the great panel of their heavenly patron, now in the Uffizi; later too they were to build the oratory known as the Bigallo, which stands opposite the Baptistry in Florence.

Outside the patronage exercised by the religious orders and confraternities, there was that offered by individual devout laymen. This patronage seems to be in no way different from that given directly by ecclesiastics. Lay donors had inevitably to consult with clergy before their offerings were accepted in church. When the Manelli wished to construct a tomb for their family in S. Maria Novella, or when the silk merchant Simone Pucci wished for a picture in San Marco, they simply left the business of commissioning the work to the ecclesiastics of the church concerned.[14] In these circumstances it is uncertain whether, for example, it was the Franciscans of Sante Croce or the Bardi family who were actually responsible for commissioning the Bardi frescoes. It seems reasonable to assume, however, that there was no difference in aesthetic sensibility between the lay and clerical world. Certainly, ecclesiastical patrons, especially within the papal *curia*, were liable to commission works which seem to have every bit as much of a 'rational' or 'advanced' character as those ordered by laymen.

In the past it has been suggested that bourgeois donations to the Church were largely the product of guilt, that they originated from the merchant's fear of damnation. These fears, it was argued, sprang from their violation of what were conceived to be the Church's prohibitions of capitalist techniques in business. This is greatly to overstate the case. It is true that the Church condemned as 'usurious' loans which exacted interest, that is to say, any interest at all, not merely high interest. But at the same time creditors were permitted to take a profit where their capital had been at risk. Accordingly, many merchants could pass the whole of their lives in speculative money-lending without any disturbance of conscience. The attacks of the Church were principally directed against 'the manifest usurer' who exacted interest against full security. Many merchants, of course, did take occasional opportunities to operate as usurers in this sense: others were frequently involved in secret usurious transactions. From these men, on their death beds, or as death approached, the Church could expect substantial donations in restitution and repentance.[15] So Folco Portinari, the father (if one accepts a common belief) of Dante's Beatrice, founded the Hospital of S. Maria Nuova as a penance for his dealings in the Cerchi bank. So too Enrico Scrovegni of Padua, son of the noted usurer whom Dante (*Inferno*, xvii) was to place within the seventh circle of Hell, built the Arena chapel in expiation, and caused Giotto to illustrate in fresco there the story of man's redemption and final judgment.

Other gifts there were, however, which were with the expression of a religious emotion less tinged with guilt, and mingled doubtless with something of social pride. So the Bardi family at the end of the century, and the Pazzi in the 1320s, erected their chapels in Santa Croce, and later commissioned Giotto to decorate them. In the same church the Baroncelli family had no less than three family chapels, adorned with their tomb-monuments, while the Alberti chapel was frescoed by the hand of Agnolo Gaddi. Nonetheless, though such gifts to the Church were common, the bourgeois in this age generally preferred to channel his religious and secular patronage in a collective form, through his community and its government.

four

Government and Patronage: I

Citizenship in the Age of Dante

The age of Dante was an important stage in that slow development of the state which forms a major theme of European history between the eleventh and the eighteenth centuries. As yet the state as we understand it hardly existed. The rights of rulers were continually contested by feudal privilege, independent corporations, and the institutions of the Church. Their machinery of administration, moreover, whether in the departments of justice, taxation, or the waging of war, was, by modern standards supremely inefficient. None the less, secular governments in this period showed a new confidence, claimed new powers and took new responsibilities. Political control assumed more impersonal forms: institutions now claimed the allegiance formerly given only to individuals. It was a time too when there grew up among intellectuals an intense loyalty to their native cities and governments.

Influenced by the current philosophic concepts of Aristotle's *Ethics* and *Politics*, these men stressed the rights of the commune against the individual with an enthusiasm which has caused them to be characterised in our own age as 'Thomistic proto-Hegelians'. With intense feeling the writers of the age, particularly the Dominicans, adapted the commentaries of Aquinas upon 'the Philosopher' to their own *polis*. 'He who is not a citizen is not a man, for man is by nature a civic animal says the philosopher'. 'The common good is without doubt to be preferred to the particular good, and the good of the multitude to the good of one person.' So wrote the

Dominican philosopher and preacher, Remigio Girolami, in his cell at S. Maria Novella in Florence. In the leading political treatise of the age, the *Defensor Pacis* of Marsiglio of Padua (1324), these accents were somewhat muted. Marsiglio was to warn against arbitrary power, and to stress the rule of law. Yet he too saw the individual as subject to 'the common good' and called for the revivification of Aristotle's concept of the city-state: that *polis* which came into being for the sake of life, but which continued in existence in order to maintain the best form of life. With these sentiments it was easy to equate, as did Ptolemy of Lucca, Christian charity with 'zeal for the *patria*', and to give new meaning to the long-standing Christian concept of Heaven itself as a city. Preaching in S. Maria Novella, Fra Giordano da Rivalto said: 'the word "City" [*Civitas*] sounds almost like "Love" [*Caritas*] and through love are cities built, since men delight in living together.' (By the same token, Hell itself, for Dante, was a *città dolente*.)

Contemporary literature shows that these feelings were not simply the product of an academic meditation, unsupported by general sentiment. For lay writers of the time, the word 'city' implied an attempt to reach a just human society, and the role of citizen was not grudgingly undertaken as a duty but welcomed as a high function of man. It was accepted in the spirit in which Caccia-guida, in the fifteenth canto of the *Paradiso* tells Dante how he was born:

> *A così riposato, a così bello*
> *viver di cittadini, a così fida*
> *cittadinanza, a così dolce ostello.*

('To so fair and tranquil a life as a citizen, to such faithful citizenship, to so sweet a refuge.')

It was given perhaps its deepest expression in the eighth canto in the exchange between the exiled poet, himself deprived of his citizenship, and Charles Martel:

> *Ond' egli ancora: 'Or di', sarebbe il peggio*
> *per l'uomo in terra se non fosse cive?'*
> *'Sì' rispos' io, 'e qui ragion non cheggio'.*

('And so he again: "Now say, would it not be worse for man on earth, if he were not a citizen?" "Yes", I replied, "and for that I seek no explanation".')

Living with these emotions, striving to support their city against the ever present menace of faction, the men of the age sought to give visible expression to the honour and nobility of the *patria*. As a result it was the city-state which in this period was the principal patron of the arts. It was the men involved in government who were responsible for the erection of the principal ecclesiastical and secular buildings, who commissioned the paintings and sculptures placed within them, and who, by their town-planning, often created the essential outlines of the cities as we see them today.

Within *trecento* Italy there were two main forms of government. The first were the signorial domains, the territories ruled by the *signori* and the kings. The second were the cities presided over by bourgeois or bourgeois-aristocratic oligarchies. Although the differences in the forms of patronage exercised by the types of government were not in fact very significant, it is worth while viewing them separately. In this chapter the patronage of the communes will be considered. By the fourteenth century the communes themselves were few enough in number, for only Venice, Siena, and Florence (though not without intervals of signorial rule), survived as republics. Elsewhere almost every city was swept by the tide which was carrying Italy to one-man governments. Padua fell finally to the della Scala family in 1328, Orvieto to the Church, while Bologna only succeeded for a few brief periods in winning back, also from the Church, independent communal rule. Where the commune survived, however, it offered the benefit of constitutions in which decision-making was based upon the free discussion of political issues by the leading families within the city. One should not think of such constitutions as being democratic, for the majority of citizens were excluded from participation in government; nor should one take at their face value their claims to embody 'Liberty', for consciously or unconsciously they often represented a means of class-oppression. Yet elements of both democracy and liberty, conceived of in an upper-bourgeois manner, were found within them.

Ecclesiastical Patronage
by the Commune

In the task of beautifying their city, to which they had set themselves, the men of the commune gave first precedence to their cathedral and greater churches. To ecclesiastics of that age the cathedral stood as a symbol of the eternal Jerusalem; to the laymen it was more, a mirror of their own holy city, a monument to its piety, a temple to the greatness of the commune itself. Here were preserved fragments of the battlewagons and standards captured from their enemies, and in it were portrayed, in fresco, the military leaders who had won glory for the town. It housed the images which in the past had brought good fortune to her politics, and the shrine of that saint who was particularly their own, that patron saint who, revered almost as a tribal god, brought prosperity to the citizens and defeat to their enemies. Here civic and religious emotions, as today in Westminster Abbey, blended without disharmony.

Accordingly, the communes from their earliest times had held themselves responsible for the building and maintenance of their cathedrals. From 1300 onwards this concern was to lead to the erection of the three great cathedrals of Florence, Orvieto, and Arezzo, to the restoration of Lucca, and to the enlargement of the cathedral at Siena. There was, of course, some consultation with the bishop, but this was largely a formality; in all these towns control was exercised by the commune, through a board of works called the *Opera del Duomo*. Generally the *opera* was supervised closely and directly by the councils of the commune, and was held responsible not to the bishop, but to the government. As the conciliar decree of Siena phrased it in 1310: 'It is evident to all that the office of the Lords Nine should have care and solicitude and love for the *opera* of the blessed Mary ever Virgin, and should concern itself with the conservation of its affairs, with curtailing useless expenses, and with accepting and preserving those things which may promote it.' At Pistoia the statutes of the *opera* expressed the same sentiment in a less tactful way: 'Neither the *opera* nor the masters of the *opera* shall be subject to the care or ward of any ecclesiastical person.' In Florence the commune's authority over the cathedral was delegated to one of the great guilds: first to the cloth-merchants, the *Arte di Calimala*, and afterwards to the *Arte della Lana*. The guild, it will be remembered, was here a major part of the governmental structure.

The tasks and constitution of the *opera* varied from town to town, but that of Siena can be taken as fairly typical. The *Opera di S. Maria di Siena* administered the patrimony confided to the cathedral, organised feasts and receptions for illustrious visitors, supervised the fabric, building, and decoration of the cathedral, and, moreover, was often held responsible for the erection of other buildings in the city. At its head was a master of works or factor, called the *operaio*, who was appointed or re-appointed by the commune every six months. He might be an artist or artisan, but more generally was some merchant who would be capable of dealing with all the business involved. (There was a brief scandal in the 1290s when it was discovered that the *operaio* appointed could neither read nor write, and the election was quashed.) The board under him, which had its own house by the cathedral, consisted of from four to six men, including, normally, a canon of the cathedral. Among these, one would act as 'chamberlain' or treasurer, and one as a notary or Clerk of the Works. Together, these men kept accounts, took in the revenues due from properties bequeathed to the *opera*, fixed contracts and wages with tradesmen and artists, and regularly reported to the commune on the condition of the cathedral. It was on their recommendation that the commune would appoint the *Capomaestro* or Master Builder, who was generally the principal professional executive of the work. In addition they sought special-ised advice by the appointment of *ad hoc* committees of tradesmen. But in all the business of the *opera* it was the commune which was the final arbiter, and it was through the commune that the *opera* re-ceived almost all the money essential for its work.

In the dispensing of money the commune exercised the tightest control. In December 1308, for instance, the *operaio* of Siena com-plained that his men went off at mealtimes to taverns or to their houses, because they were not given wine on the cathedral site. And so he proposed that the *opera* itself should serve drinks to the masters and labourers, 'for they can't be expected to stay all day working away, without drinking.' But before the board could do even this, they first had to petition the Lords Nine of the city for their consent. Again, when a general council of June 1369 authorised the expenditure of 100 florins by the *opera*, it insisted that the financial inspectors of the commune should supervise what was done with the money. All this was reasonable enough since it was the commune which provided the financial backing for every aspect of the *opera*'s activities.

Progress in building depended on the fortunes of the government, and proceeded, now slowly, now in sudden bursts of activity, as their revenues permitted or as the enthusiasm of their citizens waned and revived. Consequently the cathedrals grew up over long periods of time, slowly coming to fruition, rather than being constructed to any specific end-plan clear in the mind of the first builder. At Florence, for instance, the present cathedral was begun some time after or around 1294. The citizens, Villani explained: 'agreed to renew their greater church, which was rude in form and small in proportion to such a city, and they ordered that it should be enlarged and extended at the back, and that it was to be decorated with marble and sculptured figures.' In this first burst of enthusiasm, special taxes were raised to meet expenses, and under the direction of Arnolfo di Cambio, the first façade was erected. But at the beginning of the fourteenth century, perhaps as a result of the political crises in the city, the work languished. In 1308 a council was complaining that the building 'which for some time previously has progressed slowly, is now almost abandoned for lack of money.' Of such complaints little came. The revenues of Florence in the 1320s were poured into the disastrous war for the possession of Lucca, and into the building of the third circuit of the walls, and interest in the cathedral revived only at the end of the decade. In 1330, taxes for the work were reimposed, and the control of the *opera*, hitherto vested in the *Calimala*, was now given to the *Arte della Lana*, at this time perhaps the wealthiest among the greater guilds.

Under this new supervision more ambitious plans were drawn up and work was recommenced. Giotto was appointed as 'governor' of the *opera* in 1334, and with him the elegant campanile was begun. From the end of the 1330s however, the fortunes of the city again declined, and with them the work upon the church. When building was resumed in the second half of the century the old design was virtually replaced. The structure, excluding the exterior decoration, was only completed in 1467.

Similar delays protracted the building of Orvieto, begun in 1290. But the most revealing insight into the commune as cathedral-builder comes from Siena. By 1285, in fact, much of the present cathedral of Santa Maria of Siena (see plate 12) was already standing: the cupola, the campanile, part of the transept, and all but two of the bays of the west end. In the second decade of the fourteenth century, however, the commune decided upon its enlargement. The immediate spur was provided by the neighbouring and rival communes of Orvieto and Florence, both of which had begun work on far larger cathedrals. Faced with this challenge to their civic pride, the Sienese government decided that their own temple was inadequate. The chancel was to be lengthened over the steeply descending ground to the east, and to be supported there by a new baptistery built into a lower level of the slope. In this way the baptistery would act as a giant support and crypt for the extension of the building above.

For the moment very little came of these plans. The technical difficulties presented by the site were considerable, and work proceeded slowly. Seven years later indeed, in February 1322, a commission of five experts, which included the Sienese master Lorenzo Maitani, master-builder of Orvieto cathedral, condemned the work already done as unsound. In their report to the master of the works, which was made 'by the will and with the knowledge of the Lords Nine, and in the palace of the commune of Siena in the hall where the Council of the Bell meets', they declared that they had inspected all the new work in the cathedral, had discussed it among themselves, and had concluded that what had been done was undesirable and unpracticable. The foundations of the extension were out of line with those of the old church, and the pillars were insufficient to take the thrust of the roof. Moreover, the enlargement of the chancel would mean that the dome would no longer be over the centre of the crossing of the main building and transepts, 'where it reasonably belongs'. Accordingly:

> we think that the said building should not proceed further, because when completed it would not have those proportions of a church in length, width, and height, that the laws of a church require. Again, the old church is so well proportioned and its parts blend so well in width, length, and height, that rather than add anything to any one part, it would be better to demolish the whole church and then rebuild it in the right proportions for a church.

The committee then went on to draw up a second document proposing a wholly new cathedral:

> We advise that for the honour of God and of the blessed Virgin Mary, his most holy mother, who ever was, is, and will be in future, head of this city of Siena, that there should be begun and completed a beautiful, great, and magnificent church which shall be well-proportioned in length, height, and width, and in all those measurements which become a beautiful church, and that it should have all the brilliant ornamentation which is becoming and fitting to so great, honourable, and beautiful a church. In this way our Lord Jesus Christ and his most holy mother and his most high celestial court may be blessed and praised in hymns in that church, and the commune of Siena may be protected from harm and be held in honour in perpetuity.[1]

In these words one senses the judgment of men moved by a vision which had blinded them to mundane realities. The enormous capital expenditure required for a new building went unmentioned, and the likelihood of Siena being able to meet the cost lightly taken for granted. Presumably some were quick to note these points, and the report was shelved for the moment, work continuing slowly on the extensions already planned. Yet the citizens' very impatience at the slow speed of the extensions drove them, paradoxically enough, to demand newer and still more magnificent schemes.

So, in August 1339 the Lords Nine and 'the general council of the Bell' finally approved plans for a new cathedral; in December they called the Sienese goldsmith Lando di Pietro from Naples as consultant to the Master of Works for the building. Two ground plans, possibly drawn by Lando, which can still be seen in the Cathedral Museum, show the design. The new cathedral was to be erected along an axis bisecting the old building, and the nave of the existing cathedral was to become the transepts of the new structure. Had this plan been carried through it would have given Siena the largest cathedral in Italy.

This would not have been a distinction which the political and economic power of the city warranted. Within Siena it is clear that many doubted the wisdom of the scheme. In the General Council the plan for the new cathedral was carried by 212 votes in favour but with a considerable number of votes, 132, against. Had these men known that in 1339 they stood on the brink of a profound economic recession, it is hardly likely that the proposal would even have been considered. As it was the 1340s were a period of very great financial difficulties, and culminated in the bubonic plague of 1348. But even without this disaster it is doubtful whether the work could ever have been completed.

What building there was went ahead slowly and deficiently. In 1356 a consultant from Florence was reporting that the columns of the new nave were off the true and that the walls on one side were wider than on the other. At the same time Domenico d'Agostino, the master-builder of the time, and a colleague, were gloomily reporting that the completion of the work would cost over 150,000 florins, and, 'believe us!', would take over 100 years to finish. At this work stopped altogether, and in the following year the new rulers of the city, the Twelve Governors, gave orders for all dangerous masonry to be taken down. Today only a few over-slender piers still stand to give melancholy testimony to the ambitious dream of the Sienese. Yet, as will be seen later, this was not to be the end of the story.

In none of the Italian cities was the work of the state for the cathedral confined merely to the erection and preservation of the fabric. The communes also made themselves responsible for the interior embellishment of the building. In this field, too, there was the same easy fusion of civic and religious feeling. One thinks particularly here of the story of Duccio's painting of the *Maestà* or Queen of Heaven for the high altar of the cathedral of Siena between 1308 and 1311. With this work (now in the cathedral museum) the painter was faced with an extremely difficult task. He was called upon to replace an older picture, 'the Madonna of the Large Eyes', which, it was believed, had brought aid to the Sienese on the day of their great victory over the Florentines at Montaperti some 50 years before, and which, through these and many other associations, was dear to the men of the city. It says much for the confidence of the citizens in their own age and in Duccio himself that they should have been willing even to consider the substitution of a new painting for the old.

Whatever doubts there may have been when the *opera* first commissioned the work, the completion of the *Maestà* was received with a sense of civic triumph. It was proclaimed to be 'much more beautiful and devout and larger' than the old Madonna, and on 9 June 1311 the citizens bore it in triumph from the artist's workshop to the cathedral. The exchequer records note payments of £S12.10.0. for trumpeters, flautists, and kettledrummers who performed on the occasion, while the scene itself (which Vasari inaccurately transposed to the reception of Cimabue's *Madonna* in Florence) was described by a contemporary chronicler in these terms:

On the day it was carried to the Duomo, the shops shut up and the Bishop ordered a great and devout company of priests and friars to go in solemn procession, and they were accompanied by the Lords Nine and all the officials of the commune and all the people. And all the most worthy went hand in hand, accompanying the picture with lighted candles, and behind them went the women and children with much devotion. And they accompanied the said picture to the cathedral, processing around the Campo in the usual way, while the bells sounded a *gloria* with reverence for so noble a painting as was this. This picture was painted by Duccio and was made in the house of the Muciatti outside the gate at Stalloreggi. And all that day they stood at prayer, with much almsgiving to poor people, praying God and his holy mother who is our advocate to defend us in his infinite mercy from every adversity and all evil and to keep us from the hands of traitors and enemies of Siena.[2]

It was in this spirit, in the belief that the honouring of the Virgin and of her house was a defence of the temporal interests of the commune, that the Sienese in the period 1320–1340 were to go on to commission other paintings from Pietro Lorenzetti, Simone Martini, and Lippo Memmi, to adorn their cathedral.

This type of patronage was not confined to the cathedrals. In many towns there were certain other ecclesiastical buildings which were of particular significance to the commune. In Venice, the church of St Mark, the chapel of the Doge, whose basic structure had been raised in the eleventh century, served both for religious ceremonies and a variety of secular celebrations. In some ways it was designed as a school of moral instruction for the Doge, and was filled with inscriptions addressed to him by the commune over whose destinies he presided. Near the door through which he entered the church from his palace, for instance, he saw these words in gold letters before his eyes:

> Love justice, give to every man his rights. The poor, the widow, ward, and orphan look for a guardian in you. Be pious to all: let not fear, nor hate, nor love, nor gold, betray you. As a flower shall you fall, oh Doge, dust shall you be, and as you have acted, so shall you be esteemed after your death.

Here again there was a fusion of religious and political morality. Hence all through the twelfth, thirteenth, and later centuries it was the Republic which held itself responsible for the maintenance, extension, and adornment of the building.

In Florence, too, there were churches which had a particularly close link with the commune. In 1325, for instance, the victory of the Florentines over Arezzo, on St Barnabas' day, inspired the construction of a church dedicated to that saint. Much older and much more deeply rooted was the attachment of the citizens to their Baptistery, the church of St John. The Baptist was the patron of the city, the city itself 'the sheepfold of St John'. His church, believed, though inaccurately, to have been a temple dedicated to Mars in Roman times, was one of the most hallowed places in the citizen's life. Nowhere in Dante's writings does there appear a more authentic note of personal passion than when, as an exile, he thinks of *il mio bel San Giovanni*. Consequently, as early as the twelfth century the commune had entrusted its upkeep to the *Calimala*, the Guild of the Clothworkers, which supervised the building through a board of management, the *Opera di San Giovanni*.

From 1225 the *Calimala* gave themselves to the embellishment of this venerable centre of the citizen's life. From 1271 to the end of the century the cupola was adorned with mosaics, while from 1293 the old stone and marble tombs were removed, and a new marble surface was given to the exterior. This process of beautying continued through the fourteenth century. In the third book of the statutes of the *Calimala*, as revised in 1337, arrangements were made for the appointment each year of two 'Officials of the Mosaic Work of Saint John the Baptist' whose duties included, besides the supervision of the mosaic, all questions relating to the building, repair, and ornament of the fabric. The work done, it was stipulated, was to be 'the best and most beautiful that can be done for the honour of God and the blessed St John.' Two other men were appointed to maintain there the *carroccio* (the battle-wagon of the commune) and banners, while every January the consuls of the guild were to appoint four men who were to hold discussions with all on how the church might be best maintained: 'to the reverence of Almighty God and of his Mother and St John, and to the good state of the commune of Florence, and of the most pure guild of the *Calimala*.' The members of the guild who were principal partners in large international companies, the Bardi, Peruzzi, Bonaccorsi, Acciaiuoli, and Bilotti firms, were ordered to use their influence at the papal court, so that the Baptistery should be free of all interference from the bishop or cathedral chapter, and should remain under the control of the guild 'under whose guard and protection the said church and *opera* are directed, maintained, and governed with pure faith.' The pride with which the guild spoke of itself here was not misplaced. Between 1330 and 1336 it had supervised and financed the making of the bronze doors of Andrea Pisano, a work which Villani, himself at the time an official of the *Calimala*, had declared to be 'extremely beautiful and of marvellous workmanship and cost.' At the beginning of the next century it launched the competition which was to produce the two great gates of Ghiberti.

The interests of the communes were not confined to those churches in which their citizens had deep, specifically civic, interests. The commune assumed a measure of responsibility for all ecclesiastical buildings within its boundaries. At Siena, for instance, the *podestà*, on his accession to office, swore 'to maintain and conserve the cathedral of Siena, and the Hospital of Santa Maria, and all the venerable places of the city and *contado* of Siena'; and the government made frequent contributions towards the building or decoration of churches with which it had no clear political link. In 1309, for instance, it provided 100,000 tiles and a great quantity of mortar for the rebuilding of the church of San Domenico. In 1329, in answer to an appeal from the Carmelite friars, it contributed £S50 towards a painting that they had commissioned from Pietro Lorenzetti. Ten years later it made a grant of £S200 towards the new church of San Francesco. In 1365 it helped out the Carmelites again. They had petitioned that 'for the name and honour of the city of Siena' the commune should contribute something towards a tabernacle they wished to commission. Playing both upon the citizens' competitive civic pride and their sense of economy, they explained that it would cost 400 florins, and yet would be much more beautiful than the tabernacle in the neighbouring city of Orvieto, which, they explained, had cost a full 1,300 florins. This appeal secured 50 florins from the government.[3]

At Florence the same spirit of patronage prevailed. The statutes of 1322, for instance, claimed that the completion of the Franciscan Santa Croce and the Dominicans' Santa Maria Novella (both begun in the 1290s) should be encouraged 'for the benefit of souls and the decorum of the city'. From 1294 both churches had received financial support from the government. Other churches which benefited were Santa Maria del Carmine, Santo Spirito, the Badia, the Annunziata, and Santa Trinità. Characteristically for Florence this patronage was generally channelled through the guilds, who were severally made responsible for the *opera* of the various churches and hospitals. The *Calimala*, for instance, in addition to its control over the Baptistery and (until 1331) the Cathedral, supervised the church of San Miniato al Monte and the hospital of Sant' Eusebio. Similarly the Silk Guild administered the building of Or San Michele. In origin this was a small church dedicated to Saint Michael, standing on the grain market. After the picture of the Madonna in its loggia had been credited with miraculous powers, it was decided to rebuild the whole structure as a combined chapel and corn-exchange in the form of a palace, with a *loggia* on the ground floor, and two vaulted stories above for the storing of grain. From 1339 the decoration of the building was entrusted to the twelve principal guilds, though this was not to bear full fruit until the beginning of the fifteenth century.

It would be easy to consider this patronage of the churches by the commune and municipal guilds in a cynical light, to portray it as merely an excuse for institutional self-glorification, and it is true that an element of this entered into their policy. On the other hand the governments were also consciously acting on behalf of the deepest religious instincts of their citizens. They distributed patronage to the churches in the same way that a modern state distributes welfare benefits, not only because it made itself popular in doing so, but because it felt that this was an appropriate way for a government to behave if it wished to benefit its subjects, if it wished to fulfil the demands of justice made upon it. Throughout the whole century the demand for aid to be given in religion came from below. This can be seen, for instance, in the petition by which in April 1389 some Sienese citizens appealed to their government to repair the campanile and to make a Camposanto: 'that is to say a place of burial, in that form and manner as is found at Pisa, which is one of the most noble of those things in Christianity that appertain to the

Church.' Again, in the ponderous petition addressed to the council of Siena in 1360, we read: 'The glorious God is said to rejoice in the preaching of his saints. He rewards the devout for whatever honour is given to them, by which the cult of divine things is shown to exist. The commune of Siena, then, should turn its mind to that form of devotion whereby the pictured representation of saints, especially of the Virgin mother of God, singular refuge of our commune, are celebrated at the cross-roads of our city. . . .' In moralising documents like this, one hears the voice of the people urging governments to carry out tasks which they can properly be asked to do. When, 54 years later, the council of Siena restored the fresco put up as the result of this original petition, it may well be that it was attempting to add honour to the commune, but is also certain that its primary purpose was the gratification of its citizens' desires.

Secular Patronage

Until the thirteenth century government patronage of the arts had been largely limited to the support of the cathedrals and churches of the commune. From then, however, the cities turned to the erection of their own public buildings and to the patronage of arts which were designed to serve them in the same way that ecclesiastical art served the church.

The key building in this new movement was the *Palazzo Comunale*, the new secular cathedral of the commune, which, though it never displaced the cathedral proper in the hearts of the men of the commune, now stood beside it as the symbol of the ever more rapidly advancing claims and powers of the state. Although some communes had built communal palaces as early as the twelfth century, their construction did not become general till 100 years later, and it was only from the 1250s that they came into real prominence. Today these buildings seem an inevitable part of the Italian townscape, but it is possible that many conservative contemporaries were hostile to their erection. Dante was perhaps reflecting this opinion in his gloating though fortunately inaccurate prophecy to the Florentines in March 1311: 'The buildings which you have raised, not in prudence to serve your needs, but have recklessly altered to gratify your wantonness, these, encircled by no walls of a renovated Troy, to your grief you shall see crumble beneath the battering ram, and devoured by flames'.[4] In fact, the encroaching power of governments in the fourteenth century made these palaces less and less of a luxury to the cities. They were part of that ever-increasing secularisation, which, for all the religious quality of life, was working within Italian society. It is significant, perhaps, that both the Palazzo Vecchio at Florence and the Sienese Palazzo Pubblico distracted the communes from the work begun upon their cathedrals.

What was involved in the construction of a *Palazzo Comunale* can be illustrated from the example of Siena (see plate VII). The cathedral as it stands today is the result of a compromise between a great dream and a painful adjustment to reality. The story of the town hall is very different. The work here seems to have been undertaken, at least in its initial stages, almost reluctantly, as if only the urgent need for more space for the various government departments had forced the commune to continue with successive extensions to the building. When the circumstances are considered, the harmony of the final result seems an extraordinary achievement.

At the end of 1284, the only building that the commune possessed was a one-storey stone barn with a wooden roof. This stood on the *Campo* or central square of the city, and served both as the Mint and a residence for certain officials. The various city councils met in rooms hired in palaces throughout the town; even the prisons were in rented premises, and the very town bells hung from a hired bell-tower. It was plain that a much larger administrative centre was needed and, after frequent discussions during the 1280s, it was decided in 1293 to buy up and demolish some houses in preparation for the new work. The motion was carried by 103 to 64 votes, and it is clear that there were many who resisted the project on the grounds of expense. However, from 1295 a new brick storey was added to the existing structure, and by 1299 a second was raised on top of the first.

As with the cathedral, the building of the Palazzo was entrusted to a master of works, who seems to have held office for only a year, and under whose supervision the master builder or builders (there is no early record of their names) performed their tasks. In the construction of the palace it is impossible to see any single controlling mind devising a complete plan. Presumably designs were drawn up for each stage, as the need for further extensions became clear or as funds became available. The finished structure, therefore, is the product not of one, but many different committees, sitting at intervals over a long period.

It was in these circumstances that the work continued. About 1305 the final storey of the squat central tower was added. Above were placed the battlements, whose nine crenellations on each side did honour to the magistracy of 'the Nine' who then ruled the city. By 1310 the two wings of the building had been completed. The expense of all this, though it cannot be precisely calculated, must have been considerable. Yet money was scarce and even building materials seem to have been in short supply. In 1307 the commune bought up the tower of the Bisdomini family for £S700 and dismantled it in order to obtain the stones and bricks for the work on the palace. For the following 15 years all construction stopped. However, from 1325 the commune began the enlargement of the palace to the east, where round a courtyard were raised a new prison, offices for the *podestà* and his court, and a hall (1330–1343) in which the council could meet. In the same period the foundation stone of the great tower was laid. The chronicle of Agnolo di Tura has preserved a curious description of the ceremony:

The Sienese started to build a tower on the side of the via del Malcucinato which runs to Salicotto, and this was begun on the 12 October. And there was great festival in Siena and the canons and clergy of the cathedral came to give their blessing to the first stone and to say prayers and psalms. And the master of works of the cathedral put some money at the bottom of the tower in commemoration, and a stone with Greek, Hebrew, and Latin letters was placed in each corner of the tower that it might not be shaken by thunder or storm.[5]

By 1341 the tower was completed. In 1360 a mechanical clock was set into it, and, still later in the century, the elegant 'Chapel of the Piazza' was to be built at its foot.

The story of the Town Hall of Siena illustrates features found in all communal building of palaces in this period. So inchoate were all ideas of the 'state' that there was bound to be initial reluctance towards such a novel concept as a centre for state administration. Everywhere there was the same problem of expense, at first rejected, then shouldered with growing confidence, everywhere the same delays, and finally, the same pride in the visible expression of the commune's greatness.

Together with the patronage of secular architecture, also to be seen in erection of loggias and other minor structures, went the commune's continuous concern for the embellishment of those buildings which it had erected. As a result, the commune also emerges in this century as a major patron of the painter, and more, as a powerful shaping force on the directions in which art was developing. For neither the governments of the day nor the Church were disinterestedly bestowing money on the arts: they were seeking the aid of art in propagating their own ideals of civic morality.

The earliest examples of this civic art often show only a slight secularisation of the more customary religious motifs. Generally they took as their theme the sacred patron of the town, and placed, side by side with him or her, some figure or inscription relating the picture to the life of the city. For instance, in 1317 the town of San Gimignano commissioned Memmo di Filipuccio and his son, Lippo Memmi, to paint in the new Communal Palace a Madonna, with the two patrons of the town, SS. Gimignano and Niccolò. By their side was pictured the man who in that year was acting as the town's *podestà*, that is to say, the principal judicial officer of the commune. In this way the reverence of the whole people for their chosen saints was symbolised. This type of painting was gradually superseded, however, as the century passed, by two more secular genres. The first of these can be described as didactic, civic allegory. In Florence, for instance, above the judges' chairs in the courts were painted symbols of justice; and Taddeo Gaddi, in the hall of the Mercato Vecchio, portrayed judges tearing out the tongues of liars. Again, in the great hall of the Bargello, Giotto painted a scene showing the *podestà*, with the aid of the four virtues, preventing the degeneration of the commune. The second secular type which grew up under the stimulus of the commune, was the representation of historical events. In the Bargello, there was a painting of the victory of the city in the battle of Campaldino (1289); and in the council chamber of the Palazzo de' Priori, a large mural showing the defeat of the rebellious White Guelfs in 1303.

In addition the commune gave a variety of more humdrum commissions to the painter. One of these was the production of *Pitture infamanti*: 'pictures of infamy'. At the execution or outlawing of some particularly hated traitor or criminal the commune would order a picture of his person or crime, or punishment, to be painted on the outer walls of a public building. Nothing of this form of painting has survived from the fourteenth century, and judgment upon it is not really possible, but presumably it had little of the character of true art. Artists certainly did not seem to like doing it. In 1291, for instance, Fino di Tedaldo at Florence protested against being forced by the *podestà* to paint a 'picture of infamy'. Other work provided by the commune was more welcome. Here even the greatest artists, such as Duccio and Simone Martini, took on a variety of small decorative tasks. They could be entrusted with the painting of banners and shields, of siege machines, the covers of account books, and so on. Sometimes the commune would retain its own *pictor communis* or official painter for this kind of work. This office was held between 1291 and 1293, for instance, by one Azzo, who painted shields and siege machines and frescoed hunting scenes for the commune at San Gimignano.

The character and scope of the secular art commissioned by the communes in this period can be illustrated by considering the interior decoration of the Palazzo Pubblico of Siena. As early as 1289, when only the central, ground-floor section of the palace had been completed, there are records of payment to painters for work inside the council chambers; again, at the turn of the century, both Duccio and his pupil, Segna, produced panels, now lost, on behalf of the commune. The first major work which still survives, however, is the luminous fresco of the *Maestà*, painted by Simone Martini in 1315 in the *Sala del Mappamondo*, the large room on the first floor where the Council met. It is an example of the earliest type of civic art in which religious feeling and citizen propaganda still blended harmoniously. The Virgin, as Queen of Siena, surrounded by her heavenly court of saints and angels, sits on her golden Gothic throne and receives the homage of the four kneeling patrons of the city, SS. Ansano, Savino, Crescenzio, and Vittore, while two angels present her with vases filled with lilies and roses. In the arms of the Virgin the Christ child holds a scroll bearing the words: 'Love justice, you who rule the earth'. In a broad band around the picture are metal discs on which appear alternately the arms of the commune (the *balzana* or white and black shield) and of the Sienese people (the lion rampant). Below, a verse addresses a moral to the councillors who saw it before them in their deliberations: 'The angelic flowers of roses and lilies with which the heavenly meadow is decked, delight me no more than good counsel. But sometimes I see him who, for his own interest, despises me and deceives my land, and when he speaks it is the worst which is most praised. Let each man watch for him these words condemn.' At the bottom of the picture appears another inscription which the Virgin is supposed to address to the sacred patrons of the city: 'My beloved ones, be assured that I will answer your devout and honest prayers as you would wish, unless the powerful do harm to the weak. Your prayers are not for these, nor for anything which might deceive my land.' With these words the government of 'the Nine' had put in the mouth of the Virgin the ideals of their rule as they saw them: the ideals of a polity, which, as they chose to believe, though exercised by the powerful, did not oppress the weak, and in which the common good triumphed over the deceits of private interest. It was painted at a particularly tense moment of their rule. Two months before its completion the government had been forced to impose a truce between the Salimbeni and Tolomei, the heads of the noble factions within the city; but the peace was still uneasy. The Nine's affirmation in the verses of the fresco betrays their fear of continuing faction, as too, perhaps, does the concern in the eyes of the Virgin and the watchfulness in the face of the infant Christ. It is difficult, however, to relate the feeling in the picture as we have it to the events of any one particular year. In December 1321, there are records of £S26 being paid to Simone 'for himself, his disciples, and for gold and colours', for restoring it. Humidity from the salt (a communal monopoly) stored on the ground floor had apparently done much damage to the work produced only six years before. How far the original conception was at that time in any way modified is the object of some controversy.

Seven years later, high on the opposite wall of the same room, Simone executed another form of political art: his fresco of the *condottiere*, Guidoriccio da Fogliano, riding in triumph as Captain of the Sienese from the siege of Montemassi. In this work he celebrated a victory of the commune and of the man who had achieved it. Here is a powerful symbol of the armed strength of the city. Mounted upon his horse, Guidoriccio represents that whole Sienese army whose tents and banners appear to the left of the fresco. The mounted figure himself makes, no doubt as those who commissioned it required, a deep impression of authority and force, yet, at the same time there is something disturbing here, something almost repulsive in the coarse outlines of the face, set against the countryside seemingly laid bare by his conquests. In the lower church of San Francesco at Assisi Simone had already painted with the liveliest sympathy the scene of St Martin renouncing his arms and the military life. It may be, as Paccagnini has suggested, that in this exaltation of brute power, the artist was faced with a subject which he found distasteful.

Curiously enough Simone Martini, with all his ethereal poetry and imaginative richness, was to pass most of his life in the execution of works for civic propaganda. He completed other works in the Palazzo Pubblico in the years 1321–3, 1327, and 1329–31. But (apart from the severely damaged and ill-restored *Christ Blessing* on the ground floor which Carli has recently ascribed to him) none of these has survived. On his departure to Avignon after 1335 his position as a principal painter to the commune was taken over by

Ambrogio Lorenzetti, whose vigour and more down-to-earth qualities were better suited, in many ways, to the post.

Lorenzetti's principal work in the Palazzo Pubblico was the fresco of *Justice and the Common Good* which he painted in the 'Room of the Nine' between 1337 and 1340. Frequently, though without justification, called 'the Allegory of *Buon Governo*', it is the most elaborate political allegory which has survived from this century (see plates 7 and 8). Stretching over three walls of the room, it seeks to give in visual form complete expression to the dominant ideals of the city governors. On the wall facing the window to the right there appears the leading figure of 'the Ruler', clothed in the black and white colours of the town, and symbolising at the same time the commune of Siena and the Common Good. Above his head are placed the three theological virtues of Faith, Hope, and Charity. At his feet the Sienese she-wolf gives suck to Romulus and Remus, signifying the Roman qualities which the commune sought to emulate. By his side, and in perhaps a significantly more prominent position than the theological virtues, sit the four 'cardinal' or 'political' virtues: Prudence, Fortitude, Temperance, and Punitive Justice (this last with the gruesome head of a decapitated man on her lap). With them are Magnanimity, and slightly to one side, though central to the whole wall, the reclining figure of Peace.

This symbol of Peace forms a natural link with the left-hand side of the picture. Here is enthroned another figure representing Justice. Above her head, Wisdom, on a parallel plane to the theological virtues, holds a balance on which are the same words, 'Love Justice, you who rule the earth', which appeared in Simone Martini's *Maestà*. In its scales are two kneeling angels. The angel of distributive justice (i.e. that which gives to every one his due) beheads one man and to another gives a crown. The angel of commutative justice (i.e. that which satisfies debts and forbids deceit) rewards one man with a gift, and gives to another a sword.

Below Justice sits the magnificent, full-bodied, figure of Concord, who bears on her knees a carpenter's plane, symbolising the equality of citizens before the law. From each of the two scales above there descends a cord, which, passing through her hands, are intertwined as one. This single cord is then grasped by 24 representatives of the citizens, doubtless drawn from the permanent Council of the Twenty-four. Processing in pairs, they bear it towards the throne of 'the Ruler', who holds its other end in his right hand. On the same level of the picture, the symbolic level of everyday life, there appear, on the right, the figures of two feudal lords giving their allegiance to the commune. Underneath the figure of Punitive Justice armed soldiers watch over four bound prisoners and other rough-clad and ill-shaven figures behind them, who, though normally described as criminals, are more probably the representatives of the peasantry and urban proletariat excluded from participation in the commune.

On the wall to the right what has so far been treated allegorically finds more realistic expression. On the one side are shown the effects of the rule of Justice and the Common Good in the town, and, on the other (under the figure of Security) in the countryside. In these vivid frescoes we see, in the town, shops open, merchants trading, builders at work, pack-mules being unloaded, and the goatherd driving his flock to market. This all takes place against a background of rich houses and palaces. At the same time in the fertile countryside, the merchants go unharmed about their business along the roads, men hawk and hunt with crossbows, while the peasants plough, reap, glean, and thresh, without concern or anxiety. In the corresponding fresco on the wall to the left, there appears the allegory of Tyranny. Here the frightening figure of Tyranny sits on the throne of Justice with his feet resting upon a black goat. He is attended by a hybrid diabolical creature with a stone and a knife (the weapons of mob violence) who symbolises Fury, and by five other human symbols of Fraud, Treason, Discord, Cruelty (strangling a child), and War. Above the head of Tyranny hover the figures of Avarice, Pride, and Vainglory. By the side of this fresco is another, now much damaged, showing the ill-effects of tyrannical rule: a town of fire, rape, and violence.

Medallions in the fascia above and below emphasize the message of the central frescoes. Below the allegory of Justice and the Common

Good, Lorenzetti painted symbols of the 'Trivium': Grammar, Dialectic, and (now destroyed) Rhetoric. Above the pictures of the effects of the rule of Justice appear symbols of the auspicious planets, Venus, Mercury, and the Moon; and of the pleasant seasons, Spring and Summer. Below are the symbols of the studies of the *Quadrivium*, Arithmetic, Geometry, Music, and Astrology, together with Philosophy. The medallions around the frescoes representing Tyranny, on the other hand, show the planets of evil aspect (Mars, Saturn, and Jupiter), the seasons of decay (Autumn and Winter), and (now destroyed) five tyrants of antiquity.

The work of recent scholars[6] has made clear the sources and full meaning of Lorenzetti's allegory, which was probably devised by some notary or judge of the commune with philosophic interests. Characteristically enough for its age, it brought together the concepts of the Roman lawyers and the philosophy of such fourteenth century Thomist-Aristotelians as Giles of Rome, Remigio Girolami, and Ptolemy of Lucca. In its way it is a document of singular importance in tracing the history of the growth of the ideal of the state. It must be added, however, that consciously or unconsciously, what lay behind the refinement of its thought was a narrow class philosophy which had succeeded in equating the collective interests of the upper classes with the common good. It would be unwise to accept this version of the Sienese commune at its face value. Even on a literal and elementary plane it gives a false impression of the city of the time. A suitable mood of disenchantment, for instance, will overtake the casual viewer when he realises that the much-admired groups of dancers, clothed in Lucchese silks, were in fact contravening Dist. v, Rub. 385 of the city statutes, which forbade dancing in the streets. Yet, when all this has been said, and allowing that allegory is not now considered an appealing idiom, such was the skill of the painter that one can admire the freshness and warmth of the composition as a whole; one can forget the other side of Sienese life, the oppression of the urban poor, the unceasing labour of the peasantry for their landlords, and see the Nine and the Twenty Four as they saw themselves, as the bright preservers of justice, order, and civilisation in an unstable world.

The other works which Ambrogio carried out for the commune can be mentioned more briefly. In 1337 he painted certain 'Roman stories' on the outside wall of the *Podestà*'s palace. These no longer survive, but the fresco of a Madonna and Child in the open loggia at the back of the palace still preserves, though much damaged and repainted, Lorenzetti's original 1340 design. Here again is the theme of civic allegory. The seated Virgin holds the Christ Child who blesses a black and white globe, symbolising Siena. The scroll, with the words (from John 13.34) 'A new commandment I give unto you, that you love one another', repeats the theme of unity expounded in the other works at the palace. Also, in 1344, underneath the Martini fresco of *Guidoriccio*, Lorenzetti painted a round map of the world. This revolved on a pivot, and its constant use had, by the eighteenth century, reduced it to little more than a fragment. Nothing of it remains today though it still gives its name to the room where it was placed, the *Sala del Mappamondo*.

Siena also gave employment to its artists with the variety of mundane tasks already mentioned, such as the embellishment of shields, decoration of chests containing public documents, and *pitture infamanti*. Among these works the *Tavolette di Bicherna e di Gabelle*, a series of paintings on the covers of the account-books of the exchequer, often have a particular charm. These were sometimes executed by the greatest artists of the day. In 1291, 1292, 1294, and 1295, for example, payments of ten shillings were made to Duccio himself for working on these books.

Town Planning

During the early years of the economic revolution there had been no town planning, simply the spontaneous and haphazard erection of buildings, an unregulated growth in size, under a free enterprise system run riot. It was only from the 1250s that the governments of the cities came to direct and control the forms which this growth should take. It was this town planning, and not, as is so often claimed, some instinctive sense of form-correlation, which made the cities of Italy. In some ways it could be argued that the greatest works of art created in thirteenth- and fourteenth-century Italy were the

Italian cities themselves, for it was largely in this period that many of them assumed the form which they still possess. Certainly this is true of Tuscany, where the basic character of all the towns (with the exception of Pienza and Livorno) had been established by the beginning of the fifteenth century, and was only superficially changed in the Renaissance and Baroque eras. In considering this theme it is necessary to go beyond the years 1290–1340 and to treat the development up to the 1420s.

In general terms the rise of town planning is to be associated with the development in embryo of the state, and the idea of the state, during this period. Governments were now to seek order and stability, not only in political and economic life, but also in the outward physical form of the city. In this sense town planning was another reflection of the increasing confidence and power enjoyed by secular rulers. More specifically, the interest of governments arose, first, from the needs of defence, and then as an extension of their concern for environment in which their own buildings, the Cathedral and *Palazzo Comunale*, were sited.

From their inception the communes had held themselves responsible for the city defences. This work of maintaining and, where necessary, extending the line of the walls was a constant preoccupation during our period. The most impressive of all these fortifications was the third circle of walls at Florence, constructed between 1284 and 1330, possibly following the designs of Arnolfo di Cambio, first master-builder of the cathedral. Thirty six feet high, five to six feet wide, they extended for five miles round the city, and were interspaced with 73 towers and 15 fortified gates. This was one of the largest achievements of the age and was immensely costly. It has been claimed that the expense of the work over the 46 years of building absorbed as much as a quarter of the normal revenues of the commune.

In the commune's assumption of responsibility for defence, there was nothing new. What does seem new, however, was the aesthetic concern now brought to these projects. To the contemporary chronicler, Giovanni Villani, the walls of Florence were 'a memorial to the greatness of the city'. The gates were conceived of as works of

art, were designed by prominent builders of the time, and orna-
mented with elaborate statues of the patrons of the city. The Porta
San Gallo at Florence, for instance, erected by Jacopo Talenti (the
builder of 'the Spanish Chapel' in Santa Maria Novella), was adorned
with a group of six statues of painted stone: in the centre, Christ
crowning his mother, at the sides, the standing figures, eight feet
high, of St John the Baptist, St Reparata, St Peter, and St Laurence.
In origin these figures were themselves a part of the city's defences,
preserving it from the demons who threatened its spiritual strength.
Yet by the fourteenth century they, and the gates in which they
stood, were thought of too as objects of beauty. So, Giovanni Villani,
himself for some years one of the 'officials to the walls' who supervised their construction, complained that the San Frediano gate was
out of proportion to the others, and remarked that 'the officials
who had begun it were much blamed for this.' Later in the century,
another chronicler, Marchionne Stefani, was to echo, though with
some reservations, Villani's strictures on the work.[7]

Within the walls too the physical appearance of the city was from
the mid-thirteenth century closely controlled by the communal
administrations. In Siena the *Statutes of the Road Supervisors*, drawn
up in 1290, consisted of about 300 decrees concerned with urban
development. In these it was laid down that at the beginning of
May each year a committee, responsible to the General Council,
should survey the town in each of its administrative divisions. Then,
in the first or second week of the month, it was to draw up building
plans for the next year. For example, on 10 May 1297 this committee
sponsored no less than 18 laws. Of these, three provided for work on
the cathedral, two treated of the condition of private palaces around
the central square, two referred to arches across streets, four dealt
with well-building and lavatories, and seven with plans for the widening and paving of streets. In addition it asked for an annual budget
of £S4,000 to be assigned to the building of the Palace of the Commune, discussed plans for a new Baptistery, and inaugurated a new
committee to supervise water and wells.

For this type of supervision there was no uniform administration
throughout the Italian communes. Generally, however, overall

control was vested in one man. In Siena, Perugia, and Florence, he was called 'the Judge of the Streets', in Pisa, 'The general master of works, roads, dykes, and aqueducts'. Often the Judge of the Streets was at one and the same time the master of works of the Cathedral. His influence was considerable and high demands were made of him. Of Franceschino da Signatico, for instance, who held the post of 'General Master of Works' at Pisa between 1335 and 1365, it has been pointed out that he exercised, for those 30 years, at the same time the offices of notary or Judge, engineer, surveyor, and architect, and that this combination of functions gave him a unique opportunity for town planning. It is significant enough that with the rise of these men in the fourteenth century, there is found the first evidence for elaborate city maps. Lapo da Castiglionchio (d. 1381) in a letter written to his son described how he had seen 'some years ago a plan in which Antonio di Francesco di Barberino [son of the poet], the judge and citizen of Florence, who was a young man of noble mind, had portrayed all the city of Florence, all the walls and their measurements, all the gates and their names, all the roads and piazzas and their names, and all the houses with gardens.'

To assist them, the 'Judges' had small councils, elected once or twice yearly. In Siena there were 'the three officials'; in Perugia 'the officers of the Judge of the Streets'; in Florence the 'six of the Rights of the Commune'. Normally, these men were not building specialists but ordinary citizens. Dante served on the Florentine committee, and during his term of office took part in making arrangements for widening via San Procolo. These committees enjoyed considerable powers. They could broaden and straighten existing streets, and build new ones on both public and private property. They laid down standards for the width of roads. In Florence principal streets had to be 12 *braccia* (23 ft.) and lesser streets 8 *braccia* (15 ft. 4 in.) across, and in Siena public streets had to be 6 *braccia* (11 ft. 6 in.). The committees also attended to the actual paving, seeking to make it uniform through the town: in Florence, irregular stone blocks; in Lucca, Ferrara, and Padua, pebbles; and in Siena, brick.

The expense of such work was normally met by the commune paying a proportion of the cost, and local residents making up the balance. For the shell-form paving of the *Campo* (or principal piazza) of Siena, begun in 1327 and completed in 1349, it was decreed that the city should contribute two-thirds, and the owners of adjoining property, one-third, of the sum required. This cooperation between government and citizen was characteristic of the whole work of town planning in this century. Sometimes new measures were initiated by the 'officials of the roads', but often they were inspired by petition of local inhabitants. In December 1357, for instance, the men of the local administrative division of Fonte del Casato in Siena appealed to the General Council that they might 'give order' to a road in their district. 'Those', they said, 'who strive hard for a beautiful and honourable adornment of their city are worthy of praise and commendation. Without order no good thing is done, and you are the people who ought to give order and rule to the whole city.' Again, in 1356, two localities in Siena were petitioning for the necessary permission to erect fountains, at their own expense, in their parts of the town.

In Siena the problem of obtaining a pure water supply was always acute, and here the state made continuous efforts to supplement the work of private citizens. In 1295 the commune commissioned the master of works of the cathedral to direct the search for an underground river, 'the Diana', which, it was commonly believed, ran beneath the city (a belief which excited Dante's mockery in *Purgatorio*, xiii, 151-4). At the same time a commission was constituted by the master of works, consisting of four stone masons and the painter Duccio, with responsibility for the sinking of wells where appropriate. As the result of this and similar efforts the number of wells in 1309 (when at least 20 were in existence) had doubled by the end of the century. In this work again, humdrum enough in itself, the commune never lost sight of aesthetic criteria. Its interest is stated alliteratively in the opening words of a decree on the subject: 'Fiat fons formosus'. Still more is it revealed by the 2,000 florins paid out by the commune from 1414 to 1419 for Jacopo della Quercia's famous *Fonte Gaia*, built on the Campo.

Fragments of this work are today preserved in the Palace of the Commune.

At Florence the four bridges across the Arno were of great importance. After the disastrous flood of 1333 in which they had collapsed, the commune reconstructed them on a more impressive scale. The Ponte Vecchio was rebuilt in 1345, and the cost of the work was met from the first 20 years rents from the shops that were leased upon it. The Ponte alla Carraia was put up in the following year for 21,700 florins, and at the same time the Ponte Rubaconte (later called 'delle Grazie') and Santa Trinità.

The expensive task of bridge building was something for which the commune had to assume full control, but in other spheres the commune acted where local initiative was lacking, and gave to its committees the widest powers for subjecting private interests to the public good. All new building of houses was supervised, and normally only permitted under licence. Sometimes, on the other hand, tax exemptions were made to those who built particularly desirable houses. Communal officials paid particular attention to the construction of balconies, outer stairways, and arcades which might darken or encroach upon the width of the street. In Siena entire roads were forbidden to have any balconies; others permitted them on one side only; others again only on condition that they left a third of the road 'open to heaven'. At the end of the fourteenth century an attempt was even made in Siena to abolish all balconies, bridges, and arches over the streets.

Almost all towns, moreover, forbade the destruction of houses without licence. At Perugia in 1342 the statutes formally prohibited the demolition of towers in the city, though at the same time setting down regulations for their height. But nothing roused the communes more than encroachment of buildings upon roads or communal property. In Siena in 1370, for example, it was discovered that the new palace of the Urgurgieri family had extended three quarters of a *braccio* (16 in.) upon the *Campo*. The news aroused intense indignation; the 'Three of the Roads' at once summoned a committee of 12 craftsmen, who gave it as their opinion that encroachment had taken place, and that the offending wall should be pulled down. The 'Three' then presented their report to the General Council, who decreed by 222 votes to 77 that 'for the greater beauty of the Campo' the wall should be pulled down and rebuilt further back.[8]

Obviously much of this work was primarily functional. The cities needed well-paved good roads, an ample water supply, bridges, and so on. But the commune also paid attention to the general effect of the townscape. In 1339 officials in Florence noted that, on approaching the Piazza del Duomo from the streets on the south side, the baptistery and cathedral appeared to sink. In order to remedy this displeasing optical effect, they decreed that the surface of the streets in question should be levelled down. At Siena, in a similar spirit 30 years before, the commune had asked the Dominicans to remove a wall in front of their church upon the hill above Fontebranda, because 'it masks the view of the church from the city'.[9]

The commune also used its powers to impose an architectural harmony upon the city. In Florence great attention was paid to the uniformity and proportions of the two central piazzas. Piazza San Giovanni was reconstructed in works lasting over 100 years (1289–1389) involving the destruction of buildings within the present square, and the removal of others further back. The Piazza della Signoria was formed during the same period by the virtual destruction of a whole quarter. Those who held houses round the two squares, or in the via Calzaiuoli linking them, were forced to build or rebuild them in a uniform style, and according to the pattern or height of other buildings already standing there, or to specifications laid down by the government. In February 1363 the *Calimala* guild at Florence, acting for the government, decreed that, since around the cathedral square there were certain little houses 'which spoil the appearance and beauty of the piazza', these were to be rebuilt within a year to the height of 16 *braccia* (just over 30 ft.), and faced with good stone walls.[10]

Similar provisions were enacted at Siena. In 1310 it was decreed that all houses built of loam should be given brick walls on the side facing the street 'that such houses may give beauty to the city'.

Thirteen years before, in an attempt to bring the buildings round the *Campo* into harmony with the Palace of the Commune then being built, it was decreed:

> that if any house or palace around the Palazzo del Mercato shall be rebuilt, each and every one of those windows of the said house or palace which look upon the *Campo* shall have small columns and shall not be made with any form of balcony. And this the *podestà* shall attend to. And any one who erects such a house or palace, and fails to conform to this decree, shall be fined £S25 by the *podestà*.[11]

This decree was reissued in the statutes of 1310, and was probably an important factor in imposing that harmony upon the centre of the city around the Palazzo, which is still a feature of it today.

At the beginning of the fifteenth century the Sienese commune also intervened in private rights to permit the construction of desirable private buildings. In a session of March 1413 the Council of the People passed, first by 117 votes in favour to 19 against, and then by 200 to 19, a decree in which it was stated that citizens were often unable to build 'fine palaces, and this to the great shame and damage of the city' because others refused to sell their houses to them. It was therefore laid down that three officials, annually elected, should be given compulsory powers of purchase over houses which might have to be demolished for the building of palaces.[12]

As a supplement to its other work, the commune tried to ensure that its streets and squares were kept clean and free from disorders. In each town there were full-time street cleaners. San Gimignano, for instance, as early as 1255, had eight (today, there are only three). Householders, too, were held responsible for sweeping the area before their houses.[13] Other statutes forbade dancing, rolling hoops, or carrying on such trades as weaving or smithing in the street. Sometimes too the government would seek to preserve the particular character of a street. On 27 November 1398, for instance, a commission elected by the Council of the People of Siena made a report in the following terms:

> in every good city attention is paid to the beauty and utility of the city. You have your Piazza del Campo which is the most

beautiful that can be found, and in addition you have the Strada de' Banchi which begins at the piazza Tolomei and comes down to the Porta Solaia, and neither in Venice, nor Florence, nor in ,any other country is there a more handsome street. Now it is ruined, for shoemakers and tailors have taken up shops there, *and it is ruined.* Your lordships therefore should provide that four citizens be appointed who shall arrange that the Bankers may be together from one spot to another, the drapers and goldsmiths from one spot to another, and that within these boundaries no other tradesmen shall be able to set up.[14]

Similarly at Venice, the Greater Council decreed that the shops of the goldsmiths were to be concentrated on the Rialto.

The aesthetic criteria which informed the town planning of the fourteenth century were based principally upon an idea of 'order'. In their general pronouncements men declared that what they sought in streets, for instance, was that they should be straight, wide (though, as has been seen, this was a relative term), and that they should meet at right angles. To us, generally speaking, this is un-attractive. But the idea was born of a society where narrow, irregular roads were places of danger where one was likely to be attacked, killed, and robbed. The first to praise the beauty of winding streets was Alberti in the middle of the fifteenth century, and in this, until the era of romanticism, he was alone.

Fortunately, their chessboard ideal was one which the men of the fourteenth century were rarely able to achieve completely. Yet one often has the impression that when contemporaries speak of work being done 'for the beauty of the city', 'for the beauty of the road', they are thinking, as with the streets, of a utilitarian idea of order. Fra Giordano of Pisa, preaching in Florence, made beauty a part of 'order'. As such, it was for him an essential part of the city: 'Another reason why we call it a city, is for its order. See how beautiful the city is when it is ordered ... and this order comes from three things: beauty, strength, greatness'.

Implicit in this was the ideal of unity. Masters of the same trades were to be grouped together in certain streets, houses round piazzas

were to have the same height of stonework. The colour of stonework
in the towns was to be the same: in Florence, the bright brown
macigno (which was the dominant note until the seventeenth century),
in Siena, red brick and light travertine (as it remains today). Yet
it was a Gothic ideal of unity which was sought, one which was
based on diversity, upon every diverse thing being in its appropriate
place. Fra Giordano compared it to the articulation of various parts
of the body: the foot in its place, the head, the hands, and so on,
'and there is more beauty in this diversity than when all things are
the same.' With this aesthetic conception fourteenth century Italy
was saved from that totalitarian ideal of unity which has been the
bane of so much town planning. It was saved from it too, of course,
by the very lack of power in the governments which, with limited
resources, were always compelled to plan within the context of an
existing city, and had no desire to recreate a totally new environment.

It would be misleading to deduce from what has been written
here that the communes of the fourteenth century preserved a continuous grip upon the growth of their towns. What was written
in their statutes often went by default. In fact in 1370 the 'Three'
of Siena complained that the decrees relating 'to the greater beauty
of the city . . . have been ineffective for thirty years or more'. The
work of the town planners proceeded in spasmodic bursts of activity
and interest rather than with any steady consistency. Nonetheless
it was upon their practice that the thought of the first theoreticians
of town planning, Alberti and Francesco Martini, was based. Even
Filarete, with his imaginary city of Sforzinda, owed much to them.
It was this activity too which created in great measure the Italian
towns, considered as works of art, whose beauty has only today
begun to pass away.

It is easy enough to isolate individual factors which contributed
in the making of this harmony. In the first place, the fourteenth
century was a poor time for property speculators. Investment in
property at Florence gave a relatively small return in comparison
with money-lending, trade, or, from 1345, subscription to the public
debt. This was still truer after the population decline from the 1340s.

Again, there were no bulldozers, and it was therefore more economical for builders to follow the natural contours of the ground, rather than to level them. In this way their planning was always based upon the topography of the site, and, as Lewis Mumford has put it, 'was carried out with other ends in view than the maximum number of saleable lots and the minimum exercise of imagination'.[15] But more important than these things was the fact that the men of the time really liked cities, that they saw the city itself as having a sacred character, that they believed that 'through love are cities built, since men delight in living together'.

6 Masaccio, *Madonna and Child* (*c.* 1426)

* AMBROSIVS · LAVRENTII · DESENIS · HIC · PIXIT · VTRINQVE ·

7 Ambrogio Lorenzetti, *Allegory of Justice and the Common Good* (1337–40)

five

Government and Patronage: II

The Signorie

Ubi Dantes, ubi Petrarca, ubi Boccaccius? 'where was Dante, where Petrarch, where Boccaccio?': such was the question, the Florentine Salutati addressed to a Milanese opponent, and the expected reply was 'at Florence'. Yet it is not really an answer which corresponds closely with any truth outside rhetoric. Dante was a Florentine, but 'Florentine in my nation not in my customs', an exile who wrote his great poem in the milieu of the signorial courts. Boccaccio, or at least his family, came from the despised Certaldo, was intellectually formed at Naples in contact with the court of Robert the Wise, and on his return to Tuscany looked back with nostalgia to that bright city of his youth. Petrarch was born at Arezzo (admittedly of Florentine parents), and visited Florence for the first time at the age of 46. The truth is that from the end of the *Trecento* the Florentines launched a powerful movement of propaganda to persuade the Italian world of a palpable untruth: that it was Florence which was the sole source of Italian cultural life. So too in the sixteenth century Vasari was to distort the material of his *Lives of the Painters* in an attempt to show Florence as the unique centre of innovation in Italian art. In reality, it was not only Florence or the communes which formed *trecento* civilisation; there was a significant contribution too from the Neapolitan monarchy of the south and from the signorial courts of northern and central Italy.

The *signoria*, that is to say the rule of one single person or family, had begun to displace the commune as the principal form of government in northern and central Italy during the thirteenth century. In its attempt to incorporate all the more prosperous citizens of the town in its legislature the commune laid itself open to disunity and continual faction. In war and diplomacy it was hampered by slowness in reaching decisions, by the interference of non-professionals, and by lack of secrecy. Normally it produced a weak executive in an age when there was a real need for strong rule and the subordination of over-mighty subjects. It was a luxury which only the most wealthy and powerful cities, such as Florence and Venice, could afford. Accordingly, first in Lombardy and the Veneto, then in Tuscany and the virtually independent communities of the Papal State, the tide turned decisively in favour of the *signoria*.

In this development it would be wrong to see any change for the worse in Italian society, or to imagine that a 'free' or 'democratic' form of government fell victim to a 'dictatorship'. As early as the twelfth century communal governments were generally formed from a few oligarchs quarrelling among themselves and subject to the control of a series of 'strong men'. Usually the coming of the *signoria* was only the recognition that one of these men had now been accepted as a permanent ruler and that his descendants were to be given the same status. Basically, therefore, the *signoria* was a stabilising element in the history of the towns, for with the recognition of a single ruler faction tended to diminish. The *signoria*, that is to say, can be considered as the sophistication of an early, cruder form of government, and the *signori* as the man who saved the communes from themselves. For the ordinary person, too, the *signoria* might well be a form of government preferable to that of the bourgeois commune. The plutocratic governments of Florence, both landowners and capitalists, had every personal interest in depressing the living standards of their peasants and urban proletariat. But there was always the possibility that from among the *signoria* there might emerge a ruler whose interest lay in keeping a reasonable balance between the different classes in the state.

There is, however, little evidence to show that the *signori* ever made any determined attempt to promote social justice within their territories. Within the *signorie* there was no revolutionary ideal seeking to change the ethos of government, or to upset traditional class patterns. The only ideals, if such they may be called, were those of making governance work, which in the medieval context implied 'giving to every man his due'; and, in the smaller *signorie*, of ensuring local independence from the larger powers. Signorial rule should not be idealised. In a commune, however corrupt, the need for counsel and consent among the oligarchs could at least impose some check on the more extravagantly foolish and vicious projects or rulers. In the small *signorie*, where the Lord had to live in daily contact with his subjects, a similar stimulus to caution was provided by the threat of assassination. But in the larger states the ruler's will was unbridled, there was little to check the madness of power, and the results could be frightening. Yet by modern standards all medieval government administration was bad, all officials were inefficient and venal, whether in commune or *signoria*. In both, 'good government' meant any government at all seeking to preserve and promote some modest measure of goodwill and efficiency and seeking to support by any means the fragile fabric of society.

In Tuscany tyranny proved less attractive than elsewhere, and the individual *signori* of Lucca, Pisa, and Arezzo were unable to establish stable dynasties. In the small towns of the Papal State, however, it became firmly rooted, and families like the Malatesti of Rimini and the Montefeltri of Urbino played, for a long time, an important role in the history of the peninsula. But the most notable of the signorial houses were those of Lombardy and the Veneto: the Carrara of Padua, the della Scala of Verona, the Bonacolsi, and then the Gonzaga of Mantua, the d'Este of Ferrara, and, most important of all, the Visconti of Milan.

The Visconti had finally established themselves as lords of Milan at the beginning of the fourteenth century. Before his death in 1322 Matteo Visconti was appointed Captain General of the city for life and was invested by the German emperor with the title of Imperial Vicar. His sons and successors, Galeazzo I (1322–7), Azzone (1329–39), Luchino (1339–49), and Archbishop Giovanni (1349–54), consolidated the family's power in the commune, and extended its influence throughout Lombardy and Northern Emilia. As early as

1317 the clergy of Lombardy had declared that there would always be war in the province 'unless it have its own single king and natural lord, who shall not be of barbarian [i.e. non-Italian] birth, and who shall pass on his kingdom by natural succession'. Working upon this sentiment the Visconti established their hold upon widely disparate territories: Milan with its industries, the primitive society of the Alpine valleys to the north, the feudal world of Piedmont, and the rich agricultural lands bordering on the Po. Throughout this area the principal gift of the Visconti to their subjects was peace. They tried to abolish faction, to reconcile former enemies, and to end disputes between rival towns. However weak internally, this government was stronger than anything Lombardy had known before. At least it offered hope for the establishment of that law and order which previous rulers had failed to achieve. In return, it exacted despotic control. This despotism was in the hands of men who, even setting aside the hostile propaganda of the Florentines, emerge from contemporary sources as starkly unattractive, sometimes slightly insane, always alarming. The family vices were, among its more pleasant members, inordinate lust, among the less attractive, treachery, delight in cruelty, and unceasing desire for extension of power.

Signorial Patronage of Art

Despite the differences between communal and signorial societies, the cultural climates produced by the different sources of patronage were remarkably similar. Artists and writers passed from the world of the communes to that of the tyrants, and back again without changing their styles or ideals. For example, Boccaccio could leave the court of Naples for Florence, and Florence for service with Francesco Ordelaffi, *signore* of Forlì; Giotto could work during his life with equal ease in the palaces of King Robert the Wise, at the small courts of Romagna, at the Papal Curia, and at the public works of the commune of Florence.

In both types of society, the social purpose of patronage of the arts was much the same. This purpose was made explicit by the

Dominican Friar, Galvano Fiamma, in his history of the Visconti family. Azzone Visconti, he explained, having made peace with the papacy, decided to construct 'a magnificent palace for himself . . .':

> for as the philosopher [Aristotle] says in his fourth book of Ethics: 'It is the work of a magnificent man to erect a fine dwelling'. For people who see marvellous dwellings are deeply impressed with strong admiration (see his sixth book of the *Politics*). From this the prince is thought to be so powerful that it would be impossible to assail him. He should also make a magnificent dwelling suitable for the mass of his officials. Moreover, as the philosopher says in the fourth book of *Ethics*, when he discusses what honourable expenses a magnanimous prince should assume in relation to God, it is incumbent upon him to build magnificent and honourable temples. Accordingly Azzone Visconti built two magnificent works: the first relating to the divine cult, that is the chapel in honour of the Virgin Mary [more commonly known as S. Gottardo] and a magnificent palace suitable for him as a dwelling.[1]

This is the only full statement in this period which sets out the social purpose of governmental patronage of the arts. Although connected here with signorial activities, it should not be thought of as originating in, or being confined to, the signorial courts. The passage from the *Politics* which Fiamma cites (i.e. VI, 7, vi) in fact specifically relates to oligarchies. Those from the *Ethics* (drawn from Bk IV ch. I and 2, especially 2, xi and xvi) concern the conduct of the 'magnificent' or 'magnanimous' man in an aristocratic or oligarchical society. They had, that is to say, much more relevance to the Tuscan oligarchies than to the Lombard *signorie*. It seems probable that Fiamma was offering to the Visconti of Milan an ideal of patronage which had been first elaborated in the Dominican school of philosophy at S. Maria Novella in Florence. However this may be, Fiamma clearly believed that patronage of the arts was an important aspect of the ruler's work. Later, enumerating what he declared were the seven virtues of the Visconti as lords of Milan—that they ruled according to divine law, that they were not cruel, that they were handsome (all extremely doubtful statements)—he gave as their fifth virtue (and this was undoubtedly true) that they were *maximi muratores*, that they had built castles and bridges in the countryside, and had given great walls and palaces to the city.

In the government of the communes the provision of churches for the citizens had been seen almost as a major function of state. To be fair, the Visconti did not, in this period, wholly neglect such work. Azzone had a new campanile built for the cathedral of S. Maria Maggiore in 1335. When twenty years later it fell down, Archbishop Giovanni had it rebuilt. But of other ecclesiastical building in this period there is little evidence. Azzone's San Gottardo, with its campanile (built 1330–6), to which Fiamma referred, was little more than a huge private chapel, an appendage to his castle. Yet in other respects, there were obviously close similarities between communal and signorial patronage. The *signore*, like the commune, had the same interest in town planning and the same ideals of town order, and in this the work of both types of government followed broadly similar lines. The statutes of Faenza, drawn up for the Lord Gian Galeazzo Manfredi in 1410, contained many provisions on these themes which were identical with those of the commune of Siena, published at the beginning of the fourteenth century. The *signorie* too pursued the same type of town development. At Arezzo, the *signoria* of Bishop Guido Tarlati (1312–21) brought about the building of new town walls, the restoration of the Palazzo Comunale, and other civic works. At Mantua the Bonacolsi began the Palazzo del Capitano from 1295, and from 1303 began the demolition of houses in front of it to form a square, the Piazza Grande di S. Pietro, which was completed by the Gonzaga.[2]

At Milan, Azzone Visconti constructed a great square before the Palace of the Twelve, laid down provisions for the width of certain roads, and restored the city's perimeter of defensive walls. From 1334, the Pisan sculptor, Giovanni di Balduccio, had been called to the city, and it is probable that he gave general direction to Azzone's plans for urban development. Certainly his hand is recognisable in the votive tablets of the Comacina, Orientale, and Ticinese Gates (1335–8). At the Ticinese gate, Giovanni carved the shrine of the

Tabernacle, with the figures of Madonna and Child, St Ambrose presenting a model of the city, St Laurence, St Astorgius and St Peter Martyr. Later in the century there was a 'Judge of the Streets' who exercised an office similar to that of his namesakes in the commune, an 'engineer of the commune of Milan' and an 'engineer of the chamber of the *signore*', as well as an 'engineer of the office of Provisions' (the general administrative office of Milan).[3]

In the work undertaken at the initiative of the *signore*, however, there was a certain arbitrariness and a less truly civic spirit than in the upper-bourgeois oligarchies of the commune. There is a contrast between the slowly developing architecture undertaken by the communes, where the details of each new step forward were subject to careful discussion, and that of the *signori*, who were unrestrained by the need for conciliar approval, and able more easily to press labour for their schemes (a self-defeating situation liable to encourage shoddy workmanship). This signorial impetuosity is brought out in a passage in which the chronicler, Pietro Azario, described how Galeazzo II, building his own palace in Milan, destroyed the one previously erected by Luchino:

which palace with its decoration and pictures and fountains could not today be made for three hundred thousand florins. And in that way of his he had it destroyed and it lies as at present, to the infinite expense and detriment of his own citizens. From the citizens he pressed whoever and however many masters and workers and building material he wished in return for little or nothing. What was worse, to everyone's disgust, he would build one wall with infinite expense and labour, then have it pulled down and an almost similar one put in its place. In winter, the rainy season, and in summer heat, the work continued on walls, vaults, palaces, and the like, works of enormous width and length, which he ordered to be completed in a short space of time. Because most of the work was done with broken stones, many of the walls began to crack and some soon fell down. Still, one can say that with infinite expense he did have these two really beautiful palaces built.[4]

The *signori* did not neglect individual public buildings for the commune. Matteo Visconti, for example, built the (today much altered) Loggia degli Osii in Milan in 1316. But the private rather than the public palace was the great object of their patronage, and from such buildings the ordinary citizen was excluded. Basically these buildings were fortresses. Writing of Bernabò Visconti's restoration of Luchino's palace at S. Giovanni in Conca, Pietro Azario described the battlemented walls built around it, 50 feet high, the stables and the courtyard, wide enough for a review of troops: 'so that the palace no longer seemed a palace but rather a most powerful castle extremely strong'. Galvano Fiamma, who as chaplain of Archbishop Giovanni Visconti had penetrated into Azzone's palace and declared it to be one of the most beautiful buildings on earth, went on to remark that there was no easy way of getting in without special licence. This building, constructed round 1336, was destroyed later in the century at the time of the building of the cathedral. It was built on a quadrangle around an ample courtyard, and had long low brick external walls with towers at the corners. In its grounds it had game-preserves, fishpools, enclosures for rare animals and birds, lions, bears, and ostriches. In the cloistered courtyard there was a fountain which was surmounted by an angel holding a viper (symbol of the family), and a large basin in which were sculptured ships representing the navies of the Romans and Carthaginians. The neighbouring church of S. Gottardo served as a private chapel of the Visconti. Fiamma speaks of its paintings in gold and silver, its wonderful windows, its furnishings of ivory, and its campanile (the only part of the original building to survive today), *quod videre est quaedam magna delectatio*. The decoration of the sacristy alone, he thought, quite apart from the actual building, was worth 20,000 florins.[5] Such were the surroundings in which the lords of Milan planned the business of state or sought diversion from the fears and hates of a menacing world.

The castle, which in communal Italy was overshadowed by the municipal palace, was still the most characteristic building of the *signoria*. There was Castruccio Castracane's fortress of Sarzanello; Gradara, built in the Marche; the castle at Este, rebuilt for Ubertino de Carrara in 1334–9; and the fortress at Sirmione with its strongly protected harbour on Lake Garda. Generally speaking, however, as the century proceeded the demands of luxurious living took over from those of defence, and Azzone's sumptuous palace-castle became the prototype of all those later built in Lombardy.

Inevitably, political iconography assumed a more personal role in the *signoria* than in the commune. It was most characteristically expressed in the tomb monuments of the individual *signori*. A notable example of the use of these in signorial propaganda is the tomb of Bishop Guido Tarlati, *signore* of Arezzo. This was commissioned by his brother, and erected in the cathedral by Agostino di Giovanni and Agnolo di Ventura, between 1329 and 1333. Although mutilated by insurgents in 1341, its message can still be clearly read. The lower part of the tomb consists of 16 panels illustrating the supposed splendours of the Tarlati *signoria*. Here one sees the consecration of the Bishop, his appointment as *signore*, his rebuilding of the city walls, his coronation of the Emperor Lewis IV of Bavaria at Milan, his conquest of towns, and so on. Two reliefs in particular were designed to show the superiority of signorial over communal rule. The first, *Il comune pelato* or 'the plucked commune', shows an old man, symbolising the city, seated listlessly in his chair of office, while seven grim human figures reach forward to pluck his beard, his garments, his staff of office, and his very shoes. Here the flowing lines of the grasping hands vividly portray the avarice and lust for power that are stripping the government of authority. In the second panel, however, the old man, now revived in strength, vigorous and hale in his years, and holding firmly to his staff, sits upright on his throne. By his side is Justice, at whose feet two malefactors, with hands tied behind their backs, prepare to receive their death blows from an executioner wielding an axe. Another figure kneels before the old man to pray for mercy. Three spectators, whose dress shows them to be from the more prosperous classes, observe the scene with cold approval.

Another allegorical theme was expressed in the tomb of Azzone Visconti, carved some time after 1339 by inferior craftsmen from the workshop of Giovanni di Balduccio. (This workshop team had already some experience of the genre, for their master had carved the tomb of Castruccio Castracane, *signore* of Lucca, before coming to Milan.) In so far as one can trust the modern reconstruction, the figure of Azzone lay along the top of the coffin, watched over by four mourning figures. At the front, St Ambrose presides over a scene in which Azzone is invested with the imperial vicariate by the Emperor Lewis of Bavaria. On both sides are kneeling figures representing the towns subject to Visconti rule, each accompanied by a patron saint. More impressive, perhaps, are the tomb-monuments which abandon allegory altogether. Here one thinks of the mounted equestrian statues like the memorials to Can Grande della Scala (d. 1324) and Mastino II della Scala (before 1351) in the cloister of S. Maria Antica at Verona. In these works, whose inspiration seems to derive ultimately from thirteenth-century German sources, the effect aimed at is the presentation of simple brute force and power. The more successful examples, however, come from the second half of the century.

In painting, too, the *signori* gave a similar patronage to that offered by the communes. Under signorial government there was the same need for the decoration of account books, for the embellishment of public buildings, and for the execution of *pitture infamanti*. At Milan indeed it was decided in 1396 that this last genre should be discontinued since so much of it already existed. The decree commanding this explained that although *pitture infamanti* were indeed admirable 'for the confusion and infamy which they brought upon ill-doers', they now existed in such numbers that they were giving the impression that the city was a haven and breeding ground of wicked men, and that it had therefore been decided to paint them no more.[6] Here too, however, the principal patronage of the *signore* was directed more to the embellishment of his own palaces, to private rather than public ends. One of the earliest surviving examples of this court art are the remains of the frescoes in the hall of the Visconti castle at Angera, overlooking Lake Maggiore. These were executed by an unknown artist some time shortly after 1314. They consisted of scenes from the life of Archbishop Ottone Visconti (1262–95), the founder of the family fortunes. The parts which survive show

Ottone sparing his rival, Napoleone della Torre, after battle, the removal of the della Torre family to prison, the approach of the Archbishop to Milan, and his triumphal entry into the city. In this work the artist seems to have been forced by the realistic demands of his subject to break away at times from the stiff Romanesque manner which was native to him, and to approach the style of the new Gothic realism, especially in his careful delineation of costumes and arms. The signorial demands for vainglorious representations of their triumphs, for identifiable portrayals of themselves and their ancestors, was yet another factor which encouraged the new spirit of realism in art.

This spirit, of course, had its centre in Tuscany, and it is not surprising that the *signori* should seek here for their artists. In sculpture Azzone Visconti employed Giovanni di Balduccio; he also importuned the commune of Florence for a master of painting, and was sent no less a figure than Giotto, who served him for two years (1335–6). Matteo Visconti, before him, if Vasari is to be believed, had also given employment to Giotto's pupil, the elusive Stefano.

Nothing of Giotto's work for the Visconti survives, but he probably executed the lost frescoes in the palace of Azzone which excited the admiration of Galvano Fiamma. These consisted of representations of the battles of Altopascio and Zappolino in which Azzone had taken part, and, in the Great Hall, the pictures of Vainglory, and of heroes such as Aeneas, Attila, and Hercules. In describing these the chronicler remarked with a certain disapproval that, apart from Azzone himself, the only Christian hero shown was Charlemagne. It is a significant indication of how much the new secular attitudes of the century owed to the signorial courts. A good case could be made out, however, for asserting that the greatest triumphs of signorial patronage lay not so much in these large-scale works as the more highly personal field of the illuminated manuscript, destined for the enjoyment of the inner circle of the court alone. The great flowering of this art, the *ouvraige de Lombardie*, did not come till the end of the century, though already it was foreshadowed in such works as the *Pantheon of Goffredo of Viterbo* (now in the Bibliothèque Nationale at Paris), written by Giovanni di Nixigia for Azzone in 1331.

Patronage of Art in the Southern Monarchies

Turning from the *signorie* to consider the cultural life of the southern monarchies, the kingdom of Trinacria, or Sicily proper, can be quickly passed over. The war of the 'Sicilian Vespers' which had separated the old Angevin kingdom into the two divisions of Sicily and the mainland, largely extinguished the civilisation which the island had known in the Hohenstaufen period. The difficulties of the kings of the new Aragonese house were formidable, for they had to exercise government against the opposition both of their Angevin neighbours to the north and of their own rebellious baronage. These struggles exhausted their revenues and left them little time or inclination for the indulgence of luxury or the pursuit of culture. Accordingly there was almost nothing in fourteenth century Sicily which can be identified as court art. King Federigo III, together with Archbishop Guidotto, commissioned Byzantine mosaics in 1330 for the cathedral of Messina, but this patronage stands almost alone. The culture of the age in Sicily takes its name not from the ruling dynasty but, appropriately enough, from a leading feudal family of the island. This era of Sicilian art is generally known as *il periodo chiaramontano*, after the Chiaramonte house who built those castles which are virtually the sole architectural monuments of the century on the island.

In the kingdom of Naples to the north, however, the monarchs exercised, at least until the second half of the century, a dominant role in patronage. Charles I (ruled 1266–85), earliest of the Angevin kings, had introduced his fellow Frenchmen as artists, architects, and craftsmen during his reign, and in the years that followed their work blended with native southern styles to form a Neapolitan synthesis. A large number of churches were raised in this period. The Hohenstaufen predecessors of the Angevins had seen the friars, especially the Franciscans, as the allies of their arch-enemy, the papacy, and had looked upon their activities with marked disfavour. But with the accession of the Guelf kings, Charles II (1285–1309) and Robert

I(1309-43), they were encouraged to settle and build in the kingdom. Mary of Hungary, wife of Charles II, founded S. Maria Donna Regina; and Sancia, King Robert's second wife, who had once wished to become a Poor Clare herself, built another Franciscan church, S. Chiara.

St Francis became the principal patron of the Neapolitan kings and of their Guelf allies throughout the peninsula. King Robert's elder brother, Louis of Toulouse (1247-97), had abandoned his right to the crown of Naples, had become a Franciscan, and, after a life of privations, had died in sanctity. So splendid an opportunity for politico-religious propaganda was not to be missed. At enormous expense King Robert had his brother canonised, and determined to exploit the potentialities of his sainthood in the same way that the English kings had done with Edward the Confessor, and the French with St Louis. In Naples itself, and everywhere throughout Italy where the Neapolitan kings were welcomed as political allies, the figure of St Louis of Toulouse was to be represented as the patron of the King and the friend of the wealthy capitalists of the *parte Guelfa*. The great Florentine banking family of the Bardi had him pictured in their chapel in Santa Croce, the Sienese in the chapter house of their San Francesco. At Naples, Simone Martini painted the luminous panel in which St Louis, himself crowned by two angels, places the crown upon the head of his brother kneeling respectfully before him.

Not all of this was simply propaganda. It can hardly be doubted that Robert, who was to die in the habit of the Third Order, had a real devotion to the Franciscans. As a young man in prison in Catalonia, he had been consoled by the letters of the 'spiritual', Pietro Olvi, who had written to him of the sufferings of Joseph, and had urged him to draw joy from that inspiration. The comfort given then the King was never to forget, and even when papal hostility grew strong against them, the spiritual Franciscans, the most extreme advocates of absolute poverty, were welcome at the Neapolitan court. But the main patronage of the Angevin monarchs was given, of course, to the more orthodox conventuals.

For the church of S. Maria Donna Regina, Charles II and Robert secured frescoes from Pietro Cavallini, tempting him from Rome with payments of over 30 *uncie* of gold (120 florins) a year. Simone Martini, as already mentioned, was also employed at court, and given an annual grant of 50 *uncie* (200 florins). Giotto worked in the King's household for the years 1328–32. In the great castle at Naples, the Castelnuovo, he painted frescoes (destroyed in the fifteenth century) for a 'hall of famous men'. Here were pictured two Hebrew heroes, Solomon and Samson, and seven pagans, Alexander, Hector, Aeneas, Achilles, Paris, Hercules, and Caesar. At the same time, the king's brother Filippo commissioned Montano di Arezzo to execute paintings in his chapel at Avellino and in his house at Naples.

It is the Sienese sculptor, Tino di Camaino, however, who most fully represents the elegance and splendour of the art of the kingdom. After working in Pisa, Siena, and Florence, he was called to Naples at the beginning of 1323, and stayed there until his death 15 years later. Here, in the atmosphere of the south and amidst the influences from France, he lost the austerity which had begun to characterise his work in Tuscany. Now in his tomb-monuments for the royal house he gave himself up to an easier, freer, more Gothic manner. In these tombs there is, in contrast to the violent affirmations of the northern signorial monuments, the expression of serene confidence in the legitimacy of royal rule, a calm acceptance of death by members of a sanctified family.

After his death Camaino's influence endured, finding fullest expression in the elaborate tomb-monument for King Robert himself, which his granddaughter and successor, Queen Giovanna, commissioned in S. Chiara. This elaborate memorial, curiously appropriate to the man in its ripe blend of pomposity and magnificence, can perhaps best be described as resembling a four-layered wedding cake. In each of the layers the king appears, first among his family, then amidst representations of the liberal arts mourning his death, third among his courtiers and, finally, being presented to the Virgin by St Francis and St Clare.

The Influence of Government Patronage in Art

How far government patronage actually influenced the development of art, and whether it was responsible for any of the innovations current in this period, are matters to be treated with some caution. Yet clearly the new patronage dictated new themes: secular allegories, portraits of communal officials, pictures of identifiable places and battles. These new subjects made new demands upon the artist. Above all they stimulated a growing feeling for reality and imitation of the surrounding world; they reinforced the natural tendency of Gothic to move towards a greater naturalism. When, for instance, the men of the commune asked for the representation of a town, they sought not the portrayal of the generalised idea of a city, but a specific place known to themselves. When Simone Martini, for example, was to paint the villages of Arcidosso and Castel del Piano in the Palazzo Pubblico of Siena, he was actually sent in 1334 'with a horse and a servant' to see, and presumably sketch, them at the expense of the commune.[7] Again it is no mere chance that the first fully developed townscape and landscape paintings should have been those executed by Ambrogio Lorenzetti in the secular allegory of *Justice and the Common Good*.

As with towns and landscapes, so with people. Governments now began to ask for the representation of recognisable individuals, for portraits of the great men of their contemporary history: of Nello dei Tolomei at San Gimignano; of Guidoriccio da Fogliano at Siena (the first surviving painting of a layman without any religious significance at all); of Federico da Montefeltro in Pisano's pulpit at Pisa; and so on. Similarly, in the *pitture infamanti* they required identifiable representations of known traitors and criminals. As a result this period sees the first gropings towards the representation in art of individuals. These are not yet fully developed portraits as we understand them, for there is always too much uniformity in the basic cranial structure. Yet there is already an attempt at physical individualisation which looks forward to the full development of the art at the end of the following century. Obviously this is not something for which government patronage was alone responsible; it is heralded in the tomb monuments erected for the Roman *curia* from the 1250s, and was a consequence too of the rise of the tradition by which the donor of a painting was shown kneeling at the feet of his saint. Yet is was something to which governments gave a powerful impulse.

It is significant too that the rise of government patronage corresponded in time with what has been described as the principal achievement of *trecento* art: 'the establishment of narrative'. In the story of this development, the three men who play the leading roles, Giotto, Duccio, and Ambrogio Lorenzetti, spent most of their lives in the service of government. More noticeably governments secularised the subject matter of art. This is well illustrated by the series of political allegories executed in the Communal Palace of Siena during our period. The first of them, Simone Martini's *Maestà* of 1315, was still largely religious in form; its subject was the Virgin as the ruler of Siena. The frescoes of Lorenzetti, by contrast, painted in 1337–40, had very much less of a direct religious content. Those of Taddeo di Bartolo, carried out in 1413–14, abandoned religious motifs altogether and turned to the inspiration of Roman republican history as interpreted by the civic humanists. Perhaps unconsciously, the new secular powers, gradually in the case of the communes, more rapidly in the *signorie*, turned aside from a religious or semi-religious iconography of government, and put in their place themes derived from secular history, notably, of course, from the history of Latin antiquity.

Already by the end of the thirteenth century the communes had begun to see themselves as the heirs of Rome. To Dante, for instance, Florence was the fairest and most famous daughter of Rome, and his city was built 'in her image and similitude'. This latter, rather strange idea, for whose origin various explanations have been given, was repeated by Giovanni Villani: Florence was constructed *al modo di Roma*. With this identification of the communes with Rome, the themes of classical mythology and history came to play more and more part in art. As early as 1278 Hercules with his club appeared both on the seal of Florence and on its coinage. Hercules, Cacus, and Daedalus, symbols of human strength and ingenuity, appeared with biblical figures on the reliefs designed by Giotto at the base of the Florentine campanile. On the façade of Siena cathedral, Plato and Aristotle stood side by side with Daniel and Moses. Particularly popular was the Romulus story. Romulus and Remus were carved in the fountain of Perugia (completed in 1278) together with the

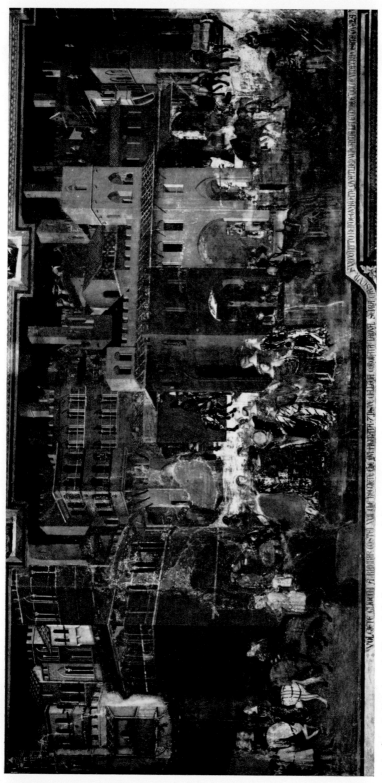

8 Ambrogio Lorenzetti, *Town Life from Justice and the Common Good*

goddess Rhea Silva; the She-Wolf was emblazoned on the arms of Siena in 1297 and was made a symbol of the city in Lorenzetti's frescoes. In 1330 Simone Martini was commissioned to illustrate a figure of M. Attilius Regulus, symbol of republican virtue, in the Offices of the Nine in the Communal palace, while seven years later, Lorenzetti illustrated certain 'Roman stories' on the exterior wall of the Palazzo del Podestà. In this way the influence of the commune combined with other early humanist influences to stress those classical motifs which in the next century were to become of predominant importance in visual communication.

The governments of the time therefore played some part in altering the direction of art and in introducing new themes within it. But they did more than this; in the communes, at least, they created an informal school of art-appreciation for their citizens. When so much of art, both religious and secular, was paid for out of municipal taxation, it was to be expected that the tax-payers themselves should come to have a concern for and interest in what their money was buying. The businessmen who had voted for or against the commissioning of a painting or building in council, the great officials who sought to bring glory to their commune by paying out money from an already overburdened treasury to an artist, had every motive for seeking to understand what they were getting in return. Throughout the community as a whole, many who would otherwise have been perhaps indifferent to art were brought to feel for it. Many who had bought what they had primarily thought of as objects of religious or political iconography must have come eventually to see them as art. Even if they failed to do this they came to see art as something which lent prestige and power.

As a result there was a deep concern for art and sometimes for artistic quality among a large number of the citizens of the communes. This is reflected, for instance, in a petition by some men of Siena to their governors in 1316. They complained of damage to a 'very beautiful' picture in the hall of the podestà's palace from smoke from the fires lit there when he ate. They did so, they explained, because: 'It is delightful to the eye, joyful to the heart, and pleasing to each human sense, and also of great honour to individual communes when their rulers and officials dwell in fair and splendid residences, both for their own sake, and, too, for those foreigners who for many and various reasons come to visit them. This, considering its greatness, is of importance to the commune of Siena. . . .'

This same note of individual appreciation sounds still stronger in the comment of the consuls of the *Calimala* on their contract with Lippo di Benivieni: 'He is at present painting figures and pictures in the church of S. Giovanni which much lighten and delight the hearts and eyes of citizens and other people who see them, for they perceive there nothing which is confused or awry.'

It is heard again in the rough verse of Antonio Pucci;

Ecci il Palagio de' Signor sì bello
Che chi cercasse tutto l'universo
Non credo, ch' e trovasse par di quello . . .

('Here is the Palazzo della Signoria, so beautiful that if you sought through the whole universe, I don't think you'd find its equal' . . .)

—or in Goro Dati's praise of the campanile of Florence: *chi non la vede non può immaginare la sua bellezza* ('who does not see it, cannot imagine its beauty'). It is the theme already heard in the Sienese petition of 1398: 'you have your Piazza del Campo which is the most beautiful that can be found, and you have the Strada de' Banchi . . . and neither in Venice nor Florence nor in any other place in the country is there a more handsome street.' It is the same personal pride which reverberates through Giovanni Villani's description of Andrea Pisano's casting of the baptistery gates: 'beautiful and of marvellous workmanship . . . and I, the author, on behalf of the merchants of the *Calimala*, guardians of the *opera* of San Giovanni was the official to commission that work'.[8]

Men like this were not to be fobbed off with what they considered to be inferior work. In August 1415, for instance, the government of Siena dismissed certain craftsmen making inlaid choir stalls for the chapel of the Communal Palace, on the grounds that their work 'did not please the eyes and minds of all our co-citizens in the beautifying of the said place'. Instead, the commission was given to Domenico di Niccolò, who, in the event, took 13 years to finish the job.[9] The incident suggests an atmosphere of delicate appreciation which distinguishes the pleasures of the eyes and the mind, and, at least among the governing classes, a patience in waiting for the completion of work which might testify to an understanding of the difficulties facing an artist.

To what extent were the works produced for the palaces of the commune available for public viewing? Was there general access, for instance, to the Communal Palace of Siena, or were its masterpieces, like the private art of the Visconti palaces, merely seen by a few, by the councillors and officials who sat in the halls where they were painted? The balance of probability seems to be that the great public buildings of the commune were open to all who chose to go and look inside them. Confirmation of this comes from a statute of Siena of 1309–10, which forbade women to enter the palace without being summoned. This passage suggests a situation where, until that time, anyone had been free to wander in and out, more or less at will.

That the new statute was ineffective is shown by a sermon of St Bernardino, delivered to a mixed audience, from all ranks of society, in the 1420s. Here he referred to the Lorenzetti frescoes:

> When, outside Siena, I was preaching on War and Peace, there came to my mind those pictures painted for you, and which certainly teach a wonderful lesson. When I turn towards the picture of Peace, I see merchants buying and selling; I see dancing, the houses being repaired, the workers busy in the vineyard. . . . And for the sake of all these things men live in peace and harmony with one another. But if I turn my eyes to the other picture I see no trade, no dancing, only men destroying men; the houses are not repaired but demolished and gutted by fire; no fields are ploughed. . . .'[10]

Obviously Bernardino expected his congregation to be familiar with the work 'painted for you'. Yet equally obviously the true allegorical meaning of the frescoes escaped him. He interpreted the painting (as Ghiberti did in his *Commentarii*) as a representation of 'Peace and War' and not, as it really is, an allegory of 'Justice and the Common Good'. Clearly, even among those of considerable culture there was no continuous interpretive tradition of the learned meaning of the work. The full symbolic implications of Lorenzetti's masterpiece can have been appreciated only by a few; its true significance was soon lost, and the attempt by the commune to create a vital Sienese myth had failed.

Patronage of Commune and Signoria
outside the visual arts

So far the patronage of governments has only been considered in the visual arts. This was the most important area of their cultural influence, but it was not the only one.

As will be seen in later chapters, they exercised some patronage over music too, while notaries in government service gave a particular cast to the development of humanism. The commune too inspired many of those chronicles of the time which can be considered as literature—those of the Villani and Marchionne di Coppo Stefani in Florence and of Ferreto de' Ferreti and Albertino Mussato in northern Italy. The commune was sometimes also the founder, patron, and administrator of universities.

In many ways, however, the signorial patronage of literature seems more impressive. One thinks in particular of Dante's stay with Can Grande della Scala at Verona—'there was I witness of your splendour, there was I witness and partaker of your bounty'—and with Guido Novello da Polenta at Ravenna. (Yet here too there was 'the salt taste of another's bread and the steepness of another's stairs'.) Yet, in literature, only King Robert of Naples stands out clearly as a patron.

In the style of the age, Robert was a cultivated man. After early difficulties in education which had caused his tutors to despair, he had been roused to enthusiasm for learning, so Boccaccio tells us, by that standard text-book of the time, the Latin version of Aesop's fables.[11] He found leisure, amidst the care of government, to pursue theological studies. When John XXII, in 1339, rashly proclaimed that the blessed would have no vision of God until after the Last Judgment, Robert was moved to write a *Tractatus de statu animae*, which gave a more orthodox opinion. From time to time, to the applause of his courtiers, he would preach sermons in which the names of the Fathers, the scholastics, and the great pagans too, were liberally bandied about. These, of which 289 survive (all said to have been delivered spontaneously, and without recourse to books), incline more to the precision of the schoolmen than the liveliness of the friars. But they were sufficient to allow flatterers to hail him as 'the Wise', and to encourage Guelph propagandists like Giovanni Villani to see in him a *grandissimo maestro in teologia e sommo filosofo*. From Avignon aspiring English academics spread the word of the royal learning, as when Master Stephen de Kettelburgh wrote to John Lutterel, Chancellor of Oxford university, urging him to take advantage of the royal bounty:

> The Lord King, who among all the clerks in the world that I have ever seen, both in oppositions and responsions [i.e. theological debate] really shows himself well and elegantly a man of great learning and as it were most perfect in every art, and very much excelling in moralities. He honours immensely men of your faculty, endears and extolls them with great rewards.[12]

These achievements were considered more coolly by those politically hostile; Dante, for instance, with an unkind sneer, dismissed him as *il re da sermone*, 'the preacher king'.

If Robert's main intellectual interests lay in theology, he did not by any means neglect the nascent spirit of humanism of his age. Virgil's Naples still bore memories, though rather strange ones, of the poet; as a magician he was said to have created the nearby Grotto of Posilipio by incantation. In the surrounding regions the visitor could enjoy the classical reminiscence of Pozzuoli, Solferata, Lake Avernus, the cave of the Sybil, and Baia. In this world it was difficult to ignore the Roman past. Yet, in the king's library, amidst the conventional works of Aquinas and Egidio Colonna, translations of Arabic medical works into Latin, and codices of civil law, only three of the hundred odd titles known to us were those of classical texts.

The king maintained a house where a group of scribes, illuminators, and book-binders, from Naples, northern Italy, France, Germany, and England, worked in his service. Other books are known to have been bought. Perhaps the small number of Roman texts known to us in his library is just the effect of chance, for it must have been one of the largest of the time. At the court and university were many of the men pre-eminent in early humanism: Barbato da Sulmona, Giovanni Barrili, Dionigi di San Sepolcro, and Paolo da Perugia (the King's librarian). Within this circle Boccaccio was first introduced to the new spirit of the age. Here too, in 1341 came Petrarch to flatter and be flattered in turn. In that curious episode, when for three days the king solemnly examined him on his qualifications as a poet, and, finally satisfied, issued letters to the Roman senate announcing his fitness for the laurel crown, is symbolised the whole world of humourless academicism which was to characterise so much of the new humanism.

PART TWO

The Age of Orcagna and Petrarch.
The Environment of Literature

six

Italy in Crisis
1340–1380

New Patterns in Cultural Change

From the beginning of the 1340s the prosperity which Italy had previously enjoyed was broken by a series of disasters. Despite this, the 40 years which span the middle years of the century still constitute an important period in intellectual and cultural development.

Though we know as yet little about the process, the change was probably most marked of all in the development of philosophy. In this age the Ockhamites and the so-called Latin Averroists developed within Italy a new and destructive criticism of the optimistic formulations of Thomism. It was an era of withdrawal from metaphysics and ideas of natural religion. Reason and revelation, philosophy and theology, it was conceded, could now no longer be reconciled by the human intellect. In their place the new Nominalism emphasized only the reality of each individual object and the primacy of each man's own experience in his attempt to grasp the meaning of the world. In this climate of thought it was natural that the schools should produce 'the idea of an experimentally grounded and mathematically formulated science of nature' which was critical of many aspects of the Aristotelian scheme.[1]

One might expect, in these circumstances, an increase in those trends towards realism in art which marked the beginning of the century. Outside Tuscany it is indeed possible to discern this development, yet at Siena and Florence visual realism was to retreat, and it is difficult to draw broad generalisations over the different schools. Whatever the position in art, literature and scholarship were marked by an optimistic tone in which the disciples of humanism proclaimed the superiority of their own age to the immediate past. Petrarch and Boccaccio were on the point of introducing an extraordinary and original periodisation of cultural history which sharply distinguished their own century from former times. Petrarch, in a remarkable reversal of Christian commonplace, declared that the centuries between the fall of Rome and the present formed 'a dark age'. For Boccaccio, Giotto had 'restored' the ancient lost art of painting, while in Dante had been reborn the skills of literature: 'through him dead poetry awakened to life'.

From these suggestions was to come a commonplace of 're-newal' and 'rebirth' which was to be constantly repeated by succeeding generations and to be applied in every context of cultural life. Finally the word 'Renaissance' was to be taken up by Michelet in 1840 and used as the basis for the definition not only of a literary and cultural era but also of an historical period. These views, developed by Burckhardt and his followers, have been accepted with remarkable unanimity ever since. It may be remarked in passing, however, that there are two essential pre-conditions for the acceptance of this 'Renaissance' formula. First, its use must be confined to Italy, where alone in Europe the idea of a 'rebirth' of the arts in the fourteenth century has any meaning. Second, one must believe that there is some point in defining historical periods in terms of their arts rather than in terms of their social and economic development.[2]

Economic Decline, political unrest, plague

At the beginning of his chronicle Matteo Villani also wrote of his era as 'a renewal of time and of the age'. Yet he used the metaphor in complete contrast to the sense given to it by Petrarch and Boccaccio. For Villani, reflecting on the disasters which had come upon Italy, what was renewed was the understanding of man's sombre destiny. In the first years of the century some cracks had already begun to appear in the Italian economy and that of Europe generally, but now there came a widespread and precipitous slump. Already Italy had begun to suffer severe famines, perhaps because its population was too great for its existing food resources, perhaps because of climatic change. Now the situation grew worse. The periods 1338–40, 1346–7, and 1373–5 were times of harvest failure and of widespread mortality in many provinces. 'In this year [1346] many people died of hunger and ate wild grass as if it were bread.' Such comments in the chronicles become more and more frequent as the century continued. In the wake of famine came plague—diseases which the chroniclers brought together under the single word *pestis*, and which were presumably those infections particularly associated with starvation: dysentery, cholera, typhus, and typhoid.

Population fell: there was a general decline in total European production and demand in agriculture, industry, and commerce. This decline was accentuated first by the disruption of trade through the outbreak of the Hundred Years War, and then through the precarious position of the international bankers of Italy, whose credit facilities were perilously over-extended and particularly vulnerable to any panic withdrawal by depositors. With the 1340s the threat to the Italian, and particularly the Florentine, banking system was becoming increasingly obvious. In September 1342, in a desperate attempt to avert the threatening financial crisis, the patriciate of Florence appointed Walter Brienne, titular Duke of Athens, as life *signore* or dictator. But confidence in his ability to master the situation was dissipated within 11 months. He was expelled from power, a new régime was formed, and the institutions of republican government were restored. Yet almost the whole structure of the city's commercial finance was ruined. In 1343 the Peruzzi bank collapsed, in 1345 the Acciaiuoli, and in 1346 the Bardi. Lesser businesses were inevitably involved in their fall, and by 1346, it has been calculated, the Florentine commercial companies had lost 1.7 million florins.

It was at this moment, when the Italian peninsula was beset by economic crisis, that there came a newer and more terrifying disaster: the Black Death, simultaneous infections of bubonic, and of the still more deadly septicaemic and pneumonic plagues. These diseases, long endemic in the east, had spread by the 1340s to the 'Golden Horde', the grouping of Mongol tribes established at

Sarai on the lower Volga. During the early months of 1347, the Mongols besieging the Genoese Black Sea trading port of Caffa had used ballistae to hurl corpses infected with the plague among the besieged. In the autumn of that year, Genoese ships returning from Caffa to Italy brought with them rats, men, and cargoes, all infested with the plague-carrying rat fleas. From the ports the infection spread rapidly through the whole country. Only Milan, for reasons which are not clear, seems to have escaped the scourge. In the two years which followed, plague moved in successive waves along the trade routes to almost all Europe. Everywhere it touched it lasted roughly from four to six months.

In the accounts of contemporary chroniclers the mortality is uniformly described as immense. De' Mussi of Piacenza, for instance, wrote of the death of 70 per cent of the population of Venice, and 68 per cent of Genoa. Many others claim that two-thirds died. These figures have a psychological interest as revealing the impression in the chroniclers' minds, though they are greatly exaggerated. Yet the more reliable conclusions of modern scholars show that the mortality was disastrous enough. At Florence in 1348 a population of about 80,000 fell to 30,000; at Siena a population of 50,000 in the city and 100,000 in the countryside was cut, perhaps, by a half. In the countryside of Pistoia a population of about 24,000 in 1344 was reduced by 1383 to 14,000. At San Gimignano a population of 13,000 in 1332 was reduced to 4,000 by 1350. The most convincing estimates at the moment suggest an overall population decline in Italy of 35 to 50 per cent. These figures are grim enough, but they do not finish the story. For the plague of 1348 did not stand by itself. It also initiated the Second Pandemic, the series of long-drawn-out, recurrent visitations which, lasting until the eighteenth century, brought every year the threat of sudden and horrible death to the inhabitants of Europe. As Thorndike has pointed out, that period which nineteenth-century historians called 'the Renaissance', that golden era of heroic men and women set in a never-never land of beauty and classical studies, fit subject for the prose of a Pater or a Symonds, might, with equal justice, be described as 'the age of pestilence'.

Within Italy bubonic plague returned with particular severity in the years 1360 to 1363 (and this time Milan did not escape), 1371 to 1374, 1382 to 1384, 1398 to 1400, and 1410 to 1412. These outbreaks were less serious than that of 1348; they moved more slowly and were less virulent. The chroniclers give the impression that the power of the disease, though still terrible, was declining, Yet in the era immediately following 1348 the plague pressed hard upon the cities of Italy. Nowhere, it is true, did the fabric of government break down; routine administration continued as ever and in some cities government finances showed surprising powers of recovery. Nor, at least in the greater centres, can the period be seen as one of uniform economic decline. At Florence, for instance, years of recovery (1349–57 and 1361–5) alternated with times of depression (1358–60, 1368–78). Again, new bankers, the Malabaya of Asti and the Alberti of Florence, came forward to take over the role of the older bankrupt firms. Yet overall there was a deep malaise and a running down of those economic entities which earlier in the century had operated with such scope and daring.

Economic decline brought political instability. At Siena the government of 'the Nine' fell in 1355. The administrations which followed were short-lived, while in 1371 the city had to face the first full-scale Italian proletarian insurrection with the rising of the wool-workers. At Florence many old fortunes collapsed and many old families withdrew from business to invest in land. In their place came 'the new men', the hated *gente nuova*. These upstarts, often enriched by the estates of those who had died in the plague, now sought a share in the control of commerce, industry, and political life. From the oligarchs who had hitherto controlled the commune they now demanded the power to which their wealth entitled them. For their own part the patriciate tried desperately to exclude from office men to whom they referred, with the customary delicacy of a threatened upper class, as 'shit-artisans' or 'money lending ponces'. Such abuse was seconded by the mockery of intellectuals. In one of the stories of the Decameron (vii, 8), a wife of one of these men is made to complain of them that 'once they get three shillings in their pockets they look for a wife among the daughters of noblemen and fine ladies, and they say: "I am of the so and so's" and "those of my line do such"'. The hate engendered by this conflict between the old and the new wealth was heightened by the constant fear of economic ruin and of threatening change, and it was in this atmosphere that the régime collapsed in the revolt and brief domination of the *Ciompi*, the urban proletariat, in the year 1378.

In external politics, too, it was a time of conflict. The growing power of the Visconti led to war between Milan and Florence in 1351 to 1353, between Milan and the Papacy in 1362 to 1364 and 1367 to 1369, between Milan and the Papacy in alliance with Florence in 1369 to 1370. In the south there was civil strife in the Kingdom of Naples between Giovanna I and the claimant to her throne, Lewis of Hungary. Meanwhile the galleys of Venice and Genoa resumed their struggle for naval and commercial predominance in the Mediterranean, a struggle now intensified by the threat to profits from the advance of the Turks in the east. In the Papal States the rule of Cardinal Albornoz (1353–63) saw the Papacy make an immense military effort to dominate the tyrants who had usurped power within its territories. Again, the imperialist ambitions of Florence led to war against Pisa (1362–4) and, in a curious alliance with the Visconti, against the Papacy itself (1375–8).

The immediate beneficiaries of these wars were the 'Companies', the huge bands of mercenary soldiers, generally foreigners, whose power made them virtually mobile states. On their release from service, these forces turned at once to more profitable careers of extortion from their former employers. 'The Great Company' of Fra Monreale d'Albano consisted of 7,000 horse and 1,500 heavily armed infantry, from which in July 1354 Florence was forced to buy immunity with payment of 25,000 florins. Other companies were those of Werner Urslingen, 'Enemy', as he boasted, 'of God, of Piety, and of Mercy'; Albrecht Sterz (3,500 horse and 2,000 foot); Conrad of Landau; Ambrogio Visconti; Hannekin Baumgarten; and John Hawkwood. Hawkwood's 'White Company', composed principally of Englishmen, was the most successful of these rapacious forces; in the three months from June 1375 alone, it was able to wring from the Tuscan communes about a quarter of a million florins in profitable blackmail. That banditry on this massive scale was possible demonstrates the impotence of commune and *signoria* alike in this period. It shows too the folly of that internecine war which distracted the peninsula; that folly at which Petrarch protested in his *Italia Mia*, with its scorn for the 'pilgrim swords' and its call for peace among those of *latin sangue gentile*.

Individual Psychology in the Age of Crisis

What psychological effects did the disasters of the age, particularly the plague, have upon men of the time? It is clear that the first appearance of the Black Death brought an immediate emotional shock. 'Is it possible', asked Petrarch, 'that posterity will believe these things? For we who have seen them can hardly do so.'

To Matteo Villani the plague was 'unheard of', comparable to Noah's flood. The celebrated Gentile da Foligno, professor of medicine, writing shortly before his death from the infection, commented: 'in former times there has been no case of so extraordinary and terrifying a plague as that which is now running through Italy.' In the face of the epidemic the medical science of the age could only diagnose the various forms of the disease and point to its origin in the will of God and in the celestial conjunction of planets. No cure could be offered and the only prophylactic was flight. With bubonic plague, signalled by the swelling of the lymphatic glands in the groin or under the armpits, death was normal within five days, though recovery was possible. More frightening were the septicaemic and primary pneumonic forms, which, invariably fatal, caused the patient to die suddenly within a few hours of the first symptom. Hence the appalled commonplace among the chroniclers: 'A man in good health today, tomorrow was carried to the grave.'

In these circumstances, amidst the fear of the unknown and the irremediable, psychological disorder was likely to be found. Although on this occasion Italy was spared the great public flagellant outbreaks and the massacres of the Jews which news of the plague sparked off in northern Europe, hysterical fantasies flourished. Michele da Piazza, writing a few years after the disaster, captures

something of the feeling of this period when he describes how at
Messina during the plague demons in the shape of dogs attacked
the corpses, how a black dog with a sword between its paws,
gnashing its teeth, broke up a procession asking for divine aid, and
how the statue of the Madonna, six miles from the city, refused at
first to participate in the citizen's service of intercession. These are the
tales of an excessively superstitious Sicilian cleric, but the atmosphere of horror in which such delusion could flourish is vividly
presented in all the contemporary accounts. It comes out most
strongly, perhaps, in the words of Agnolo di Tura, recorded in a
Sienese chronicle:

> The mortality began in Siena in May. It was horrible and cruel,
> and I know not how in its frightfulness this cruelty began, for it
> seemed that those witnessing it were stupefied with sorrow. And
> it is not possible for human tongue to tell of the horror, and one
> can well call that man happy who has not seen it. Father abandoned
> child; wife, husband; one brother, another; for the illness struck
> both through breath and sight. And so they died. None there were
> who for money or friendship would bury the dead. Members of a
> family brought their dead to the ditch as best they could without
> priest or divine office, and the bell did not sound for them. And in
> many places in Siena huge pits were dug and the multitude of the
> dead were piled within them ... And I, Agnolo di Tura, called
> 'the Fat', buried my five children with my own hands. And there
> were those so poorly covered with earth that the dogs dug them
> up and gnawed their bodies throughout the city. And there were
> none who wept for any death, for everyone expected to die. And
> so many died that everyone thought it to be the end of the world
> ... and there was so much horror, that I, the writer, cannot think
> of it, and therefore will tell no more.

These emotions are echoed in all chronicles which add to Tura's
account only the precision of more details: the rotting bodies and
the problems of their disposal, the stench of numberless grave pits,
the cattle wandering in the fields without guardians, ships whose
crews were all dead, driven as the waves took them until wrecked on

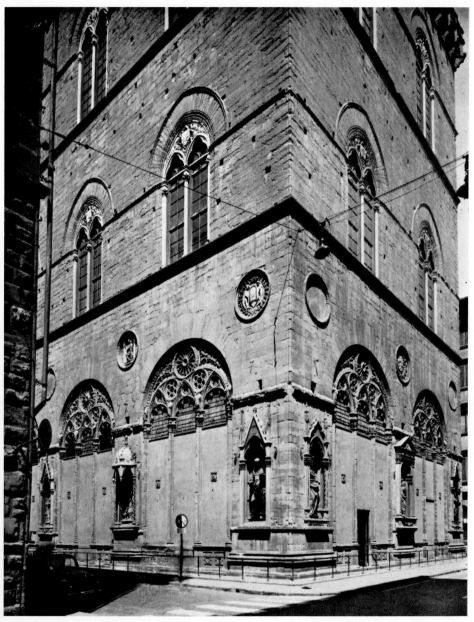

10 Or San Michele, Florence

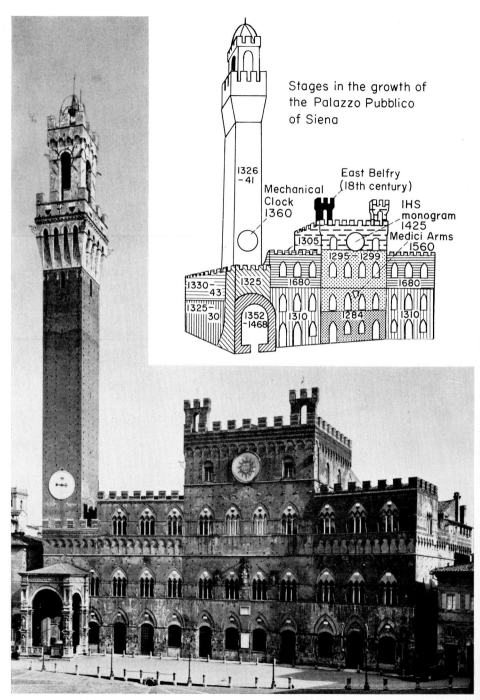

Stages in the growth of
the Palazzo Pubblico
of Siena

1326
-41

Mechanical
Clock
1360

East Belfry
(18th century)

IHS
monogram
1425
Medici Arms
1560

1305

1295 - 1299

1330 -
43

1325

1680

1325 -
30

1352
-1468

1310

1284

1680

1310

11 Palazzo Pubblico, Siena. Inset: stages in the growth of the Palazzo (sketch by Phyllis Carr)

strange shores. Most terrible of all perhaps was the resurgence under fear of death of inhumanity within man himself, the abandonment of friends and relatives, the refusal of doctors to visit the sick, of priests to attend the dying.

In these circumstances men faced the crisis each according to their characters. The celebrated introduction to Boccaccio's *Decameron*, though based in part upon Paul the Deacon's account of plague in seventh-century Rome,[3] chronicles the various responses. Some gave themselves up to apathy and refused to carry on their customary work; some shut themselves away in solitude, ate and drank in moderation, listened to music, avoided all sound of the outer world; some took refuge in excess; others fled to the country 'as if God's anger had only been confined within the walls of the city'. Yet others, followed the counsel of the Florentine versificr, Antonio Pucci, and confessed, performed pious works, visited the sick, and 'thought it foolish to flee a death which God had decreed but prepared their souls for it in courage'.

It is as well to bear in mind this diversity of reaction to the immediate experience of the plague, when we consider the more difficult question of long-term psychological effects. Did the pandemic, as many have argued, leave a deep scar upon the collective psyche of the societies it attacked? To such improbable allies as Coulton and Gasquet, Thorndike and Renouard, the year 1348 saw the origins of vast changes in European thought and feeling; these changes affected not only the generations which experienced the plague, but extended beyond them and into the sixteenth century.

In the period up to 1380, there is certainly some evidence to show this time as an era of profound pessimism and renunciation of life. One could contrast the introduction of Giovanni Villani's chronicle, begun in 1300, with that of his brother Matteo, begun in 1348. Giovanni wrote, he explained, because 'considering the nobility and greatness of our city at the present time', he wished to explain the cause of this greatness to future generations. His aim, that is, was to tell a success story. Matteo, on the other hand, began his work by referring to 'the stain of sin through which the generations of men are wholly subject to temporal calamities, and to much misery and innumerable ills'. He detailed these at some length: 'wars, battles, the fury of peoples, change of kingdoms, tyrannical usurpations, plagues, deaths, famines, floods, shipwrecks,' etc. and remarked that, through their failure to understand divine judgment, men were surprised when these came upon them. The purpose of his history, then, he continued, was to prepare men in good or bad times for the worst, and to show them *l'uscimento cadevole e il fine dubbioso delle mortali cose*, 'the doubtful doom of human kind'.[4]

Those who reacted to disaster in this spirit turned for support to a religion which was now likely to portray the relationship of God and man in much more sombre terms. Since it was almost universally believed that the plague was the punishment of sin by a wrathful deity, God was considered again as a remote and terrible Jehovah, rather than a Being who shared, albeit in exalted and mystical form, the humanity of ordinary men. Symbolic of the change in religious sentiment is the difference between the sermons delivered in S. Maria Novella at Florence by Domenico Cavalca (*c.* 1270–1342), with their emphasis upon divine love and charity, and those of Jacopo Passavanti given in 1354, which laid stress instead upon such themes as the decay of human flesh, the need for penitence, the eternity of the pains of hell. Passavanti's teaching echoed in part that of the Augustinian friar, Simone Fidati, who in his *De gestis Domini Salvatoris* (begun 1338, unfinished at his death in 1348) presented a life of Christ whose austerity is in sharp contrast to those earlier lives in the tradition of the pseudo-Bonaventura. Fra Simone was on terms of friendship with Taddeo Gaddi, and it has been suggested that it was his moral influence which led both him and Daddi, in their later works, to eschew the portrayal of love and affection between their holy figures.

In the period as a whole religious feeling assumed more tortured and melancholy forms. Religious intensity grew. Some followed orthodox paths, enrolling in the lay-societies, the *Laudesi*, and the confraternities of penance in which the practice of penitential self-flagellation now came to be more common. Others, noticeably among the urban proletariat, turned to the heretical movement of the Fraticelli, with its exaltation of poverty, and its belief that the

Pope, with his vast wealth, was the anti-Christ. In Tuscany, at least, the 50s, 60s, and 70s were certainly the decades of spectacular saints: the blessed Giovanni dalle Celle in his hermit existence above Vallambrosa, the English eremite William Fleet at Lecceto, the blessed Giovanni Colombini, former Sienese merchant-banker and member of 'the Nine', who founded the order of the *Gesuati*. Above all, it is the age of St Catherine Benincasa of Siena (1347–80). That the fantasies born of profound psychological disturbance, which moved this admittedly highly intelligent girl, should have been welcomed by the Church, shows more clearly than anything else the atmosphere of hysteria to be found in the religion of the time. Yet in the face of this emotionalism which often bordered on the heretical, the Church sought to lay new stress upon its own institutions, its role as the guardian of orthodoxy, and as the guiding authority which brought salvation.

But if those who turned to religion brought a new intensity of feeling to their devotions, the generality of men, to the surprise of the chroniclers, gave proof of the essential resilience of the human mind before even the greatest disasters. It seems wise to discount much that has been written on the supposed long-term effects of the Black Death. In an interesting chapter ('Would the living envy the dead?') in his *On Thermonuclear War*, Herman Kahn has discussed the possible psychic effects of a nuclear attack on the United States in which half the population were killed. His conclusions, fortified by the findings of the Rand Foundation, are that one can dismiss all possibilities of permanent or semi-permanent mental malaise in such circumstances. Life would go on (as too, presumably, would nuclear wars). Speculative studies of hypothetical situations obviously provide poor analogies. Nonetheless it may be that here we encounter an unchanging element in human beings, their capacity for endurance and for hope in the future.

In many ways, it should be added, the survivors of the plague were often better off than they had been before. It has been seen, for instance, how 'new men', enriched by inheritance from those who had died, now came forward at Florence to claim their share in government. Similarly the Black Death brought an increased demand for labour and a rise in wages and working conditions which did much to better the lot of the poorer classes. Although prices rose too, the balance of advantage still lay with the employed. A recent study of the countryside around Pistoia, for instance, has shown how during the century before the plague urban landlords had been able to exploit a large rural population by the exaction of extremely high rents in the leasing of land. With the demographic decline rents fell, profits shrank, and what can be considered as a more equitable rural social order came into being. One striking example of a new lower-class prosperity is the fact that it is apparently in the fourteenth century that the Italian peasant first began to wear underwear.

Inheritance benefited the poor; it also made the rich richer. So, in an apparent paradox, this age of profound economic decline was a period of personal extravagance and conspicuous consumption. It was the age of 'the new clothes', new luxurious styles of dress which shocked the chroniclers of the time both by their immodesty and their cost. It was a period, too, of sumptuous public and private entertainments. At the marriage of Lionel, Duke of Clarence, the third son of Edward III, to Violante Visconti in 1368, the celebrations at Milan were rumoured to have cost 200,000 florins. They included a monstrous 18-course meal, of which 16 were double courses, of both meat and fish. Between each course lavish gifts were given to the guests: greyhounds, mastiffs, bloodhounds, sparrow-hawks, peregrine falcons, suits of combat armour, of jousting armour, small and large coursers with gilded saddles, jousting steeds, precious clothes and jewels. In its tasteless extravagance the celebration serves as a symbol of the profligate largesse of the new age.

Accordingly, it need cause no surprise that though the first three chapters of Matteo Villani's chronicle deal with the effects of the plague, the fourth should bear the title: 'How men were worse than before'. He observed how after 1348 it was believed that men 'having seen the extermination of their neighbours' would become holy and virtuous and full of love and charity towards each other. In fact, he continued, 'forgetting what has passed as if it had never been' the survivors gave themselves up to profligacy:

passing the time in idleness they dissolutely indulged the sin of gluttony, in banquets, taverns, and feasts, with delicate foods: in gambling, in running without bridle to lust, in wallowing in strange clothes and unwonted fashions and unchaste manners, and in giving new forms to all their everyday goods. And the common people, men and women, for the vast abundance of goods that they possessed, did not want to work at their accustomed trades, and sought out the dearest and most delicate foods, and at their will they married, clothing their low-born women in all the fine and costly robes of the ladies who had died in the horrible death. And without any restraint almost the whole of the city rushed to unchaste life, and so too and worse, did the other cities and provinces of the world. And from the information we could gather there was nowhere where men restrained themselves in continence. Having escaped from the divine fury, they thought the hand of God was tired. But as the prophet Isaiah says: 'His anger is not turned away, and His hand is stretched out still.'

The tone of this need not be taken too seriously: the thought that the lower orders are enjoying prosperity rather than devoting themselves exclusively to work has always been deeply disturbing to the bourgeois spirit. But the passage does give evidence of a new affluence in certain classes. With this in mind it is easier to consider the effects which the Black Death may be supposed to have had upon the course of literature and art.

Patterns of Patronage, 1340–1380

In this age of economic and political crisis, which was yet in many ways, as we have seen, a period of affluence, were there any substantial changes in patronage? With the difficulty in maintaining levels of tax revenue during population decline, and with the need to devote much of the money obtained to facing dangerous political situations, it might be expected that there would be a decline in the amount of art and architecture to be commissioned by governments. But it is difficult to present any sustained interpretation of what happened in these terms.

Only in the kingdom of Naples, where the accession of Queen Giovanna led to a weakening of central control, was there any marked cessation of patronage. In Tuscany, though the 40s present a rather blank period, the years which followed show the maintenance of, what is in the circumstances, a remarkably high level of artistic production. At Florence the expulsion of the Duke of Athens as *signore* on St Anne's day (26th July 1343) caused the grateful commune to arrange for the building of a church to her in the city. At the same time the Priors caused a fresco to be painted in the Bargello, showing the saint giving banners to the insurgents with her right hand, while protecting the Palazzo Vecchio with her left. (This picture, perhaps by Taddeo Gaddi, is now in the house of the Società Filarmonica in via Ghibellina.) More continuous work was carried out in Piazza San Giovanni and Piazza Signoria. During the 50s Alberto Arnoldi worked on the reliefs illustrating the sacraments in the second storey of the campanile, and the years 1376 to about 1381 saw the construction of the elegant Loggia dei Lanzi in front of the Palazzo Vecchio. Work on the cathedral was resumed in 1357 and advanced steadily. By this time standards of taste had changed. The new master-builder, Francesco Talenti, abandoned Cambio's façade and projected a new design. This was in its turn to be swept away in the sixteenth century, and replaced by the present decoration, an object of much criticism, in 1887.) During the 1360s work went forward on the nave and tribunes, and after another pause in the 70s the chapels and choir were begun. Similarly work continued on Or San Michele. In 1346 the *Arte della Seta* commissioned Bernardo Daddi to paint there a picture of the Madonna in place of the old miracle-working image. Between 1352 and 1360 the same guild entrusted to Orcagna, who had already acted as master-builder to the whole structure, the carving of the tabernacle to enclose Daddi's painting. The costly silver altar-dossal of the Baptistery was made by the workshop of Leonardo di San Giovanni in the years after 1367.

However, the final problem of the erection of the cupola upon the cathedral was abandoned until the 1420s. So, too, the further decoration of Or San Michele stopped, despite ambitious projects, until the beginning of the next century. The commune seems to have suspended much of that financial assistance it had given in the past to other churches of the city. The nave of S. Trinità was built in 1350–70, but the rest of the church was not constructed until the 1380s. Many of the churches which had been begun earlier, S. Spirito, the Badia, S. Croce, and S. Maria Novella, were left without façades. Indeed all but the last named lacked them in the nineteenth century. Commenting on this, Fiumi has spoken of sixteenth-century Florence as a city of unfinished monuments. It is possible that the popular temper of the city had in some measure turned against the idea of government patronage. With his customary surliness Matteo Villani growled a complaint that the plans for the Loggia dei Lanzi had been drawn up 'because the Priors had nothing better to do'.

Yet the commune still achieved much during these years, and even supplemented the patronage of private individuals upon occasion. The banker Lenno Balducci, for instance, secured some government support for the erection of the Ospedale di San Matteo. At the same time the financial position of the religious orders and the religious guilds had greatly improved. All had been suddenly enriched, either through legacies from victims of the Black Death, or gifts prompted by terror or gratitude from survivors. In 1348, for example, the Company of the Madonna of Or San Michele received goods valued at the staggering sum of over 350,000 florins. At the same time both the hospital of S. Maria Nuova, and the Company of S. Maria della Misericordia were left over 25,000 florins. Villani pointed out that these increases in wealth came precisely at a time when the opportunities for charitable work had shrunk, since many of the mendicant and sick had died in the plague, and many of the surviving poor had suddenly been saved from their poverty by inheritance. Consequently these bodies were in a strong position to give patronage to the arts, as did the Misericordia, for instance by building in 1352 the oratory known as the Bigallo which stands opposite the Baptistery of Florence.

Moreover, individuals who with new wealth had acquired new ambitions of ostentation gave money to the Church for art. It was in these years that the statesman Niccolò Acciaiuoli planned his

Charterhouse, that his soul 'if it is immortal, as my lord chancellor says', might delight in it from beyond the grave. Others, it is likely, had acquired new fears. So, in 1348, Turino Baldesi gave a large sum to Santa Maria Novella for the painting of a narrative cycle on the Old Testament. In the same church the construction of a new chapter house, 'the Spanish Chapel', was undertaken with the money given by Buonamico Guidalotti, a wealthy merchant whose wife had died in the plague. Seven years later he gave more money, which was used to commission Andrea da Firenze to paint there the great fresco glorifying the Dominican order (about 1366–8). All this meant that the private individual and private corporation came into much greater prominence as patrons. Yet it would still be too much to claim that the initiative had passed to these from the Florentine government.

At Siena too the commune maintained its predominance. The project for the new cathedral (see pages 68–70) was finally abandoned in 1356. Yet this was not the end of the story. In turning from their great dream, the Sienese did not abandon all plans for the glory of their church. Instead they returned to the more modest project of an extension of the existing fabric on the basis of the scheme of 1315. By 1370 the choir had been extended to the east over the Baptistery, and between 1377 and 1382 the west façade was completed. In all the work of the cathedral the technical difficulties to which the 1322 committee had referred were skilfully overcome. Nonetheless, those defects of proportion which had been criticised in the original plan can still be seen in the final result. The naves have been raised so high that the dome appears to be set far too low upon them, while the displacement of the cupola from the centre of the crossing has given clumsy balance to the middle of the church. But the cathedral, on which the commune had been engaged for some 150 years, has still a remarkable consistency in general effect. Meanwhile, from 1352 the 'Chapel of the Piazza' was begun at the foot of the Palazzo Pubblico, perhaps as the result of a vow taken during the Black Death. It was erected under the initial supervision of Domenico d'Agostino, master of works of the cathedral. Despite a decree of the General Council in 1369 authorising the expenditure of 100 florins a year upon the building, the work proceeded slowly. Only in 1376 were the square pillars raised, and the marble brought from Carrara for its statues. In the following year commissions were given to various sculptors for the adornment of the building. During the same period further decoration was completed inside the Communal Palace. In 1352 Lippo Vanni executed a *Coronation of the Virgin* on the ground floor. Later he painted the huge monochrome battle scene showing *The Victory of the Sienese over the Company of the Capello* which still survives in the Sala del Mappamondo. Then there was a lull of some 40 years in which work within the building largely ceased.

Outside Tuscany, government patronage seems, if anything, to have grown in volume in the years following the 40s. In central Italy Cardinal Albornoz, who had brought war to all the provinces of the Papal State, sought to reinforce his control by beginning the great fortresses of Assisi, Narni, and Spoleto at the end of the 60s. Nor did he neglect the arts of peace. As a result of his beneficence the Collegio di Spagna was erected at Bologna, under the supervision of Matteo Gattapone, for the benefit of Spanish students at the university. At Venice the Doge Andrea Dandolo (in office, 1343–54) commissioned the mosaic work in the Baptistery and the Chapel of St Isidore which so strikingly combines Byzantine solemnity and International Gothic elegance. He also caused the Pala d' Oro, the tenth-century altar-screen within St. Mark's, to be richly embellished. Gold, polychrome, and a fantastic wealth of jewellery (86 enamels, 1,300 pearls, 300 sapphires, 300 emeralds, etc.) were added in order to give the work new splendour. From 1340 the Hall of the Great Council in the Doge's Palace was enlarged, and from 1365 Guariento was called upon to begin its decoration with frescoes. An anonymous sculptor carved Dandolo's own monument in San Marco, and Nino Pisano came north to erect the tomb for the Doge Marco Cornaro (d. 1367) in SS. Giovanni e Paolo.

Among the *signorie*, too, it was an important age for patronage of the arts. Petrarch, in a treatise on government written in 1373 for Francesco Carrara, Lord of Padua, had called upon his 'ancients' to justify the importance of this. A just *signore*, he explained, should follow the example of Augustus, whom Livy had called 'builder and restorer of temples', and of whom Suetonius said that he found Rome brick and left it marble. So, today, ecclesiastical and public buildings should be raised, and the streets should be freed from 'these hellish vehicles of ours (*nostris his tartareis curribus*) which are destroying the roads and houses, and more, the minds of those living inside them'. Princes too, of course, should honour men with uncommon skills in literature and learning. By these means the ruler would be able to attract the love of his subjects.[5]

Despite these amiable sentiments, signorial patronage in this age was directed mainly towards the delectation of the *signori* themselves rather than to public beneficence. The tradition of equestrian monuments, begun with the early tombs of the della Scala family in the cloister of S. Maria Antica at Verona, was continued with the memorial to Mastino II (d. 1351) and the 'magnificent Gothic machine' which commemorates Cansignorio della Scala, executed by Bonino da Campione between 1370 and 1374. The most successful of all this genre, however, is the same sculptor's earlier equestrian statue of Bernabò Visconti (see plate XI). The contemporary Azario described how Bernabò had this *mirabilis et pulchra opera*: 'sculpted in marble, armed as if setting out for war, brandishing his baton of lordship'. At its sides were two statues of virgins representing his justice and strength, 'those virtues by which he ruled'.[6] During his own lifetime Bernabò had this statue placed above the high altar of San Gottardo, from which effective if bizarre setting it can be imagined as menacing the congregation upon their knees before it.

Many castles were built in this period. Francesco Carrara built the elaborate Porta Legnago at Montagnana; and Cangrande della Scala erected the castle and fortified bridge at Verona (the latter now authentically reconstructed). But in this field the Visconti were still supreme. Azzone Visconti's magnificent fortified palace (see page 104) served as a model for many of the buildings put up by the family throughout their territory. Of these the most celebrated surviving example is Pavia, constructed for Galeazzo II between 1360 and 1365. Petrarch wrote in admiring terms to Boccaccio of this work: 'the huge palace situated on the highest point of the city, an admirable building which cost a vast amount . . . built . . . by a man who surpasses others in many ways and in the magnificence of his buildings excels himself. I am convinced, unless I be misled by my partiality for the founder, that, with your good taste in such matters, you would declare this to be the most noble product of modern art'.[7]

Within the castles elaborate decorative works continued. Some of these took a religious theme, such as the *Scenes from the life of Christ* (c. 1350), executed by an unknown artist in the Visconti castle of Montiglio. But secular motifs were much more in evidence, noticeably those cycles commemorating 'Famous Men'. Around 1370 certain artists, probably Altichiero and Jacopo Avanzo, with, possibly, Giusto de' Menabuoi, decorated the palace of Francesco Carrara at Padua with figures drawn from Petrarch's biographical study of classical heroes, the *De viris illustribus*. In the same period Altichiero worked in the palace of the della Scala at Verona. Here he painted medallion portraits of famous men of his own time above frescoes illustrating Josephus's account of the Wars of Jerusalem. In Lombardy there was fierce competition for the services of artists. Already, in the 1330s, Galvano Fiamma had written of Azzone Visconti's palace as filled 'with ironworkers, sculptors, writers, glassworkers, carpenters, and all manner of artisans'. In May 1366, Galeazzo II was writing to the Lord Guido Gonzaga of Mantua with a request that he should send all the painters that could be spared to Pavia. Fourteen years later, Giangaleazzo sent a letter couched in virtually identical terms to Ludovico Gonzaga: 'In order that certain rooms in our castle of Pavia be decorated we require a great number of painters. Please therefore send four to six from Mantua, for we understand there are good painters there.' In addition to paintings the *signori* adorned their palaces with exotica. Jacopo Dondi, for instance, built for the Carrara palace at Padua an ornate astronomical clock which showed not only the hours of the day but the courses of the planets. His son, Giovanni, one of the most prominent physicians of northern Italy, and one of Petrarch's closest friends, designed a still more elaborate time-piece for the library of the Visconti castle at Pavia, a work which, to judge from surviving descriptions and plans, had the highest claims to be considered as a work of art.[8]

Finally the *signoria* provided a certain measure of patronage to literature. In all, considering the economic difficulties with which the Italian governments were confronted, their record of achievement in the arts in this period is remarkable. It is particularly so in that Italy was now faced from outside the peninsula with the competition of another major cultural centre which acted as a lure to the artist and the intellectual. The Papacy was by this time firmly established at Avignon, and its interests were beginning to be distracted from Italian concerns. At first the Popes did not entirely forget their obligations in Rome. John XXII sent 5,000 florins for the restoration of St John Lateran in 1320, 3,000 florins for St Peter's in March 1321, and 1,000 florins in September 1322 for the monastery of S. Paolo fuori le Mura. In 1340 Benedict XII sent 5,000 florins for the repair of the Papal Palace, and the following year another thousand florins for St Peter's. He is also said to have put aside a full 50,000 florins for the general restoration of the basilicas. In the 1340s the city saw the building of the staircase of the Aracoeli and the hospital of the confraternity of *Salvator ad Sancta Sanctorum* at the Lateran. Then, with the decision of Clement VI (1342–1352) to build the Papal Palace at Avignon, interest waned. Provence proved a magnet for such Italian artists as Matteo Giovanetti of Viterbo, and a host of lesser followers. Urban V diverted revenues to churches and monasteries in the Massif Central, and to his Benedictine college and monastery at Montpellier.

Urban's temporary return to Italy (1367–70), inspired a short burst of artistic activity. In 1369 Giovanni da Milano, Agnolo and Giovanni Gaddi, and Giottino di Stefano, were decorating two chapels in the Vatican for the pope. In the same year di Stefano was being employed as *architector* (roof-mender?) for the renewal of St John Lateran, partly destroyed by fire in 1360. Coluccio Salutati wrote exultantly to Petrarch, describing the rebuilding of the Lateran, and the repairs to St Peter's and S. Paulo, and concluding that Rome was once again rising from its ruins.[9] But these hopes were not fulfilled. The return of the Papacy to Rome in 1378 was followed almost at once by the outbreak of the Great Schism, and the return of a large part of the papal *curia* to Avignon. In the generation which followed it was to be Avignon, together with other northern courts, Prague, Paris, Angers, and Dijon, rather than the cities of Italy, which were to be the principal centres determining the characteristic tone of European art.

Changes in Art, 1340–1380

Though the full development of the so-called 'International Gothic' style lay in the future, art in Italy, or, more precisely, in Tuscany, did in some circumstances radically change its character both in form and content. These changes, which have been brilliantly analysed by Professor Millard Meiss, give the appearance, above all, of a reassessment of the relation between God and man. In Florence, the tradition of Giotto gave way to the art of Andrea di Cione, called Orcagna, his younger brother Nardo, Andrea da Firenze, Giovanni del Biondo, and Giovanni da Milano. Significantly, in the 1370s, Benvenuto da Imola could record that he had heard from experts that Giotto had at times made 'great errors' in his painting. In Siena, similarly, the tradition of Duccio yielded to the styles of Barna, Bartolo di Fredo, and Andrea Vanni. In both cities there was a return to pre-Giottesque ideals, an indifference to the art of the previous generation, and a turning-away from the religious ideals which had inspired it. Christ, his humanity diminished in favor of his Godhead, was no longer represented as the lovely child or the man of sorrows, but became again a figure raised far above man and remote from him. He was depicted frontally, without any real attempt to give volume, as if to emphasize his transcendence, his separation from the merely human. He is immobile or, if he moves, he threatens. Yet even his very immobility is, as in Orcagna's Strozzi altarpiece, charged with a certain menace.

In the portrayal of the divine, a new prominence was given to abstract themes such as 'The Trinity'. This was accompanied by similar changes in representations of the Virgin. In the *Maestà* in the church of S. Agostino in Siena, painted by a follower of Lorenzetti in the 1370s, one can see this new spirit most clearly (see plate 4). The theme is no longer the glorification of the Virgin in Majesty, but the supplication of helpless man to remote powers. Of the eight saints portrayed, four—St Apollonia, St Bartholomew, St Catherine, and St Agatha (with her severed head)—are the victims of brutal martyrdom. At the centre of the picture, the Christ-child in the arms of a cold and indifferent Virgin withdraws his hands in fear and disgust from the goldfinch, symbol of plague, that she is holding. By her side kneels St Michael the Archangel who, according to a legend of St Gregory the Great, had power against the plague.[10] This dehumanisation of the divine went with an abandonment of those narrative elements, those human stories, that had meant so much to the previous generation. Art now turned 'from narrative to ritual'. Symbols were all, and the symbols given particular prominence were those of the Church and the Priest. These dominate, for instance, Giovanni da Milano's *Expulsion of Joachim* in S. Croce, Florence, and Andrea da Firenze's *Road to Salvation* in the chapter house of S. Maria Novella.

There was too a particular fascination with the morbid treatment of such sombre themes as 'the woes of Job' and the sufferings of the plague saints, Sebastian and Bartholomew. This new mood is best illustrated in three frescoes, probably executed in the 1350s by Francesco Traini (now in the Museo Nazionale di San Matteo at Pisa, formerly in the Camposanto). *The Triumph of Death* was the new generation's answer to that hope in the temporal state which had sustained their fathers and which had been illustrated in Lorenzetti's allegory of 'Justice'. This vast fresco shows, to the left, 'the meeting of the quick and the dead'. Here a hunting-party, with King, Queen, Emperor, and nobles, riding in the prime of life, comes suddenly upon three coffins, whose putrefying corpses show them what they will become. The Emperor holds a handkerchief to his nose against the stench; a hermit stands by to point the moral. To the right, there is a sylvan idyll; nobles and ladies feast with cupids, oblivious of the terrible figure of death threatening them from above with his scythe. Only the wretched, the lame, and the poor, in the centre of the painting, can see him. They lift up their hands towards him asking to be relieved of their miseries, and, ironically, are ignored. Around, angels and demons fight for possession of the souls of the dead, and the damned are borne off to the mountain of hell. Finally, in the section called 'The Legends of the Anchorites', stress is laid upon the virtues of the eremitical life, on the spiritual supremacy of those indifferent to death which frightens the worldly.

The same atmosphere is found in the surviving fragments of Orcagna's *Last Judgement* and *Hell* in S. Croce in Florence; and in the decayed corpse, consumed by snakes and toads, in the predella of Giovanni del Biondo's Vatican *Madonna*. Both life and death here have intense horror. In the new art only the enigmatic Barna of Siena, in his frescoes for the Collegiate Church of San Gimignano (probably painted 1350–55), succeeds in rising above a mere morbidity of feeling, an excitement with physical corruption, to a human acceptance of brutality and pain and to a sustained tragic vision of the life of Christ and of man.

A change has come over Tuscan art in this period. The morbidity of subject matter and the new stress upon the priest can obviously be related to the plague, the attempts of the Church in these circumstances to draw its own moral from disaster, and the damage done to individual sensibilities by the enormous mortality. The change in style, the rejection of the Giottesque in favour of a more transcendental portrayal of the divine, has received other divergent interpretations. It has been suggested, for instance, in the neo-Marxist analysis of Antal, that the more conservative styles, now fashionable, particularly reflected the tastes of the *gente nuova* or 'new men' coming forward to claim their part in Florentine government. These men (who are, inaccurately,[11] equated with the whole of the lower middle class) are said to have been without the cultural traditions of the old ruling groups which had patronised Giotto, and to have preferred the supposed simplicities of pre-Giottesque art to which Orcagna and his followers were moving. A major difficulty here is that there seems to be no evidence that it was in fact these 'new men' who were giving patronage to the new art. Yet the old patriciate, as the name of the Strozzi altarpiece reminds us, certainly were. Antal meets this objection by asserting that the old upper class were seeking by means of the new art to 'conciliate' the tastes of the *gente nuova*. All this is an inadmissable hypothesis. The evidence to show that by the middle of the century Giottesque naturalism required a greater measure of sophistication from those who viewed it than the new art is slight, merely one ambiguous remark by Petrarch. And everything suggests that 'conciliation' was the last reaction of the directing class to the challenge to their power by the 'new men'.

Others have suggested that the plague, in carrying off the older generation of artists, had left the survivors with a new freedom of innovation which had allowed them to develop fresh styles and to abandon what has become by now a traditional orthodoxy. Though more plausible, this argument is inconclusive. It is true that many of the older artists died or were heard no more of from around 1348 to 1350, men like Maso di Banco and Bernardo Daddi in Florence, the Lorenzetti in Siena. Yet others, such as Taddeo Gaddi, lived on. Even if one were to accept that a younger generation of artists had taken over, it is still difficult to see that this by itself should lead to a general preference for pre-Giottesque influences. More satisfactorily, the change in style is to be seen as the consequence of the new subject matter, and the change in religious feeling which it expressed. The techniques of Giotto and his followers were abandoned, the attempts to give volume and form were ignored, because it was no longer thought necessary or desirable to give humanity to the divine. Artists no longer sought the delineation of nature because nature was no longer a good in itself, an ideal to be rendered in paint. Nature had proved the enemy of man. Under the psychological stress of the plague those values which had sustained man earlier in the century: those beliefs, that is, in what may be called the humanity of God and the nobility of man created in his image, had disappeared.

Turning from Tuscany to other centres in Italy, it can be seen at once (and the reflection must warn us against any schematic socio-logical interpretations of the arts) that there is no similar pattern of withdrawal to earlier styles, of turning away from Giottesque traditions. In Venice Lorenzo Veneziano still pursued without noticeable change the modified Byzantine styles of the earlier part of the century. In the Veneto the Paduan school was seeking Giottesque values precisely at the time when they were being

12 Siena Cathedral

abandoned in Florence and Siena. Altichiero, Avanzo, and Giusto de' Menabuoi (a Florentine by birth), worked here in a style which sought depth recession and portrait naturalism. In the Po valley and at Bologna, Vitale da Bologna was blending realism and graphic refinement in a way which looked forward to the full maturity of the International Gothic. In any age, art is too complex and subtle to be compressed into simple explicative formulas, and every generalisation made must be given with reservations.

Changes in Literature, 1340–1380

In literature too it is difficult to trace any signs of the mid-century crisis. Obviously the plague did not pass unnoticed in the writings of the time. To Petrarch, for instance, it meant the tragic deaths of old friends: the Cardinal Colonna, Franceschino degli Albizzi, Roberto de' Bardi, and, above all, Laura herself. Writing to a friend in the first letter of the *Familiares*, the poet reflected: 'Time slips through our fingers. Our old hopes are buried with our friends. The year 1348 has left us alone and forlorn, for it has taken from us what the wealth of the Caspian or India cannot replace. These final losses are irreparable. The wounds dealt by death are past cure.'

Nor did these tragedies pass unremarked in his verse:

> *Lasciato hai, Morte, senza sole il mondo*
> *oscuro e freddo, Amor cieco et inerme,*
> *leggiadria ignuda, le bellezze inferme,*
> *me sconsolato, et a me grave pondo . . .*

('Death, you have left the world without sun, dark and cold; Love, blind and disarmed; grace stripped; beauties ailing; myself saddened and weighing on myself')

or again, in the sonnet:

> *Rotta è l'alta Colonna e 'l verde Lauro*

('Shattered is the high column [i.e. Cardinal Colonna], and the green laurel [i.e. Laura]')

Yet beyond the immediate memorial, it is hard to discern any permanent psychological affliction in the tranquil final years of Petrarch's life. Even in the lines quoted above, and still more in Petrarch's letters, there is a certain coldness and artifice in which the poet's delight in words seems almost to transcend the grief he is seeking to express.

The question of literary sincerity is a difficult one; convincing writing does not necessarily mean depth of feeling. There are some other guiding reflections which should be borne in mind if the failures of Huizinga and Stadelmann as 'historians of sensibility' are to be avoided. First, generalisations must not be made from the work of any one writer, since any one in a specific age is as likely to be a melancholic as an extrovert. Second, one must look at all that the writer has written, not merely select what is useful to one's thesis. The Shakespeare who wrote *King Lear* is the same man who wrote *Twelfth Night*. Third, it must be recognised that to think about death is not morbid, is not a sign of immaturity but of maturity. Morbidity and psychological disorder enter in only when the thought becomes obsessive. Finally, everything must be seen in context. Those who make a special study of wills or obituaries will easily come to the conclusion that every age has been preoccupied with death.

With these criteria in mind we can turn to Giovanni Boccaccio. It is his writings which have been most frequently quoted to show the effects of contemporary disasters upon fourteenth-century literature. The first argument follows these lines: in the 1330s Boccaccio was the poet of the gay, chivalric, careless life of Naples. This mood continued through the immediate horror of the Black Death, and was still present in the *Decameron*, written between 1348 and 1353. Then suddenly all changed, as the psychological pressures of the age made themselves felt. In the *Corbaccio*, written in 1354-5, Boccaccio turned to misogynist gloom and despair. Love was vile, sex disgusting. This mood continued with the *De casibus virorum illustrium*, written between 1355 and 1360. (These are the tales of misfortunes to the great which so upset the Canterbury Pilgrims when Chaucer's gloomy monk tried to tell them.) Then in 1362, when he was sent a message by a strange religious fanatic, Boccaccio wondered whether he should repent of his life and abandon literature. In 1372, finally, he was writing to Mainardo Cavalcanti, saying how appalled he is to hear that the ladies of Cavalcanti's household have been reading the *Decameron*: 'they will think me a filthy pimp, an incestuous old man, shameless, foul-mouthed, an eager narrator of others' wickedness'.[12] With these words, the new age, dominated by the spirit of religious revival, has triumphed over the old.

Such is the thesis. But there are many objections to it. It seems curious in the first place that the effects of the plague of 1348 should have been delayed until 1354. Some scholars are convinced that the bitterness of the *Corbaccio* arose not from social causes but from the personal fate of Boccaccio being rejected in love. If Boccaccio were tempted to abandon literature in 1362, he did not, in fact, do so. Seen in context, his letter of 1372 to Mainardo is very much better interpreted rather as a piece of humorous self-caricature than as a disavowal of his work. And where, in this thesis, can room be found for his *Praise of Famous Women* (written after 1360) which, although dotted with conventional moralising, makes reasonably cheerful reading? But suppose that it were all true, that there were a straight line of depression in Boccaccio's work from 1354, is it then proved that this is in any way connected with the condition of contemporary Italy? Advancing years bring sobriety and a new awareness of the virtues of piety and chastity, and old men chill more quickly than youth at the thought of death.

Another and rather different sociological interpretation of Boccaccio has recently been advanced.[13] Following the hypothesis of Raffaelo Ramat, the *Decameron*, far from being, as most have imagined, merely an intelligent, amoral entertainment for Florentine bourgeois-aristocratic society, is in fact an intensely serious and ethical affirmation of the values of the Commune. It is the work of a writer who is profoundly *engagé*. In the face of that crisis of the 40s, in the face of that plague which forms the *grave e nojoso principio*, the *orrido cominciamento* to the work, the ten young men and women are reaffirming the ideals of their city and their class. The stories of the *Decameron* in this view, are all specifically intended to illustrate the virtues of bourgeois *cortesia* and the continued vitality of bourgeois ideals despite the threats to the society which embodies them.

How can such a thesis be proved or disproved? All that can be said is that it springs from a remarkably professorial view of literature, and though it may be granted that the later Boccaccio had something of the professor about him, it seems inappropriate here. Is, for instance, the story of the Innkeeper of Mugnone (G. IX, no. 6), the story retold by the Reeve in the Canterbury Tales, really the passionate outpouring of a socially committed writer? In an area where complete subjectivity holds the field, an amateur in this world may perhaps be allowed his own interpretation. Why not then this? Briefly, the *Decameron* is above all a work of pure escapism. The purpose of the frame story of the plague is solely to remove the ten young people from the *città*, that is to say, from all the ordered social framework of values in the workaday city, and to transport them into a never-never land where nothing is real, although everything has the appearance of reality and where everyone speaks realistically. The mood of the *Decameron* has something in common with that of International Gothic art, where realistic peasants appear in the midst of dream fantasies. Accordingly, to seek here for information about contemporary moral attitudes, or to see, with Scaglione, these stories as illustrating the claims of nature and love against contemporary society, is to follow a blind alley, for it is wholly a world of dreams. The dream over, the young people return once again to the *città*, to the real world in the piazza before S. Maria Novella, from which they disperse to their homes and their everyday life.

Men's dreams, of course, are not insignificant. Those of the *Decameron* have for the most part an immense humour, health, and balance. This impression of balance, of human resilience in the face of disaster, is the strongest feeling gained from the work. In the introduction Boccaccio apologises 'to the ladies' for beginning his book with 'the dolorous memory of the plague mortality'. This beginning:

is but a journey over a harsh and steep mountain placed before a beautiful and delightful plain, which seems the more pleasurable, through the very difficulty of having gained it. For as unhappiness reaches upon the boundaries of joy, so sorrow is ended by the happiness which takes its place. To this short fatigue (I call it short in that it is contained in few words) there follows straightway the sweetness and pleasure that I have promised you.

Reading these words it is difficult to see Boccaccio either as the writer who will succumb to a negative view of life or as one who is writing as the intellectual apologist of the Florentine *popolo grasso*. It can be concluded perhaps that in the works of Boccaccio, as in the general literature of the age, there is no detailed correlation with any specific change in society. On the other hand, Tuscan art, which in this context is religious art, showed the strain to which the Italian world was subject in these years because it had, unlike literature, a direct relation with the Church, a Church which sought to dramatise the disasters in order to bring men, in despair of their condition, to the cross.

The Origins of Humanism

Certainly the development of humanism was to be unaffected by the miseries of the age. Within Italy this movement was to become supremely important during the next 150 years, and to exercise far-reaching effects upon all aspects of culture.

The word 'humanism' today implies a certain secular philosophy or 'ethics without God'. But this use of the word is comparatively modern. In the fourteenth century 'humanism' implied, not a specific outlook, but a sphere of study, more precisely, the intensive study of the classical world. Whereas other intellectuals were primarily interested in such subjects as science, metaphysics, law, and theology, the humanists gave themselves up to what Cicero had called the *studia humanitatis*: 'the humanities'. Humanists were those who studied grammar, rhetoric, poetry, history, and moral philosophy from Latin and, less frequently, from Greek texts.

The Latin classics had been studied long before the fourteenth century, often with considerable sophistication, as by the masters of the school of Chartres 200 years earlier. But there was an essential difference between these men and the new humanists. The scholars of an earlier age saw these Latin writings as having less importance than biblical exegesis or theology. They had not looked on them as a primary source of inspiration, and so, in a sense, had never read them for their own sake. But from the time of Petrarch this changed. In Italy there now appeared men who believed that in many fields the classical world offered a model for study superior to the Christian centuries which succeeded it.

As with so much else in Italian cultural life of this period, the origins of the new movement were to be found in thirteenth-century France. In Italy before 1300 there had been little writing of Latin poetry, and few commentaries upon classical authors, though both these activities had been common in French university circles. Italian libraries were far less well-stocked with classical texts than those of France and Germany. Only at the end of the thirteenth century did Italians take over the French humanist interests. Then, almost simultaneously, scholars at many different centres began to turn to the ancient authors, and to develop their studies with a passion unknown to the French, and to a point where they far excelled those north of the Alps. At Padua, the circle of Lovato de' Lovati (d. 1309) brought a new enthusiasm to the reading of Latin literature; the poetry of Albertino Mussato drew inspiration from Ovid and Horace, and his historical writing was modelled on Livy. At Verona, Giovanni de Matociis brought a new critical spirit to the study of antiquity. At Florence, Forese Donati and Franceschino degli Albizzi pursued research into classical mythology, while Geri d'Arezzo wrote in classical Latin. During this period, too, the *studia humanitatis* became a part of the curriculum in the Arts faculties of the Italian universities.

From these beginnings, which were no more than a linear development of medieval Latin studies, humanism was taken up in the next generation, and became a central part of the Italian cultural scene. It was Francesco Petrarch (1304–74) who was principally responsible for the consolidation and expansion of its disciplines. By his textual scholarship—his search for the manuscripts of the classics, his works in Latin of poetry, history, moral reflections—he provided a model of what the scholar's task should be. More, in his life, in his diligent cultivation of literary friendship, in his relations with the great, he showed how the scholar should live.

For his heirs in the fifteenth century, for men like Flavio Biondo, it was he who had begun the task of reviving classical civilisation. Others, like Bruni, might temporarily modify his ideals and might ask for a more active participation by intellectuals in the work of government, for more engagement in social life. Others cultivated that knowledge of Greek which Petrarch lacked. But in essence their standards of judgment and their attitudes to culture derived from him. It was his setting up of the classical world as a standard of life, his obsessive approach to the classics, and above all his realisation of the vast difference between his own and the classical world, which set a precedent for all the humanists who came after him. He was not alone in his generation. Others furthered the great advance in knowledge: at Naples there was the circle of Niccolò Acciaiuoli, which included Barbato da Sulmona, Giovanni Barili, and Zanobi da Strada; and at Florence the companions of Giovanni Boccaccio, Bishop Angelo Acciaiuoli (uncle of Niccolò), Francesco Nelli, and Lapo da Castiglionchio.

It is not difficult to explain the enthusiasm for classical studies which marked Italy during these years. In the first place government demanded skill in expression, elegant diplomatic letters, propaganda, and high-sounding orations at formal state occasions. In councils and law courts speeches had to carry conviction. In all this the style of the ancient world was found to exercise a particular force over men's minds. In the first half of the fourteenth century the skills of humanists such as Tanto dei Tanti at Venice and of Benzo d'Alessandria, chancellor of Cangrande della Scala at Verona, were already consciously being employed in the service of governments. Benintendi (d. 1365), chancellor to the Doge Andrea Dandolo, believed that the entire object of humanist study lay in the political field and in the preservation of republican freedom. In consequence, he thought that those parts of humanist studies, such as poetry, which did not lie strictly within it were not 'worthy of a free man', not worthy to be included among the liberal arts.[14]

Such a view was too extreme ever to gain anything like general acceptance: humanism cannot simply be considered as a stylistic innovation and as an enhanced concentration upon a merely verbal classical imitation. It must be taken too to imply a dominating admiration for the classical world. This admiration is understandable enough. To a society which was becoming increasingly secularised, where, for instance, the *Ethics* of Aristotle were constantly quoted, there was an irresistible fascination in the picture of the secular society discovered in the history and literature of Rome. In Italy there were particular factors which strengthened this interest. In the first place there was the influence of Roman law in whose study Italy had long been supreme, that incomparable inheritance from the past which may be supposed to have drawn men inevitably to ask themselves what society it was that had produced it. In this respect it is not surprising that so many of the early humanists were lawyers and notaries or originated from legal families.

At a time too when France and Germany looked to Charlemagne and England to Arthur, it was natural that Italians should turn back to the great era of their past. Dante wrote: 'it is the duty of all Italians to love the capital of Italy as the common source of their civility'. Within the peninsula there lay all around the ruins of Rome's past. Petrarch has described the intensity of his emotions at sitting on the roof of the baths of Diocletian and feeling the silence and solitude of the immense city in the pure air.[15] What more natural than that a cult of Livy should grow up at Padua, of Virgil at Mantua? At Mantua, the very coinage of the town had from the mid-twelfth century borne upon it simply the words VIRGILIUS or PUBLIUS VIRGILIUS; from the mid-thirteenth it carried his image too.

In these circumstances an interest in the Roman past developed which was not purely confined to scholars. During the second half of the thirteenth and first half of the fourteenth century there were a large number of translations of the classics into Italian, works by Cicero, Virgil, Seneca, Boethius, Livy, and Sallust, which widened popular fascination in the past. The friars themselves, with their sure instinct for current general taste, laced their sermons with popularised classical knowledge. Fra Remigio Girolami (1265–1319) referred in his preaching to Suetonius' *Lives of the Caesars*, to Cicero, and Seneca. His colleague at S. Maria Novella, Fra Giordano da Rivalto, spoke of the descent of Orpheus into the underworld, the destruction of Troy through Helen, and the rivalries of Pompey and Caesar. In the same period some clerics even began to be alarmed by this diffusion of knowledge of a non-Christian world, and Fra Uberto Guidi from the same house at Florence as Remigio and Giordano set himself to combat 'the pagan stories and the poet's fables'.[16]

This Italian pride in the past, upon which much of humanism was plainly based, found its most remarkable expression in political life with the career of Cola (Nicola) di Rienzo (1313–54). Cola, born on the left bank of the Tiber, son of an innkeeper and a washerwoman, had qualified as a notary, and in his early life devoted his leisure to the study of Latin literature and those epitaphs and inscriptions of the classical world which he found in his native city. These investigations, together with the influence of strange Joachimite prophecies which he had absorbed in the circles of the heretical Fraticelli, persuaded him that the Roman people should once again seize the pre-eminence which they had enjoyed in their golden age. This extraordinary dream was expressed with such charismatic power that it worked for a time upon even so sober a spirit as Petrarch. Moreover Cola's ambitions provided a useful tool to those, for instance, who wished to break the power of the Roman nobility, or to humble still further the claims of the German emperor. So, for a time, he prospered. In 1347 'Nicola the severe and clement, the Tribune of freedom, peace, and justice, and liberator of the Holy Roman Republic' drove out the local aristocracy and assumed control of the city in the name of the Roman people. From there he sent out messages to all the courts of Italy announcing his intention of summoning a council to discuss 'the security and peace of the whole Roman province' and 'the question of the Roman empire'. Seemingly he was seeking an Italian national confederation to be headed by Rome. Amazingly enough he secured some recognition, and ambassadors of a few powers appeared at his synod. Here, amidst lavish celebrations, the jurisdiction of the Romans over the whole world was solemnly affirmed, Roman citizenship was extended to all Italians, and the cities of Italy were declared free.

In political terms all this was, of course, completely unrealistic: '*opera fantastica*' wrote Giovanni Villani '*e poco da durare*'. Yet it was likely to appeal particularly to Italians. Cola is only one in a series of demagogues: Alberic, Arnold of Brescia, Mazzini, and Mussolini, who have across the centuries sought to overcome reality by their rhetorical hold upon the Roman people. In his case the dream was short-lived, and by 1350 his power had dissolved. When he returned to the city in 1354 it was as a puppet of Cardinal Albornoz; his magic had disappeared, and within two months he was killed by his own Romans. Yet his appearance on the Italian scene, the sudden irruption of his fantasy world, shows better, perhaps, than anything else the dominion which the idea of Rome now held over the minds of the Italian peoples.

In all this, the problem facing the historian is not so much to explain why humanism should be received so enthusiastically in fourteenth century Italy. It is rather to explain why these studies should have been deferred until then and why they were not flourishing in the century before. Without going into this in detail, three summary reasons may be offered. First it can be suggested that in the thirteenth century Italy had too close a relation with the German Empire across the Alps, which claimed and was universally acknowledged in the west to be 'the Roman Empire', to be able to assess clearly enough its Roman heritage. Second, at Bologna at least, and perhaps at other universities, the growing complexity of legal studies had impelled the students at the beginning of the thirteenth century to insist that the preliminary study of Latin grammar and rhetoric should be reduced to the minimum in order to permit more time to be given to their central preoccupation. Finally, as has been previously mentioned, the libraries of Italy, with the exception of Montecassino, were much poorer in classical texts than those of northern and central France. It was only in the fourteenth century that Italy had an opportunity to acquire a deep knowledge of classical literature. At that time Italian clerics were first appointed to French benefices, and the papacy moved to Avignon. It was in this period that Landolfo Colonna, 'provided' to a canonry at Chartres, came upon the texts which John of Salisbury had read there in the twelfth century, and that Petrarch 'discovered' Cicero's *Pro Archia* at Liège. Avignon itself was a centre where scholarly emigré Italians came together to exchange news of those discoveries of their own past which they had made in the libraries of France.

By the years 1340 to 1380, the new disciplines were already beginning to affect the course of the arts. In literature they produced Petrarch's Latin epic *Africa* and a variety of prose works. In painting too they had their influence. Francesco Carrara, Lord of Padua, had the main hall of his palace decorated with the portraits of 36 heroes of republican Rome, drawn from Petrarch's biographical study, *De viris illustribus*. Here too were portrayed the monuments of the city of Rome, the Pantheon, Colosseum, Castel Sant' Angelo, and the Vatican obelisk. Considered purely as exercises in classicism, both Petrarch's writings and the art here in Padua were defective. To the discerning of later ages, to Erasmus, for instance, reared in a longer tradition of humanist studies, Petrarch's Latin was still semi-barbarous. In so far as the Padua frescoes can be reconstructed, it would seem too that the paintings had no proper classical form, that the costume, for instance, was of the fourteenth century. Yet in these early works are the origins of that classicising movement which, strengthened in the next generation, was to come eventually to dominate almost all aspects of the arts in Italy.

Curiously enough this development of reverence for an essentially pagan society took place against the background of the plague and a sharp intensification of religious feeling. It might be that the study of the classics would have gathered greater momentum in these years but for the disasters which had overtaken the peninsula. Writing in the middle of the fifteenth century, Ghiberti told a curious story about a Venus Andiomene, a Roman copy of a statue by Lysippus, which had been dug up in the foundations of a palace in Siena in 1325. It had been sketched by Lorenzetti, and was perhaps used by him as a model for the figures of 'Caritas' and 'Securitas' in his fresco of *Justice and the Common Good*. Ghiberti speaks first of two other ancient statues which had also been discovered, and then continues:

> One other similar to these two was found in the city of Siena, at which there was much rejoicing. And by those who understand it was held to be a marvellous work and on the base was written the name of the master, who was a most excellent master called Lysippus. . . . And with much honour they placed it above their fountain as something of much distinction. All gathered with great rejoicing and honour when it was put there, and it was built magnificently into the top of the fountain. But it reigned there only for a short time. As the city had many disasters in war with the Florentines, when the flower of the citizens gathered in council one of them rose up and spoke about the statue in this fashion . . . 'My lord citizens, considering that from the time we found this statue, everything has continually gone wrong, and considering that idolatry is very seriously forbidden by our faith, we ought to believe that it is God who has, for our errors, sent us these afflictions. And in fact we see that from the time we gave honour to this statue, things have gone from bad to worse for us. I believe certainly that for as long as we have it on our soil things will continue to go badly. I am one of those who counsel that it should be taken down, broken up and smashed, and then be sent to be buried in the soil of the Florentines'. All agreed with the speech of their fellow citizen, and so it was put into effect; the statue was buried in our [Florentine] territory.

At first sight this story has about it the improbable air of some Boccaccian tale of superstition and malice. But it finds confirmation both in more contemporary chronicles and in the records of Sienese council meetings. The conciliar register of 7 November 1357 has the note: '*Item*, that the marble statue at present placed on the fountain of the *Campo*, be taken away from there quickly as possible, since it is seen to be a cause of scandal, and let it be dealt with as seems appropriate and pleasing to the Lords Twelve.'[17]

Despite the misfortunes of the period, this reaction to the products of the pagan world was not general. Lombardo della Seta, disciple of Petrarch, continued to keep a *Venus pudica* unearthed at Florence, in his house at Padua. The tide of humanism continued to flow. The artists and intellectuals preserved a basic psychological health. Amidst possibilities of ruin, the bourgeois too averted their minds from the transcendental and maintained that pragmatism which was their main strength. Bernabò of Genoa speaks for them all when, in the Decameron, addressing his fellow merchants, he remarks: *Io son mercatante e non filosofo, e come mercatante risponderò*—'I'm a merchant, not a philosopher, and it's as a merchant that I'll reply to you'.

seven

Literature and Music

From Sound to Sight

The most basic intellectual development of the later middle ages was the transition from a primarily oral culture to one which was principally literary and visual. Before the eleventh century knowledge was thought of as something one received from hearing, from speech, and from people; then it gradually came to be considered as the product of sight and of things (especially books). This change has for some time past been attributed to the invention of printing, which certainly played an important part in the process. Yet many of the features which have been ascribed to the Gutenberg revolution are found before the middle of the fifteenth century. The invention of printing, that is to say, was in many ways an effect rather than a cause in the emergence of a visual culture. Ultimately the reasons for the decline of oral learning must be sought rather in the 'rationalisation' of European society which came with the economic revolutions of the twelfth and thirteenth centuries.

In considering these economic revolutions it has already been seen that by the end of the thirteenth century the Italian bourgeoisie had become dependent upon reading and writing. The continual refrain of the merchant's handbooks: *non perdonare mai alla penna*, 'never spare the pen', is the same counsel which is repeated insistently in the naive, jingling verses of an anonymous Genoese businessman, writing in his own dialect at the beginning of the fourteenth century:

ma sempre aregordar te voi
de scrive ben li faiti toi
perzò che non te esan de mente
tu li scrivi incontanente

('and seek when venturing from the toun
to write your ilka business doun
ere it sall gang from your mind away
ye should write it doun that day.')

and:

chi è peigro faxeor
e lento in so faiti scrive
senza dano e senza error
no po longamenti vive

('he who's made of idle stuff
in writing what has gang
wi'oot trials and passage rough
canna live for lang.')

'These merchants', wrote Boccaccio, 'always ill at ease, calculating, worrying about every little occurrence, now in England, now in Flanders, now in Spain, now in Cyprus, now here, now there, they don't so much write letters to their partners as volumes'.[1] In the archives of the Datini firm at Prato there are over 500 account books, 120,000 letters, and many thousand more miscellaneous business documents mainly from the years 1382 to 1410. In the eight years 1392 to 1400 the branch of the firm at Genoa received 16,000 letters (an average of six a day) from 200 different towns in Europe. In the fourteenth century the merchant was an avid correspondent, and, in Florence at least, a compulsive private diarist. Writing had become for him an everyday activity. Merchant wealth itself was seen to exist only in so far as it was written down. In a letter to Datini a friend expressed this idea forcibly: *Ma fatti vostri sono in inscritture oggi sì, domani no*, 'Your business is just in your account books, here today, gone tomorrow'.

While oral culture was still very strong, there was a considerable growth in bookishness and in habits of reading. This is seen in the advice of Paolo di Pace of Certaldo: 'Keep well in mind that you should read many books and learn many things'; and in the counsels of Giovanni Morelli, who, writing some time after 1403, suggested that a young man of independent means should spend at least one hour a day reading Cicero, Aristotle (in Latin translation), scripture, and the *Divine Comedy*. Before the mid-century Boccaccio was complaining that 'It is a characteristic of the fool to believe nothing that he hasn't seen in a book, as though reading a thing made it true.'[2]

In literature the praise of the book as the companion of the lonely emerged as a new commonplace. It is found particularly in Petrarch:

> The country folk
> Marvel that I despise those rare delights
> That seem to them supreme. They do not know
> My joy: my company of secret friends.
> They come to me from every century
> And every land, illustrious in speech . . .
> . . . when I am bowed
> With sorrow, they restore me: when I meet
> With fortune's favour, they restrain my pride. . . .[3]

With Petrarch there is found too that academic cast of mind in which books are preferred to the things they describe. In a letter (*Epistolae familiares*, iii, 18), written probably in 1346, he says:

You certainly should not think me immune from all human faults. There is one insatiable passion which holds me and which hitherto I have been neither able nor willing to check (for I assure myself that it is a passion for something decent rather than otherwise). Do you want to know the nature of the disease? I cannot glut my appetite for books. And I have more perhaps than is proper. But as in other things, so it is with books; success in obtaining them is a spur to avarice. For there is a particular pleasure in books. Gold, silver, jewels, purple clothing, a marble house, a fertile field, painted pictures, high-stepping armoured steeds, and other things of that kind, give a mute and superficial pleasure. Books please us to the marrow of our bones; they speak to us, give advice, they bind us to a lively and witty companionship. And not only does each introduce itself to the reader. It thrusts upon him the names of others, kindling his desire for them.

The activities of the humanists, such as the attempt of Petrarch to establish a correct text of Livy and the interest of Petrarch and Salutati in orthography, show the emergence of a tradition in which the written word was coming to have more and more importance. When in 1382 Salutati received a copy of Filippo Villani's *Liber de civitate Florentiae*, and wrote to the author expressing his enthusiasm but complaining of his spelling conventions, he was marking an important milestone along the road which led to the predominance of the pen in western society.[4]

During the fourteenth century this development was furthered by two noticeable innovations, apparently minor in scope, but of far-reaching significance. The first of these was the increased use of magnifying glasses and spectacles. These were invented at the end of the thirteenth century as a result of the theoretical studies at Oxford, stimulated by the twelfth-century translations of Arabic works on optics. By 1300 they were being manufactured commercially at Venice. This discovery increased the potential reading public, giving scribes, scholars, writers, and readers a longer working life. Moreover, most great scholars require time to mature, and the use of spectacles now permitted them to pursue their studies into extreme old age. Even though eye-glasses were not at first either widely used or wholly satisfactory, they are an underrated factor in explaining the growth of humanism. Petrarch, who boasted of the good sight he possessed as a young man, had to wear glasses from his sixtieth year. Although he employed copyists extensively, it is doubtful if without spectacles he could have produced the fifth version of the *Canzoniere*, could have completed the *De remediis* and *De viris illustribus*, could have compiled the *Epistolae seniles*, or could have written at all the *De ignorantia*, the *Letter to Posterity*, the *Treatise on Princely Government*, or the Latin translation of Boccaccio's *Griselda*.

The value of this technical invention at the beginning of our period was enhanced by a stylistic innovation at the end. The handwriting of books produced in the fourteenth century, even in Italy where the modified *rotunda* style was used, is cramped and angular, marred by numerous abbreviations of common words, and painful to read for long periods. In one passage Petrarch complained that this script, though more 'beautiful and luxurious' than that of earlier times, was written 'as if it was made for anything rather than reading'. As a result scholars sought out books which had been written in the twelfth century or before the introduction of Gothic script. In these circumstances, the invention by Poggio Bracciolini of italic script around the years 1402–3, a clear, rounded, very little abbreviated handwriting, based ultimately upon the *lettera antica* of ninth-century Europe, was one of the greatest possible contributions ever made to the popularisation of reading. With Bracciolini's script, too, there came a change in aesthetic sentiment. The clarity and restraint of the lettering came to be seen in the next century as visually more pleasing than the ornate luxuriance of Gothic script. This development, however, though important for the future, had obviously only a minor influence at the beginning of the fifteenth century.

The Audience for Literature

Despite the increasingly visual character of culture in this age, literature still retained very strong oral elements. Poetry, for instance, was thought of as being very much more closely connected with music than it is today. 'If we are rightly to define poetry', wrote Dante, 'it is nothing other than a composition structured in verse according to rhetoric and music'.[5] Accordingly he questioned whether one could speak of a *canzone* (the lyric verse form whose name means literally 'song') which merely consisted of words without music. His conclusion was that what made a *canzone* was the act of writing the words, but that the object in doing so was that the words should be set to music. Such poetry was meant to be intoned; and poets seem to have done so in the act of composing. In his working copy of the *Canzoniere* Petrarch wrote against one piece: 'I must make these two verses over again, singing them and I must transpose them: 3 o'clock in the morning, October the 19th.'[6] In performance, poems were not generally recited but sung. When in 1353 Gano Colle composed a sonnet complaining that Petrarch had settled at Milan with the Visconti, the enemies of Florence, he actually sent it to Francesco by the hand of a minstrel called Giovanni di Firenze, whose duty it was to sing it to the poet.

The reading of prose by this time was largely a private activity, but very often it was read aloud in company. It was in this way that Petrarch's Latin version of Boccaccio's *Griselda* story was given to the learned public of Padua, and his *Letter to Cicero* to that of Vicenza. The very character of Gothic manuscripts, with their difficult script, rudimentary punctuation, and lack of any orthographical standards, suggests that these works were designed primarily for oral recitation. Certainly they are much easier to read aloud or with a movement of the lips. The contemporary tradition of reading aloud is perhaps responsible for the highly rhetorical character of early Italian literature: something which is still characteristic of the language today, and which makes so much of its prose distasteful to the Anglo-Saxon reader. In so far as the fourteenth century is concerned, this oral emphasis assured a very wide audience for authors. The illiterate were not excluded from knowledge and enjoyment of the greatest works. In one of his *novelle* (which, if not true, have a social accuracy), Sacchetti tells of a blacksmith at Porta S. Piero 'singing Dante as a *cantare* is sung'; in another he tells of a drover interspersing his 'singing of Dante's book' with cries of encouragement to his ass. As early as 1319, a verse letter of Giovanni di Virgilio had reproached Dante for writing in Italian rather than Latin, the effect of which was, he pointed out, that unlearned and common people were bringing out his verse 'at the crossroads'.

For the humanists this public enjoyment was a profanation of poetry; a leading attraction of writing in Latin was that one was

spared such common appreciation. In a passage of the *De vulgari
eloquentia*, Dante had remarked that writings in Italian had given
high honour to their authors. 'Does not their fame surpass that of
kings, marquises, counts, and all other magnates?' Yet Petrarch, in
the next generation, saw this very fame as deplorable. In the celebrated letter to Boccaccio, the aim of which, imperfectly achieved,
was to dispel the charge that he was envious of Dante, the poet
wrote:

> He [Dante] has long been buffeted and wearied by the windy
> plaudits of the multitude ... among the rude fellows who
> frequent the taverns and public squares. .... I can only give voice
> to my irritation when I hear the common herd befouling with
> their stupid mouths the noble beauty of his lines. .... I feared for
> my writings the same fate ... my apprehensions were not idle ...
> I am continually tortured by the tongues of the people as they sing
> the few productions which I allowed to escape me in my youth ...
> everywhere I find my Damoetas ready at the street corner 'to
> murder with his screeching reed' my poor song. .... Should I be
> jealous of the hoarse applause which our poet enjoys from the
> tavern-keepers, fullers, butchers, and others of that class, who
> dishonour those whom they would praise? Far from desiring such
> popular recognition, I congratulate myself, on the contrary, that
> along with Virgil and Homer, I am free from it, inasmuch as I
> fully realise how little the plaudits of the unschooled multitude
> weigh with scholars.[7]

The plaudits of the unschooled multitude, however, so distasteful
to scholars, were sought for with some zeal by the Church, which
provided sermons, a large literature of devotion, and the ecclesiastical drama of the *laudesi*. A form of secular drama was cultivated too,
though we know little about it. In December 1389, the ladies of the
Porta Vercellina district of Milan put on 'the story of Jason and
Medea' to raise money for the building of the new cathedral. From
the list of props, it must have been an exciting occasion, and not
unduly tramelled by any niggling over-adherence to the original
plot:

For the skin of a ram for making a lion, and for another skin for making tail and legs . . . 8s.
For a wax spear to be placed in the neck of said lion . . . 3s.
For head of a lion in relief and gilt for covering the skin . . . 2s.
For iron for nails and teeth of said lion . . . 2s.
For painting a drape of flax with water, fish, and ships . . . 3s.[8]

Certainly, the play was a financial success, raising £M477 14s. 1d. for the cause.

It is obvious that there was a wide audience for literature in the vulgar tongues. Whether the different types of literature made a particular appeal to different sections of society is a question which it is more difficult to answer. Looking at individual libraries and manuscripts, however, some sort of pattern emerges. Histories, translations from the classics, works of religious edification, and *novelle* seem to have been the books particularly favoured by the bourgeoisie. The *Decameron*, for instance, in which so many of the stories have merchants as heroes, and whose moral climate, with its admiration given to moderation and utility, was that of the merchant, was particularly popular in commercial circles. Three-quarters of the surviving manuscripts from the fourteenth and fifteenth centuries were owned by members of prominent bourgeois families. On the margins of their texts are often to be found evidence of their business interests: notes of loans, leases, and other financial transactions. Some of these men, like Giovanni Capponi, who was Prior of the Greater Arts at Florence in 1378, passed their leisure in writing the work out in their own hand, as another merchant Filippo d' Andrea puts it, 'for the benefit of his relatives and friends'.

On the other hand, the *Decameron* was received with some coolness by the learned world of the time. After all, it was written not in Latin but 'the vulgar tongue'. Petrarch, though he was the author's best friend, wrote a chilling appreciation of it. Similarly almost none of the surviving manuscripts come from famous libraries or from the hands of noblemen's copyists. By contrast the manuscripts of Boccaccio's other Italian works, those of the *Filocolo*, *Filostrato*, and the *Teseide*, those which draw ultimately upon the inspiration of courtly epic, are mainly found in signorial libraries. The *signori* were drawn above all to those tales of *courtoisie* and knight-errantry found in the French romance tradition. In courtly circles of the north, Italians still continued to write chivalric epics in that Franco-Italian dialect which had been a major literary language of the peninsula in the thirteenth century. Niccolò da Verona, for instance, who dedicated his *Pharsale* to Niccolò I d'Este, Lord of Ferrara, also produced a Carolingian story, the *Prise de Pampelune (c.* 1330). In the second half of the century Niccolò da Casola, a Bolognese notary who had been exiled to Ferrara, composed a poem, *The War of Attila*, which was dedicated to the Marquess Aldobrandino d' Este. This work exalted the ancestors of the d'Este family, who are supposed by the poet to have played a major role in the Italian resistance to the barbarian invader.

The works of this genre look forward to the north Italian courtly epic of Ariosto and Tasso which flowered in the sixteenth century. In individual psychology they come much closer to the character of the modern novel than did the bourgeois *novella* or short story. So much has been heard from the sociologist on the novel as a middle-class art form that this aristocratic aspect has been rather neglected. Undoubtedly the *novella* first flourished in the bourgeois world of the fourteenth century—the anonymous *Novellino* (composed 1281–1300), Boccaccio's *Decameron (c.* 1350), Franco Sacchetti's *Trecentonovelle* (1392–6), and the late fourteenth-century compilations of Giovanni Sercambi and Giovanni Fiorentino. But, with the exception of Boccaccio's stories, they lack that interest in human personality which is the mark of the novel, and which is found much more clearly in epic poetry. The whole tradition of the *novella* derives from the medieval *exempla* (collections of stories for use in sermons); the *novella* itself is a bare anecdote whose interest is wholly exhausted in the curious facts it relates. Boccaccio's sense of style, his vivacity, and the interest he shows in the way people speak, was able to draw him above the customary work of the genre; but in this he was alone. When Giovanni Fiorentino, in his *Pecorone*, for instance, first told the story of 'the Merchant of Venice', what emerges is merely a *bon mot*. The only interest of the story is in what later writers have made of it. The origins of a literary interest in human personality do not lie in the bourgeois *novella*, but in Cicero's letters, in St Augustine's *Confessions* (a work of great popularity in this age), and in the courtly epic tradition of the twelfth century Chrétien de Troyes.

Naturally enough the courts of northern Italy and the kingdom of Naples were also drawn to French works written in the *langue d' oeil*. Our knowledge of twelfth- and thirteenth-century French poetry owes much to manuscripts transcribed in the peninsula during the fourteenth century. In 1342 Petrarch sent a copy of the *Roman de la Rose* to Guido Gonzaga, Lord of Mantua, as he had been asked to do, but at the same time wrote that he would have much preferred to meet a request for a Virgil, Ovid, Propertius, or Catullus. Complaints such as these found little response among aristocrats of the age, for in the literature of chivalry they thought to find a pleasing mirror image of their own lives. In the library of the Visconti there were more works in French than in Italian, yet still not enough to satisfy them. In June 1378, Luchino Visconti, about to set sail for Cyprus, was writing to the Gonzaga court to ask for 'a romance speaking of Tristan or Lancelot or of some other fair and delightful matter to repel the tedium of shipboard life'.[9] When they came to name their children it was of the heroes of these stories that they thought, and in the fourteenth century there was a plethora of aristocratic Lancellottos, Palamedes, Sagomaros, Isottas, and Ginevras. Yet it would be misleading to think that chivalric literature in Italian was appreciated only in aristocratic circles. There was a whole literature of chivalry in the fourteenth century: works like Paolino Pieri's *Storia di Merlino*, the anonymous *Tavola ritonda*, which were written by and for the bourgeoisie. The most celebrated of these 'aristocratic' works, like the sonnets of Folgore da San Gimignano, can often be seen most convincingly as exotic, middle-class fantasies of aristocratic life.

Turning to literature written in Latin, the audience narrows very considerably indeed; to a small well-educated governing class, some clerics, and professional men. Not even all those who had a working knowledge of the Latin of the day were able to understand or appreciate the Latin of the humanists. At Padua in the early years of the fourteenth century, the Guild of Notaries, men whose education had been almost exclusively in Latin and who passed their days in drawing up Latin documents, were forced to ask Mussato to write for them a work which was less elevated than his *Ecerinide*: something, they explained, 'easy and close to common understanding'.[10] The very quality of humanist learning sharpened the distinction between popular and élite culture, reduced the public for literature, and began that process which has made its enjoyment a solitary activity restricted to the educated.

Music in Society

As with literature, so with music, the fourteenth century was the first time that Italians contested a European primacy with France. From the middle of the twelfth century musical composition had been dominated by Paris and the cathedral of Notre Dame, and, as far as the evidence goes, there seems to have been little significant musical activity in Italy. Some two-part settings of liturgical offices from Padua, written about 1300, have survived, and these suggest the presence of an earlier polyphonic tradition. But Italian music only rose to prominence with the beginning of the fourteenth century when a native school of the *Ars Nova* emerged in Lombardy and Florence. By 1318 Marchetto da Padua's *Pomerium* gave full details of a specifically Italian style of musical notation, where the minim is first found. However, French influence still remained very strong. Much of our knowledge of French music in this period is derived from Italian manuscripts, a point which testifies to its continuous popularity in Italy. From the 1340s, when the treatise of Philippe de Vitry began to be known in the peninsula, French practice again came to predominate. By the end of the century France was once more able to claim musical pre-eminence; northern styles of composition and notation drove out their rivals; and as a result, by the 1420s Italy became 'a musical province of Burgundy'.

Although classified among 'the Liberal Arts', music does not at this period seem to have been taught in the Italian universities,[11] and the various speculative treatises on the subject produced at the time were the fruits of solitary meditation outside strictly academic circles. But the church and the secular governments provided a measure of patronage. There were the religious confraternities of the *Laudesi*, who, in the singing of their *laude* to Christ, the Virgin, and saints, played a part somewhat similar to that of choral societies today. The Company of Or San Michele at Florence, for instance, appointed an organist, a 'master of instruments', and four singing teachers.[12] Probably the societies concentrated on simple monodic measures, descending often to a mere rhythmic recitation. More important were the establishments of the cathedrals and greater churches. Here two modes of music were popular. The friars, ever anxious to gain attention, concentrated, it seems likely, on *canto figurato*, the 'figured' or elaborate style, while the secular clergy stuck to the traditional homophony or plain chant. All the greater churches had organs (S. Maria Novella in Florence had two in 1350), choirs, and singing teachers.

These could be extremely expensive to maintain. In Milan, at the end of the century, Fra Martino de' Stremati, of the order of the *Umiliati*, built a 'splendid' organ for the cathedral, for which he received 600 *milanesi* florins, in addition to other considerable sums which he had spent on materials. (Despite this the instrument did not prove very satisfactory. The wheel operating the bellows required two men to turn it, and by 1407, when it was replaced by a less cumbersome mechanism, made so much noise that the music was often drowned.) The organist, maestro Monti of Prato, was given a salary of 30 *milanesi* florins a year in 1395, 50 florins in 1396, and later a lease on a house near the cathedral. In 1402 Matteo of Perugia was taken on as *cantor* at 48 florins a year, a salary which 'for his sweet and mellifluous songs and measures' was raised, three years later, to 50 florins. His duties were to sing on feast days at mass and vespers, to teach music for a fee to all who wished to learn, and to teach free of charge three boys nominated by the cathedral board. He promised to teach only in the cathedral. His successor in 1411, Ambrosio da Pessano, was taken on at 24 *milanesi* florins a year, in the words of the document, 'that the church might be honoured with mellifluous voices and sweet and beauteous songs'.[13]

The organs of cathedrals were almost always built by clerics, and clerics often composed. Vincenzo da Rimini and Bartolomeo da Bologna were both abbots. Donato da Cascia was a Benedictine monk, and Bartolomeo da Padova probably was too. Antonio da Cividale, Corrado da Pistoia, Egidio and Guglielmo da Firenze were all Dominicans. Several of the organists of Venice came from the order of the Servi di Maria. But organists and cantors were often laymen; the most famous was the organist of Florence cathedral, Francesco Landini (1335?–97). Blinded by an attack of smallpox when three years old he managed, none the less, to acquire a liberal education. He exchanged Italian sonnets with Franco Sacchetti and others of the age, wrote a Latin poem in defence of William of Ockham's logic, and so attained a reputation in learned circles. In youth he visited Lombardy, was at the court of Verona, and wrote songs celebrating the birth of two Visconti princesses in Milan. In 1364 he was crowned with the laurel wreath at Venice, perhaps as a poet rather than musician, by King Peter I of Cyprus. However, in a competition at Venice for playing the organ, he seems to have lost to the organist of St Mark's. By 1375 he had returned to Florence as cathedral organist, and perhaps took orders. He was skilled in many instruments and invented a sort of one-man band called 'the Siren of Sirens'. He died in 1397 and was buried under an elegant tombstone which still survives in San Lorenzo. In the *Paradiso degli Alberti*, written around 1420, Domenico da Prato remembered him as a friend, a leading light of the humanist circle around Salutati, and a performer upon the *organetto* or hand-organ whose playing could attract the nightingale.

Although Landini occupied an ecclesiastical post, most of his 70 *ballate* which survive are on the theme of love. One of the principal features of Italian music of the fourteenth century is its secular character. The most common genres were *ballate* (for a single voice, generally to accompany dancing), two-part madrigals (though rather different in form from the sixteenth-century madrigals), and *cacce*. The *caccia* (a word related to the English 'catch') was for three voices, with the top two in canon, and described exciting scenes such as hunts, battles, and the putting out of a fire. It introduced such natural sounds as bird calls, the blowing of horns, and barking of dogs. In all, Italian sources preserve the music of 175 madrigals, 25 *cacce*, and 420 *ballate* from this period.

During the first half of the century the principal centres of composition seem to have been the courts. Of the two treatises of Marchetto da Padua on music, one was dedicated to King Robert of Naples, and the other to a prominent officer of his household. In the preface to his *Pomerium*, Marchetto speaks of Robert as having inherited his father's love of music, and as being surrounded by 'a crowd' of singers. The court of Verona under Mastino II della Scala (1329–1351) was also particularly prominent. Here were found the young Francesco Landini, Giovanni da Cascia (who had previously served as cathedral organist at Florence), and Jacopo da Bologna. It was for another of the della Scala, Alberto, that Antonio da Tempo wrote his treatise on music and poetry in 1332. In music only Venice among the communes seems to have rivalled the importance of Milan, Verona, Padua, and Rimini.

Thenceforward, however, the communes came into their own, and here patronage from governments doubtless achieved something. In the fourteenth century there were ten and then twelve 'musicians of Florence' in the service of the city. Some of these men were probably trumpeters, kettledrummers, pipers, and such like, who filled a ceremonial rather than a strictly musical role. In April 1396, for example, we find the commune employing five trumpeters at a salary of three florins a month each. Yet there were official musicians of another type. In July 1333, for instance, the commune decreed that: 'Since in almost every noble city, whether in Lombardy or Tuscany, fine singers are retained for the delight and joy of the citizens ... to whom the rulers of those cities give robes ... and since among other worthy and fine singers is messer Prezzivalle di Gianni who dwells in the city of Florence, who follows each day the office of his song ... the said Prezzivalle shall receive every three months an honourable robe from the *podestà*.'[14] Similarly, at Perugia in 1407, the Priors and Chamberlain decreed that: 'since the office of the Magnificent Lords Priors and of the Chamberlain of the Guilds of the city of Perugia is accompanied by the burden of melancholy cogitations and seems to be lacking in any recreations by which from time to time they may seek swift relaxation', therefore, 'for the honour, convenience, benignity, and magnificence of the said commune the circumspect and virtuous youth, Jacopo di Filippo' would be reappointed for a further year as 'guitarist to the Palace of the Priors'.[15] It was the commune too which provided money for the purchase of the cathedral organ, paid the salary of the organist, and met the expense of running repairs upon it.

More than any other of the arts, however, music flourished independently of ecclesiastical or government patronage. A very large number, perhaps the majority, of middle-class men and women were able to sing or perform on some instrument. Noble ladies preferred the harp, girls the viola and *mezzo canone* or short recorder. Men and women played the lute, the lyre, the rebec, and the *organetto* or portative organ, and men the double flute. In the evening entertainments after each of the ten days of the *Decameron*, all the young girls are expected to sing. The dancing begins with a song, and is carried on to the accompaniment of a servant playing the bagpipe. Sometimes a girl plays the *cembalo* or tambourine; sometimes one of the men will accompany a song with a guitar. In town and country it was still customary to serenade the loved one before her house, singing to the music of guitar, lute, or viola. The Florentine statutes of 1325 sought to regulate the practice by laying down the penalty of confiscation for instruments played at night.

From the middle class came a large number of composers. Giovanni Frescobaldi (d. 1327) from the great Florentine banking family, who played the guitar, lute, and viola, set his own poetry to music. So did Franco Sacchetti, though complaining still that too many others were doing the same thing:

> *Pieno è il mondo di chi vuol far rime ...*
> *Così del canto avvien: senza alcun arte ...*

('The world is full of people who want to make rhymes ... so it is with songs too: without any skill'.)

A madrigal of Landini made the same complaint:

Ciascun vuole narrar musical note
Conpor madriali, cacce, ballate,
Tenend' ognum le sue autentica.

('Everyone wants to arrange musical notes, to compose madrigals, *cacce*, *ballate*, believing that his own are fine.')

In this song we hear again the authentic voice of the fourteenth-century intellectual. The sweetness of music, he continues, once prized by nobles, is now deserted for the songs of the people. Once again, the dedicated man of learning is protesting against the culture which is common to the everyday world. Yet this attachment to music must have been a real sweetener of the harsh life of four-teenth-century Italy, and even the humanist could not complain for long about it. When Vergerio drew up his treatise for the educa-tion of youth in 1401 he noticed that the Greeks refused the title of 'educated' to those who could not sing or play, that Socrates had considered music of benefit to the harmony of the soul, and con-cluded that the young should learn both its theory and practice.

Minstrels and 'Men of the Court'

In addition to amateur enthusiasts and ecclesiastical and government pensioners, there was also a class of paid entertainers who satisfied the popular demand for music and poetry. The names given to these men sufficiently indicate their precarious status; they were called *giullari* (which might mean 'minstrel' or 'jester'), *buffoni* ('entertainers' or 'buffoons') or *uomini del corte* ('men about the court'). Any one of these titles could be given equally to men who, like Antonio Beccari, might exchange sonnets with Petrarch, or to those travelling tumblers and street musicians who entertained the crowds of the towns on market day. In Italy they had a long tradition behind them. At the court of the counts of Monferrato at the beginning of the thirteenth century, Peire de la Mula, writing in Provençal, had complained that 'there were more *ioglars* than little hares' and had added for good measure that he 'didn't give a turnip for their ill-speech'. In the fourteenth century they were still very numerous: at the feast for the knighting of the sons of the Malatesti at Rimini in 1324, no less than 500 were present, and at the marriage of Galeazzo Visconti to the sister of the Marquess d'Este, more than 7,000 robes were said to have been distributed to them.[16]

Sometimes these men were employed by the communes. In 1290, for instance, the Priors of Florence gave three of them clothing at public expense. More generally they were found in the signorial courts, dependent upon the casual gifts of the *signore*. They seem to have been particularly favoured by the Visconti. In a lament for the death of Bernabò Visconti, one of their number asserted that:

> *Buffoni, giocolari e altre gente*
> *della tua corte erano i be' signori.*

('*Buffoni*, jugglers, and others, were the fine lords of your court'.) Among those who practised as minstrels, not many attempted original composition. Petrarch, in a characteristic letter, complained about:

that widely distributed and vulgar set of men who live by words, and those not their own, who have increased to such an irritating extent among us. . . . They haunt the antechambers of kings and potentates, naked if it were not for the poetic vesture that they have filched from others. Any especially good passage which someone has turned off, they seize upon, more particularly if it be in the mother tongue, and recite it with great gusto. In this way they strive to gain the favour of the nobility and procure money, clothes, or other gifts. Their stock-in-trade is partly picked up here and there, partly obtained directly from the writers themselves, either by begging, or, where cupidity or poverty exists, for money. . . . You can easily imagine how often these fellows have pestered me, and I doubt not others, with their disgusting fawning. . . . Sometimes when I knew the applicant to be humble and needy I have reflected that my aid might be of permanent use to the recipient, while it cost me only a short hour of work. Some of those whom I have been induced to assist, and who had left me with their wish fulfilled, but otherwise poor and ill-clad, re- turned shortly after arrayed in silks, with well-filled bellies and purses, to thank me for the assistance which had enabled them to cast off the burden of poverty.[17]

Yet some of these men were poets in their own right too. We know little about them, though one thing they seem to have in common is a faint suggestion of social descent or failure in life. Most strictly 'literary' among them was Fazio degli Uberti, from a branch of the great Florentine house which had fallen on evil days. Found at the courts of Padua and Milan, he exchanged sonnets with Luchino Visconti and was author of a substantial, encyclopaedic poem, the *Dittamondo*. More typical were Marchionne di Matteo Arrighi, author of the lament for Bernabò Visconti, cited above; Francesco di Vanozzo, servant in turn to the Carrara, della Scala, and Visconti families; and Antonio Beccari of Ferrara, found at the signorial courts of Emilia and Lombardy. All three, individually, developed the theme in poetry of how gambling had brought them to poverty. Braccio Bracci, again, another of the Visconti's minstrels, was from an exiled Florentine family, and had been driven by poverty to become a *giullare*. Simone Serdini, panegyricist of Giangaleazzo Visconti, seems to have been forced to leave his native Siena through crimes committed in his youth.

Most famous of these men was Dolcibene de' Torri of Florence, poet and composer, who sang his compositions to his own accompaniment on the lute and hand-organ. He was a favourite of Galeazzo II Visconti, the elder Francesco da Carrara of Padua, the Este of Ferrara, the Ordelaffi of Forlì, and of Galeotto and Malatesta Unagaro Malatesti of Rimini whom he accompanied on a pilgrimage to the Holy Land. On Charles IV's first visit to Rome, Dolcibene was knighted by the Emperor and given a diploma, declaring him to be 'King of all the *istrioni*' (i.e., in this context, 'entertainers'). He enjoyed wide esteem too as a wit, and figures often in the *novelle* of Sacchetti.

The precarious trade of high-class minstrel, combining the cultures of the courtier poet and the crossroads minstrel, was particularly suited for the educated gentleman down on his luck. But it was, one would imagine, very much a last resort, for he was very directly dependent upon the whim of his patron. Although there was a demand for variety in manner—the minstrel could be called upon to produce *frottole* (popular songs in local dialect) or courtly sonnets—the choice of theme was restricted. The greater part of the demand he met was for poems lamenting the death of the great, the praise of his lords as 'saints and saviours', prophecies of their future conquests, and kindred matter.

Below these men were the *cantastorie*, the entertainers of the people, travelling from town to town, half story-tellers and musicians, half jugglers, tumblers, and mountebanks. They were a cosmopolitan crew. At Florence in 1384, we find three Germans, Heinrich Johann, Angel Johann, and Petrus Hermann, 'pipers and players of bagpipes and other instruments', being imprisoned for playing in the early morning.[18] And earlier Folgore da San Gimignano's ideal world had included:

> music to greet the morn
> And amorous girls to sing
> To new instruments from Germany . . .
> Trumpets, flutes, and tambourines.

Most of the *cantastorie*, of course, were Italian. They would sing the old tales of Roland and Oliver, chant *cantari* (narratives) and *serventesi* (political songs for whose public performance they were doubtless paid by private patrons), and then perform tricks and tumbling. Often they sang not in Italian but in Franco-Italian. (In a somewhat similar way, British pop singers of the twentieth century, until recently, would sing their lyrics in a bastard American.) A passage of a Latin poem written by Lovato de' Lovati at the beginning of the fourteenth century tells of these singers at work:

> I was going by chance through the town of the springs
> Which takes its name from its three streets, [i.e., Treviso]
> Passing the time by strolling along,
> When I see on a platform in the piazza
> A singer declaiming the story of Charlemagne
> And the *gestes* of the French. The rabble hang round,
> Listening intently, charmed by their Orpheus.

In silence I hear it. With a crude pronunciation
He deforms the song written in French,
Mixing it all up at his whim, without heed
To art or the story. Still, the mob liked it . . .[19]

Disliked by the friars, to whose sermons they provided a counter-attraction, they were accused by them of effecting their conjuring tricks in league with the devil. In the statutes of Bologna of 1288 (and then again of Faenza in 1410), 'the singers in the French manner' were forbidden to perform before the Communal Palace. Yet their traditions harkened back to the multilingual Breton minstrels of the eleventh century who first carried the stories of Arthur into Italy. So long a history, combined with all the life and colour which they brought to the little towns, was not to be extinguished through ecclesiastical petulance or the scorn of the respectable, and the *giullari* remained popular throughout the century.

Finally, among the crowds gathered round the *cantastorie* in the villages and market places were those who would take up their material and form it into the dialect songs of harvest and marriage festival or work in the fields, or into those old European non-Christian hymns which greet the coming of March and May. Here too were the simple rhythms and the freshness of *stornelli*, and the popular lullabies of infancy. Such is the cradle song found in the margins of a codex containing the scholastic Latin of Benvenuto da Imola:

> *Ninna, nanna*
> *Li miei begli fanti*
> *Giammai non fu cotarti.*

('Hush-a-bye, bye-byes,
My bonny babbies,
Never were any just like you.')

Very little survives of this material. It is known to us only through fragments on the corner of a manuscript or the occasional doodlings of a notary in his protocol book. Yet there are still echoes of it in Italy today, in the songs of children's round-games, which in their simplicity never lose their ability to press strongly on the emotions.

eight

The Environment of Literature: Books, Libraries, Education

The transition from an oral to a visual culture was one of the long-term results of the economic revolutions of the twelfth and thirteenth centuries. It was expressed in and assisted by a growth in the number of books and libraries, and by an increase in educational facilities at many levels. The work of booksellers, copyists, and teachers provided the essential background for the development of literature at this time.

Booksellers

The trade of bookselling only came into existence with the foundation and rise of the universities in the thirteenth century. At that time it was only in university towns, and to meet the needs of universities, that the 'stationers' enjoyed any real prominence, and their principal role was not so much to sell as to lend books. The stationers stocked all those texts which were prescribed in the university course and, in return for a small fee, lent them out for copying. Normally they dealt not in whole books but in *pecia*: a measure which was standardised at Bologna at 16 double columns of writing, each column consisting of 62 lines, each line of 32 letters. The breaking down of books into *pecia* greatly facilitated the production of texts. Each scribe working for a stationer could specialise in producing one brief piece. His constant repetition of this *pecia* gave him a familiarity with it which rendered transcription almost mechanical. Moreover the turnover of *pecie* lent for copying was obviously much more rapid than that of books would have been. Students did not have to wait around for necessary texts while their fellows laboriously copied out whole books at a time.

The activities of the stationers were closely controlled by the universities. In the fourteenth century at Bologna, Padua, and Florence, the number of texts they had to keep in stock (119 in the civil and canon law faculties alone), their accuracy, and the price which could be charged for their hire (4d. a quire), were all carefully laid down by statute. Six students were appointed each year to ensure their enforcement and to impose fines for infringement. During the first half of the fourteenth century most of the work of the university stationers was still concerned with the loan of texts and only gradually did purchase become more frequent than hire. The regulations of the universities were specifically designed to make the sale of books fairly unprofitable to the stationer. Under these the student took the books which he wanted to dispose of to the stationer, who then sold it for him in return for a commission fixed by the statutes (e.g., 1s. for a book sold for below £3; 4s. for a book sold for £40 to £60). These profits were small, but on the other hand there was a rapid turnover, since as late as the 1330s no student was allowed to take books of any kind outside the town of his university without special permission. Often they were searched at the town gates to ensure that they were not violating this prohibition.

In these circumstances university stationers did little more than provide cheap textbooks for the courses which the students attended. However, booksellers who were independent of the university, and who had wider functions, had already begun to appear by the beginning of the fourteenth century. At Florence in the 1290s, they were found in and around the via del Proconsolo, though at this period they were principally concerned with producing account books and notebooks, and only later produced literary texts. At Milan, on the other hand, according to Bonvesin de la Riva, there were 40 'transcribers of books' in 1288, and these men probably formed the nucleus of a book industry. By the 1340s such an industry obviously existed in Italy. The grandiloquent booklover, Richard de Bury, Bishop of Durham, in his *Philo-biblion*, written shortly before 1345, boasted that he gave advances to Italian as well as to French, English, and German stationers and booksellers in the expectation that they would send him texts he wanted. By then these men held themselves responsible as entre-preneurs for all the operations of book manufacture. For instance, in Florence around 1404, Dino di Piero, bookseller and miniaturist, bought paper and parchment, and arranged for the writing, il-lumination, binding, and rebinding of books.[1] Sometimes, like Giovanni d' Arezzo, who was active at Florence from 1375 to 1417, they sent scribes to monasteries to produce copies of works. By the second decade of the fifteenth century they also kept in stock a selection of works, presumably in most cases second-hand, which had not been specifically commissioned by customers. In 1416, for instance, Leonardo Bruni spoke of hunting through the bookshops at Florence for a Priscian, while two years later Ambrogio Traversari wrote to a friend asking him to go through them all for a *Decretals*. By this time too there were highly specialised manuscript dealers, men like Giovanni Aurispa (1369–1443). But books were not exclusively sold by booksellers. Others such as silk merchants might include manuscripts among their other merchandise.

Even small and unimportant books in everyday use were quite expensive. The valuer of some books from the papal library de-posited at Assisi in 1327 judged a number of missals as worth two, three, four, and 15 florins; psalters from less than a florin to one ('very beautiful') at five florins; breviaries from less than a florin to 12 florins. A Cassiodorus cost a florin, a book of sermons two florins. A bible he assessed at 15 florins, though ten books of another bible, with glosses, reached 40 florins. A volume containing Cicero's *De officiis*, Macrobius' *Dream of Scipio*, a translation of Plato's *Timaeus*, and some writings of Seneca, he valued at two florins.[2] The worth of these can be judged by thinking of two florins as being a week's salary for a branch manager of an important banking house.

Yet the availability of paper meant that books were becoming cheaper to manufacture. Paper had been imported from the Moslem world through Genoa in the twelfth century, and had been used in

public documents. By the 1270s the Italians were making it themselves; in the fourteenth century it was manufactured at Colle di
Valdelsa, Bologna, Forlì, Parma, Padua, Treviso, and above all,
at Fabriano in the Marche, where by 1330 no less than 20 paper mills
were in operation. In 1327 the Florentine businessman Jacopo
Orlandi was supplying paper to the papal *curia* at Avignon. By the
1330s Italy was exporting paper to France and Germany. This was
to make possible a notable reduction in the cost of producing books. For
a bible of parchment, for instance, it was necessary to have the skins
of 300 sheep; a paper bible cost only a sixth of the sum for this.
Moreover paper made the physical act of writing easier. To write on
parchment takes real strength and if continuously sustained demands
physical fitness of the whole body. The weary concluding glosses of
so many medieval scribes had much justification.

> This work was done by Martino da Trieste in the school of
> master Bonaventura da Verona.

> *Dextra scriptoris careat gravitate doloris*
> *Detur pro penna scriptori pulcra puella*

('I can't feel my hand, my head's in a whirl, I'd swap for my pen a
beautiful girl.')

This inscription, from a manuscript of Lucan's *Pharsalia*, executed in
1338,[3] can serve as a typical epitaph to those who had to labour on
parchment. With paper the task of the scribe became much easier.

Yet the main benefits of paper lay in the future, for collectors
continued to prefer works in more durable parchment, or in the
still more expensive vellum. In the library of the Lords of Este in
1436, for instance, only four out of 243 books were written on paper.
The prices of books produced for this luxury market were correspondingly high. In 1358, for instance, a missal made in Florence for
the monastery of S. Felicità cost in all £115 10s. (at this period about
40 florins), about the annual salary of a cashier in one of the great
banks. The expense was itemised as follows:

For parchment	£23 4s. 0
For scribe	£54 0s. 0

> For the miniaturist   £30 0s. 0
> For binding   £8 6s. 0

Scribes were generally either notaries or clerics working part-time. Though painters often undertook commissions as miniaturists, there was also a class of men who considered themselves as 'miniaturists' simply, and who in documents referred to themselves as '*miniatore*' rather than '*pittore*'. The anonymous *De arte illuminandi*, a handbook written for their guidance in the late fourteenth century, takes pains to distinguish their work from that of painters. These men were generally clerics, there were some notaries, and in one case a miniaturist was a barman. Normally they seem to have been paid piece-rates. But sometimes, like Don Simone, a Camaldolese monk working for the Carmine at Florence, they might receive the cost of the materials plus a day-wage, in his case three shillings a day, excluding Sundays. Miniaturists did not normally have any role as scribes. The *De arte illuminandi* assumes that the miniaturist will have before him when he begins his work a book which had already been ruled and written.[4]

Libraries

Books were not only expensive; at the end of the thirteenth century, outside a few standard and basic texts, they were often difficult to obtain. In the *Convivio*, for instance, Dante remarked that Boethius' *Consolations of Philosophy*, a work which was immensely popular in the northern world during the middle ages, was at Florence 'known only to a few'. Dante himself, it is beginning to be realised, had not, by the standards of the second half of the century, read very widely. This is especially true in regard to classical authors. If, as a recent book calls him, he was '*juge du monde grèco-latin*', he was handing down his conclusions on the basis of inadequate evidence.[5] This is understandable enough in that at Florence there was probably no body of classical texts at all until 1359, when Niccolò Acciaiuoli presented a collection to his Charterhouse. In these circumstances, libraries and the making of new collections of books assumed a very great importance. It was the work of a handful of Florentine book-collectors during the second half of the century which remedied the lack felt in the city at the beginning of the period, and which made Florence the first centre of humanist studies at the beginning of the fifteenth century.

Of principal importance were the ancient monastic and cathedral libraries, Cremona, Ivrea, Novara, Monza, Vercelli, Pomposa, and Farfa, in whose *scriptoria* the works of antiquity had been transcribed throughout the darkest periods of the middle ages. Of these, some, such as the library of the monastery of Bobbio, which in the tenth century already had 666 books, were almost wholly neglected in our period. Others were small; the chapter library of Bologna, for instance, had only 43 manuscripts in 1420. But others played an important part in the rise of the humanist movement, noticeably the chapter library of Verona, with perhaps 1,000 books, among them the unique manuscript (now lost) of Cicero's *Letters to Atticus* and a complete Catullus. The library of Montecassino, the oldest monastic house in Western Europe, was important too. Boccaccio left a description of the library in his own day which sought to show it to be neglected and in complete disorder. But no less than 100 manuscripts were added to its collections in the fourteenth century, and his account was probably coloured by the attempt to justify his own thefts from it.

Supplementary to these were the new libraries of the orders of Friars established in the thirteenth century. Here the Dominicans led, with collections of books in all their principal houses: 100 volumes, for example, in their house at Lucca in 1278 and 472 at Bologna in 1386. The Franciscans too, despite the prohibition of their founder against the possession of books, had numerous libraries: 86 chained and 291 unchained books in the convent of Pisa in 1355, 234 volumes at Gubbio in 1360, 183 volumes at La Verna in 1372, 181 chained and 537 unchained at Padua in 1396, 649 at Bologna in 1421, and 781 books at S. Croce in Florence in 1426. In these libraries the chained books could only be consulted on the spot, but the unchained could be lent out, often on very long loan, to those allowed to use the library. But the collections were built on utilitarian principles and generally had little literary value. They mainly consisted of books of sermons, biblical commentaries, legal texts for those friars studying civil and canon law, theology, and philosophy. Of the 100 books at the Dominican Library at Lucca, for instance, no less than 74 consisted of glossed books of the bible, and indeed the only non-theological work there was a copy of the canon-law text of the *Decretals*. However, occasionally a private collector left his books to the friars, and so widened the scope of their libraries. For example, Boccaccio left his overwhelmingly secular collection of books to the Augustine friars of S. Spirito in Florence. At San Francesco at Pisa there were some copies of Martial, Suetonius, Seneca, Sallust, three comedies of Terence, Caesar's *Commentaries*, the *Rhetoric* and *Friendship* of Cicero, and a Horace. A fine collection of secular works came to S. Croce in Florence, when the Franciscan friar Tedaldo della Casa bequeathed his 70 volumes to the library in 1406. But in most libraries of the friars this sort of book was rare.

None of the communes had libraries. In 1362 Petrarch proposed to the Venetian government that, 'in honour of St Mark, in memory of myself, and too for the encouragement and benefit of those noble and superior minds in the city who would take delight in such things', his own books should be preserved in a house there as the nucleus for what he in fact called 'a public library'. He hoped that the commune would buy books for it, and that private individuals would leave their collections to it at death. 'In this way there could easily be established a large and famous library equal to those of antiquity'.[6] Petrarch's plan was that the commune should assign him a house, that he should live there, and that at his death it should become the seat of a library. The project was accepted by the *Serenissima*, and Petrarch took up residence. But by 1371 he had grown disillusioned with Venice and went to Padua, at which the scheme foundered. It was not to be until 1469, with the Cardinal Bessarion's bequest, that Venice was to have its own library.

Though there were no public libraries in the communes, certain scholars had limited access to some magnificent signorial libraries. These often had a much wider selection of books than anything found in the ecclesiastical collections. Particularly important were the royal library at Naples, begun by Charles I (d. 1285), the library of the Gonzaga of Mantua (with 400 manuscripts by 1407) begun by Guido Gonzaga (1360–9) and notably enriched by Ludovico I (1370–82), and that of the Este lords of Ferrara (243 manuscripts by 1436). But the most magnificent was that of the Visconti. This collection was probably begun by Azzone (d. 1339), and developed by Luchino and Archbishop Giovanni. It was most noticeably enriched by Giangaleazzo, who added manuscripts taken from the library of the della Scala at Verona (which had fallen to him in 1387), of the Carrara of Padua (conquered in 1388, 35 books from this collection are still extant), and from the collection of his own secretary Pasquino Capelli (disgraced 1398). The inventory of 1426 listed close on 1,000 books. Of these 844 were in Latin, 90 in French, 2 in Provençal, 1 in Spanish, 52 in Italian, 2 in Greek, and 2 in Hebrew. A very large number of these were still the same sort of biblical commentaries, liturgical books, collections of the fathers, works on theology, philosophy, and science, to be found in ecclesiastical libraries. But in addition the collection contained all the standard classical texts known in the middle ages, and a large collection of Tuscan (though not so much north Italian) vulgar works. There were four copies of the *Divine Comedy*, two of the *Decameron* and other works of Boccaccio, in addition to an almost complete selection of Petrarch's Latin, though not Italian, writings. However, as in the Este and Gonzaga libraries, the number of works in the French of the *langue d' oeil* outnumbered those written in Italian. A high proportion of these books, of which many today are in the Louvre at Paris, were objects of extreme luxury, with their press boards bound in worked and coloured leather, velvet, gold brocade, or brocaded silk, their pages adorned with illuminations and the Visconti arms, works of art in their own right.

In contrast to these signorial libraries, that of the papal court at the end of the thirteenth century was drab. In 1295 its 443 volumes consisted almost entirely of treatises on theology, civil and canon law, and medicine. At Avignon the position may have improved, for Petrarch sought access to the papal collections there, but in Italy it was only with the establishment of the papacy at Rome under the pontificate of Martin v (1417–31) that the foundations were laid for the establishment of the Vatican Library later in the century.

Despite the existence of the signorial collections, there was little in most libraries useful to the reader who was indifferent to theology and philosophy. Those with other tastes had to rely principally on such books as they could collect themselves, and this period is notable for the rise of the impassioned private collector. Such men had been known before: the great jurist Accursius, for instance, had left a library of 200 volumes on his death in 1273, though these were all on legal topics. It was only with the fourteenth century that there were large collections of literary works. Petrarch (1304–74) probably had as many as 200 books; 46 volumes, not including six of his own works, have been identified from his library.

The learned physician, Giovanni Dondi, left 100 volumes in 1389. These included seven of his own works, 17 of Aristotle, collections of Aquinas and Albertus, but also French and Italian poetry, two works by Petrarch, and a good number of classical texts by Terence, Cicero, Statius, Ovid, Livy, Pliny, and Vitruvius. According to Poggio, Coluccio Salutati (1331–1406) was said to have possessed 800 books, of which today 111 have survived and been identified. Book collecting on this scale assumed ever-increasing importance at the end of the century, especially at Florence. Here the rich rentier, Antonio Corbinelli (d. 1425), had 194 Latin and 79 Greek codices consisting overwhelmingly of classical authors; the banker Palla Strozzi had 277 books by 1431; Cosimo de' Medici had acquired 80 manuscripts by 1418; while Niccolò Niccoli (1363–1437) was rumoured to have acquired as many as 800 volumes and to have ruined himself in the process. Other notable collections were made by Zanobi della Strada, the Franciscan Tedaldo della Casa, and Sozomen of Pistoia.

But collections of this sort were exceptional. If an educated person had a large library, it was likely to consist almost entirely of books connected with his profession, or of works with a religious character. For instance, the 113 books of Ugolino Montecatini, who taught medicine at Florence University from 1393–5, consisted principally of medical treatises and works on natural science, some theology, one or two books on philosophy, and only three or four lighter works such as Marco Polo's *Milione*. The 200 volumes owned privately by Pope Gregory XII in 1411 consisted almost entirely of works on theology, philosophy, and canon law. Libraries on this scale were unusual. It would be very rare for educated people to have more than 40 or 50 books. The library of the wealthy Mantuan noble and poetaster, Bonamente Aliprandi (d. 1417), is typical of the sort of collection made for pleasure rather than professional reasons. This consisted of 19 books:

1   A translation of Boethius
2   Town statutes on the elections of certain officials
3   Egidio Colonna's *De regimine principum* (a treatise on political thought)
4   A chronicle of Mantua
5   A 'Jewish History' (Josephus?)
6   A book on morals
7   *unus liber nasionis qui tractat usque ad mortem* (?)
8   A book on vices and virtues
9   A book on the function of virtues
10   A chronicle of Mantua
11   'A certain book in the French language'
12   A story of the Trojan War
13   A book of physic
14   A missal
15   Stories of vices and virtues
16   A book of many orations
17   A book of expositions of the Gospel
18   A book of the blessed St Francis
19   A book of Dante.[7]

At a more learned level there was the collection of Antonio di Persico, a notary of Verona, who married a descendant of Dante and died in 1418. His 27 books included seven *codices* of Ovid, the *Thebaid* and *Achilleid* of Statius, Lucan's *Pharsalia*, Horace's *Ars Poetica*, Aesop's *Fables*, the *Epistles* of Sidonius, and a Boethius.

Such libraries were built up by purchase from booksellers, private treaty with special dealers, and often the direct commissioning of scribes. Petrarch, for instance, retained as many as six at a time in his service. Ordinary copyists, earning about 3s. a day, were cheap and easy to come by. Yet as Petrarch pointed out, it was difficult to get a copyist who was educated enough to do the work well. Until he found a good secretary in Giovanni di Ravenna, he would copy valuable texts himself, and indeed very many book collectors were forced to do this for works they wished to possess.

Education

Though libraries were growing in size, scope, and number during the fourteenth century, they were still by any post-printing standards pitifully sparse. Moreover, despite the many signs of growth and development in education, higher lay culture rested upon a narrow base. Even so, by 1400 Italy led the rest of the west in the literacy of its population, and in an educational system which responded to the needs of the lay society, created by the economic revolution and the growth of the state.

Until the middle of the thirteenth century elementary education was the virtual monopoly of the Church. In the hundred years from 1150–1250, it was the cathedral schools which dominated this field, and obviously these were primarily intended to satisfy the needs of ecclesiastical society. Their concept of teaching was that traditional within the church. According to Fra Remigio Girolami, *lector* of the Dominican school at S. Maria Novella until his death in 1319, all human learning served merely as a preparation for theology. Clearly lay society made different demands upon learning and needed an educational system which would be adapted to them. Gradually, as it became increasingly necessary for the cities to meet the demand for lawyers, notaries, administrators, and merchants, this religious monopoly of education was broken and lay schools predominated. The first certain reference to a lay teacher in Italy appears in a document of 1130. Towards the end of the thirteenth century lay schools became common, while in the fourteenth century the secular school which had been established by the commune, and especially by the small commune, became general throughout the whole peninsula. By the middle of the century it was exceptional for any commune not to have its own school.

The effects of this growth, at least in the major cities, can be assessed by considering the statistics which Giovanni Villani gave for Florence in 1338. Here in a population of about 92,000 (that is to say, in a society of this sort, of about 15,000 boys and girls between eight and fourteen years old), Villani claimed that 8,000 to 10,000 were being taught to read, that 1,000 to 1,200 pupils were at business schools, and that 550 to 600 were in attendance at four 'large' grammar schools. This would imply that in Florence the children in elementary schools comprised 10 per cent of the population, and that no less than 60 to 80 per cent of the whole lay population in the city were to some extent literate. This figure seems extraordinarily high, and it takes no account of those being instructed in ecclesiastical schools, or by private tutors at home. In 1863 students in elementary schools comprised four per cent of the population, and the ratio implied by Villani for Florence in 1338 was only surpassed in Tuscany as a whole after 1937. In these circumstances the doubts which have been expressed on the precision of these figures must be allowed full weight. None the less, and granting their inaccuracy, they do give a contemporary impression of the educational facilities which existed at the time. A similar picture is given for Milan by Bonvesin de la Riva in 1288, and by Galvano Fiamma in the 1330s. According to these men the city possessed 8 to 15 grammar school teachers with a 'great multitude of scholars', and 70 elementary schoolmasters.

At the base of education were those masters and mistresses who taught reading and writing. Sometimes they held their own schools, often they made their living by visiting their pupils' homes, presumably for a set number of hours each week. So we find a master being paid 1s. 6d. a month (a surprisingly small sum) for teaching Perotto of the Ammonnati family to read at Florence between January and August 1290. In August another master received 2s. a month for teaching him to write. In the following year one Master Bonno received 9s. for a further three months' instruction in writing.

Shortly afterwards the child was apprenticed to the workshop of a smith. On other occasions the master was paid by results, and was given a fixed sum when the skill had been imparted. These contracts were a particular feature of adult education. In Venice in 1405, to give one notable example, a priest offered 8 ducats (roughly 8 florins) to a master to teach him Latin.[8]

A large number of women were taught reading and writing, a practice which was normal in princely families in thirteenth-century Europe. It had been advocated, for instance, by Guillaume Perrault (d. 1275) in his *De eruditione principum*, though the Italian bourgeoisie seem to have been chary about the idea. In his *Ragionamento delle donne*, Francesco da Barberino (1264-1348) brooded heavily upon its wisdom. Certainly, he thought, they should be instructed in singing and dancing, but might not reading expose them to the dangers of sensual literature and over-stimulating poetry? He concluded, and it is perhaps significant that he should have gone out of his way to say so, that the daughters of artisans and peasants should not be threatened by these dangers. Again Paolo da Certaldo, in his *Libro di buoni costumi*, written after 1350, advised that boys should start to read at six or seven, but that girls, unless they were to be nuns, should be taught not to read but to sew. Despite this sort of prejudice, and though women wrote no literature in this period, nevertheless there were women teachers. For example, one Clemenza taught reading, writing, and Latin (i.e. Donatus, the Psalter, and the drawing up of notarial instruments) at Florence in 1304; and a certain Lucia was a quite prosperous school-mistress at Venice in 1413. Most masters at this level, however, enjoyed very little prosperity, and from their ranks was formed a proletarian élite which was likely to take the lead in fomenting social disturbance. Among the leaders of the Ciompi revolt at Florence in 1378 was Gasparre di Ricco, the owner of a school for children in via Ghibellina; 25 years before, he had been branded by the Inquisitor as a heretic.

With this initial instruction, given between the ages of eight and eleven, the formal education of most boys and of all but an insignificant number of girls, ended. On the other hand, some went forward to the business schools or 'schools of the abacus' as they were called. Villani tells of six schools at Florence in 1338, and they were common in all the major commercial centres. Here the pupils, generally between the ages of 11 and 14, learnt arithmetic, particularly the use of the abacus, calculation in arabic and roman numerals, calculations of interest and discount, and something of commercial practice. Then they would go on to be apprenticed to a commercial firm, and this apprenticeship was a form of further education. A smaller number of pupils, those destined by their parents to be notaries or to study at the university, would, after learning how to read and write, be sent to a grammar school, generally one of the lay-schools which had been founded or which was endowed by the local commune.

Normally the masters who taught in such schools were called 'masters of grammar and logic'; what they principally taught was Latin. The course at the communal school at Pistoia in 1397 is typical. Here the younger pupils learnt the elements of the language and then proceeded to such simple texts as the Psalter, the Catechism, Cato's *Moralia*, and the Latin version of Aesop's *Fables*. Then they went on to study the grammar of Donatus. At this stage they became *latinantes* proper, reading more difficult authors, and studying the art of prose style, the *ars dictaminis*, or *ars dictandi*. If the master were particularly keen he might read Virgil, Lucan, and Terence with his boys, though this would not be very common. In general, the aim of this education was not the creation of cultured men, but was primarily utilitarian: the training in the adequate expression of ideas in legal or state documents, and the imparting of a sufficient fluency in the language to be able to benefit from lectures, and to take part in disputations in the universities. In this the committing to memory of stereotyped forms of expression found in the textbooks of the *ars dictaminis* played an important part. Closely connected with the *ars dictaminis* was the notarial art, and in many schools the elder boys would learn the forms in which notarial documents were drawn up. Some schools made it their primary aim to produce notaries, and notaries themselves, like Benvenuto da Imola's father, actually directed the school.

This emphasis upon the *ars dictandi*, with its ideal of a formal verbal perfection, its stress upon a system of highly stylised rhetorical expression and its store of *topoi* or commonplaces, was one of the most important features in the formation of Italian culture of the age. Its influence can be discerned in all medieval literature, but it is particularly prominent in Italian. Its strong hold from childhood on the pupils of the grammar schools explains not only the rhetorical character of writing in the age, remarkable even in such an apparently unrhetorical work as the *Decameron*, but also the highly rhetorical character of the Italian language as it was formed in that period and as we know it today. However much this may jar upon the modern Anglo-Saxon sensibility, it must be recognised that this rhetoric, 'sweetest of all the other sciences' as Dante calls it, was an essential element in the formation of Italian modes of speech and writing. Moreover the habit of mind imposed by this intense form of verbal training allowed Italians from the age of Petrarch to proceed easily to the study of the equally artificial rhetoric of the classical world.[9]

The masters who taught in the grammar schools were fairly well paid, and their salaries seem to increase as the fourteenth century continued. By the middle of the century the grammar masters at San Gimignano, Siena, Lucca, Pisa, Volterra, Colle di Valdelsa, and San Miniato, all received stipends of between 60 and 100 florins from their communes. These men had an ungrateful task and were not often well regarded. Their role was seen simply as the imparting of certain techniques, without any of that civilising gloss which was to be later required of them. In a notorious letter (*Epistolae familiares*, iii, 18) to Zanobi della Strada, Petrarch, by a familiar depreciation of the profession, attempted to persuade him to leave schoolmastering behind and to seek the patronage of the court of Naples:

> Let them teach boys who cannot do greater things, men of an industrious officiousness, a slower mind, a dull understanding, an unfledged intellect, cold blood, a body attuned to hard labour, a soul contemptuous of glory, those who seek small profit, who are unsqueamish, men of a very different sort from yourself. Let those watch over unstable bands of children, their wandering attention

and confused noise, who take pleasure in the work and in the dust and noise and the cry of screams, mingled with prayers and tears, under the rod; those for whom it is pleasant to become a boy again, who do not like to treat with men, who are reluctant to live with their equals, who prefer to lord it over their juniors, to have always someone whom they can terrify, torture, hurt, whose subjects hate them while they fear. . . . They best teach children who are most like them.

Frequent complaints against schoolmasters were that they were pedants and pederasts (for this offence Dante placed Priscian, author of the doubtless much hated school grammar, in the *Inferno*). Parents complained that they accepted bribes to give children holidays, that they did not beat their pupils enough, and (less frequently) that they beat them too much. Much of this can be discounted. In the formation of such men as Petrarch, Boccaccio, and Dante, it would be rash to brush off the influence of those men who first led them along the paths of grammar. Petrarch's old school-master, Convenevole da Prato, who later acquired the laurel crown; Zanobi della Strada himself, who was crowned as Latin poet by the Emperor Charles IV; Zanobi's father, in whose school Boccaccio and Niccolò Acciaiuoli sat side by side; Marzagaia of Verona, the historian, who probably taught Guarino; these men, had not, one imagines, much in common with the stereotype of the brutal usher. Nor, perhaps, had the majority of their colleagues. Yet the stereotype was still there, and the given role of the schoolmaster in this age was uninspiring. In these circumstances, the educational thought of the generation of humanists after Petrarch, which transformed the methods and ideals of the educator, and assigned a new and more exhilarating role to the teacher, or at least to the teacher of the upper classes, was of inestimable benefit to the cultural development of Italy, and later, of Europe.

At 14, sometimes later, sometimes earlier, those who had passed out from the grammar schools, or those born into wealthy families who had pursued the grammar school course under a private tutor at home, could enter the university. At the end of the thirteenth century only Bologna and Padua possessed major flourishing universities, and these easily preserved their pre-eminence. There were other foundations which still precariously struggled for existence, or where the mere *de iure* right to hold a university was claimed: Naples, Vercelli (extinguished by the 1350s), that of the papal court at Rome; but of these almost nothing was to be heard during the following century. Some attempts were made to found other universities: at the city of Rome (1303), Treviso (1314), Pisa (1343), Arezzo (1355–73), and Piacenza (1398–1412). These came to grief almost immediately. Siena (from 1357), Ferrara (in 1391), and Turin (in 1405) enjoyed no prosperity before the middle of the fifteenth century. Only Perugia (from 1308) and Pavia (founded by Galeazzo Visconti in 1361) managed to attract any large body of students. Florence, whose university was founded in 1349, never attained real prosperity, although it had a very considerable cultural influence through the teaching of one or two professors at the turn of the century. It was only the fame of the two older foundations, Bologna and Padua, which could hope to attract foreign students. The number of Italian boys who had been educated in grammar schools and whose parents could afford to maintain them for another seven or eight years, was too small to permit any expansion of higher education. This was particularly true after the fall in population from the 1340s. This meant, incidentally, that there was a high premium in Italian life on the university graduate.

There were two basic university faculties: the first, Law, the second, Medicine and Arts. A doctorate in civil law demanded seven years study; canon law, six. Law is not generally considered as a subject which is conducive to literary or artistic development—nor was it then; indeed there were many complaints among the humanists at its alleged aridity. Yet in two ways it did much for the development of humanism. First it gave its students the technique, found pre-eminently among the *glossators* (or commentators upon legal texts), of close textual criticism, the ability to point conflicts between authorities and to reconcile or choose between them. It was, in other words, in the law schools of Bologna that Petrarch learnt those skills which made him one of the greatest of textual critics. Second, it spoke in every line of the greatness of the Roman secular society from which ultimately it derived.

The study of medicine, with its attendant disciplines of philosophy, natural philosophy (including mathematics), and astrology, was less fruitful. Yet incorporated within the medical faculty was that of Arts, that is to say those studies of grammar, rhetoric, and logic which were considered as preliminary to other courses. The faculty of Arts sometimes provided very basic grammar-school type courses for the younger boys at the university, but also, from the end of the thirteenth century, more advanced teaching. At Bologna, for instance, in 1321, Giovanni di Virgilio, with whom Dante exchanged Latin verses, lectured upon Virgil, Statius, Lucan, and Ovid. The arts faculty of Padua, both at the beginning and end of the century, was a notable centre of humanist enthusiasm. All this, however, was a recent development, for in the thirteenth century the universities, as we have seen, had turned away from any intensive study of the classics.

The universities were not the only centres of higher learning. In towns without *studia* there were sometimes private and free-lance teachers whose personality guaranteed an audience, and who, for payment or friendship, would give informal instruction in the field which they had made their own. Such teachers, it may be assumed, were the Florentine chancellor, Brunetto Latini (d. 1294) who was Dante's own master, and the judge, Lovato de' Lovati (c. 1237–1309) who gathered a circle of humanist enthusiasts around him at Padua. Theology was not taught in Italian universities before the establishment of a faculty at Bologna in 1364, but it could be studied by both clerics and laymen in the *studia* of the friars. Both Franciscans and Dominicans gave instruction in theology, philosophy, and, sometimes, in the basic preliminary studies of logic, grammar, and rhetoric. The philosophic teaching of the two schools of S. Croce and S. Maria Novella in Florence played an incalculable part in the creation of the *Divine Comedy*. To Dante's contemporaries too, these schools, with their links in international orders, brought news of the latest developments which were taking place at Paris and Oxford the principal centres in this era of European theology and philosophy.

In the universities proper, however, all teaching, almost without exception, was performed by laymen. The professors were paid by the city commune or *signoria*, but were controlled and disciplined by the *universitas* itself, or guild of students. Instruction consisted solely of morning and afternoon lectures, and normally students were given no supervision over their studies or their employment of time. That is to say that in the universities the aims of education were still functional. Its purpose was merely to inculcate certain disciplines, and all teaching was directed towards the passing of an exam. The considerable academic and social difficulties likely to be encountered by students who were often very young boys were almost wholly ignored. Such was the general rule. However, occasionally, for a minority of pupils and in return for substantial fees, some of the professors would take into their own homes the sons of those parents who desired and could afford a more personal academic and moral supervision. In these circumstances a much closer relation between teacher and pupil, and a much more humane system of education, could develop. For instance, at Padua towards the end of the century, three humanists, Barzizza, Vittorino da Feltre, and Guarino, all supervised undergraduates in this way.

It was perhaps partly from their experience of this system that the new educational ideals of the fifteenth century were to be born. It has been seen that in many ways education in fourteenth century Italy was almost wholly directed to utilitarian ends, that it was narrow in aims and content. At the end of the century, however, a new body of educational theory began to form which, considering principally the problems of educating the children of the upper classes, stressed the need for an instruction which was to be primarily non-vocational and literary. Its earliest exponent was Pier Paolo Vergerio the elder in his *De ingenuis moribus*, written in about 1400–2 and addressed to Ubertino Carrara, the eleven-year-old heir to the *signoria* of Padua.

In Vergerio's treatise, vocational training for medicine, law, or even theology (though the last is somewhat obscurely passed over) was regarded as being outside the education of 'a free man'. So too, of course, was education for trade. The purpose of education, following Aristotle, whose authority was appealed to in this, was the production of citizens (that is, of an élite class) who should be active and valuable members of the community. The ideal education in these circumstances was to be both physical and mental. Physical activity and training in arms were to alternate with the study of 'the Liberal Arts'. These, of course, had been prescribed in the traditional educational pattern of previous centuries. What was new here, however, was the emphasis given to the specifically literary branches of these studies. Arithmetic, geometry, and astronomy were passed over with a formal acknowledgement; logic was considered to be no more than a branch of eloquence. The true centre of study was henceforth to be Latin and, where possible, Greek grammar, rhetoric, history, and moral philosophy. These studies, Vergerio held, were those which bestowed 'virtue and wisdom'. Their purpose was in part non-utilitarian (he emphasised their value as recreation in later life) but were also designed to make the child useful as a citizen. Vergerio thought that the ability to speak and write with true eloquence were of very large importance in the administration of government and the services of the ruler.

This change in emphasis in the syllabus was accompanied by a new emphasis upon pedagogy proper, a new theory of how children should be educated. Vergerio believed, and this view was adopted from the signorial households, that boys were best educated away from home and the possible over-indulgence of their parents. The teacher should pay great attention to their moral development. Their appetites were to be disciplined, there was to be no excess in eating, drinking, or sleeping. Ideals of 'moral worth and fame' were to be inculcated by reference to ancient and contemporary heroes. In learning itself the teacher was supposed to recognise that mental endowments differed and that children of modest powers required more attention than others. He should work by encouragement and rewards, and though he should avoid over-leniency, he should not be too severe 'for we must avoid all that terrifies a boy'.

This new ideal of education was drawn partly from the old disciplines of the *trivium* and *quadrivium*. Partly too it came from the traditions of character-training found in the leading feudal houses of

Europe and expanded in such treatises as Vincent of Beauvais' *De eruditione filiorum nobilium* (*c.* 1246–7), Guillaume Perrault's *De eruditione principum* (second half of the thirteenth century), and the *De regimine principum* of Egidio Colonna (*c.* 1243–1316). But the largest element of novelty within it was its enthusiasm for the classical world and the literary discipline of Greek and Latin learning. As such its two primary sources of inspiration were Plutarch's treatise *On Education*, translated by Guarino in 1411, and, above all, Quintilian's *Education of the Orator*. Though the complete text of this work was only discovered by Poggio in 1416, mutilated copies had been known to earlier writers, and had been received with particular enthusiasm by the Colonna family, Petrarch, Lapo da Castiglionchio, Salutati, and, of course, by Vergerio himself. In this treatise the orator was regarded by Quintilian as the complete man; to be successful he had also to be wise and good, and therefore his training was equated with the ideal education of a free citizen.

These ideals, as expounded by Plutarch, Quintilian, and now Vergerio, were to have an immediate and extraordinary influence. They inspired the schools of Guarino and Vittorino during the first half of the fifteenth century, became the educational goal of the whole of Europe in the early sixteenth, and were revived, in some at least of their aspects, in English public schools of the nineteenth. All this was a development which can perhaps in some ways be regretted. Some Italian critics have noted how this non-vocational education proceeded in public esteem *pari passu* with the decline of the Italian economy. Moreover, it limited the content of education to a narrow field, though, of course, to a much fuller comprehension of what actually was studied. In this respect Vergerio pointed out that a thorough mastery of one subject could take a lifetime, and that most have only sufficient ability to pursue the one thing which is most suited to their intelligence and tastes. Therefore: 'Let the boy of limited capacity work only at that subject in which he shows he can attain some result.'

This sounds a liberal note, but on the other hand the humanists were by and large determined that the specialisation should be exclusively in their own discipline. In his *De studiis et literis*, written around 1405, Leonardo Bruni observed that 'subtleties of arithmetic and geometry' (which were lumped together with astrology) 'were not worthy to absorb a cultivated mind'. Nor, of course, was 'that vulgar and threadbare jargon' of theology, unless by chance expressed in some fairly reasonable prose style, such as that of Lactantius, Augustine, and Jerome. But morality itself was more likely to be absorbed when read in the prose style of the classic, though perhaps unfortunately pagan ages, in the writings of Plato and Cicero.

The obsessive concern in education with classical culture, which has lasted until today, came about at the beginning of the fifteenth century. It was, perhaps, an important factor in explaining the regress of Italian science in the fifteenth century from the advances made in the fourteenth. Its fruits were obvious: the universal classicising of art and literature, the adoption of Greek and Latin themes, myths, and style. The total effect was perhaps disappointing: the fifteenth century may have had an educational system based upon 'letters'; the fourteenth had Dante, Petrarch, and Boccaccio. Yet the establishment of a new educational ideal moulded the whole of Italian and European thought for the next century, and beyond. The values of pagan Greece and Rome were to co-exist in greater or lesser tension with those of Christianity in the consciousness of every educated man. This was part of the attraction of the new studies; they widened the possible areas of moral debate, and extended the potentialities of men beyond the purely Christian conception of the world. For this reason too, the more percipient (and not, as is so often asserted today, the more stupid) of the Christian clergy attempted vainly to stem the tide of the new educational movement. Such a man was Fra Giovanni Dominici (c. 1356–1419), *lector* in that same school of S. Maria Novella where, a hundred years before, Dante had studied philosophy. In the old days, the friar complained, children learnt their Psalter and Catechism, then perhaps went on to read Cato, Aesop's fables, Boethius, and St Augustine. Now however, they were imbibing the *Ars Amatoria*, stories of Jupiter and Saturn and Venus, before they knew anything of the Trinity: 'so that they're pagans before they're Christians, and the faith is despised, sin is established ... all comes from the poisonous malice of the ancient serpent.' The humanist's counter contentions: that the fathers knew the poets or that no one took the fables of the ancient gods seriously were disingenuous. However sincere they were as Christians, and most of them were, they must have realised that there was a profound and ultimately irreconcilable conflict between Roman *virtus* and Christian morality. Their true, perhaps unrecognised, desire to hold both ideals at once in their souls was essentially the reflection of that still Christian but deeply secularised society in which they found themselves living, that world in which the economic revolution and slow growth of the state had transformed the older Christian ideals of life.

The end of the fifteenth century sees the beginnings of a new emphasis upon the education of upper-class women. It has already been seen that a comparatively large number of women had begun to receive some sort of education by the middle of the fourteenth century. Yet none really played any part as patrons or authors of literary works until the fifteenth century. The first of the learned ladies who characterise that period is the poetess, Battista da Montefeltro (1383–1450), wife of Galeazzo Malatesti of Pesaro. At first it was perhaps difficult for the humanists to give recognition to these feminine aspirations. Vergerio ignored them altogether, but Bruni, in his *De studiis et literis*, specifically written for Battista, had encouraged the idea, though with some reservations. It was a difficult case to urge from classical precedent. Bruni, seeking for examples of cultured women from the classical world, found it easy to refer to 'Cornelia, the daughter of Scipio Africanus, whose letters survived for centuries through their elegant style', but was then driven back upon rather less fortunate examples: 'Sappho, the poetess, held in the highest honour for her singular skill' and 'Aspasia, the most learned woman, from whom Socrates was not ashamed to confess that he had learnt'. Reading between the lines it can be judged that his championing of feminine education is somewhat lukewarm. He remarks, for instance, that history, being an easy subject, consisting simply of the narrative of readily understood matters of fact, was eminently suitable for a studious lady. But other humanists of the time, such as Guarino and Vittorino da Feltre, were more wholehearted in this cause.

nine

Authorship

Authors as Amateurs and Professionals

The overwhelming majority of authors in this period were amateurs. The numbers of minstrels and 'men of the court' who actually composed their own work was small, and in an age without publishers or copyright the possibilities of making money directly from literature were few. In these circumstances almost all writers either had independent means or followed a trade or profession. If Petrarch is to be believed, one should add that almost anyone who followed a trade or profession was an author. In a letter to a friend he complained that others seemed to have caught from him the disease of writing, that every day letters and poems for comment descended on him not only from Italy, but from all over Europe. The mania has spread far and wide, and scarcely does he dare venture out: 'If I do wild fellows rush up from every side and seize upon me, asking advice, giving me suggestions, disputing and fighting among themselves. . . . If the disease spreads, I am undone. Shepherds, fishermen, hunters, ploughboys, all will be carried away. Even the cows will low in numbers and ruminate sonnets.'[1] Most educated men, it seems probable, were likely, at some time in their lives, to have turned their hand to some secret verse-making.

Ignoring this general activity, and looking only at those who left a fairly significant or substantial corpus of works, one can roughly distinguish five classes among those who wrote in Italian. First were clerics. Predictably enough in the overwhelming majority of cases their writing was confined to sermons, *laude*, lives of the saints, and general works of piety. Their writings were didactic, or, as in the case of Jacopone da Todi, have the character of a spontaneous upsurge of mystical religious feeling. In this class can be placed the only two women whose works attained fame in this century, St Catherine of Siena (1347–80) and the Franciscan tertiary Angela da Foligno, though the mystical outpourings of these ladies were taken down by others since both were illiterate. Apart from works specifically dealing with religion, clerics played some part as translators of the classics. Noticeable here is the Carmelite friar, Guido da Pisa, whose *Fiore d' Italia* consisted of prose stories of the early kings of Latium, and the Dominican Bartolomeo di San Concordio (d. 1347), who translated Sallust and an anthology of Latin passages called the *Ammaestramenti degli antichi*.

The second class of *volgare* writers are men from substantial merchant families: historians such as Dino Compagni, the Villani, Andrea Dandolo, Marchionne Stefani, and Gregorio Dati, whose motives for writing seem best summed up as 'patriotic'; poets, such as Bindo Bonichi and Dino and Matteo Frescobaldi; and the *novellista*, Giovanni Sercambi. The third and fourth classes, both very much smaller, are formed by aristocrats and teachers. Aristocrats, men such as Guido Cavalcanti (d. 1301); Guido Novello da Polenta, Lord of Ravenna (d. 1330); and Brizio Visconti, a natural son of Luchino Visconti, were all poets, for the writing of verse was considered a desirable 'gentle' accomplishment. Among teachers no more than three men stand out as writers in Italian: the poet, Cecco d' Ascoli, a professor of astrology, who was burnt for heresy in 1327, Bartolomeo di Castel del Pieve (*fl.* 1370), a schoolmaster poet, and Donato Albanzani (*c.* 1330–1411), the friend and translator of Petrarch and Boccaccio. Only two men from the working class have been claimed as authors, and both seem rather doubtful cases. The first is Antonio Pucci, (*c.* 1310–88) the Florentine towncrier, who is better considered as a 'professional' author. The second is the Florentine Agnolo Torini (*c.* 1315–95) who wrote a *Brieve collezione della umana condizione* and other pietistic works. Torini's claim to be of the working class however rests on the slim foundation that he calls himself *colonaio* i.e. 'bedspread-maker'. Since, however, his

Brieve collezione suggests a knowledge of Innocent III's Latin *De contemptu mundi* and Boccacio's will made him ward for his children, he appears to have been a manufacturer rather than an artisan.

The last, and by far the largest class of authors in Italian, was composed of notaries, judges, and jurists. These provided the greatest number of poets, the majority of translators of Latin classics, and a large body of chroniclers. This connection with the law appears everywhere in Italian literature of the time. Even the mystic poet, Jacopone da Todi, had been a notary before joining the Franciscans in middle age; Boccaccio had studied canon law at Naples; and Petrarch, civil law at Bologna. A high proportion of these lawyers seem to have been connected with the administration of government. From the chancery of Florence, for instance, came Dante's master, Brunetto Latini, author of the *Rettorica* and the *Livres dou trésor*; the poet, Ventura Monachi; and the chronicler, Nofri delle Riformagioni. Officials in other governments were Graziolo Bambaglioli, the author of a commentary upon the *Divine Comedy*; the Venetian poet and chronicler, Nicoletto d' Alessio; the poet, Antonio di Giovanni da Legnano, notary to the della Scala lords of Verona; Domenico da Montichiello, translator of Ovid's *Heroides* into verse, who was vicar of Piacenza for Galeazzo Visconti II; and Battista da Verona, poet and chancellor of Verona. Judges figure prominently: Armanino di Tommaso of Bologna, the author of the *Fiorita* (a prose and verse account of the human race from the creation to the death of Pompey), Cino da Pistoia, the poet and friend of Dante; Dante's son, Pietro Alighieri, also a poet; Giovanni de' Boni, a judge for Giangaleazzo Visconti; and Andrea di Anfuso, author of verse in Sicilian dialect.

This predominance of notaries and the legal profession becomes almost overwhelming among those who wrote in Latin. Although the aristocracy were likely to be able to read Latin (there is an interesting letter of Petrarch which felicitates Count Guido di Battifolle on his son's progress in the language), few among them are found as authors. (An exception here is Niccolò Orsini, count of Nola, who had received notarial training, became governor of the Patrimony of Tuscany within the papal state, and corresponded with

Salutati.) Similarly, until the end of the fourteenth century there were few men from substantial merchant families. There were some clerics who wrote in Latin on themes not directly connected with religion. Francesco Nelli, Bishop Angelo Acciaiuoli, the Augustinian friar Luigi Marsigli, and the Camaldolesi monk Ambrogio Traversari (who might also qualify as an aristocrat), were closely associated with the development of humanism, and Fra Francesco da Buti was the author of commentaries on Horace and Dante.

Among teachers, the Latin poets, Giovanni di Virgilio and Giovanni Malpaghini, and the great Ciceronian scholar, Gasparino Barzizza, were professors of rhetoric. Pier Paolo Vergerio, who took orders and ended his days in the chancery of the Emperor Sigismund, began his career as a university teacher. The Latin poet, Zanobi da Strada, abandoned schoolteaching to join the Neapolitan chancery and then became a papal secretary. The careers of Convenevole da Prato, the master of Petrarch, and of Giovanni di Conversino went in the reverse direction. Convenevole had originally been a notary before he adopted the schoolmaster's profession at Avignon. Conversino was trained as a notary and served for a few years as Chancellor in Padua and Ragusa, but seems actively to have preferred the life of the school to work in government. So too did one of the most influential of all the humanists, Guarino da Verona (1374–1460). Guarino's father was a smith who died when his son was only 12. None the less the boy was able to obtain a considerable education. Then in 1403, with the financial assistance of Paolo Zane, a Venetian ambassador and merchant, he went to Constantinople for four years to study Greek under Chrysoloras. On his return he earned his living as a teacher at Verona, Florence, and Ferrara.

It was men connected with the law, however, who were principally responsible for Latin writings in the century. The Paduan proto-humanist circle of the late thirteenth and early fourteenth centuries was presided over by the poet-judge, Lovato de' Lovati, and the poet, historian, and notary, Albertino Mussato. At Verona in the same period were the notary Benzo d' Alessandria and the jurist Guglielmo da Pastrengo, while Vicenza boasted the chronicler and notary, Ferreto de' Ferreti. The notaries, Paolo da Perugia and

Barbato da Sulmona, and the jurist, Giovanni Barili, were among the first humanists of southern Italy. In Venice, early humanism was intimately connected throughout the century with the chancery: with men like Benintendi de' Ravagnani and Raffaino Caresini, who both served as Chancellors.

Only with early Florentine humanism of the middle of the century in the circle of Boccaccio and Bishop Angelo was this legal predominance eclipsed. Yet lawyers were still found there: men such as the notary, Francesco Bruni, later to become apostolic secretary to the papal curia, and the judge, Lapo da Castiglionchio. Moreover others, who at first sight seem remote from the legal-administrative class, can be found to have some connection with it; men like Boccaccio and Zanobi da Strada and the cleric, Francesco Nelli, who all became secretaries at the Neapolitan court.

In the next generation the domination of the legal class, and more especially of those concerned in the administration of government, was again confirmed. In the north of Italy, Paolo di Bernardo and Pelegrino Zambeccari were chancellors of Venice and Bologna, respectively, and Pasquino Capelli and Antonio Loschi in turn headed the Visconti secretariat. At Florence during the same period the position was more complex. Many of the humanists came from old, extremely wealthy bourgeois families and were often very powerful men. Such were Cino Rinuccini and the Corbinelli brothers, whose families had made great fortunes from the wool trade, Agnolo Pandolfini, landlord, merchant, and important office holder, Palla di Nofri Strozzi, powerful banker and politician, and Roberto de' Rossi, magnate and landowner. Together with these were others in more ambiguous circumstances, men such as Pietro di Ser Mino, from a family of notaries, who was chancellor from 1406 to 1410, but who then retired to a monastery; and Niccolò Niccoli who, though from a wealthy family and of independent means, was in reduced circumstances towards the end of his life.

But the three most important men of Florentine humanism in the period, Salutati, Bruni, and Poggio, were all trained as notaries, and from comparatively humble backgrounds. They all managed to break into the city's élite. Coluccio Salutati (1331-1406) had been born of wealthy parents but his father had died when he was ten, and for 15 years he was forced to be a village notary in his native Stignano. In 1367 however, his skill in Latin composition secured him the chancellorship of the commune of Todi, and then subsequently of Lucca. Finally in 1375 he was appointed Chancellor of Florence, a position which brought him an annual income of 600 florins, and the possibility of acquiring large capital assets. Leonardo Bruni (c. 1370–1444) was the son of a grain dealer from Arezzo, whose parents died during his youth. Through keeping a hard eye on the main chance and through placing his talents at the service of the papal and Florentine chanceries, he was by 1427 among the top one per cent of taxpayers within the commune. Poggio Bracciolini (1380–1459), whose father was an impoverished apothecary, enjoyed a comfortable living in government service by the 1420s, and by 1458 was extremely wealthy.

The success of these men prompts a rephrasing of our judgement upon 'authors as amateurs' in this period. For authorship itself was a primary means of obtaining lucrative positions within government service, and this serves in large part to explain the predominance of the legally trained administrator among authors. In the first place, it is clear, successful authorship already contributed to social distinction. Authorship brought fame, and authors in this century were almost uniformly obsessed with fame. The contention of those who have argued that before printing authorship was held in little esteem and that authors were indifferent to their reputation, can only be considered as an extended paradox. In Dante's words, speaking of writing in Italian: *Quod autem honore sublimet, in promptu est . . . Minime hoc probatione indiget*: 'That it raises one up, is evident. . . . This has no need at all of proof.'[2]

But more than this, the study of rhetoric and composition, particularly in Latin, was considered, under Ciceronian influence, to be a particularly important aspect of the art of government.[3] 'Tully', wrote Dante's master, Brunetto Latini, 'says that the noblest part of all sciences in governing a city is rhetoric, that is the science of speech'. In Italian society, therefore, to demonstrate ability in written expression was to reveal that one possessed a technical skill of supreme importance in the development of governments into 'states'. The books produced by those who worked in the Florentine chancery were written for pleasure, but also as exercises which demonstrated the suitability of their authors for the positions they held. This explains the large amount of 'chancery' writing in Italy and the intimate connection, from the very beginnings of humanism, between literature and government circles.

There is a sense then in which the professional writer already existed in the Italy of the fourteenth century. Yet over and above this, three men, and these the three greatest of Italian writers, by the intensity of their devotion to writing look forward to the post-printing era of the professional author.

Dante Alighieri: 'Man of the court'

Dante claimed aristocratic descent. In the *Paradiso*, he asserted that his ancestor, Cacciaguida, had been knighted by an emperor, and had died on crusade. It seems an unlikely story, though the early history of the family is obscure. His father and uncle both engaged in money-lending; one of his sisters married a money-lender, and another a towncrier. In fact the Alighieri seem to have been a minor Florentine family which, in the generation of Dante's father, had made some money by usury, had bought properties in the countryside, and had recently acquired social pretensions.

At the age of 12, Dante was betrothed to, and later married, Gemma di Manetto from a junior branch of the powerful house of Donati. Dante's mother died during his youth. His father remarried and had children by a second wife. By the time the poet was 18, the father himself had died. He left his sons sufficiently well off, presumably from the rents of his rural properties, to live without following any profession or trade. Dante's step-brother, Francesco, lived out a quiet life as a small landlord. Since he and Dante borrowed money ($227\frac{1}{2}$ florins in April 1297, 480 florins in December 1297), this may indicate some dwindling of the paternal patrimony. On the other hand, nothing is known of the circumstances, and the possibility of obtaining credits on this scale might equally suggest that they enjoyed a considerable prosperity.

In his early years Dante lived the life of a man-about-town. In June 1289 he fulfilled a citizen duty by taking part as a mounted soldier in expeditions of the commune against Arezzo and Pisa. There is no good evidence that the poet studied at university, either in Bologna or Paris. But he formed a friendship with Brunetto Latini, the chancellor of the commune, whose circle cultivated the arts of rhetoric and took pleasure in acquiring an encyclopaedic learning. In the courtly milieux of the city there was a passionate interest in music and Italian and Provençal poetry, and the ability to write poetry was considered a part of *cortesia*. Here Dante discovered his inherent and individual genius. At the age of 18 his poem, *A ciascun' alma presa*, directed to 'the many who were at that time famous *trovatori* of the city', won him the friendship of the aristocratic Guido Cavalcanti. Ten years older than Dante, already famous as a poet, Guido introduced him to the notary, Lapo Gianni, and other kindred spirits whose society stimulated his early verses. The poets of central Italy, Gianni Alfani, Bernardo da Bologna, Dino Compagni, and Cino da Pistoia, all knew each other and exchanged sonnets. Literature here was, in the first place, an entertainment between friends. But from these narrow circles the fame of the author was diffused, to the courts of Italy and then right down to the peasant driving his ass, by the *giullari* or minstrels. This world of Dante as a young man is reflected in the *Vita nova*, the story in verse and prose of his love for Beatrice, a lady whom his son and other close commentators identified as Bice di Folco Portinari, wife of Simone de' Bardi, from the prominent banking family. This work was first circulated shortly after the lady's death, in 1292–3, when Dante was 27 years old. For Florence it announced the appearance of a great poet.

In the years which immediately followed, Dante's life matured in two directions. In the first place it was a period of intensive study, both in philosophy and theology at the schools of the Dominicans and Franciscans in Florence, and then privately in the Latin prose-writers, moralists, and historians. At the same time Dante gave himself over to a passionate commitment to 'the active life'. He had perhaps hoped to take honourable and profitable service with the

Angevin, Charles Martel, heir to the Neapolitan throne, who visited Florence in 1294. But the prince's death in the following year banished these hopes, and Dante turned instead to the political life of his own commune. In order to play a part here, membership of a guild was obligatory, and accordingly in 1295 he enrolled in the Art of Physicians and Apothecaries, a formal gesture which did not imply that he wished to follow these callings. From then on he was deeply involved both in the official and unofficial councils of the commune, and in June to August 1300 was elected to be one of the six priors of the city.

It was a dangerous time to be involved in politics, and it is perhaps as difficult for us today as it was for Boccaccio, the poet's first biographer, to understand what motives, what combination of ambition, idealism, or personal loyalties, caused Dante to pursue this life. Possibly he was moved to it by Brunetto Latini's Ciceronian doctrines on the connection between rhetoric and politics. But such teaching could only have reinforced his native instincts. No other poet has had so strong a will to political power, and no other great poet, at least before the French revolution, was ever so prominently and closely caught up in party political struggles. This is the more remarkable in that it is difficult to see any ideological or even class interest in these struggles or indeed any motive at all beyond the fight for power of rival factions. Fortunately, for otherwise it may be assumed that the poet would have been lost in the politician, Dante had chosen the wrong side. His own party, 'the Whites', were shortly to be overwhelmed by 'the Blacks' (led by his wife's kinsmen, the Donati), who had secured the powerful alliance of Pope Boniface VIII and the French royal house. In October 1301 he was one of three ambassadors of the commune at Rome seeking to negotiate with the Pope. In his absence 'the Blacks' seized power, and set about the systematic destruction of their rivals. In the following January Dante was called to answer charges of disturbance of the public peace, hostility to the Pope, and misappropriation of public money. On his failure to appear before the judges, he was condemned in March to be burnt alive if he fell into the hands of the commune. At that time he was 36 years old. He was never to see Florence again.

From 1302 to 1304 he took part in the attempts of the banished 'Whites' to regain power. Yet in that period he lost sympathy with his companions, 'a wicked and foolish company', and abandoned them. To live he now had to solicit the hospitality of the great. He had to adopt the harsh life of 'the man of the court'. His fame as poet and politician preceded him, but he was still forced into dependence upon others. In the seventeenth canto of the *Paradiso*, Cacciaguida prophesies the poet's life at this time:

> As Hippolytus was sent from Athens through his cruel and perfidious stepmother, so you must part from Florence.
> So it is willed, so already it is sought, so it will be done by he [Boniface VIII] who plots there where Christ each day is put on sale [the Roman *curia*]. . . .
> You will abandon each thing loved most dearly, and this is the arrow which the bow of exile shall first shoot.
> You will learn the salt taste of another's bread, and how hard the path to go down and mount other's stairs.

The years 1304 to 1310 were a period of migrations from petty court to petty court of which little is known. Perhaps he was at Verona. There is a glimpse of him in the castle of the Marquisses of Malaspina in the Lunigiana, and then he is gone again, possibly to the fiefs of the Conti Guidi in the high Appenines, possibly to Lucca or Treviso. He has summed up his life in that period in the *Convivio*:

> Through almost all the regions in which our speech extends, I have gone as a pilgrim, all but begging my way, showing against my will the wounds of fortune—wounds for which the blame is normally given to him who has endured them. Truly I have been a ship without sail or helm, driven to diverse ports and river mouths and shores, blown by the dry wind of wretched poverty.

In these straits, Dante made overtures for reconciliation with the ruling Florentine 'Blacks'. He was conciliatory and sought their pardon. He began the writing of the *De vulgari eloquentia* and the *Convivio* in an attempt to turn back fortune, and by a demonstration of his learning to persuade the Florentines to recall him from exile.

Both works were unfinished. For in 1310, the Emperor Henry VII invaded Italy, and Dante, seeing in him the hope of breaking the government in power at Florence, put aside prudence, and returned to politics. The poet hastened to meet his saviour in northern Italy, and, kneeling before him, he tells us, exclaimed within himself: 'Behold the Lamb of God, behold he who taketh away the sins of the world.' It was a period of profound emotion in his life. From the castle of Poppi, where he was the guest of the Conti Guidi of Battifolle, he wrote letters as a propagandist in the imperial cause. In these he expresses first hope and triumph and then, as the power of the Emperor wavered and collapsed, a concentrated venom born from the anguish of exile and the acceptance of despair.

Despite the imperial failure, Dante was given a chance to return to Florence. In 1315 he could have taken advantage of an amnesty which required from him only an acknowledgment of guilt. But this his spirit refused:

> If I can enter Florence by no other means, then I in Florence will never enter. And what of it? Can I not, wherever I may be, contemplate the spheres of the sun and the stars? Can I not in any place under the vault of the sky meditate the sweetest truths— provided only that I have not first made myself contemptible, nay abject, before the people and your city?

Dante had at last disowned the social world of the city, to which hitherto he had been wholly attached. From then on, and it is from this that the immense power of the Comedy derives, though once intimately linked with the world of his age, he has become now utterly alone within it: *una sola vox, sola pia et hac privata.*

He found refuge at the court of Cangrande della Scala, Lord of Verona. Here was a haven of munificence and *cortesia*, which he was to recall in moving lines both in the seventeenth canto of the Paradiso, and in his dedication of the poem:

> I came to Verona to test with my own eyes what I had heard of you and I saw your magnificence; I saw and experienced your generosity. And whereas I had previously believed that the

reports of your fame were excessive, I came to realise that it was the reality itself which was measureless. So that though, through hearsay, I had previously, with a certain reverence of soul, come to hold you in esteem; on first sight of you, I became your devoted servant and friend.

But though he lived in this court he was not of it. The world was now his country: 'as the sea to fish'. It was in these years, as I believe, and not amidst the expectations of Henry VII's coming, that Dante sat down to write those serene pages of the *Monarchia* in which he reasserted the eternal need of mankind for a unitary world-empire. At the same time his studies concentrated on those authors who had turned away, both in church and state, from the pursuit of power and the hopes of the world. He chose his books now from the writings of St Peter Damiani, of St Bernard, of Richard of St Victor. Yet out of his very despair was now born the apocalyptic belief that all would change: that the Empire would again reign supreme, that the church would be reformed, that he himself would return again to Florence not as a suppliant, but as a victor.

It was in this mood that during these years Dante gave final form to the *Divine Comedy*. Those many who have treated the poem as if it were in the central line of thought of the time, as if it were in any way representative of 'medieval' orthodoxy, are mistaken. Only its deep ambiguity and its author's genius for synthesis disguise the fact that it is a bizarre and highly personal chiliastic fantasy, just how bizarre and how personal is revealed by the place of Beatrice within it. The theological progenitor of the poem is not so much St Thomas Aquinas as that strange eremite mystic of the twelfth century, Joachim da Fiore. Hope here is concentrated on the mystic Veltro and Saviour, of whom Dante conceived himself, quite literally, to be the prophet. It is a work which reflects the society of the age only so far as it appears in the powerful distorting mirror of a man who has been frustrated in his every social ideal and who has attained tranquillity by a subconscious resolve to accept impossible beliefs.

In the last years of his life Cangrande sent the poet to Ravenna and the court of Guido Novello da Polenta to negotiate on the supply of salt to Verona and to secure a firmer alliance between the two powers against Venice. Such were the tasks in which 'a man of the court' if sufficiently eminent, could be employed. There can have been few places where the poet might more appropriately have ended his days. Ravenna, once the capital of the world, then a small provincial town, with its continual sense of lost greatness, must intimately have matched his mood. Returning from an embassy to Venice on behalf of the Lord Guido Novello in 1321, the poet contracted malaria, and died here on the night of 13–14 September.

At the end of his life, from a financial point of view he can have lacked for little. His children were adequately provided for. Jacopo acquired a canonry and other benefices in Verona. Thanks to the patronage of Guido Novello, his other son, Pietro, secured the revenues of two parishes in Ravenna, and then entered on the expensive legal training necessary to become a judge. His daughter, Antonia, became a nun at Ravenna and assumed the name in religion of Beatrice. Already, as the epistles of Giovanni di Virgilio testify, the poet enjoyed a wide fame in northern Italy. In Ravenna itself he was revered by a small circle of notaries who attempted in their own way to pursue Latin and Italian literature.

At the same time he seems, emotionally, to have acquired a precarious serenity. Boccaccio tells us how those who had known Dante at the end of his life described him: 'ever melancholy and thoughtful, grave and mild, and wonderfully composed and civil both at home and in public business, rarely speaking, only when asked and then most eloquently; very lonely, friendly with few; assiduous in study; of high and most disdainful soul'.

Boccaccio: Bourgeois, 'man of the court', Cleric

Boccaccio's career by contrast missed the tragedy and passion of Dante's. His family came from Certaldo, within the countryside subject to Florence. At the end of the thirteenth century his father, Boccaccino, and his uncle, without abandoning their local interests, had moved to Florence and with great success had taken to commerce. Boccaccino served twice as 'consul' in the guild of Money

Changers, and attained, as Dante had done, the office of Prior. In 1313, the year of Boccaccio's birth, his uncle established himself as a merchant in Paris. Giovanni himself was illegitimate. Of his real mother he never speaks, and we know nothing of her. But his father had him legitimised and raised as a true son. It was a small world, this fourteenth-century Florence; when, later, Boccaccino married, his wife was related to Dante's Beatrice.

At the age of six, when, Boccaccio tells us, he already knew something of reading and writing, he began to attend the school of Giovanni da Strada, where among the pupils he met Zanobi, son of his schoolmaster, and a future Latin poet, and Niccolò Acciaiuoli who was to have a great career in the political world. In 1327, some seven years later, Boccaccio's father went to Naples to direct there the interests of the Bardi company. In this position he had close links with the court of King Robert, and was eventually appointed as his councillor and chamberlain, honorary posts, but ones which reflected his importance in the commercial world of the southern kingdom. With him went Giovanni, and here in the Portanova district, where the moneychangers had their 'benches', the boy began his four-year apprenticeship in commerce. His days were passed with the scales of assay, the abacus, and the account books of his company, and here he first met those men who were taking part in the great epic of Italian capitalism, those men later immortalised in the *Decameron*.

It was not a life which appealed to him. In middle age he looked back on it merely as pointless expenditure of 'irrecoverable time'. It was rather poetry, he tells us, which obsessed him: he had been born *ad poeticas meditationes dispositum ex utero matris*. It was an Ovidian reference which Pope has made familiar to us in English:

While still a child and yet a fool to fame
I lisped in numbers, for the numbers came.

Seeing his distaste for commerce his father decided that he should study canon law instead: 'as a good way to get rich'. From his eighteenth to twenty-fourth year accordingly he was enrolled in the classes of the university of Naples, wasting yet more time: 'so great was my passion for poetry'.

Not all was waste. At the university he attended the lectures of the jurist, Cino da Pistoia, poet and friend of Dante. Here too he made the acquaintance of Dionigi da Borgo San Sepolcro, lecturer in theology and friend of Petrarch, from whom perhaps he first heard the name of the man whose influence was so greatly to mould the pattern of his life. He had access to the royal library where Paolo da Perugia, the king's librarian, author of commentaries on Persius and Horace, first gave him his taste for encyclopaedic learning. Yet for the moment it was the glamour of the court which most appealed to him. Thanks to his father's position he had access to the great; the young nobility visited his father's house and drew him to the culture of France and Provence.

The attractions of the court shone all the more brightly at that time through the extraordinary triumph of an old schoolfellow. In 1331 the young Niccolò Acciaiuoli had arrived at Naples to follow, like Boccaccio, the merchant's trade. But a burning ambition had driven him to the court, where in a brief time he had become councillor to the chamber of the princess Giovanna and 'man of confidence' to the King's step-sister, Catherine de Valois. Within four years of his arrival at Naples, and aged only 25, he had been knighted and had become chamberlain to the King. Boccaccio hoped for a similar success, but where Niccolò had triumphed by charm, he would succeed through the pen. It was some such thought as this, combined always with his native passion, which in the years from 1334 to 1340 caused him to write his verse romances in the French tradition: the *Caccia di Diana*, the *Filostrato*, the *Teseida*; and the prose story, *Filocolo*.

It was a world of day dreams. Niccolò, for social reasons (his own legitimacy was not untainted) had boasted of his descent 'from Phrygian gods'. In these pages Giovanni, to alleviate a private pain, invented a mother who was a French princess, prevented by the stern laws of society from marrying his father. Niccolò had won the heart of Catherine de Valois. Giovanni dreamed as he wrote of a successful love affair with a daughter of King Robert. But it was not by dreams that Niccolò was coming to dominate the real world, and once in the real world Giovanni's dreams collapsed. In Naples he found no patron, and all the works he wrote there were dedicated to imaginary people, to Fiametta and other mythical ladies.

His father, Boccaccino, had left Naples in 1332 and in the hope of new profits had gone on to Paris. But during the late 30s Florentine commerce was heading towards disaster, and his own business interests were affected by the current malaise. By 1341 he was forced to return to Florence. He recalled Giovanni back to Tuscany and put an end to his life of expensive but unprofitable studies. For the son, then 27, it was a bitter blow. He appealed to Acciaiuoli for a position which might have kept him in the southern capital, but was ignored. That old friend, now Bailli of Morea, Baron of Kalamata, Lord of Andromonasti, Justiciar of the Lavoro, was too busy among the great affairs of the world to notice every call for help from those whom he had left behind on his climb upward. Boccaccio had to return to Florence. Here, after the gay, chivalric 'douceur de la vie' of the south he found, he complained, 'a house, dark and silent and sad', a father, 'old, cold, coarse, and mean'.

These thoughts, for which, with all his inherent warmth, he was to make handsome amends in the following year, were merely the product of a temporary bitterness. Boccaccio did not repine. After the first few months he threw himself into such literary society as Florence then boasted, making the acquaintance of Forese Donati, Franceschino Albizzi, and others of the upper bourgeoisie with a taste for poetry. At the end of 1341 he dedicated his *Comedia delle Ninfe* to Niccolò di Bartolo del Buono, an influential Florentine politician. In rapid succession there followed the *Amorosa visione*, which spoke in flattering terms of his father, and the *Fiammetta* (1343–4?), which has a good claim to be considered as the first realistic, psychological novel, and which is thus to be seen as demonstrating the influence of the realism of bourgeois society upon the author. From this period his father's fortunes began to recover. Boccaccino was appointed to an office in the commune, and his revived economic circumstances allowed his son a greater measure of independence.

None the less Giovanni decided upon a career outside the paternal roof. For a brief period he resolved to seek his fortune as a 'man of the court' in the little principalities of Romagna on the other side of the Appenines. At the end of 1345 he was with the Lord Ostasio da Polenta at Ravenna, and there probably translated and dedicated to him the fourth decade of Livy's history. Here too he gathered memories of Dante's last days. At the end of 1347 and the beginning of 1348 he was at the court of Francesco Ordelaffi, Lord of Forlì. Here he made the acquaintance of Cecco di Meleto, secretary to the Ordelaffi, whose circle of friends pursued the Latin rhetorical interests which had been diffused through Emilia in the previous generation by Giovanni di Virgilio. This position was not without a certain conflict of loyalties or interests. The Lord of Forlì was in alliance with Lewis of Hungary, who at that moment was preparing to dispute possession of the throne of Naples with Luigi of Taranto. And the Prince of Taranto had as his principal councillor Niccolò Acciaiuoli. In these circumstances Boccaccio was called upon to make propaganda against his old friend, a task to which, with a certain inability to grasp the realities of politics, he fell with a will.

In fact the Hungarian expedition melted away before the onset of plague, and Boccaccio soon abandoned the service of the Ordelaffi. At the same time his writing on Naples veered round to match the new political circumstances. His Latin *Eclogues* now returned to praises of the Neapolitan court and of Acciaiuoli. His earlier attacks upon them, he explained, had in fact only been dictated by fear. Niccolò's *mot* against him as 'Johannem tranquillitatum', 'fair-weather Giovanni', does not really seem in any way unjust. All we can say is that Boccaccio was too great a man to be pinned down by a politician's witticism. However this may be, by March 1348 he was back in Florence and there witnessed the great plague, in which his father, step-mother, and uncle all died. He was left as head of the family. Moreover he had certain obligations to his illegitimate children, of whom there were by this time at least two boys and three girls. In these circumstances, during the first half of the 1350s Boccaccio sought the profits of public office in the Florentine commune, positions to which his friendship with prominent members of the upper bourgeoisie secured him easy access. He was chamberlain of the *camera* of the commune in 1351, ambassador to the Marquess of Brandenburg in 1352, to the courts of Forlì and Ravenna in 1353, to Pope Innocent VI at Avignon in 1354, and Officer of the Mercenaries in 1355.

At the same time the character of his writing and of his interests was changing. The *Decameron*, which reached its final form in 1351, the human comedy of Italian literature, was virtually the last work of the purely literary Boccaccio. It was a work which drew its inspiration from the three different cultural milieux in which Boccaccio had lived: the southern court with its penchant for French literature, Florence and the bourgeois world, and the Romagnol courts with their tradition of rhetorical study. From then on, however, the first two of these sources were neglected by Boccaccio, and he turned to the world of humanist rhetoric. Was this, as has been claimed, a drying up with age of creative ability? Perhaps so; but much too was owed here to the ever growing influence of Petrarch, and Petrarch's plan of studies, over Boccaccio's mind. He met Petrarch for the first time in September 1350 when, together with Francesco Nelli, Lapo da Castiglionchio, and Zanobi da Strada, he had welcomed him to Florence. In March of the following year the commune had sent him to visit the poet at Padua to offer him the chair of rhetoric at Florence. For Boccaccio's circle Petrarch's decision to settle instead with the Visconti in Milan was a bitter blow, but their reverence for him was such that it survived even this.

In the second half of the 1350s Boccaccio was working upon the *Genealogia deorum gentilium* and the *De montibus*, the *De casibus*, and the *Trattatello in laude di Dante*. Little is known of his life during this period. In 1355 he made a brief visit to Naples, where he met with a further rebuff from Acciaiuoli, and then visited the great library of the Abbey of Montecassino. In 1359 he was serving on an ambassadorial mission to northern Italy. By that year Boccaccio had taken holy orders, and two years later was in possession of a benefice. This supplement to his income came opportunely. In December 1360 some of his friends among the bourgeoisie were implicated in a plot against the commune, and Niccolò del Buono, to whom he had dedicated the *Fiametta*, was executed for treason. Boccaccio himself was now regarded with some reserve in official circles, and until 1365 he was to receive no other public office.

Boccaccio seems to have thought it wise to leave Florence for a time. From the summer of 1360 he had had Leonzio Pilato in his house, and from October of that year until 1362 his guest had been lecturing on and translating Homer, Euripides, and Aristotle, in the university. Despite this attraction Boccaccio retired to the family estate at Certaldo. Then in the winter of 1361 he was found again at Ravenna. In the following year he seems, on the recommendation of Petrarch, to have been offered the important, and immensely lucrative, office of apostolic secretary at Avignon, a post which had fallen vacant through the death of Zanobi da Strada. But he rejected this, and, rashly enough, accepted instead the post of secretary to Niccolò Acciaiuoli, now Grand Seneschal of the southern kingdom.

In October 1362 he set off with his half-brother and his library for Naples. But between two such men as Boccaccio and Acciaiuoli, with their respective histories, any satisfactory relationship was doomed. Niccolò did not feel any personal loyalty to 'fair-weather Giovanni', nor did he have any respect for his abilities. Had Petrarch accepted his invitation to come to court he would have given him all honour. But he believed Boccaccio to be in a different class of writers, and due therefore for indifferent treatment. If anything he looked on him with the characteristic contempt of those who have made their way in the world for those who have failed. Had Boccaccio, like Nelli and Zanobi before him, knuckled under as an obedient and flattering servant, all might have been well. But for Boccaccio himself, who had known the great seneschal as a younger, penniless companion, this was an impossibility.

By March 1363 Boccaccio was back in Tuscany. His fury at his treatment spilled out in a ten-page letter (*Epistolae*, xii) to Francesco Nelli, who had been his predecessor in the post. He describes the greeting of 'your Maecenas': 'as if I had just returned from the suburbs of Naples, scarcely giving me his right hand'. In the re-

splendent palace, Boccaccio continued, there was an obscure corner
shut away and guarded by a maze of spiders' webs, flourishing among
fetid dust. It was here, as if he were unwholesome, to which he had
been exiled. For his benefit a small wretched bed, full of hemp
fibres, was dragged out from below the slumbering form of a mule
driver, and with it a shred of stinking coverlet and half a blanket.
Around midnight a room was assigned to him as well, dimly seen by
the half light of an earthenware lamp. Warming to his theme,
Boccaccio goes on to describe the dining arrangements: a little table
of thick, filth-encrusted canvas, stained either by dogs or old age,
with beneath it 'not so much a bench as a little piece of wood with
maimed feet'. This bench, he believed, was expressly formed to
harmonise with the food placed before those who sat on it. And the
company—all around swarmed gluttons, flatterers, pages, cooks,
scullions, 'put it another way, dogs of the court and domestic mice'
who filled the house with discordant noise and their own stench.
Acciaiuoli himself, 'to show how important he is', in the fashion
of royalty, had porters before his door who forbade access to those
who might be coming to complain of these conditions.

Such could be the life of the 'man of the court'. From these
conditions Boccaccio had been temporarily rescued by Mainardo
Cavalcanti, a powerful baron of the kingdom, who had taken him
into the peace and comfort of his own house. This was to be but a
brief respite. Acciaiuoli transferred to his villa at Baia, and Boccaccio
was forced to follow. Then his patron decided to return to Naples;
Giovanni and his brother were left alone with their books, without
food or drink or word from anyone on how they were supposed to
live. It was more than enough; Giovanni took a final leave of his
former friend, and then returned to Florence.

From 1365 he was once again employed in government posts: as
'official of the militia' again, and on embassies to Genoa and Avignon. In April 1367 he was appointed by the captains of the Company of Or San Michele to a committee to consider 'if the work for
the adornment and safety of the tabernacle of Our Lady in the arch
of the building above the tabernacle should be carried out or not'.
In the same year he was on embassy to the Pope at Rome. But he

was getting older and his enthusiasm for such posts was waning; especially now when financially he seems to have been under no real pressure.

These were important years for the growth of his contemporary reputation. In the autumn of 1370, by which time Acciaiuoli had been dead for five years, he visited Naples again. Now he was received with courtesy not only by the literary circle of the capital but by the great too. His old friend, Mainardo Cavalcanti (to whom he was to dedicate the final version of the De casibus), Mainardo's brother, now viceroy of the kingdom, and the powerful baron, Ugo di San Severino, gave him access to the highest circles in the court. Queen Giovanna offered him a post of honour. Niccolò Orsini, governor of the papal patrimony in Tuscany, invited him to his castles. Boccaccio, however, no longer wished for those things which he had struggled to possess in youth. He found it easy to refuse, though the refusals were not without a certain sweetness.

From then on his life was uneventful: with visits to Petrarch, writing and study, friendships with the Florentine writers and humanists of the coming generation, and the spiritual consolations of the Augustinians of S. Spirito. From August 1373 he began his lectures on Dante's Commedia in the church of S. Stefano di Badia, a few steps from the family house of the Alighieri. It was a task to which he had been appointed by the commune in return for 100 florins, and it was his last tribute to his prima fax. He died two years later in December 1375.

Petrarch: from 'man of the court' to 'man of letters'

Of the three most eminent writers of the fourteenth century, Petrarch in his life had by far the greatest success. He acquired both a large income and an immense fame by his pen without any significant loss of personal independence. In this he was aided, as compared with Dante, by having a merely romantic, rather than practical, interest in politics, which saved him from large gestures. Again, his real liking, for the company of the great was accompanied, necessarily, by the possession of acute antennae for the discovery and expression of what was likely to be acceptable to them.

He was the son, grandson, and great-grandson of notaries. His father, Ser Petracco, had been of sufficient eminence to take a part in the political struggles of Florence, had, like Dante, followed the cause of 'the Whites', and was exiled from the city on the same day as Dante. He had retired to Arezzo where two years later, in 1304, Francesco was born. Then, in 1312, like so many other Italians drawn by the magnet of the papacy, the family had transferred to France, where the father managed to build up a successful practice among the merchants and ecclesiastics of the Avignon court. Petrarch began life as an exile with all that awareness of nationality which exile brings. It was in France that he developed that fierce love of Italy and of the Roman world which was the source of so much of his writings.

He was given an excellent education. His schoolmaster, the Italian, Convenevole da Prato, who had in earlier life been a notary, was a man of literary ambitions, even though they had never been sustained. He would, Petrarch explains, find a magnificent title, write a splendid preface, and then turn to some other project with a still more splendid title, and so on. Although occasionally hard up (he may, as Petrarch claims, have pawned a copy of Cicero's manuscripts which the poet had lent him), he was probably a fashionable teacher among the Italian community. It was he who gave Petrarch the foundations of the Latin style with which he achieved fame. He was, said Petrarch: 'a teacher whose equal I have not known.' Among the fellow pupils whom he met at school, he was, characteristically enough, to form a particular friendship with Guido Sette, destined for a great future in the world as Archbishop of Genoa.

In a letter written towards the end of his life, Petrarch, perhaps carried away by the desire to tell a good story, wrote of how his father, disturbed by his son's youthful fondness for Roman authors, had hurled his copies of Cicero and Virgil on the fire. If this is so, Ser Petracco must have been a wealthy man, for the destruction of a book was an expensive gesture. Moreover, it hardly fits in with what else we know about him, for he had personally commissioned a manuscript of Virgil now found in the Ambrosian library. In Petrarch the natural desire to repudiate the father (who may well have been the first to inspire him with humanist interests) was sharpened perhaps by an intense devotion to the memory of his mother who died in 1318, and by the shock of his father's remarriage in 1325, a year before his death. Amidst all his voluminous personal writings Petrarch never mentioned his step-mother.

At the age of 12 or 13, as was fairly common at the time, Petrarch, together with his brother Gherardo and Guido Sette, entered the arts faculty of the university of Montpellier. Then in 1320 the three went on to Bologna. Here the young Petrarch studied civil law, perhaps the greatest inheritance of Roman civilisation. In his *Letter to Posterity* he described it as 'great and full of that Roman antiquity in which I delight'. The professors, he wrote in later years to Sette, 'looked lawgivers of ancient times come to life again'. Yet these studies were too narrow to appeal greatly to his active mind, and though he continued in them till 1326, when his father died, he never troubled to graduate. Instead he returned to Avignon. Here, as Petrarch claimed, the executors of his father's will cheated him and his brother out of the estate. None the less he was still able to use his father's influential connections, and he resolved to pursue a life of poetry and scholarship by following a career in the church.

Almost at once he attracted the attention of Giacomo Colonna, Bishop of Lombez and member of the great Roman aristocratic family. He took minor orders, and through the Bishop's influence was taken into the service of the cultivated Cardinal Giovanni Colonna. Here until 1337 he fulfilled what were largely nominal duties as household chaplain, wrote verse, and built up a wide range of influential contacts. In Colonna's household were the scholars Lello Tosetti and Ludwig van Kempen. In the curia at Avignon were Raimondo Soranzo, a book-collector and enthusiast for Roman history, and Giovanni di Firenze, whom Petrarch calls 'an outstanding literary scholar'. Here he knew and admired the painter, Simone Martini, and met and described such visiting notables as Dionigi di Borgo San Sepolcro, and the English bibliophile, Richard Bury, Bishop of Durham.

Although his verse proclaimed a passion, albeit platonic, for the celebrated Laura, this did not, in the secular world of the curia, hinder his prospects of promotion. Any fears for his reputation which there might have been were attenuated by the doubts, whether legitimate or merely well-fostered, which many held as to the reality of her existence. Nor did more fleshly though less well publicised loves, which resulted in two illegitimate children. In 1335, on the recommendation of Colonna, Benedict XII appointed Petrarch to the canonry of Lombez, and the poet began that exploitation of ecclesiastical posts which was to provide his main source of revenue. In some of these positions Petrarch rarely, in most of them never, actually fulfilled any duties, but confined himself to drawing their revenues. This was the normal practice of the time. Petrarch was an example of the much-condemned absentee pluralist.

It was the patronage of the Colonna family which had obtained Petrarch his first benefice. In the following year (December 1336– July 1337) a branch of the family entertained him on his first visit to Rome. On his return he found that his income from the canonry allowed him to establish himself in a country property at Vaucluse, some 15 miles from Avignon. The city itself, transformed suddenly from a small provincial town to the papal capital, had become an intolerable place to live in without a great deal of money, which Petrarch did not have. At Vaucluse, with two manservants and an overseer for the farm (whom occasionally he would beat for real or imagined dereliction of duty), he was able to live in comfort, though not luxury, and had the additional benefit of being able to speak in Horatian vein, though without Horatian irony, on the joys of country life. Here too he cultivated the friendship of the local bishop of Cavaillon, Phillipe de Cabasolles. As ever Petrarch's instinct was unfailing. Philippe was later to become Vice-Chancellor of the Kingdom of Naples, and through him Petrarch was to gain the friendship of Niccolò Acciaiuoli and King Robert. Meanwhile the poet's withdrawal to Vaucluse did not prevent him from continuing the diligent cultivation of the powerful who still resided in Avignon, to whom he addressed elegant prose and verse letters.

14 Façade of Florence cathedral (drawing of sixteenth century)

15 Agostino di Giovanni and Agnolo di Ventura, *above* 'The plucked commune', *below* 'The commune under *signoria*'

Certainly, although no longer an active member of Colonna's household he continued to act in many ways as his client and friend.

Up to 1341, when Petrarch was 36, he had already achieved much as a poet and scholar. He had written many of his Italian lyrics, published 12 Latin verse epistles, and begun work on his Latin epic, the *Africa*, and on his Roman biographies, the *De viris illustribus*. Already too he had produced the first scholarly edition of the first four *Decades* of Livy. None the less, to all but a rather limited circle it is fair to say that he had shown, at least in Latin letters, promise rather than profound achievement. In this year however, he suddenly achieved European fame through his crowning as poet in Rome. He was crowned, it should be emphasised, not for his skill in Italian, but in Latin, verse. Some brief classical references seem, at the beginning of the fourteenth century, to have led in Italian universities to the occasional crowning of poets. Descriptions of these had fired Petrarch's imagination, and by 1336 he had already begun to lay the grounds for a still more splendid poetic ceremony. He wrote to his friends of his hopes in this, and engaged his patrons to use their influence here. These efforts were to lead to a ceremony which was as bogus as a modern Eisteddfod but which would have delighted the heart of the most energetic publicity man of our own time.

On 1 December 1340, as Petrarch claimed, he received from the chancellor of the university of Paris, and from the Roman Senate, separate invitations to appear before them and be crowned with laurel as a poet. The precise coincidence of dual invitations of the same date has aroused scepticism, but for some time Petrarch had been angling in many directions for a ceremony of this sort. The Parisian chancellor, Roberto de' Bardi, a scion of the banking house, may have wished to gratify his powerful friends at Avignon, and it is just possible that his invitation was drawn up at about the same time as that of the Roman senate. The Roman offer itself was clearly inspired by the Colonna, and was powerfully backed by King Robert of Naples. At the king's court were men like Dionigi di Borgo San Sepolcro, who had known Petrarch at Avignon.

Bishop Philippe Cabasolles was already a client of the king's and must have drawn Petrarch's name to his attention. By this time Petrarch had been emboldened by these friends to exchange letters with the king. In these circumstances, Robert, who lost no opportunity of affirming his devotion to culture, needed little urging to participate in a high-flown ceremony.

It was, of course, this invitation which Petrarch accepted: he set off for the Neapolitan court in February 1314. Here he was examined for three days by the king on his qualifications as a poet. Having satisfied himself that Petrarch was adequate for the role, the king gave him a robe to wear for the coronation, regretted that his health did not permit him to attend it in person, but appointed a representative to go to Rome to witness the ceremony. At Rome, on the Capitoline, he was presented with a privilege declaring him to be *magnum poetam et historicum* and citizen of Rome. Petrarch delivered an oration on poetry, and was then crowned with the laurel. From that moment his contemporary fame and material prosperity were assured.

In Rome he made friends with the da Corregio lords of Parma, and visited them in their home city before returning to Vaucluse. It was the first of the many friendships he was to form with the *signori* of northern Italy, and the very fact that he could now do so shows the new eminence which the laurel crown had bestowed upon him. For Petrarch the future was bright. The new pope, Clement VI, proved to be one of Petrarch's most generous patrons and, through the mediation of Cardinal Colonna, presented him to a rich selection of ecclesiastical posts: a canonry at Pisa (1342, resigned by 1365), a rectorate at Castiglione Fiorentino (1342), and a canonry and the archdeaconry of Parma (1347-8). In the following year he received another canonry at Padua, and later Innocent VI was to give him a canonry at Monselice, near Arquà, and some other benefices. Moreover, in 1352, he secured a canonry at Verona for his illegitimate son, Giovanni, then aged 15.

These posts made Petrarch a free and comparatively wealthy man. He was no longer dependent upon Colonna patronage though in these years he still carried out certain tasks for them. In 1342 he wrote to Pope Clement on their behalf suggesting a return to Rome; in the following year he served on an embassy for Cardinal Giovanni at the court of Naples. But he was now able to give fuller rein to his admittedly somewhat ambiguous sympathies for Cola di Rienzo, the arch-enemy of the Colonna in Rome. By 1347 he felt secure enough to criticise Cardinal Giovanni in a private epistle. Only those with little knowledge of human nature will be surprised to learn that Petrarch here accused his former patron of ingratitude.

Had wealth and position alone been Petrarch's goals, he could have risen still further in the ecclesiastical world. Clement VI repeatedly offered him both a papal secretaryship and a bishop's mitre; and the offer of the secretaryship was revived later by Innocent VI. Alternatively he could have accepted that offer of a professorship in the university of Florence, which Boccaccio conveyed to him. But his ecclesiastical benefices preserved him from having to seek onerous posts. There are reasons for thinking that he might have been tempted by the offer of a cardinal's hat, but this never came. As it was, by the early 1350s he was free to devote himself almost exclusively to letters.

He was also able by now to leave the hated 'Babylon', and to return to live in Italy. In 1343–5, and again in 1348–1351, he had visited the peninsula and cultivated the *signori* of the north. Then in 1353 he accepted the invitation of Archbishop Giovanni Visconti, Lord of Milan, to settle in that city. He was to stay there for eight years. The Visconti assigned him a house at the edge of the city, looking over green fields to the distant Alps, and promised him what he sought, freedom and solitude. It was an arrangement which brought benefit to both parties. For the rulers of Milan the presence of the most widely acclaimed intellectual in Europe was a notable status symbol. By now Petrarch enjoyed a very wide fame. When the laureate poet acted as godfather to Bernabò Visconti's son, wrote metrical epistles in praise of his rule, and delivered the funeral panegyric of the Archbishop Giovanni, he was bestowing a real prestige upon the family. In other ways too he served their purpose: as orator in embassies to Venice, to the Emperor Charles IV at Prague and Mantua, to John II at Paris; and as their direct propagandist in his writings. For the Visconti he wrote to the French court and the Imperial Vicar, delivered orations in praise of their military victories, and made attacks on their enemies: those Pavians who resisted Visconti conquest, and, rather surprisingly perhaps, his former friend, Pandolfo Malatesti, Lord of Rimini. When his Florentine friends had protested to him that in residing at Milan he would be serving the interests of 'tyrants' and enemies of their city, they had much justice on their side. In brushing away these pleas with the observation that he was completely free, he was perhaps being disingenuous. A less tactful but truer answer would surely have been that he saw no reason to adapt his private interests to the state interests of that commune which had expelled his father from it in shame.

These private interests were real enough. For his part, Petrarch acquired from his association with the Visconti a pleasant home and a freedom to study and write, which were only rarely broken into by the claims of state. Most important of all, he gained a new entrée to the great of the world, and so a new foundation for the building up of the fame which he sought so avidly. Believing, inaccurately as it happened, that he might have influence with the rulers of the great Visconti domains of Lombardy, statesmen and cardinals treated him with a new respect. He had always written to these men, solicited their attention; now they replied. His relations with the Emperor are revealing. He had addressed an epistle to him in February 1351, and then again in 1352. No reply. Then in November 1353, five months after the poet's arrival in Milan, there came an imperial answer to the 1351 letter. The timing of the reply, one may suspect, was not caused by any delay in the posts, but by a suspicion of Petrarch's influence in the signorial world. It was Petrarch's association with the Visconti which allowed him to form a literary friendship with the imperial chancellor, persuaded the Emperor to receive him in audience, and secured his appointment as Count Palatine and Councillor.

In later life Petrarch estimated that he had lost only seven months of his life in the service of princes, and these all in the service of the Visconti. It was perhaps the feeling that he could gain still greater independence and freedom which now persuaded him to leave Milan. In part too he was driven on by natural restlessness, and perhaps by consideration of the possible dangers implicit in being linked too closely with any one dynasty. In 1361 he left Milan and took up residence in the cathedral close of Padua, then under the rule of Francesco da Carrara. On this occasion his stay was brief, for in the following year he decided to establish himself at Venice. In 1362 he proposed to the Grand Council that a house 'not large, but respectable' be given to him for his books and himself, suggesting that after his death his books should remain there to serve as the nucleus of a public library. The council replied that 'for the honour and fame of our city, that offer made by Francesco Petrarch, whose fame in the whole world is such that within the memory of man there was not for a long time and is not among Christians any moral philosopher and poet who can be compared with him, shall be accepted . . .' A house was assigned to him on the Riva degli Schiavoni, and here he was to make his home for the next six years.

Then in 1368 he returned to Padua. Perhaps the indifference of the new Doge, with whom he had little contact, had something to do with the change, perhaps the presence of too many younger scholars at Venice, who regarded him with less than the overwhelming hero-worship to which he had become accustomed. He was exceptionally thin-skinned, and the casual remark of some Venetian patricians that 'he was a good man but wanted learning' had, for all its absurdity, wounded him deeply. In the signorial courts they were more accustomed to flattery. At Padua the Lord Francesco gave him a country property at Arquà in the Euganean hills. Here he had a house built, south-facing, amidst vines and olives, where he resided until his death in 1374.

On his deathbed Petrarch could look back upon a career in literature whose success was unparalleled in the middle ages. His wealth was not, as he repeatedly pointed out, excessive. His annual income, estimated at the equivalent of over 400 florins, was not as great as the controllers of the great banking houses, the cardinals of the papal *curia*, or the more eminent lawyers of the day. Yet his self-description as living in 'a fortunate mean between poverty and riches' was rather less than the truth. It was true that as his wealth grew, his expenses grew with it. Yet he lived with an assured revenue from ecclesiastical posts for which he was compelled to do no work, with two pleasant properties in France and Italy, respectively, plenty of servants, five or six copyists, a picture by Giotto, a large and expensive library, and his surviving child well provided for. Few writers today would ask for more. If he had wanted riches in themselves he could always have accepted the invitation of the Emperor to Prague, of King John to Paris, or of the Popes to Avignon.

In addition, he had gained, and this was more important to him, an outstanding reputation. Even in distant England the fame had spread of:

> 'Fraunceys Petrak, the lauriat poete,
> ... whos rethorike sweete
> Enlumyned al Ytaille of poetrie.'

Already in 1350, on visiting Arezzo, he was gratified to learn that the commune had decreed that no alteration should be permitted to the house in which he had been born. Private admiration went further. The Florentine humanist, Francesco Nelli, for instance, wrote in 1350: 'I see you as pefect, you do not seem a mere man ... you are for me in heaven and I long to have you descend to me on earth ... you are Parthenias, the virtuous one. You have no avarice, pride, ambition, anxious concern for earthly things'. In less-learned milieux the same sentiments were expressed. Not without some complacency, Petrarch himself has described how Enrico Capra, goldsmith of Bergamo, had come to 'worship' him, turning his house into a virtual Petrarchian museum, filling it with mementoes, pictures, and copies of his writings. Under this inspiration he had given up his trade and had come to devote himself to study. In response to repeated requests Petrarch resolved to grace his humble admirer with a visit. He was received at the gate of Bergamo by the governor, officials, and a large crowd, was invited to stay in the Palazzo Comunale or in the houses of the nobility, but decided instead to rest with the reverent goldsmith who had made such extravagant preparations for his coming. The bed in which he slept, he was assured, had never before been lain upon by man, nor would ever be used in future. As for the goldsmith: 'He seemed to have reached the absolute peak of his dearest hopes and to be meta-morphosed by joy.'

There were dangers in all this, noticeably the possibility that Petrarch's head would be turned or that the image would engulf the real and private person. Yet Petrarch's eminence and the fame he achieved did much to raise the esteem in which letters and learning were held. If princes vied for his favour, if the Emperor took him by the hand, they were not paying tribute to one man alone. In securing his social position Petrarch was campaigning, whether he knew it or not, for all his humbler colleagues and successors too. His careful cultivation of patronage made the way smoother in their struggle to earn a living from their pens.

It remains to be asked how, if at all, the patronage which Petrarch exploited came to affect his writing. Probably it made little difference, for socially and politically he was largely a conformist, and therefore fell easily into the clientage system. The embarrassment of patronage, however, did make for a certain disharmony between his life and writings which contrasts forcibly with the career of Dante, and led sometimes to certain inner inconsistencies within the total body of his work. Behind the moral philosopher the figure of the absentee pluralist looms uncomfortably. His violent attacks upon the alleged corruption of the papal court in the *Epistolae sine nomine* do not read easily together with the humble letters he addressed to the *curia* in the hope of advancement. His public praise of living popes clashed harshly with his private denigration of them after death. It has been suggested that the *Epistolae sine nomine* were primarily dictated by his fury at being refused a cardinal's hat. More probably they resulted from a feeling that the demands of gratitude become over a long period burdensome, and the instinct to seek for pretexts to shuffle them off.

A Footnote on 'men of letters'

To many the contemplation of the private lives of artists is attended by disillusion. This is the more particularly so when these lives are considered from the point of view of the individual s social and economic development. Admirers of *A la recherche du temps perdu* are disappointed to find that Proust's letters treat obsessively with the rise or decline of his investments in steel. When they learn that these were prospering they find it difficult not to turn against him.

Certainly a Dante without hatred, a Boccaccio at peace with his patrons, a Petrarch without vanity, would all doubtless have been more pleasant people. In particular, as it is often urged, a Petrarch less skilled in securing the friendship of the great, would have been altogether more amiable. But there is an extraordinary triviality in such considerations. The story of Petrarch's inner life is of a man in whom the instincts of humanity eventually triumph over the isolation and reserve of genius, and this coexists with the history of his social triumphs. Yet even this is perhaps not the true story, which is to be found in his writings and the influence he had upon European thought and letters.

This is not to say that consideration of the artist's social circumstances is unimportant. First reflections upon the careers of these three men will perhaps lead us to conclude that they had almost nothing in common. It is perhaps interesting, psychologically, that all three had step-mothers, but one would hardly base a theory of creativity upon such a chance. Yet there is one important generalisation one can make from them. All three men, starting, admittedly, from a bourgeois base, had no difficulty in carving out for themselves a position in society where they had ample leisure to devote themselves, almost exclusively, to letters, and where they were able at the same time to attain an acceptable bourgeois standard of living. Both Petrarch and Boccaccio, if they had been willing to sacrifice their leisure, could, in addition, have become very wealthy indeed in the papal secretariat. For genius, at least, there was, in the fourteenth century, great fame, and a standard of living in which the writer could live at ease.

PART THREE

Italian Culture and Society in Transition (c. 1380–c. 1420). The Environment of Art

ten

Social and Cultural Change
1380–1420

Art and Literature

The period 1380–1420 forms no anti-climax to the story of fourteenth-century culture. Although disappointing in some aspects, noticeably in literature and painting, it is difficult to take seriously the contention sometimes advanced that we are faced here with 'an inner exhaustion of creative forces'. Italy achieved much in this age, while at the turn of the century the foundations were laid and extended for new triumphs in the *Quattrocento*. In art it was the 'International Style' (otherwise 'International Gothic' or '*weicher Stil*') which dominated the peninsula. The cosmopolitan city of Milan absorbed and developed the styles current in the northern courts of Paris, Dijon, Cologne, and Prague. Gothic was stronger here in 1400 than it had been a century before and emphasis was now laid upon a chivalric decorative world of courtly splendour where realism and idealisation consciously blended. This is seen at its best in the manuscript illuminations of the *ouvraige de Lombardie*, whose finest practitioners were Giovannino de' Grassi (recorded 1389, 1396, dead by 1398) and Michelino da Besozzo (worked 1394–1442). Their pictorial illustrations of plants and animals, with intense concentration upon natural detail, look forward to the sketchbooks of Leonardo da Vinci. In larger works too the style has its triumphs in northern Italy with Gentile da Fabriano (1360–1428) and the young Pisanello (1395–*c.* 1455). Even in the bourgeois environment of Tuscany the International Style influenced painting. But it could never be fully harmonised with the Florentine preoccupation with form. Only the Camaldolese monk, Lorenzo Monaco (*c.* 1370–1424), with his two-dimensional, dreamlike exoticism, was able easily to draw inspiration from this source. Among his Tuscan contemporaries Taddeo di Bartolo (recorded 1386, d. 1422), Spinello Aretino (recorded 1385, d. 1410), and many others, were driven by its influence into a rather clumsy eclecticism.

In sculpture the International Style had easier triumphs. This is the age of the subtle ivory and bone carvings of the Embriachi school of Venice, the heavier effigies of the dalle Masegne brothers, and, in Tuscany, the earlier works of Jacopo della Quercia (1374–1438) and Lorenzo Ghiberti (1378–1455). It was an important period too for ecclesiastical building. The cathedrals of Milan, Monza, and Como were all begun in this period, as were the Charterhouse of Pavia, the 'Flamboyant' churches of S. Zanipolo and S. Alvise in Venice, and the great temple of S. Petronio at Bologna. In secular architecture Bartolino da Novara introduced a more lavish style with his castles for the Este family at Ferrara and the Gonzaga at Mantua.

More than this it is a period which sees the first impulses towards a new visual world. Here, once again, the developments which were to be most fruitful for the future were found in Florence. By 1420, Ghiberti was nearing completion of the second set of Baptistery doors. Donatello and Nanni di Banco were seeking a classical spirit in the treatment of the human body. Brunelleschi had drawn plans for the dome of the cathedral and was intriguing for their adoption. Masolino was instructing Masaccio in those techniques which were to restore the monumental to painting. The sense of the third dimension which Giotto and Duccio had brought to art was intuitive; with the artists to come in the fifteenth century, with Brunelleschi and Alberti, this vision was to be given consistent scientific expression and applied to the techniques of full perspective. Moreover the ever-growing influence of classicism was to drive them to a search for a complete naturalism which would have been alien to the spirit and taste of Giotto and his contemporaries.

In Italian literature it is easier to accept the idea of a decline. Sacchetti's verses on the death of Boccaccio seem all too true:

Or è mancata ogni poesia
e vote sono le case di Parnaso.

('Now all poetry is lacking and void are the houses of Parnassus.')
Despite the interest of Sacchetti himself, versifier and writer of
novelle, and a few contemporaries of equal stature, there was a
considerable decline. Yet this loss, in a certain sense, is to be balanced
against the work of the 'civic humanists': Coluccio Salutati (1330–
1406), Leonardo Bruni (*c.* 1370–1444), and their circle. These men,
building upon the foundations of the previous generation, were to
introduce and diffuse an influential reinterpretation of the classical
world. At the same time, first among the Florentine humanists,
and then in northern Italy, the study of Greek literature was initiated.
The propaganda of these men in favour of the utility of classical
studies and the desirability of a just appreciation of the classical
world was to be of deep importance for the future of European
culture.

The Economy

The economic background to the culture of the age is obscure.
Although it is generally recognised that there was a contraction
of the economy in the 1340s and in the decades immediately following, the position of Italy at the turn of the century is still the object
of controversy. Some scholars maintain that the peninsula did not
recover from the Black Death until the sixteenth century. In Italy,
following this thesis, the period 1340 to 1500 was an era of slump, and
the economic situation of 1500 was much less healthy than that of
1300. Certainly, from 1380 to 1420, plague continued. There were
severe outbreaks in 1382 to 1384, 1398 to 1400, 1407, 1409 to 1412,
and 1417. These must have prevented any restoration of population by
1420 to pre-1340 levels and have eliminated the effects of that increase in fertility which normally follows demographic disaster.
It is true too that many areas declined economically. In the south
agriculture contracted, a third of the villages disappeared and, as
man retreated, malaria advanced. Old towns such as San Gimignano

and Siena (whose population had fallen by the end of the century to below 15,000), once foci of international trade, now became local market centres. At Genoa, with the exception of the 1370s, there is real evidence of a catastrophic decline in commerce which lasted at least until 1400. In that year the city's turnover of trade was still probably less than half that of 1284.

Florence in the 1330s had a population of about 90,000; by 1427 it had fallen to about 37,000, of whom a third were too poor to be taxed. Whether Florentine commerce similarly declined is an object of some controversy. Among those who most strongly assert the hypothesis of continuous economic stagnation, Enrico Fiumi has attempted to link the pattern of economic change with social and cultural developments in the city. Following this thesis, the safe returns from state loans (which could be as high as 60 per cent) and from land (which were between 4 and 30 per cent) seemed preferable to the now highly speculative investments in trade (which yielded an average 12 to 15 per cent.) Consequently, he claims, capital was diverted from business into other channels, and as a result society came to be dominated by an élite which no longer possessed the predominantly mercantile sympathies which it previously had. Accordingly, for Florence the fifteenth and six-teenth centuries in terms of the economy made up 'a sunset rather than a renaissance'. At the same time, the cultural achievements of the fifteenth century, owed to the patronage of a few families, are contrasted with those of the fourteenth century which, he points out, can be considered as a product of the city as a whole.

However, Fiumi's hypothesis is not universally accepted. Against it can be placed the arguments of the schools of Cipolla and Melis who claim that already in the *Trecento* there appears strong evidence for a pronounced revival in economic activity. Certainly there was plague in the period, yet the attacks were much less dramatic than those of the 1340s to 1360s, and by and large men were coming to take them for granted. Perhaps population did decline, but commerce and industry revived, particularly in Lombardy. At Milan the cloth trade was growing and banking facilities expanded. From the mid-fourteenth century Milanesi merchants, for the first time, were found at the fairs of northern Europe, and new upper bourgeois dynasties appeared in society. In Lombardy there was a new agricultural revolution with the development of capitalist methods of farming and the introduction of rice cultivation.

At Venice, pursuing this argument, the position would seem to be favourable. At the beginning of the fifteenth century huge cargoes of spices, valued at 200 ducats or over, were still arriving from Alexandria and Beirut, while from 1376 the commune had begun to organise regular sailings of convoys to England. In the 1430s a Venetian statesman could assert that the port possessed 45 galleys, 300 ships of over 120 tons, and 3,000 lighter vessels, and that the ship-building industry of the Arsenal employed 6,000 workers. State securities in 1345 could be marketed at 100 per cent of their nominal value. In 1381 they stood at 18 per cent, but rose to 40 per cent in 1382 and to 63 per cent in 1400.

In Tuscany there are similar signs of renewal. Although the annual output of 'pieces' of cloth at Florence fell from 100,000 in 1309 to 10,000 to 19,000 in 1382, a recent historian has argued that the period 1360 to 1400 is the 'golden age of Florentine cloth', and that owing to the use of better (English) wool, the total cash value of the cloth output had actually increased within these years. New banking houses, the Medici in Florence from the 1390s, the Chigi in Siena, came to take the place of the old firms which had collapsed in the 40s. If Lucca lost her virtual monopoly of silk manufacture, Florence in Tuscany, and Milan, Venice, Genoa, and Bologna outside, had all begun by the end of the century to develop their own industries.

These conflicting interpretations of economic activity are paralleled by other conflicting theories of their supposed effects upon cultural development. Baron has claimed that humanism took root among the Florentine upper bourgeoisie in this period because its members were turning from commercial to industrial activity. Antal, by contrast, has claimed that the developments of the age are to be explained by a bourgeois withdrawal from industry.[1] The known facts are hardly adequate to support either contention, and industrial capitalism itself, it should be added, was always of very much less importance than financial in the Florentine economy. In seeking to resolve the clash of evidence in the wider field and in attempting to decide whether this was a period of depression, the most one can hope for is an informed guess. This might be that in Italy economic production was still by 1420 below its level in the 1290s. Yet in certain cities and in certain areas there had been significant advances and, in all, the position was not too gloomy. For though there may have been a decline in capital and production, this is likely to have been offset by an even greater demographic decline. Accordingly less goods were being produced in general terms, but more *per capita* to the now smaller population. Thus at the beginning of the fifteenth century there might be greater individual prosperity than at the time of earlier economic expansion. (So, for comparison, individual prosperity is greater in Britain today than in the 1860s, though the economy is expanding at a much slower rate.) Certainly, when considering the patronage of art, it is clear that some governments could still draw upon very large taxable resources, and that individuals could still make large fortunes.

The Great Schism and the Political World

In this period the life of the peninsula was greatly disturbed. In 1377 the Papacy had returned from Avignon to Rome. Yet in the following year a disputed election caused Europe to be split between the authority of two rival ecclesiastical heads and organisations. In Rome Urban VI and his successors commanded the allegiance of England, the Italian governments, and the Emperor. At Avignon Clement VII was given the support of France, Scotland, and the Iberian kingdoms. In this, the Great Schism, which was to be complicated by the election of a third pope at Pisa in 1409, and which was to endure for some 40 years, the authority, prestige, and power of the institutions of the papacy were greatly weakened. Theorists within the Church, 'the conciliarists', argued against the monarchical claims of the popes, while practical politicians exploited its divisions

16 Bonino da Campione, *Statue of Bernabò Visconti* (before 1363)

17 Michelino da Besozzo, *Giangaleazzo Visconti crowned by the child Jesus*

18 Detail from Lippo Vanni, *Battle of Val di Chiana* (1373)

for their national or party ends. The Church was to be united again only by the Council of Constance, held from 1414–17.

At the same time Italy was convulsed by great political struggles. The most important of these was the clash between the expansionist aims of the two leading powers of the peninsula: the Visconti and the Republic of Florence. In 1375 Florence abandoned her old alliance with the Papacy and for three years waged 'the war of the Eight Saints' against the Popes, a war which intensified already deep anti-clerical currents in the city. Turning to territorial aggrandisement, Florence absorbed Arezzo in 1384, and from then on pressed south, against Siena, north against Lucca, and east against Pisa. This policy was described by her humanists, and has been thought of by some modern historians, as an attempt to preserve the freedom of Italy. Putting the most favourable construction on Florentine actions in this period, however, her real aims seem to have been to acquire Pisa (conquered in 1406) and thus to become a maritime power, to secure hegemony in Tuscany, and to prevent domination of the peninsula by any other government.

These territorial ambitions hindered Florence considerably in her attempts to deal with the Visconti. Her neighbours looked upon her policy with alarm and in the ultimate analysis decided that they preferred the rule of Milan. At the same time within the commune the already oligarchic bias of the constitution was still further narrowed. From 1382 control passed to elements in the *Popolo Grasso*, the great capitalists of the city, dominated by Maso degli Albizzi until his death in 1417, and then by his son, Rinaldo, from 1417 to 1434. The appearance of popular rule was maintained, although the government itself was directed by, and in the interests of, a small class—some 30 families—of extremely rich men.

From 1385 the lands of the republic's greatest rival, the Visconti family, were held under the single rule of Giangaleazzo, son of Galeazzo II. These territories included Milan, the great city with its substantial industries, the rich agricultural areas of the upper Po valley, Pavia, an important banking centre, Como, Brescia, Bergamo, much of Piedmont, a semi-feudal world, and the primitive pastoral communities which controlled the passes through the Alps. An intellectual and a solitary, Giangaleazzo combined knowledge of the academically fashionable astrology with a real taste for illuminated manuscripts. Without the cruelty of his family, temperate and prudent in action, punctilious in the forms of religious observance, he was yet mastered by an ambition which placed no bounds upon the means necessary to its achievement. That brutality of expression and those menacing eyes in the sketch attributed to Pisanello suggest the true image of the man within.

From 1385 to 1388 he advanced into Eastern Lombardy and the Veneto. His progress alarmed Florence; attempts at formal recognition of mutual areas of influence failed; and for all the period 1390 to 1402 the two powers were either at war or in a state of armed truce in preparation for war. It was a conflict in which, while he lived, Giangaleazzo held the upper hand. Extending his influence deep into Tuscany and Umbria, he was recognised as *signore* of Pisa (in 1399), of Perugia (early 1400), of Cortona, Chiusi, Spoleto, Assisi, Siena, and, to the south-west of Florence, of Massa and Corneto. In June 1402 he was hailed as Lord of Bologna. Florence was surrounded by a strong ring of Visconti power and the arteries of her commerce were about to be cut. At this moment of imminent disaster she was saved only by the death of her enemy. When Giangaleazzo died (3 September 1402) the power which he had created collapsed. His son, Giovanni Maria (1402–12), incapable, and faced with the economic exhaustion of his territories, could do nothing to prevent the disintegration of the empire his father had built up. Only with the accession of Filippo Maria (1412–47) was Milan once again able to dominate Lombardy. It was to be another 20 years before she could effectively challenge the power of Florence.

Till then the Florentine oligarchy had little to fear from its rivals. Their propagandists sought to arouse the same fears against King Ladislaus of Naples that they had tried to evoke against Giangaleazzo, and to suggest that he too was seeking an Italian kingdom. But his actions are more easily interpreted as a defence against French pretensions to his crown, and certainly, after his defeat at Roccasecca in 1411, he presented no menace to the republic. Elsewhere in Italy,

Venice seized the opportunity of Giangaleazzo's death to expand on the mainland. Turning from the sea for the first time, she occupied Padua, Verona, Vicenza, and the Trevisan Marches. Meanwhile Genoa, her old rival, defeated in the war of Chiogga, fell to France. French influence was particularly strong in these years. The claims of the French line of the Angevins upon the Neapolitan kingdom caused them to build up their Italian connections. Duke Louis I of Anjou invaded Italy (1382–4) in an attempt to dispossess Charles III of Naples, and was followed by his son, Louis II, in an equally unsuccessful attack upon King Ladislaus in 1411.

Giangaleazzo had been married to Isabelle de Valois, a sister of King Charles v of France, and accordingly was related to the Dukes of Berry and Burgundy. His daughter, Valentina, married Louis of Orleans, brother of King Charles VI. These contacts with the northern world contributed something to the vogue of the International Style which radiated north and south of the Alps from the Visconti court and provide the best social explanation for its success in this age. It has also been suggested, though in passing and without attempt at detailed treatment,[2] that it should be seen as a self-assertion of European aristocratic sentiment. Following the serious proletarian revolutions of the 20 years between 1365 and 1385 (the Jacquerie in France, the Peasants' Revolt in England, the *Ciompi* in Florence and Siena) the aristocracy, the argument runs, had been forced to replace feudal ideals by a new economic philosophy borrowed from the upper bourgeoisie. Precisely because of this, the nobility looked with nostalgia to the spirit of chivalry present in the International Style and were followed in this by a bourgeoisie attempting to ennoble itself. All this seems somewhat far-fetched and the historical aspect of the thesis cannot in any way be documented. It is particularly difficult, for instance, to see in what way 'feudal' ideas were replaced by 'a new economic philosophy' at this time.

Changes in Humanism

In 1392, at a time of temporary truce between Florence and Milan, Coluccio Salutati, chancellor of Florence, wrote to Pasquino Capelli, secretary to Giangaleazzo, of the bonds between the two men:

> God does not wish that the errors of our rulers, who threw land
> and sea into confusion by war and set at risk themselves and their
> states, should succeed in breaking the chain of reciprocal affection
> between us. Speaking for myself I know only that the more the
> war raged the more I thought of you. I will not hide from you
> my fear then that the madness of our rulers might, to the profit
> of other nations, bring ruin to these two pillars of Italy.[3]

When the war resumed and the struggle between the two powers
grew more bitter, this spirit of friendship between fellow scholars
was not lost despite the propaganda attacks upon each other which
their masters commissioned from them. Salutati's political *Invective*
against Capelli's successor, Antonio Loschi, changed nothing. Loschi
continued to speak of Salutati as his master. The Florentine, Bruni,
in his turn found no difficulty in dedicating to Loschi his translation
of the *Phaedra*. The political passions in these attacks and counter-
attacks upon each other were produced at a surface level and did
not engage their whole personalities. Salutati himself, at the very
height of the war between Florence and the Visconti, divided
his time between writing public propaganda tracts in favour of
republican liberty and penning in his *De tyranno* a private defence of
Dante's monarchism.

This divorce between official writings and private sentiment may
lead one to doubt the claim of Hans Baron that it was the propaganda warfare of this era which led the Florentine humanists to a
single-minded and militant dedication to classicism. Might it not as
probably be asserted that their writings assumed their particular form
because their authors had already, under the influence of Petrarch,
become passionately devoted to the classics? None the less this
propaganda had a certain influence upon the development of
humanism. For the Milanesi humanists the themes to be used were
comparatively simple. Like Loschi and Manzini they could point
to the advantages of monarchy and empire, and claim that the
conquest of Italy by their master would destroy petty tyrannies

and restore the golden age of 'ancient Italy'. They could set 'the terrifying brigandage' of Liberty, equated with licence, against the *unmota pax* of single-person rule, and dwell upon the evils of Florentine oligarchic government. These topics were to a very large extent in harmony with the secular political concepts of the medieval world.

To counter these claims the Florentine humanists had to seek more original lines of argument. Part of their efforts here were purely mendacious. They claimed, for instance, that Florentine government sought merely the independence of other states, that within Florence there flourished a political order which fostered the liberty and equality of all, where rank depended not on wealth but on merit, and where all citizens were free to take part in government. The Florentines themselves on occasion blushed at these flights of fancy. In 1427, for instance, Poggio was writing: 'we who are born in free cities are accustomed to execrate tyrants. . . . Yet I would plead against that liberty in which injustice may take the place of justice and which serves the rich in private rather than the poor in public.' None the less, these men were putting forward an ideal, even if the ideal had little correspondence to reality. In addition to this they advanced other new theoretical concepts. They came, for example, to glorify the Roman history of the Republic rather than that of the Empire. They praised not the medieval hero, Caesar, but the republican hero, Brutus. As a result, they broke free from the medieval historical obsession with the idea of a divinely ordained empire and developed new historical perspectives. In order to justify the desire of the citizen to participate in government, they contrasted unfavourably the contemplative life, the life of the scholar withdrawn from the world, unmarried, and abstaining from participation in society, with the *vita activa*, the life of the intellectual who was linked by bonds of marriage to society and who participated in its political fortunes. Patriotism and civic life became objects of praise, and ethical thought was further secularised.

These ideals were not wholly new. In the thirteenth century Ptolemy of Lucca had written in laudatory terms of the Roman republic, and, in his younger days, at least, Petrarch had questioned the role of the Caesars. In an age which looked to St Augustine's *City of God* with deep reverence it was difficult to give an unreserved admiration to the traditions of the Roman Empire. Nor was there anything new in the claim that the scholar should be committed to an active life in society. It has already been seen how the Venetian chancellor, Benintendi, had contended that the entire object of humanist study lay in the preservation of republican freedom. Civic patriotism and the secularisation of intellectual life were as old as the commune itself. Yet such ideas had never before been brought together at one time and propagated with such intensity. As a result 'civic humanism' was created, a climate of thought which mirrored these ideals. Roman history came to be reassessed and the active life to be praised. This 'civic' humanism was not the only form of humanism in Italy or in Florence in this period, but for the following 50 years it was destined to be extremely influential.

Still more influential, ultimately, in establishing the character of European intellectual life was the development of Greek studies. It was something which Petrarch's cultivation of Latin literature had made inevitable. He himself, though praising *ex ignorantia* the superiority of Latin to Greek classicism, was aware that Greek literature lay behind and had a supremely powerful influence upon Latin. Although in the twelfth and thirteenth centuries a considerable body of Greek scientific and philosophic work had been translated, Platonic, historic, and literary texts had been ignored. (Dante explained the neglect of literature by pointing out the impossibility of translating poetry satisfactorily from one tongue to another.) Moreover, few Latin Christians knew Greek during the fourteenth century. In Apulia and Calabria, however, there were still areas where Greek was spoken and where the clergy owed allegiance to the Orthodox Church, and a Frankish nobility ruled in the Peloponnese. It was in contact with these areas that the West in the fourteenth century began its quest towards the discovery of Greek literature.

From 1341 until his death in 1348 a distinguished Byzantine intellectual and cleric, Barlaam, who had been born in Calabria, served out his exile from Constantinople, first at Naples, where he worked in the library of King Robert, and then at Avignon, where he met Petrarch. His pupil, Leonzio Pilato, another Calabrian Greek, was persuaded by Boccaccio to go to Florence between 1360 and 1362, and there in the university he translated and commented upon Homer, Euripides, and Aristotle. In this Boccaccio laid the foundations for the Greek studies of the following generation; it was the enthusiasm he generated which fired Bruni and his circle.

Their opportunity came when Manuel Chrysoloras arrived as ambassador to Venice in 1394 to seek aid for the Byzantine Empire against the Ottomans. Two Florentine members of the upper bourgeoisie, Roberto Rossi and Jacopo d' Angelo da Scarperia, sought him out there and began to learn Greek in his household. Jacopo followed him back to Constantinople in 1395. As a result of these contacts, Salutati sent Manuel an official invitation to teach in Florence. After holding a chair in the university from 1397 to 1400 he moved to Pavia until 1403, where under the patronage of Duke Giangaleazzo he collaborated with Uberto Decembrio in translating Plato's *Republic*. Following this he returned to Constantinople. Later, he travelled through France, England, and Spain (1408–1410), joined the Court of the Pisan pope John XXIII at Bologna in 1410, and followed its peregrinations to Rome, Florence, and then finally, in the year of his death (1415), to the Council at Constance. His influence was maintained by his pupils, notably Guarino Guarini who, after spending five years with him at Constantinople, returned to hold the chair of Greek at Florence from 1410 to 1414.

By 1420 knowledge of Greek literature was still confined to a very small circle of scholars. Yet already it had produced some important translations into Latin and had started to influence humanist thought and writings. Above all it was recognised now that for an understanding of the classical world a knowledge of Greek was essential. Although this new enthusiasm owed something to the patronage given by commune, *signoria*, and papacy, its principal stimulus was undoubtedly the tastes and propaganda of certain individuals.

Humanist Influence in Art and Italian Literature

The influence which humanism had already begun to exercise in art before the 1380s was strengthened in this period. At Padua the medallion effigies of Francesco I and Francesco II Novello da Carrara, produced around 1390, show a real attempt at portraiture modelled on Roman coinage. Some 12 years later the Duc de Berry in France possessed a copy of one of these medallions and bought four gold medals of Emperors from two Florentine merchants. Whether these Emperors were palmed off on him as genuine antiques (which they were not) or as original works of art in a classic vein is uncertain, but one of them, the Constantine medallion, was copied in his *Très Riches Heures du Duc de Berry*, the famous illuminated manuscript executed for him by the Limbourg brothers.[4] At Venice, the Sesti family, who for a century had worked as coin-makers, turned now to the introduction of ancient themes, producing coins with such motifs as the head of Galba, Perseus freeing Andromeda, and Androcles and the Lion.

In Florence, Niccolò Niccoli, who was one of the leading figures in the humanist movement, had a deep interest in ancient buildings (an interest which roused the contempt of his enemy, Guarino) and was a close friend of Ghiberti, Brunelleschi, and Lucca della Robbia. It was doubtless under his influence that Brunelleschi and Donatello made their journey to Rome to study the surviving antiquities. In the enthusiastic classicism of the Florentine humanists are to be found the origins of Donatello's imitation of classical forms and Brunelleschi's search 'to revive the ancient way of building'.

The influence of the new 'civic' humanism finds full expression in the allegorical frescoes painted by Taddeo di Bartolo in the antechapel of the Palazzo Pubblico of Siena (1413–14)[5] (see plate 9). In the lunettes at the top of the east and west walls are representations of the four 'political' virtues: Magnanimity, Justice, Prudence, and Fortitude. Below Justice are portraits of Cicero, Porcius Cato, and Scipio Nasica, three men who defended Republican civil life against tyranny. Below Magnanimity are Curius Dentatus, Camillus, and

Scipio Africanus, three military leaders of the Republic. Below Fortitude appears the biblical military hero, Judas Maccabeus, and below Prudence, the Sienese saint, the Blessed Ambrogio Sansedoni, who had persuaded Pope Gregory x to raise his interdict upon the town in 1273. Around all these figures appear 16 medallions containing portraits of other heroes of the Roman Republic.

On the south wall the figure of *Religio* fills the lunette above the main entrance. Although this image holds the figure of Christ, it is seated among pagan deities and is the symbol rather of the Roman civil and moral cult than of the Christian virtue of *fides*. Under the arch of the entrance there appear a map of Rome, the gods of war, Mars and Jupiter, and the civic deities, Apollo and Pallas. Below, on the right, Aristotle, the inspiration behind so much of the new secular philosophy of government and the symbol of human wisdom, points the moral in a *titulus*: 'Render just counsel like these men. Remain united and you will ascend to the sky with all glory as did the great people of Mars [the Romans] who obtained victory in the world.' Siena must seek the same unity and inspiration as the Roman Republic. Facing Aristotle, in the opposite wall of the arch, are the figures of Caesar and Pompey, no longer considered as heroes, but serving as a warning against those discords which ended the existence of the Republic and brought the tyranny of the Emperors to Rome.

The famous Romans here are not the Emperors and their servants, so popular in other towns, but are exclusively from the Republican period. This iconography seems closely related to the thought of Bruni's circle in Florence, with its exaltation of Brutus against Caesar and its praise of Cicero as a republican statesman. Pietro de' Pucci, one of the two men responsible for devising the scheme of the work, is known to have been in Florence in November 1413, and, as Professor Rubinstein has suggested, probably discussed the programme with Bruni.

Turning to literature, some contemporaries, such as Cino Rinuc-cini and Domenico da Prato, believed that the humanists of this age were hostile to Italian and that they despised the *volgare* writings of Dante, Petrarch, and Boccaccio. These views, taken up by nineteenth-century scholars who postulated a complete divorce between classical and *volgare* literature in this period, were much exaggerated. Many of the humanists wrote in both Latin and Italian and expressed admiration for the vernacular. Where humanist criticisms of the *volgare* occur they are insufficiently emphatic or continuous to be taken very seriously. Granting this, it should be added, however, that the ever increasing prestige of the classics inevitably minimised the influence of the vernacular. From the last years in which Dante was writing almost all intellectuals regretted that he had chosen to cast the *Divine Comedy* in Italian. Why, Giovanni di Virgilio asked him, throw pearls, prodigally, before swine, why clothe the Castalian sisters in unworthy dress? When the highest ideal for the educated became the writing of a pure Latin, many who might otherwise have written in the vernacular must have given themselves exclusively to the classics. The young man who learnt from Coluccio Salutati that Dante did indeed produce 'a most divine work' but that he would have surpassed Homer had he written it in Latin, was given a judgment against which only the strongest minded could stand out. The decline of Italian literature in this period, though it was but a temporary phase, is not unrelated to the rise of classicism.

If the Latin of the humanists had produced a Catullus or a Tacitus, the gain might have outweighed the loss. But for these men Latin was more dead a language than it was either for St Bernard in the twelfth century or for Erasmus in the sixteenth. Was a humanist study of classical Latin, however, as some have urged, necessary for the creation of a fully structured, flexible Italian language? (It is a kindred argument to that of the schoolmaster who urges that only those who have been exercised in Latin composition are capable of just expression in English.) It seems doubtful; even Boccaccio's *Decameron* followed the rhythms of the medieval *dictamen* rather than those of Cicero. None the less, the humanist's passion for the classical tongue was bound up with enthusiasm for the discovery of the classical world, and the one would not have been possible without the other. What the culture of Italy and

Europe may have lost in language from these 40 years, it gained in knowledge and understanding.

Papal and Governmental Patronage

However much Italy was ravaged by war in this period, governments still continued to spend money upon the arts. The Papacy was an exception, for the Roman popes had few resources. Boniface IX (1389–1404) made some changes in the defences of Castel Sant' Angelo and converted the Senate House at Rome into a fortress. But these works, together with some rather undistinguished tomb sculptures for cardinals, are the sole artistic monuments in the city from this period. In 1420 Rome was still a great field of ruins, with roofless churches and destroyed buildings. Even the portico of St Peter's had collapsed. None the less the Popes in Italy did much for humanism. Jacopo da Scarperia, Poggio, Bruni, Vergerio, and Francesco da Fiano, served in the *curia* of the Roman popes, Boniface IX and Innocent VII. Later, these men, together with Chrysoloras, Loschi, and Zabarella, served under the Pope of the Pisan allegiance, John XXIII. With the convening of the Council of the Constance (1414–17) humanists in the service of the three popes had opportunities for meeting each other. No greater number of intellectually eminent men, it has been said, had ever before been together for so long in one place. Constance, like Avignon, was a meeting place for Italian scholars and the northern world, and here Poggio, as papal secretary, seized the chance to search for manuscripts in the monasteries of Reichenau, Weingarten, and St Gall.

Among secular governments both *signorie* and commune were still the principal patrons of the arts. Within the principalities this patronage produced such varied and distinguished works as the medallions of the Carrara family at Padua and the tomb of Illaria, wife of the Lord Paolo Guinigi, executed by Jacopo della Quercia at Lucca. But the most eminent centres of signorial munificence were the courts of the Visconti, the Este of Ferrara, and the Gonzaga of Mantua. Ferrara under Niccolò II d'Este (1361–88) gave patronage to scholars and saw such impressive building works as the Castello, begun by Bartolino da Novara. A few years later the construction of the Palazzo Schifanoia was initiated though, like the Castello, its form was to be much changed in succeeding centuries.

At Mantua Francesco Gonzaga (ruled 1388–1407) was an important patron. The buildings around what is now Piazza Sordello were brought together in his reign to form the Palazzo Ducale, and the little Casa Giocosa was constructed near the cathedral. In the same period the dalle Masegne brothers, Jacobello and Pier Paolo, erected a marble façade upon the cathedral (now disappeared) and carved the monument to Francesco's wife, Margherita Malatesta Gonzaga. Here too, probably as the result of a vow made in time of the plague, Francesco caused the temple of the Madonna delle Grazie to be built in the years between 1399 and 1406. The beginning of this work (much changed today through subsequent alterations) is probably to be associated with Bartolino da Novara who was in Mantua from 1397 to 1401. It was he who from 1395 erected the castle of San Giorgio in the city, which developed the tradition of the Visconti castles of the mid-century and had much more the character of a princely dwelling than a military strongpoint. Lord Francesco's interests were not confined to the visual arts, for his library had 292 manuscripts. That 67 of these were French, as compared with only 33 in Italian, shows the long-enduring influence of French literary culture in Lombardy.

Within the republics too patronage flourished. At Venice government interests in the arts was more pronounced than ever before. At the end of the fourteenth century the northern façade of San Marco was refashioned. Its previously simple outline was crowded with pinnacles, tabernacles, finials, and pointed arches, which still today give it its incongruous sense of over-elaboration. Inside, the church was enriched with the vast iconostasis of the dalle Massegne brothers. The late fourteenth and early fifteenth centuries also saw the construction of the new façades to the Doge's Palace. Here again, the dalle Masegne sculpted elaborate capitals with the Drunkenness of Noah and the Temptation and Fall. Inside the building Pisanello and Gentile da Fabriano worked together between 1415 and 1420 on (now lost) frescoes in the Sala del Gran Consiglio.

At Bologna there was a temporary re-establishment of communal government in the last quarter of the fourteenth century, after the rule of a series of tyrants and papal officials. This event led to the building of one of the greatest of Italian churches of this period, the temple of S. Petronio. The decree of the Council of Six Hundred of 31 July 1390 proclaimed that the church was to be built because:

> we wish, with God's help, to prolong for ever the popular state and most happy liberty of this fair city of Bologna. By this means we and our descendants may more readily avoid that severe yoke of servitude which seems now yet more bitter through the joyful taste of the fresh liberty which God has brought us. For we believe that this was given not through human merits but through God's own mercy and through benign intercession of the [spiritual] protectors of the city. By this work, our God, through the intercession of Saint Petronio, the perpetual protector and defender of this city, may incline more intently in his clemency to the protection, defence, and perpetuation of this liberty and popular state.[6]

In this period churches were still being built as the visible symbol of a particular form of government, and of a government which still invoked 'our God' and 'our protector' in its aid. The building proceeded until 1410 when the city fell under the domination of Pope Alexander v who looked with hostile eyes upon this manifestation of civic independence. The work was then stopped, and the materials gathered for it sold and dispersed. It was only to be resumed later in the century with the coming of the Bentivoglio family to *signoria.*

At Siena, whose population and prosperity had much declined in this period, there were plans at the end of the 1380s for rebuilding the Campanile and for creating an adjacent Campo Santo or burial place on the model of that of Pisa. These came to nothing. But during the first two decades of the fifteenth century the *opera* was again busy. In this period Taddeo di Bartolo, Giovanni Fei, Andrea di Bartolo, Spinello Aretino, and other painters executed frescoes in the cathedral and in the Communal Palace. In the *Campo,* Jacopo della Quercia sculpted the Fonte Gaia at a cost of 2,000 florins. Inside the Duomo, Fra Ambrogio Biondo was commissioned to produce stained-glass windows, and Ginevra di Piero to embroider altar cloths for the high altar. At the Baptistery the font was built and Lorenzo Ghiberti entrusted with the execution of two of the panels set within it.

Still at the end of our period the contracts show a community filled with pride and love for its cathedral as a symbol of the community itself. It is the spirit in which the Master of Works for 1407 petitioned the government for a new sacristy. The one at present standing, he complained, would not be good enough for a village church; so praiseworthy and honoured a cathedral should have in its place a sacristy, 'great, beautiful, and honourable, as the beauty of your church demands'.[7] Looking back from that time the government and men of the commune could have reflected that, despite the setbacks of the 40s and 50s, the sacrifices they had made for 'their church' had given to the city something of permanent worth by which they would be remembered among future generations.

Among the republics however the patronage of Florence was still supreme. In this era its principal fruits lay in the fields of humanism and in sculpture. At the cathedral, under the direction of the *Arte della Lana* (wool guild), teams of sculptors (Giovanni di Ambrogio, Pietro di Giovanni Antonio and Nanni di Banco, Donatello, Ciuffagni, Niccolò Lamberti, and others) worked on the statuary for the Mandorla Gate, the third storey of the Campanile, and the third storey and main portal of the façade. At Or San Michele the guilds combined in the first decade of the fifteenth century to fill the 13 vacant niches within the supporting piers with statues, thus completing a project first planned in 1339. In the same period the *Calimala* (cloth guild) arranged for the completion of the chapel of Niccolò Acciaiuoli at S. Maria Novella and the church of S. Domenico at Fiesole.

The most interesting incident in guild patronage in this period, however, was the competition, or *combattimento* as the sources more expressively put it, for the commission given by the *Calimala* for the new bronze doors of the Baptistery. Announced in the winter of 1400–1, applications to take part came from all parts of Italy. This preliminary field was narrowed down to seven contestants: Brunelleschi, Ghiberti, Niccolò Lamberti, Niccolò Spinelli from Arezzo, Simone da Colle, and two Sienese, Jacopo della Quercia and Francesco da Valdambino. Each was to execute a panel on the theme of 'The Sacrifice of Isaac', and the judgment was made on technical and on aesthetic grounds. At the end the choice lay clearly between Ghiberti and Brunelleschi, and it was only, apparently, after considerable acrimonious debate that in late 1402 or early 1403 the commission was assigned to Ghiberti.

With these projects the story of state patronage in Florence in this period comes to an end. But it was still the guilds who were pointing the way to the future. By 1420 the *Lana* had completed the drum above the crossing of the cathedral and was negotiating with Brunelleschi on his plans for the cupola. Already the silk guild was laying plans for the Ospedale degli Innocenti. A classical architecture was about to be born. With Donatello's David for the Mandorla gate (1405–9) and his St George, executed at Or San Michele for the armourer's guild (1417?), 'Renaissance' sculpture had come into existence. In the patronage of the new visual world of the fifteenth century the government-guilds were still influential, though by the 1450s it was more and more to be individuals rather than collective bodies that played the decisive part.

Signorial Individualism and Popular Community: The Cathedral of Milan

In some ways the pattern of future development in Tuscany can already be seen in this period in the story of Visconti patronage. Within the smaller *signorie* it was still possible in the fourteenth century to find that sense of community which we have discerned in the art patronage of the communes. But in the lordship of the Visconti, which extended over and transcended the local traditions of very different communes, and where loyalty was claimed by a distant *signore* rather than by a local city, this was lacking, and with it the communal and public patronage which it encouraged. Here the *signore* began to disassociate himself from the artistic demands of his subjects and to concentrate on satisfying his own social and aesthetic requirements.

By this time the real centre of Visconti patronage was the court and the *signore*'s library at Pavia. It was for the library that men such as Imbonate, Michelino da Besozzo, and that most versatile and talented of all North Italian artists in the century, Giovannino de' Grassi, produced the *ouvraige de Lombardie*. Their illuminated manuscripts, designed for the private enjoyment of the collector, make a striking contrast to the statuary in public places which the Florentine Republic commissioned in the same period. The library was a natural meeting place for the humanists of the court. Giovanni Manzini tells of discussions here 'in the notable library of our prince' between Pietro Filargo (the future Pope Alexander v) and Bartolomeo di Jacopo of Genoa on the theme of 'the superiority of men over women'. In the preface to his translation of Plato's *Republic* Uberto Decembrio wrote of 'the piety of that celestial prince, Giangaleazzo' who 'among his other splendid enterprises' had gathered together 'not only the most celebrated men of the world, but every type of book to which the greatest and holiest of the Greeks and Latins consigned the fruits of their divine minds'. This is a courtly overstatement. Although Giovanni di Ravenna and Vergerio praised the Duke's munificence, the most celebrated men of the time were not by and large at his court, and, as far as we know, there were only two Greek books in his library. But certainly the Visconti did give considerable private patronage to the learned world.

The private character of Visconti patronage appears again in their programme of church-building and decoration. In the governments of the communes it has been seen that the provision of churches for the citizens was almost treated as a major matter of state. To be fair the Visconti did not wholly neglect such works. Giangaleazzo probably had some part in the arrangements for the construction of the new tomb for St Augustine of Hippo in San Pietro in Ciel d'Oro at Pavia, and for the carving of the marble *paliotto* of the high altar of S. Astorgio at Milan. Moreover, he and his son, Filippo Maria, provided funds for the building of the Carmelite churches of Pavia (still unfinished in 1420) and of Milan (still unfinished in 1446).

But in general the ecclesiastical building of the family was confined to the erection of what were in fact huge private chapels. One example is S. Maria della Scala (from whose site the Opera house takes its name) built from 1381, in accordance with the wish of Regina della Scala, wife of Bernabò. Such too was the mausoleum and monastery of the Charterhouse of Pavia. It was founded by Giangaleazzo as the result of a vow taken by his wife Catherine in 1390. Endowed with large grants of lands and revenues in 1393, work upon it began in July 1395. The foundations were completed in 1402, and in 1409 the Embriachi workshop was being paid for its ivory and ebony altar triptych. Yet this impressive foundation (only completed in the second half of the fifteenth century) was, despite its magnificence, little more than the family church of the adjacent castle. Here, as before in the history of the Visconti connection with the arts, artists were occasionally pressed forcibly into service. For work within the castle of Pavia in 1395, Giangaleazzo compelled nine goldsmiths of the town to take employment with him.[8]

In cathedral building which engaged the principal attention of the governments of the communes, the Visconti showed much less interest. During the rule of Giangaleazzo there were at least five cathedrals whose buildings were restored or initiated within his territories: Vigevano (restored by Bartolino da Novara), Mortara (1375–80), Monza (façade completed 1396), Como (probably started in 1396, no work done 1402–50), and Milan itself. The Visconti were not actively hostile to these projects; they could not have taken place without the approval of the *signore*. So vast a creation as the cathedral of Milan, for instance, which involved the whole of society in its construction, could not have been begun without the consent of the ruler. In fact, Giangaleazzo did much for the building. He provided funds of 500 florins a month, gave exemptions, privileges, and exclusive use of the Candoglia quarries to the *Fabbrica*, and secured help from the Pope. But the real driving force behind the project was not the *signore* but the archbishop and people of the city. It is clear that any great enthusiasm the Duke ever had for the project soon waned. Disputes sprung up between him and the controllers of the Cathedral building about his employment of their 'engineers', workmen, and materials, in his own project, the Charterhouse of Pavia. In his will he left money for a church at Rome dedicated to S. Maria delle Nevi, and ordered the construction and endowment of chapels at Verona, Pavia, and elsewhere. Yet the Duomo of Milan was almost passed over in ostentatious silence. His only reference to it was to ask that a monument to his father, Galeazzo II, should be placed within it (a request which was ignored).

The building of the cathedral, together with a Camposanto and Baptistery (from 1394), can be attributed principally to the Archbishop Antonio da Saluzzo and to the citizens of Milan themselves. They had long considered it as a work necessary to establish the greatness of their city, for the old basilica of S. Maria Maggiore had been built in the twelfth century and the population of the city had outgrown its size. Moreover, it had been damaged by the fall of Azzone's campanile in 1353. To confront the enormous task before them without the whole-hearted support of the government, the citizens had virtually to create a government administration for themselves, modelled on the institutions of the commune over which the Visconti had triumphed. In 1386 a general council was convened of 100 'noble and prudent citizens' called 'Deputies to the Fabric'. Their numbers were increased to 200 in 1388, and to 300 in 1395. These men met together regularly with the Vicar and the Twelve of Provisions (the ordinary administrative body of the city), with Doctors of Law and the leading ecclesiastics, to decide upon the course and form of the operations to be undertaken. They also elected the engineers and principal permanent or semi-permanent officials who actually executed the work. By 1402 these included two business supervisors with a notary, two accountants, one paymaster, and two receivers of money with a notary.

In the archive of the *Fabbrica* in Milan one finds the first full documentation of the building of a cathedral. In the first place

money had to be raised from the citizens to supplement the archiepis-
copal revenues and signorial grant. Arrangements had to be made
for the collection of donations from the citizens. In some cases this
meant that the *Deputati* had to concern themselves with the administration and liquidation of large commercial enterprises, such
as that which the merchant Marcuolo Carelli bequeathed to the
Fabric in 1394. Carelli's businesses, valued at 35,000 ducats, involved
the administrators in such questions as the price of sugar at Venice,
the value of land leases in the *contado*, the finding of suitable markets
for the disposal of cotton, and the rates for the cashing of bills of
exchange. On other occasions they had to settle such trivial matters
as the complaint of a husband that his 'half-witted' wife had given
48 silver and gilt buttons to the Fabric without his consent. (They
were returned to him.) They had to arrange for the authorisation
of an indulgence from the Pope to raise money. This was an extremely costly transaction. Half the money raised went to the Pope
himself, in addition to the original 1,500 florins paid for the papal
bull. When the indulgence was preached and a priest was heard to
'say certain monstrous things' against it, they had to ensure that
he should only be released from prison on promising to be silent
about the subject in future.[9]

They had to arrange for the sale of gifts in kind given to the
cathedral and such delicate questions as what to do with the cloth
of gold given by the Queen of Cyprus. Friars who begged for the
cathedral had to be licensed and those who begged without licence
had to be imprisoned. Notaries drawing up wills had to be instructed
that it was their duty to inform the Fabric of all legacies made to it.
Constant record had to be made of moneys owing to the Fabric,
and all financial accounts submitted to strict audit.

Another major problem was the provision of materials. The marble
and granite required came principally from Monte Candoglia
above the Toce valley near Lake Maggiore, some 60 miles from the
city. Work here was generally supervised by the 'official and engineers in the district of Lake Maggiore'. Another 'official of the
mountain' exercised immediate control over the principal quarry.
Here the Deputies of the Fabric arranged for the lease of the castle

of Albo to house the labourers, for the building of a barracks at the foot of Candoglia (after lodging prices had risen at neighbouring Mergozzo), and for the building of an inn for their leisure. They even saw to such details as the provision of sheets and hempen mattresses stuffed with leaves for their beds. Arrangements had to be made for the import of glass from Germany, lime from the Alpine foothills, iron from Bonino and Brescia, charcoal from Angera, and oak from Mirasole. Transport presented difficulties. Although the granitoid gneiss of the Morena hills was much closer to the city than the quarries of the Val d' Ossola it was virtually impossible to use in an age when the transport of heavy goods along roads was extremely expensive. The Deputies had to draw upon the stone-works of the Lake Maggiore district. From Candoglia the barges transported the marble down the river Toce to Lake Maggiore, then down the Ticino to Abbiategrasso, and so along the canal of the Naviglio Grande to the Ticinese gate at Milan. Within Milan itself other canals ran to S. Stefano and the site of the cathedral. For all this the Deputies had not only to arrange contracts with conveyors and bargemasters; they had also to take an active interest in the inspection and maintenance of the whole transport system. Consequently, they were driven to alter the course of the Ticino river at certain points, to construct dykes and what seem to be primitive forms of locks within the city canal, and to build roads from the quarries to the barge-ports. In bringing the oak from the forest of Mirasole they had to arrange for the feeding of the oxen on the way.

A difficult problem for the Deputies was labour, skilled and unskilled. The Fabric had to solicit the services of engineers, sculptors, and craftsmen from all over Europe, to decide upon their wages and conditions of work, and to take the responsibility of dismissing them when necessary. They had to persuade the Duke to prohibit stone workers from leaving his lands without licence. They had to investigate the claims of those who offered machines which would cut down labour costs. In 1402 the Council advanced money to Antonio da Gorganzola and then to Francesco Pessano to construct a horse-operated stone cutter which, as they each claimed, would be able at the expense of three shillings a day to do one-third more work than four men paid together 13s. 4d. a day. In a similar way, the Deputies were called in February 1407 to consider Giovanni Clerici's claim that his new invention could reduce the numbers of men necessary for giving power to the organ from two to one. They had to feed their labour force, and attempt to secure from the Visconti exemptions from taxation payable upon the food and wine they brought into the city to do this.

Their most responsible task was to judge the merits of the various aesthetic and engineering projects put up to them by the rival cliques of foreign and Lombard experts whom they had called to their service. In addition to the building and embellishment of the church they arranged for the construction of an organ, the appointment of organists, the provision of a library, and regulations for library use. In all they were responsible for an enormous body of work which affected every level of Milanese society, and to achieve it they had to form themselves into a virtual government which expressed, as that of the Visconti did only doubtfully, the true aspirations of the Milanese people.

During the digging of the foundations from September 1387 representatives of, one day, a guild, on the next, a parish, would gather to make their oblations and then to give a free day's work to the Fabric. In this manual labour the guild of Armourers took their share on 17 September, the Judges and Notaries on 30 October, the Nobles on 7 November, and so on. At their lunch-breaks these men sat down side by side with the paid labourers and drank wine and soup from the same earthenware bowls and jugs. This involvement of the whole city, of all classes within it, in the building of the cathedral is brought out again in running down the lists of oblations made to the Fabric. Among those of the first week of November 1387,[10] for instance, we find:

1 November   from Franceschino da Carcano for the soul of
              his friend, Simpliciano—£ [Imperiali] 1. 12. 0.
              from collecting box at the door—£[I.] 33. 4. 0.
2 November   from officials of Milan who came to work for
              nothing—£[I.] 23. 6. 6.

in collecting box at S. Tommaso—£[I.]6. 17. 6.

3 November   from collection box at door—£[I.]25. 7. 6.

from collection box at S. Tecla—£[I.]15. 11. 0.

from Dimono Pessina and his wife and servants —£[I.]1. 9. 4.

4 November   in collection box at door—£[I.]45. 15. 6.

from Emanuele Zuponerio who bought back a fur given to the Fabric by the indigent Caterina da Abbiategrasso, and restored it to her—£[I.]1. 0. 0.

from the men of the administrative district of Porta Orientale who came to work for nothing—£[I.]426. 4. 3.

from a woman called Raffalda, a prostitute— £[I.]3. 4. 0.

5 November   from Giovanni da San Gallo who came with 25 masters and 50 labourers to work for nothing —£[I.]30. 5. 4.

in collection box at door—£[I.]13. 0. 0.

6 November   from the chancellor of the most illustrious lady Valentina, daughter of the most illustrious, magnificent, and high lord of Milan.—100 florins

from the priests of the Humiliati order from Vicoboldono and Mirasole and their servants who worked in the day for nothing— £[I.]25. 5. 7.

in collection box at door—£[I.]15. 7. 8.

7 November   in collection box at door—£[I.]8. 18. 0.

in collection box at S. Tecla—£[I.]2. 10. 0.

from nobles and noble youths of Milan who came to work for nothing—£[I.]272. 6. 4.

from Giovanni Fidele and the men from Vittorzino and from the robe-makers of Milan who all came to work for nothing— £[I.]12. 14. 8.

(In this period 32 shillings Imperiali were the equivalent of 1 Florentine florin.)

These records reveal the last of that civic spirit of the fourteenth century which enlisted all citizens in the task of making their city beautiful. Though the building of the church was to continue until the end of the eighteenth century it was only in these early years that the work retained its popular character. In the following century the ever-increasing predominance of the princes was largely to set aside that tradition in most fields of art and was to bring to the fore a culture produced, not by and for the community as a whole, but by and for powerful individuals. Despite all the achievements of the new art, despite too the recognition that the art of the *Quattrocento* was more truly 'aesthetic', concerned less with satisfying religious needs, one can still regret that the intimate link between the community and the world of art found in the fourteenth century had to pass away. One can still regret that the living relationship between the major work of art and the whole of society should have been broken by the new signorial art designed primarily for an élite.

eleven

The Artist in Society
I.   The Idea of the Artist

It is in the fourteenth century that the Italian artist can first be seen as an individual. For this period there is an increasing body of evidence about his daily life in the workshop, his apprenticeship and training, the art market, and the distribution of patronage, while the relationship of art to the intellectual world of the time and the changing state of the artist in society can be assessed in the writings of contemporaries.

An initial difficulty in this subject is the word 'artist', which has anachronistic overtones and which is used here only to avoid such inelegant alternatives as 'practitioners of the visual arts'. There are two or three passages in the *Divine Comedy* where Dante may be giving the word a value closer to the present-day sense, but normally in the fourteenth century *artista* (or *artifex*) is to be translated as 'artisan'. That this should be so reflects the social circumstances of the overwhelming majority of those who practised the arts. Most artists were recruited from the artisan class, and never rose above it. Their principal tasks were the painting of coats of arms, saddles, standards, caparisons, and so on; and for this sort of work they were paid and treated like artisans. It is not these men who are to be considered here, but rather those few who attained the greatest reputation and who were thought of as the leading painters or sculptors of the time.

In the early medieval world, two principal traditions of thought about the artist had rather uneasily co-existed. The first, which could be called the Ecclesiastical-Roman-Imperial, has been noticed when treating religious aesthetic (see pages 47–52). In the words of the second council of Nicea quoted there ('. . . the construction of images is not the invention of painters. . . .'), and in Gregory the Great's famous assumption that art was an activity particularly appropriate to the understanding of the illiterate, the artist is seen as an artisan, whose function was to illuminate the truths of religion, commanded and guided by the ecclesiastic. This view of the artist as a mere hand, subordinate to the directing mind of the priest-patron, also drew strength from the traditions of the Roman world. Here the artist had normally been a slave, and in consequence the visual arts had been excluded from the category of 'the liberal arts', those activities worthy of a free man. In his preface to the *Life of Pericles*, Plutarch casually remarked that no young man of good breeding who admired the statue of Jupiter at Olympia or of Juno at Argos would actually wish to become either Phidias or Polykleitos. Art could be admired, but not the artist.

Seneca, whose thought was so influential in the middle ages, had gone out of his way to remark that painting and sculpture were not primarily intellectual but rather manual activities, and were inherently servile. He would, he explained, no more include these within the liberal arts, than he would wrestling, perfumery, or cooking. In the Roman world even emperors had occasionally tried their hand at sculpture, and the cultivated society of the age of Pliny had indulged a passionate connoisseurship of the arts. Yet disdain for the artist himself had remained, and the distinction between the liberal arts and the mechanical arts, with painting and sculpture firmly in the inferior category, was taken up and schematized in the encyclopedias of the early middle ages. By the twelfth century this concept was a commonplace in scholastic discussions on the range of human activities.

However, another tradition was slowly developing which unconsciously challenged the official and dominant view of the artist. In the northern world a *topos*, derived ultimately from Pliny, became current. This was of the artist who 'far excels all others' and who, like Jehanz, the fabulous master artist and craftsman in

Chrétian de Troyes' *Cligés*, had a world reputation:

> *N'est terre, ou l'an ne le conoisse*
> *Par les oeuvres, qui il a feites.*

But in contemporary Italian literature this theme is absent, and the sole evidence for the new sentiment is found in works of art themselves. Yet these are revealing. As early as the eighth century Italian artists had acquired sufficient self-confidence in the value of their personal art to sign their own works. A ciborium in the church of S. Giorgio at Valpolicella, bearing the date 712, carries the prominent inscription: '*Ursus magister cum discepolis suis Juvinto et Juviano*'. As time passed these simple inscriptions were expanded. At the turn of the eleventh and twelfth centuries, for instance, the sculptor Wiligelmo placed a tablet in the façade of Modena cathedral bearing the words:

> Among sculptors how greatly are you worthy in honour,
> Now, oh Wiligelmo, your sculpture shines forth.

On the portals of Ferrara, and, in a very slightly different form, of Verona cathedral, a pupil of Wiligelmo, working in the 1130s, announced his own fame in a similar way:

> Coming together men will praise for generations
> That Niccolò the skilled *artifex* who carved these things.

On the tympanum of the Church of St Zeno at Verona he inscribed the words:

> Niccolò, the skilled *artifex* who carved these things,
> We all will praise, and we will ask the Lord Christ
> To bestow on him the high kingdom of heaven.

From this period inscriptions of this type appeared quite frequently in other centres in northern Italy, as they did at the same time in France. Obviously they were not just put up at the whim of the artist, but were permitted to him and approved by his patrons. It is clear that there already existed an admiration for art in itself as opposed to art as a cult object, and an admiration for the man who had produced it.

Yet, turning from the early middle ages to the period following the mid-thirteenth century, there are still very many suggestions that the visual arts were often little valued for their own sake. Some ecclesiastics, following a possibly mistaken interpretation of the Nicaean decree, looked to the arts for authentic historical images of Christ and the saints (see p. 48). With this assumption, the older the picture the better it must be, and artistic originality or individuality could only be seen as blasphemy. Even those who rejected this view considered the arts unworthy of intellectual examination. Philosophers ignored them. In the schools, following scholastic tradition, beauty itself was treated merely as a symbol or similitude of the divine. This is the attitude of Guillaume Durand's *Rationale Divinorum Officiorum*, a work which specifically and exhaustively discusses the decoration of churches, and yet shows a complete lack of interest in aesthetics. Durand's sole consideration is the symbolic meaning of the church itself, and of the paintings and images which adorn it. Though he acknowledges Pope Gregory's formula, he seems almost to suggest at times that art, rather than being a prop for the ignorant, should be an arcane, symbolic language for those extremely well educated in ecclesiastical rhetoric. Much of religious art in the fourteenth century was, of course, just that.

For followers of a different tradition, one which had been expressed by St Bernard in the twelfth century, art and artists were to be treated with a continuous reserve. Their views were given expression in what was for contemporaries Petrarch's most popular, because most conservative work, the *De remediis utriusque fortunae*, written between 1354 and 1367. In the *De remediis*, 'Reason' remonstrates with 'Delight' and with 'Hope' in order to induce a contempt for things of this world. So, when Delight speaks of his enjoyment of pictures, Reason replies:

Vain pleasure . . . Oh strange frenzy of a human soul, admiring all save He whom among all works not alone of art but of nature there is nothing more wondrous. . . . You dare not look up to heaven and you have forgotten the framer of the sun and moon, so great is your pleasure in examining most fragile paintings and you despise the route which leads on high and your mind flees the good yonder.[1]

When Delight persists, Reason answers again, suggesting, flatteringly enough, that this is a vice characteristic of higher spirits, and precisely because of that, it must be particularly resisted:

You delight in brush and colours in which both price and skill and variety and curious conjunction please. Here living gestures come from the lifeless, movement from immobile forms. Here are images bursting from their frames and the lineaments of breathing faces, so that you expect shortly to hear the sound of their voices. It is herein that the danger lies, for great minds are greatly taken with this. While the rustic passes these things with a brief, joyous surprise, the cultivated man is drawn to them with sighs and veneration. It would clearly be a laborious task, and not one for this work, to lay bare the origin and progress of this art, its miraculous works, the labours of its craftsmen, and the madness of princes who at enormous cost traded it across the seas and consecrated it at Rome in the temples of the Gods, in the chambers of the Caesars, in public squares and porticoes. This did not suffice them. They applied to it their own right arms and what in their souls was owed to greater matters, as before did the most noble philosophers of the Greeks. And so it was that for a long time among us, painting, as being closer to nature, was held in esteem before all the mechanical arts. Among the Greeks indeed it was considered to be in the first rank of the liberal arts. I pass over these things since they are not strictly in harmony with my aim of brevity or the present point. They could seem to feed the ill which I was promising to cure and, considered too closely, to justify the folly of those benumbed in this way. But as I have said the greatness of those who err takes nothing from the error . . . But as for you, if these feigned and fictitious things with their empty sweets still give delight, lift up your eyes to him who painted human bone with the senses, the soul with the mind, the heavens with stars, the earth with flowers, and spurn those *artifices* whom you admire.

In the following dialogue, when Delight remarks on his pleasure in statues, Reason is assured that since sculpture is more permanent, it is, if anything, more harmful than painting. Certainly it is no plebian taste: emperors have indulged it, while among the ancients the fame of sculptors was acknowledged, not just among the mob but in the writings of the élite. But all this serves to make the evil more pervasive. Again, is not the sense of pleasure here bound up with avarice? An admirable skill can be discerned in any craft at all. Is not, therefore, what one particularly admires in sculpture the cost and expense which has gone into it? To Delight's dying protestations, Reason finally replies:

> To take pleasure in men's abilities, especially of those who excel in skill, if done with moderation, is tolerable. So too to take pleasure in sacred representations which remind those who see them of heavenly blessings, may often be pious and may be a valuable incitement of the soul. But profane images, even though they may, now and then, stimulate and move to virtue by kindling lukewarm souls with the memory of noble matters, should not be equally loved and honoured lest they become witnesses of folly or agents of avarice or rebels against faith and true religion and against that celebrated command: 'Preserve yourself from images.' Assuredly if you should look from here to Him who made the solid earth, the moving sea, and the revolving heavens, and who gave not false but true things, living men, the beasts of the field, fishes of the sea, and birds of the air, I think that you would despise Protogenes and Apelles and Polykleitos and Phidias too.

All this is very literary; Reason has clearly been greatly influenced by a recent reading of the chapters on the arts in Pliny's *Encyclopaedia*. (In the following dialogue, Delight is reproved for his pleasure in Corinthian vases, hardly a major temptation to Italian souls in the fourteenth century.) More, these passages are pervaded by a deep, characteristically Petrarchian ambiguity. They are part of Petrarch's unceasing interior debate between the rival attractions of the austere Christianity embraced by his brother, the Carthusian monk, and the pagan world of the ancient texts. Yet what clearly emerges here, the more so in that Petrarch himself was obviously keenly responsive to the visual arts, is the old Christian distrust of aesthetic pleasure. There are echoes of St Augustine's suspicion of 'the various arts and crafts . . . vases, paintings, and every kind of statue, far exceeding any necessary and modest use or pious devotion.'

Petrarch's scorn here for art and the artist, though contrived, and existing, as will be seen, side by side with other sentiments, is found again in the commentaries written during the fourteenth century on the *Divine Comedy*. In discussing that part of the eleventh canto of the *Purgatorio* where, among the proud, Dante meets the miniaturist, Oderisi da Gubbio, the commentators show attitudes to artists which, in part at least, reflect the still pervasive influence of the Ecclesiastical-Roman-Imperial tradition. In these lines Dante first takes Oderisi as the symbol of that pride which is punished in Purgatory. At the same time he reflects on the fleeting glory of human achievement by comparing the contemporary fame of Giotto with the dimming memory of Cimabue.

> 'O' dissi lui, 'non sei tu Oderisi,
>   l'onor d'Agobbio, e l'onor di quell' arte
>   che 'alluminare' è chiamata in Parisi?'
> 'Frate', diss' egli, 'più ridon le carte
>   che penelleggia Franco Bolognese:
>   l'onore è tutto or suo, e mio in parte.
> Ben non sare' io stato sì cortese
>   mentre ch'io vissi, per lo gran disio
>   dell 'eccellenza, ove mio core intese.
> Di tal superbia qui si paga il fio;
>   ed ancor non sarei qui, se non fosse,
>   che, possendo peccar, mi volsi a Dio.
> O vana gloria dell' umane posse,
>   com' poco verde in su la cima dura,
>   se non è giunta dall' etati grosse!
> Credette Cimabue nella pittura
>   tener lo campo, ed ora ha Giotto il grido,
>   sì che la fama di colui è oscura.

*Così ha tolto l' uno all' altro Guido
la gloria della lingua; e forse è nato
chi l' uno e l'altro caccerà di nido.'*

('Oh', I said to him, 'are you not Oderisi, the honour of Gubbio
and the honour of the art which in Paris they call "illumination"?'
'Brother', he replied, 'the pages worked by Franco of Bologna
shine more brightly. It is his now, all the honour, and mine in
part. I would not have been so courteous as this while I lived,
through that great desire to excel on which my heart was set.
For such pride here [in Purgatory] we pay the price, and I would
not even be here were it not that having power to sin I turned
to God. Oh empty glory of human power; how briefly does
its freshness last at its peak unless it is followed by an age of
dullness! In painting Cimabue thought to hold the field and
now Giotto has the cry so that the other's fame is down. So
has the one Guido [Cavalcanti] taken from the other [Guido
Guinizelli] the glory of language; and perhaps there has been
born one [i.e., Dante himself] who will drive off both from the
nest.')

In discussing this passage the author of the *Ottimo Commento*,
which was written around 1333, remarked that the reader might
well be surprised that Dante here should give 'these rude mechanicals
[*artefici meccanichi*] honour and fame.' This remark was taken up
and developed further in Benvenuto da Imola's commentary written
some 40 years later:

And note this: that some through ignorance have been surprised
at this, and have asked why Dante should have named here unknown men of a low art, when he might more suitably have
referred to most excellent men, avid for glory, who had executed
beautiful and noble works of glory. In fact the poet has shown
here his great skill and best judgment, for in this he has tacitly
let it be understood that the appetite for glory is found indifferently
among all so that even small craftsmen have been eager to

acquire it. So we see that painters attach their names to works, as Valerius [Maximus] points out in his *De pictore nobili*.[2]

So far it has been said that, certainly up to the last quarter of the fourteenth century, there was still in Italy a current of thought which reflected a traditional, early medieval view of the artist as artisan. However, this was been overtaken by a new tradition. This can be seen from the commentaries on Dante just cited, which, after speaking of artists in derogatory terms, turn straightway to praise of the artist, Giotto, and to speak in Benvenuto's words, 'of the excellence of the mind and skill of this noble painter.' Already a new attitude has begun to appear, which will provide, up to the eighteenth century, the framework in which men were to develop their ideas of the artist's true role.

This development is heralded in the careers of two men, Giovanni Pisano and Giotto. Of Giovanni Pisano (recorded 1265, 1314; dead by 1319) we know very little. Yet everything we do know seems to reinforce his claim to be the first known artist whose emphasis upon his own personality makes him break out of the artisan world. His first appearance in our documents is in his father's contract with Siena Cathedral in October 1266, and it seems to reflect a characteristic waywardness. Nicola Pisano and his apprentices Lapo and Arnolfo di Cambio will carry out work on the pulpit; Nicola's son, Giovanni, may perhaps join them later. From then on his career passes through a maze of dimly discernible disputes with fellow artists and employers, and unexplained clashes with the law. Throughout there comes the suggestion of Giovanni's attempt to preserve his own individuality in his art. In November 1288, when the sculptor Ramo di Paganello, his brother, and great-nephews were taken on to work upon the façade of Siena cathedral, their contract specifically laid it down that: 'they shall not interfere in the work of master Giovanni di fu Nicola, unless the said master Giovanni wishes that the said master Ramo, and his brother and nephews, shall work with him in his work; then they can and are permitted to, and they ought to work with him in his work.'

Cum eo et in suo opere; it would be too fanciful to read in this affirmation of 'his work' by itself anything of particular significance.

It would be too much to construct from a handful of documents alone a picture of 'artistic temperament'. Yet when we align these suggestions with the remarkable series of inscriptions which Giovanni left behind on his sculptures, it is difficult to dismiss these thoughts out of hand. The most famous of these were chiselled on his pulpit at Pisa. There was nothing new in artists announcing their own skill on the works which they had executed. The sculptor who had carved the pulpit which Giovanni's work replaced had done the same. After 1311 this had been sent to the cathedral of Cagliari in Sardinia, where it can still be seen, with the date 1162 and the declaration that its maker, Guglielmo, was 'more eminent in art than any of the moderns'. But the scale and tone of the clumsy, rhymed Latin verses of Giovanni Pisano's inscription are unparalleled. The first, below the reliefs, might be translated as follows:

I praise the true God, through whom comes the best of things, who has allowed a man to form these pure figures. In the year of our Lord thirteen hundred and eleven the hands of Giovanni, born of the late Nicola, by their craft alone, carved this work, when, in concord and division, Count Frederico da Montefeltro ruled the Pisans, and when Nello di Falcone was Master of the Building, both over its works and its rights. He is a Pisan as is that Giovanni, skilled above all in the order of the art of pure sculpture, carving splendid things in stone, wood, and gold. Even if he wished he could not carve what is ugly or base. There are many sculptors but to him remain the honours of praise. He has made noble sculptures and differing figures. Let anyone who wonders at them test them with the proper rules. Christ have mercy on him to whom such gifts are given.

Along the step beneath the pulpit there is a further inscription. There has been much debate about its meaning, but its tone is unmistakable:

Giovanni has encircled here the rivers and provinces of the world seeking without reward to learn many things, and preparing everything with heavy labour. Now he calls out: 'I have not taken heed, for the more I have achieved, the more I have experienced hostile injuries. But I bear the pain with an indifferent heart and a calm mind.' That I [the pulpit] may take this envy from him, soothe his sorrow and aid his glory, join tears to these verses. He who condemns the man worthy of the diadem, proves himself unworthy: so he who reproves him, shows himself worthy of reproof.

What Giovanni has done here is to take the simple affirmation of artistic worth, and the prayer found in other inscriptions of the age, in for instance the words painted on Duccio's *Maestà* in 1308— 'Holy Mother of God—Give peace to Siena—Give life to Duccio— because I have painted you this'—and turned them into a passionate personal plea which speaks as much of himself as of his work. However, though the inscription reaches its peak with him, in the following years of the fourteenth century these direct apostrophes of the artist's audience are found no more. Artists signed their work much more frequently, but they left its praise to other men.

Giovanni was a lonely figure, whose struggle for personal recognition found no such strident followers as himself and (at least for a long time) no great posthumous, public acknowledgement. Giotto (recorded 1301, died 1337), on the other hand, was destined to become, while still living, and for the century which followed his death, the popular type of the artist. In so far as any personal impression is gained from the documents of his life, it is of a man who combined the highest artistic skills with an acute business sense. In 1312, for instance, like any other Florentine bourgeois, he leased out for six months a loom valued at £10 to a weaver, who in return was to pay him 20 shillings a month (a profit of 120 per cent per annum). He seems too to have stood as guarantor for loans which were unlikely to be repaid, in the hope that he would be able to impound the securities which backed them. In 1314, four, perhaps even six, notaries were watching over his business interests. He was able to support at least eight children, four boys and four girls, and to become a landowner at Colle. We cannot be certain that he wrote the poem sneering at 'those many who praise Poverty' to which his name is attached, but there is nothing in his life which makes it improbable.

No other artist was likely to make such an appeal to the Florentine middle class. Moreover, he was the most original artist that Italy was to see for centuries. As a result his personality released something new in European society, an almost unremitting paean of praise for the artist by non-artists. It began in his lifetime with the passage in the *Purgatorio* which was probably written some time around 1312. In the same year the will drawn up by one Richuccio di Puccio of Florence left oil for a lamp burning in S. Maria Novella before 'the crucifix painted by the distinguished painter whose name is Giotto di Bondone'. Where private individuals led, the commune followed. Some three years before his death the council of Florence, in appointing him as a 'skilled and famous man' to the position of 'Governor' of the building works of the commune and of the cathedral, declared:

> It is said that in the whole world no-one can be found who is more capable in these and other things than Master Giotto di Bondone, painter of Florence. He should be received therefore in his country as a great master and be held dear in the city, and he should have cause for agreeing to a continued domicile within it. With this many will profit from his knowledge and learning so that no little beauty will come to the city.[3]

It would be superfluous to catalogue here the continuous acclaim of Giotto, which rings through the fourteenth century. Other artists occasionally receive their share of praise: Arnolfo di Cambio, and (lavishly in the works of Petrarch) Simone Martini, but it is to Giotto that men continually return. His name is the touchstone by which contemporaries make the distinction between the mechanical artisan and the great artist.

It was with the attitudes towards the artist, revealed in their different ways by Giovanni Pisano and Giotto, that a wholly new conception of the artist grew up in Italian *trecento* thought. This development can be broken down into three stages. The first can be thought of as extending to the 1340s: in this period, certainly by 1324, a distinction has been drawn between the various types of 'mechanical' arts. Working from a passage in Aristotle's *Politics*, Marsiglio of Padua in the *Defensor Pacis* distinguished within 'the mechanical arts' between those which served for the necessities of life, and those others which 'are rather for pleasure and for living well . . . such as the art of painting and others like it.' A similar distinction to this lies behind the programme for the reliefs executed between 1334 and 1337 on the Campanile of Florence, which were designed to illustrate 'the work of men'. Here representations of the three visual disciplines—painting, sculpture, and architecture—were separated from those portraying the mechanical arts, and were set in a separate section between them and the liberal arts.

From the middle of the century the position of the artist rose much higher. Here the principal spokesman of the new views was Giovanni Boccaccio, surprisingly enough, if it is true, as recently claimed, that he had no feeling for art. The key passage is found, again surprisingly perhaps, in his *Decameron* (vi, 5), written about 1350. Speaking of Giotto he says:

> He had a mind of such excellence that there was nothing given by Nature, mother and mover, together with the continuous whirling of the skies, of all things which he, with style or pen or brush, could not paint so like, that it seemed not so much similar, but rather the thing itself, so that often, in things done by him, the optical sense of men was deceived. And he brought back to life that art which for many centuries had been buried under the errors of those who in painting had sought to give pleasure to the eyes of the ignorant rather than to delight the minds of the wise. It is, therefore, with justice that he may be called one of the lights of Florentine glory.

In this brief passage there appear for the first time two ideas destined to be profoundly influential in European thought. The first is the idea that art, after being 'buried for many centuries' has now 'been brought back to light', a view of cultural change which reached maturity 200 years later with Vasari. The second is the concept of an art of the élite which is distinguished from an art of the people, the idea of an intellectual artist who delights the minds of the wise and the few rather than the eyes of the ignorant many. Boccaccio's scorn here for the painting designed for *gli occhi degli ignoranti* provides a vivid contrast to those traditionally hallowed words of Pope Gregory, in which he had praised painting, *quia in ipsa ignorantes vident quod sequi debeant*. Petrarch echoed the same thought when in his will, drawn up in 1370, he bequeathed to the Lord of Padua 'my picture, or icon, of the blessed Virgin Mary, the work of the distinguished painter Giotto, given to me by my friend, Michele Vanni of Florence, whose beauty amazes the masters of the art, though the ignorant cannot understand it.' The influence of Petrarch, Boccaccio, and, more remotely, Pliny can be seen in the *Commentary* of Benvenuto da Imola, written around 1376. Benvenuto expounded a 'rude mechanicals' view of artists; yet when he discussed Giotto his tone changed: 'Giotto still holds the field because no other painter more subtle has yet appeared, although sometimes he made great mistakes in his paintings as great minds have explained to me. This art of painting and sculpture had once more wonderful practitioners [*artifices*] among the Greeks and Latins, as can be seen in Pliny's *Natural History . . .*'

So far the commentator has seemed to have a certain scorn, not only for Oderisi, but for painters in general. However, perhaps reluctantly, but clearly under the influence of the literary tide of the day, he continues with praise for Giotto:

And note this, reader, that our poet justly commends Giotto, by reason of his city (as being a fellow Florentine), by reason of his skill, by reason of having known him personally. [Benvenuto believed that they had met at Padua.] For two other Florentine poets, Boccaccio and Petrarch, mention and praise him. Boccaccio writes that such was the excellence of the mind and art of this noble painter that nature produced nothing which he could not represent in such a way that the eye of those who saw it was not often deceived: taking the painting for reality.

It is against the background of these humanist observations that in the generation after Petrarch and Boccaccio, two men, Cennino Cennini, and, with much greater emphasis, Filippo Villani, advanced new claims for the artist. The *Libro dell' arte* of Cennino Cennini is a treatise on painting written by one who was himself a painter of Florence at the end of the Century.[4] This work gives a deep sense of the dignity of the painter's art. Here is a more modest but more securely confident affirmation of what had been claimed by Giovanni Pisano at the beginning of the century. His book, Cennino says, is written in reverence of God and the saints, but also 'in the reverence of Giotto, of Taddeo [Gaddi], and of Agnolo [Gaddi]'. As a result of the Fall, man has to seek a living from his own exertions, and to cultivate 'the arts'. The most noble of these is *la scientia*, that is to say, the mental discipline of the liberal arts, such things as theology and philosophy. But next to this, and springing in part from it, is painting: 'for which we must have imagination and manual skill in order to discover things unseen, hidden under the shade of nature, and in order to form with the hand and present to the sight that which did not before appear to be there. It is in the second place to *la scientia* and crowned by poetry. For this reason that by the help of *scientia*, the painter becomes free and able to compose and bind together, or not, at the pleasure of his will.' It is an art, he says, which requires love, reverence, obedience, and perseverence, and the apprentice to it should follow a mode of life as if he were studying theology, philosophy, or any other *scientia*. Cennino's pride is obvious, though his book, taken as a whole, suggests a man who still lived often in the craftsmen's world.

Some 20 years earlier, Filippo Villani, resuming the humanist tradition of Boccaccio and Petrarch, had gone much further. Villani elevates the artist finally above the artisan level in which he had been found for so long and proclaims that the practice of art could indeed be superior to the study of *la scientia*. In the first version of his book *On the famous citizens of Florence* (1381–2), Villani took the original step of devoting a chapter to Florentine painters. It is worth citing the passage in its entirety:

Concerning Cimabue, Giotto, Maso, Stefano, and Taddeo, painters. The ancients, who drew up their histories with such distinction, included the best painters of pictures and sculptors of statues together with other famous men in their volumes. Again the ancient poets admired the intelligence and industry of that Prometheus who [following fourteenth-century interpretation] pretended to have made men from the loam of earth. These prudent men, I infer, thought that the imitators of nature who strove to construct the forms of men from stone and bronze, would have had no success without the power of a most noble skill and singular memory and a delicate and profound control of the hand. So among the other illustrious men in their annals they places Zeuxis, Polykleitos, Pheidias, Praxiteles, Myron, Apelles, 'Conon' [?], and others distinguished in this type of art. To me too then it seems right, *pace* those who may mock, to mention at this point those distinguished Florentine painters who revived that bloodless and almost extinct art.

Among these the first was that Giovanni called Cimabue. By his craft and intelligence he began to recall to the similitude of nature that antiquated, and, as it were, long dissolute and wayward painting, which through the ignorance of painters had childishly diverged from nature. For it is a fact that before him Greek and Latin painting had lain for many centuries under the rule of gross lack of skill; as may be fully seen in the figures and images that adorn the panels and walls of the churches of the saints.

After he had paved the way for new developments, Giotto, who was not only the equal of ancient painters in the glory of fame, but their superior in craft and mind, restored painting to its high renown and pristine dignity. For the images pictured in his paintings so conformed to the lineaments of nature that they seemed to attentive observers as if they lived and drew breath. He made them too with such exemplary motions and gestures that they appeared to speak, weep, rejoice, and do other things which gave great delight to those who, seeing them, gave praise to the mind and hand of the constructor.

According to the view of many intelligent people, indeed, painters are not inferior in mind to those made masters by the liberal arts, since the latter obtain by study and learning in books what is required by their arts, while painters depend only on the high mind and tenacious memory which is manifest in their art.

Quite apart from his art Giotto was clearly a man of great judgment who understood the working of many things. He had a full knowledge, moreover, of the stories [ie. that he painted] and he stood out as a rival to poetry for it seemed to the careful observers that he painted what was acutely imagined. He was also, as becomes a judicious man, eager for fame rather than money. And so, wanting to extend his reputation, he painted something in prominent places throughout almost all the famous towns of Italy, notably at Rome, at the entrance to the church of San Pietro di Trastevere [i.e., the great St Peter's] where he represented in mosaic the apostles in peril on the ship so that he might give a demonstration of himself and his art to those from the whole world who flowed to the city at times of indulgences. Moreover, with the help of mirrors he painted himself and his contemporary, Dante, on the altar panel of the chapel of the palace of the *podestà*.

From this praiseworthy man, as from a most abundant and clear fount, there flowed the brightest streams of painting, those men who formed the precious and pleasing renewed style, emulous of nature. Among these most delightful of all, Maso di Stefano, painted with a wonderful and incredible grace.

Stefano was nature's monkey; so well could he imitate it that in his pictures of the body, even for doctors, the arteries, veins, nerves, and the minutest human lineaments, were so disposed that in his paintings only breath and respiration seemed to be lacking.

Taddeo [Gaddi] again, painted buildings with such art that he seemed to be another Dinocrates or that Vitruvius who wrote 'The Art of Architecture'.

To number the innumerable who, following them, ennobled the art, would be a wider function and a theme of greater extent. Consequently, satisfied in this of having spoken of these men, I come to other matters.[5]

At first sight this reads flatly enough. Yet within it is to be discerned a striking picture of seminal humanist attitudes to the arts. Taking up Boccaccio's words that art 'has been brought back to light', Villani claims that, after being long inflicted 'with a gross lack of skill', a 'lost and almost extinct art' has been restored to life and a 'similitude of nature.' Here a periodisation and a value judgment is established which, taken up in the fifteenth century and formalised by Vasari in the sixteenth, was to last almost until our own times.

Turning to Giotto, Villani then proceeds to project a wholly new image of the artist. The men who have brought back dignity to painting have dignified themselves. Giotto is now not only the equal but, in contrast to the views of Benvenuto da Imola, the superior of ancient painters. Seeing his work, men praise not alone his hand but his mind. This thought in its turn provokes a striking affirmation: painters are not inferior to professors of the liberal arts; they are, by implication, superior to them. The one are masters only of book-learning, but the painters depend on their *altum ingenium* (high mind? genius?) and their faculty of visual memory. Giotto, by the acuteness of his imagination, rivalled the poets.

This striking assertation, that artists were at least the equals of those who practised the liberal arts, makes Villani's passage the artists' Magna Carta. It implied that the old religious view of the artist as manual worker had at last fully given way to a secular view of the artist as creative intellectual. He is a fellow spirit of the humanist. Both are seeking to renew and go beyond the learning of the ancient world, long overlaid by barbarism. As a result the person of the artist himself suddenly acquires new dignity. Giotto was, we are assured (though it seems the reverse of the truth) 'eager for fame rather than money'. His wandering throughout Italy was the result of a wish to extend his fame, not, as one might have thought, a mere desire to find wealthy patrons. His mosaic of the Navicella at Rome he specifically executed there that it might give to those who flocked to Rome a demonstration, not certainly of the glory of God, nor solely of Giotto's own art, but also *de se* 'of himself'. Art is no longer a method of religious contemplation, but a manifestation of human ingenuity. Moreover, the interest in the artist's person, and the assumption that Giotto was seeking to gratify it, led Villani to mention where the self-portrait could be seen.

This new attitude to the artist depended upon the vast expansion in the demand for art which characterised the fourteenth century. The increasing calls upon the artist's services make the claims of a Giovanni Pisano intelligible. Also important was the emergence of the commune as the major patron of art, and the effect this had on art appreciation. This was paralleled by the rise of humanism in the intellectual sphere, where Pliny was a major inspiration. In *Purgatorio* x, the poet sees a wall:

> *di marmo candido, e adorno*
> *d'intagli sì che non pur Policreto*
> *ma la natura lì avrebbe scorno*

('of shining marble, and adorned with reliefs that would put to shame not only Polykleitos, but nature itself').

Obviously Dante knew of Polykleitos only from a literary source; already Italians were coming to a knowledge of those chapters on the arts written by the elder Pliny. In the middle years of the century the extent of this knowledge has already been seen in Petrarch's *De remediis*; it can be studied further in his annotations to his still extant copy of the author. It was probably Petrarch who initiated the controversy in the second half of the century on the relative merits of ancient and modern art. This curious example of the *querelles des anciens et modernes* drew for one side of the argument very largely upon the authority of Pliny, whose written praises of lost masterpieces were favourably contrasted with those works of contemporaries which could actually be seen.

In one important respect, however, Pliny was misunderstood. Reading in his work of the admiration excited in the Roman world by the works of Apelles, Praxitiles, and Polykleitos, Italians assumed, quite mistakenly, that the artists themselves, as opposed to their art, had received a high personal esteem. From this they had gone on to give honour to their own artists, to Cimabue, Giotto, and

Simone Martini. From the end of the century these erroneous assumptions about the Roman world were greatly strengthened by the rising interest in the world of classical Greece. For here, indeed, in contrast to Rome, the artist had genuinely enjoyed great status. So, for instance, in his educational treatise, the *De ingenuis moribus*, written in 1404, Pier Paolo Vergerio pointed out that 'the figurative art' was one of the four liberal arts in which Greek boys were instructed:

> There were four subjects that the Greeks taught their boys: letters, gymnastics, music, and design, which they also called 'figurative art'. . . . Of these the fourth, design, is not to-day taught as a liberal art unless one includes within it writing, which is in fact an aspect of drawing. It belongs wholly to the painter's profession. However, as Aristotle observed [Politics, viii, ch. 3, i, vii], knowledge of design was not only a decorative accomplishment, but of practical use. For in the acquisition of vases and pictures and sculptures, in which the Greeks took much pleasure, their knowledge of the art was of great use to them, both in not being cheated over the price, and because it helped them to distinguish what was beautiful and graceful whether in nature or art. These are things which men of distinction should be able to discuss and judge.[6]

Petrarch, it has been seen, had learnt from Pliny that among the Greeks art had been placed in *primum gradum liberalium*. But the conservative half of his mind had rejected this as a folly. Vergerio, however, was now taking the knowledge much more seriously. Petrarch too had still clung to a vision of a primarily ecclesiastical art; Vergerio here seems to think wholly in terms of lay connoiseurship. In the growth of this new vision of art, Manuel Chrysoloras, the Byzantine teacher of Greek who was in Italy from 1394, is probably of great significance. It was he who introduced the society of classical Greece to the Italian humanist world, and he himself was a man with an interest both in works of art and in aesthetic theory. Why is it, he asks in a letter written in 1411, that when we see an object in reality we ignore it, and yet when we see it painted we come to admire it? His answer, and it again raises the artist from any artisan status, is that what we admire is a 'philosophic activity', the mind which has shaped nature into the forms of art.[7]

Despite such passages older attitudes could still prevail outside the humanist milieu. In his book of advice for Florentine families written between 1400 and 1405, the Dominican friar Giovanni Dominici continued to recommend the use of paintings and sculptures in words drawn from Gregory the Great: while scriptural study was for the educated 'these representations are the books of the man in the street'. The dabblings in art patronage of a self-made merchant like Francesco di Marco Datini of Prato show too how remote humanist thought could be for many among the bourgeoisie. Even for the intellectuals of the opening decade of the fifteenth century the alliance of humanist and artist was still being formed. Alberti's *De pictura* and Ghiberti's *Commentarii* had still to be written. As late as the sixteenth century Castiglione in *The Courtier* still felt it necessary to justify by reference to the Greeks an accomplishment in design 'which today may seem mechanical and inappropriate for a gentleman'.

Nor was the esteem which the great artist received in any way yet comparable with what it was to become. He was not, like Michelangelo, 'divine', nor, like Leonardo, 'the God and creator of his work'. He was utterly remote from those twentieth-century followers of Kandinsky who would claim for him an absolute aesthetic and moral freedom. As yet no general system of the arts nor any secular aesthetic had been formulated. 'Art' still did not exist, and was not perhaps invented until the eighteenth century. Yet a real change had come. It was in the fourteenth century that the first decisive break was made in the way in which the arts were conceived, and it was then that the artist first came to enjoy any measure of status in the intellectual world.

twelve

The Artist in Society
II.   Workshop and Guild

Work of Artists

In the fourteenth century the words 'art' and artist' carried different connotations from those they bear today. 'Art' implied not merely visual arts, but any human activity or skill. No 'artist' at this time thought of himself as such, but rather as a painter, a goldsmith, or a stonemason. Creative artists were still intimately linked with the artisan world and much of the work undertaken by artists had an artisan character. A typical painter at Florence, for instance, was Ghigo di Salvato (*fl. c.* 1340) described as 'a scabbard-maker or painter'. Another was Bartolomeo di Gaggio, who, in September 1330, formed a partnership with six companions for the painting and selling of leather caparisons for horses. These, it was agreed, were to be marketed at 2 florins each. Later in his life, this Bartolomeo attained a certain fame as a *pittore di camera*, that is, a painter of rooms inside private houses. (The contemporary Florentine writer, Franco Sacchetti, tells a story of how Bartolomeo was commissioned by Piero Brunelleschi to decorate a room in his palace. When the work was completed, Piero complained that there were not enough birds in the composition. Bartolomeo, somewhat the worse for drink, replied: 'Sir, I painted a great many more, but your servants left the windows open, so most of them got out and flew away!'.) Other men, like that Master Mino of Siena, who appear in another of Sacchetti's stories, concentrated on the repetition of one theme. Sacchetti wrote that in Mino's shop there were always four or five unfinished crucifixes, covered with a cloth, lying around ready for sale. Much of the work done in Florence and Siena was of this type, the equivalent of what one might now call sacristy art, almost mechanically produced, often for the export market.

Some craftsmen, more ambitiously, might specialise in both the making and decoration of *cassoni* (wedding chests), strong boxes, and caskets. Typical of these were the brothers Alluzzino and Ammanatino of Florence. (Their house, incidentally, was one of those compulsorily purchased and demolished in 1389, during the enlargement of the cathedral piazza.) Ammanatino was the father of the painters Jacopo and Manetto, and the carpenter Michele, who together carried on the family trade. It was work in which it was possible to gain considerable prestige. Domenico de' Forzerini, whose name came from the caskets (*forzerini*) which he made, was one of the eleven painters summoned in July 1366 to discuss plans for the building of the cathedral, and his son Guido (recorded 1405) seems from his tax returns to have enjoyed a comfortable income in the same business.

Not only was there artisan specialisation among members of artists' guilds, but the workshops of the greatest painters accepted artisan tasks as part of their everyday business. For example, in 1327 the account-books of Siena show the following entries:

> Also to master Simone [Martini], painter, for 720 gold double lilies at 10d. a double lily: £30.
> Also to the aforesaid master Simone for 16 double lions on the arms of the *Popolo* at 16 shillings each: £12. 16. 0.
> Also to the aforesaid master Simone for the silver border along the windows, at eight shillings each. There were 16 borders: £6. 8. 0.
> Also for painting 20 lances at four shillings each: £4.[1]

There is no evidence that Martini carried out these commissions in person at this time. Presumably they would be executed by his apprentices, but certainly he would have done work like this during his own apprenticeship.

Celebrated artists not only accepted artisan tasks, they were also ready to undertake several very different forms of art. Orcagna, for instance, was painter, sculptor, and master-builder. Giotto was painter, 'Governor' of the building works of Florence cathedral, mosaic worker, and perhaps town planner. Giovannino de' Grassi was both a miniaturist and an 'engineer' in the building of Milan cathedral. Goldsmiths were particularly versatile. They repaired silver mass-cruets at Orvieto, fashioned silver trumpets, 'well formed, well sounding and pealing, with the arms of the commune in gilt upon them', for the commune of Siena, or were employed as consultants in architectural and engineering works.

Lando di Pietro, for instance, who made the gold crown for the coronation of the Emperor Henry VII at Milan in 1311, also founded the bells of the commune in the Palazzo del Popolo of Florence in 1322, and repaired the bells of Siena in 1321 and again in 1332. He was building fortifications at Montemassi in 1328 and walls at the little town of Paganico in the Maremma in 1334. As recent studies have shown, he also carved the wooden crucifix in the church at Paganico. Finally, after service in Naples at the court of King Robert, he was appointed as master builder to the cathedral and commune of Siena in 1339. Michele Memmi, who made a new silver seal for the commune of Siena in 1340, undertook mosaic work in the façade of the cathedral in 1358. He was master builder of the chapel of the *Campo* in 1360 and held at the same time the office of master of works of fountains and aqueducts. In 1369 he was supervisor of bells and clocks for the commune.[2] Occasionally people called 'goldsmiths' are found who, though they may from time to time exercise their craft, seem to gain their living through moneylending or other business. Lorenzo di Donato, for instance, goldsmith of Florence, who produced six lamps for the parish church at Prato in the first decade of the fifteenth century, also dealt in wood and slaves, and acted as an intermediary in land sales.[3]

Recruitment and Training

A comparatively large number of men were needed to fulfil all the demands for art in the Italian towns. There are examples of smaller communes actually soliciting craftsmen to stay with them. In November 1307 the council of San Gimignano, 'seeing that in San Gimignano there is no richness and adornment of a goldsmith as there once used to be', gave Lupo Berti, formerly a resident, a retainer of £10 a year, 'as his father received', 'to dwell there, exercise his art, and teach anyone wishing to learn it'. Later, the same commune was to pay the painter Memmo, father of Lippo Memmi, a retainer of £8 a year for his residence in the town.

In larger centres artists were more in evidence. An incomplete taxation record from 1311 of the Terzo di Città, one of the three administrative divisions of Siena, shows that here alone were living ten painters, 21 goldsmiths, two miniaturists, and 24 stoneworkers. In Siena as a whole in 1363, which at that time had a population of about 25,000 people, there were 30 master painters, 21 master goldsmiths, and 62 master stone-workers. The number of master painters increased to 64 in the 1370s, to 100 at the turn of the century, and only dropped again to about 32 in the 1430s, when the population of the city itself had probably fallen to below 15,000. For each of these men one has to multiply, perhaps by two or three, to find the number of workers and apprentices who were subject to the guilds without being masters. So at Siena around 1400 there might be 300 men and boys engaged in painting. Obviously many of these men produced work and possessed talents appropriate to craftsmen, yet many were genuine artists.

A similar picture emerges at Florence. In 1320, 70 men were enrolled in the painters' guild. These included mattress-makers, wax-workers, the makers of jewel boxes and *cassoni* who had their shops in via Nuova near the Cathedral, and so on. But by 1327, 36 men, exclusively painters, had been newly matriculated. In the following year, as Davidsohn has calculated, there were 48 goldsmiths in Florence (and, of course, there were others who had emigrated to Rome and Avignon). In the period 1353 to 1386, 58 painters were matriculated, and from 1386 to 1409 another 34. For the period 1290 to 1420 we know the names of 428 painters who practised some form of art at Florence: 100 who principally exercised their craft in the years 1290 to 1340, 151 in the years 1340 to 80, and

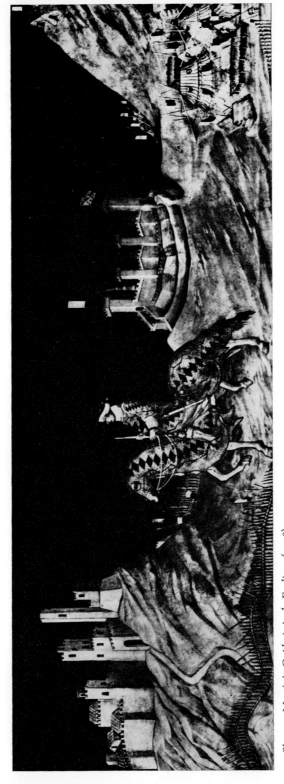

19 Simone Martini, *Guidoriccio da Fogliano* (1328)

20 Andreolo de' Bianchi, *Four Workmen*

21 Tommaso da Modena, *Cardinal Hugh of Provence* (1352)

177 in 1380 to 1420. Of these, 12 in the first period, 19 in the second, and 12 again in the third definitely came from areas outside the republic, such as Forlì, Camerino, or Milan. Yet towns like Florence and Siena, though of leading importance, did not, like the modern art metropolis, suck dry all talent from elsewhere. Other cities in Italy had comparable forces of workers, and even small centres could boast their native practitioners of the arts. At Perugia in the 1360s there were over 50 painters enrolled in the guild. At Arezzo there were over nine goldsmiths in 1353. These men cannot simply be dismissed as provincial hacks unable to get a job elsewhere. The very real skill that they could achieve is shown, for instance, by the reliquary bust of St Donatus, executed by Pietro and Paolo of Arezzo in 1346, still preserved in the *pieve* of the town.[4]

Many of those who practised the arts came from families already engaged in them. Ugolino di Vieri (*fl.* 1329–85), for instance, the creator of the tabernacle of the cathedral of Orvieto, was the son of a goldsmith, with two brothers and a nephew who exercised the same art. Lorenzo Maitani (1275?–1330), the principal builder of the cathedral of Orvieto, was the son and brother of stonemasons, and the father of two men who continued his work after his death. The sculptor, Tino di Camaino (*fl.* 1312–36), was the son of a stone-mason, and his daughter married a painter. Andrea di Bartolo (d. 1428) was the son and grandson of painters, and the grandson of a goldsmith. Simone Martini's connections with other painting families are complex enough to demand a brief genealogical tree:

				Memmo (painter)		
		Martino				
Giovanni di Biondo (miniaturist) *fl.* 1294–1315	Donato (painter) d. 1347	Simone Martini (painter) *c.* 1284–1344 (no issue)	= Giovanna	Lippo (painter) d. 1356?	Tederigo (painter)	
Giovanni di Sera (painter) *fl.* 1340–1373	= Caterina	Giovanni (notary)	Bernaba (goldsmith) (1345–1418)			

The genealogy of another Sienese family, that of Buoninsegna, gives a similar impression:

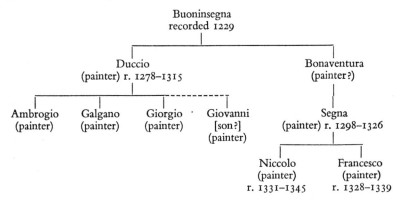

Many men, though, took to the arts with no family background behind them. Lorenzo Ghiberti, for instance, in a story which was later to be repeated by Vasari, told in his *Commentaries* of how the greatest of Italian artists was set on his career:

> In a village near the city of Florence called Vespignano, a boy was born of marvellous talent, who was drawing a sheep from life when the painter Cimabue passed by on the Bologna road. He saw the lad sitting on the ground drawing the sheep on a stone. He was struck with admiration for the boy who, being so young, yet drew so well, and, realising his natural skill, he asked the boy's name. 'My name is Giotto; my father's is Bondone, and he lives in that house nearby', replied the boy. Cimabue went with the boy to his father, and as he was of distinguished appearance, and the boy's father was very poor, they agreed that Cimabue should take Giotto with him as his apprentice.[5]

This tale is most unlikely to be true. It combines, as Dr Ernst Kris has pointed out, three standard biographical formulae found in hero-myths: the attempt to find links between two famous men; the element of chance in the discovery of the hero; and the element of social ascent (employment as a shepherd is an especially frequent motif in such tales). Moreover, it was written in the early 1450s, well over 100 years after Giotto's death. Coming closer to Giotto's own time, an anonymous commentary on the *Divine Comedy*, written in the 1340s, provides another account: 'It is said that Giotto's father had apprenticed him to the wool trade, and that every morning going to work he would stop at Cimabue's workshop. When his father asked the wool merchant how his son was doing, he replied: "It's a long time since he's been here. I found out recently that he stays with the painters, where his nature draws him." So, having taken Cimabue's advice, the father took him from the wool trade and put him to paint with Cimabue.' It seems a more probable story, but true or not, it shows at least, what one author thought was likely to be accepted as probable. In Manetti's *Life of Brunelleschi* there is another description of how an artist was recruited. Manetti was writing at the end of the fifteenth century, and so describing something which had happened 100 years before, yet there is much in his account which can be checked against contemporary material. Brunelleschi's father was a notary of good family, who held quite high posts in the Florentine administration. In 1398 at the age of 24, Filippo matriculated in the silk guild, to which the goldsmiths were subordinate. He became a master six years later in 1404. Manetti's account tells how Filippo, from an early age:

learnt reading, writing, and the abacus, as most boys of good family in Florence do, and also received some knowledge of letters [i.e., Latin], for his father was a notary, and perhaps had the idea that he should be one too. At that time, few persons among those who did not expect to become doctors, lawyers, or priests, were given [Latin] literary training. . . . Even as a very little boy he took a natural delight in drawing and painting and was much attracted by them. So when his father, as usual, came to put him to some trade, Filippo chose to be a goldsmith. His father consented, for he was a sensible man and saw that Filippo had the talent. His son became proficient in all parts of his craft, particularly as regards design, in which he showed himself to have marvellous skill. In a little while he became a perfect master of *niello*, enamel, and coloured or gilded ornaments in relief, as well as in the cutting, splitting, and setting of precious stones.[6]

Brunelleschi, it should be added, whose family had around 2,000 florins in the communal debt, was, as far as we know, the one artist to come from a socially elevated milieu in this period. Other artists, if not the sons of artists themselves, were likely to be children of notaries of modest means, or of artisans such as barbers and tailors.

When a boy wished to become an artist, his family would arrange for him to be apprenticed to a master in one of the guilds. Although there was no strong idea of specialisation, it was normal practice to enrol in one guild only. On particular occasions, for instance when a goldsmith was called upon to do sculpture in stone, he would enrol temporarily in the other appropriate *arte*. In Florence the guild authorities insisted that the apprenticeship of painters should be registered by a notary. But often this was ignored, the agreement was informal, and no deeds were drawn up. We hear in one instance of a master having no legal redress against an apprentice who had run away from him, precisely because no contract existed between them. Possibly only the legalistically minded went to the trouble of having the contract of an apprenticeship registered by the notary. The contracts which were drawn up, however, do tell something of the apprentice's standing, and show masters accepting boys under a variety of different conditions.[7] Apprentices were engaged for various periods of time, running from one to eight years. It is possible that where they stipulated a brief period, both parties simply wanted an opportunity to get to know each other before reaching a more permanent arrangement. On the other hand, no contract has been found which specifically says that the apprenticeship is being renewed, and it may be that the whole system was much more flexible than is generally imagined. It is generally assumed, for instance, that the apprenticeship lasted for seven years. Yet no guild statute actually lays this down, and it could well be that if, after three or four years, a boy had shown himself to have acquired the skills of his art, then he was no longer treated as an apprentice, and was paid a man's wage.

The age of the boy is never mentioned, though by analogy with other guilds it would normally be between ten and twelve. Here again it is difficult to see any general rule. Brunelleschi was 24 when he became an apprentice, and 30 when he was enrolled as a master goldsmith. Occasionally, a man who had already qualified in one trade would bind himself as apprentice to another. At Siena, in June 1414, the painter Giacomo apprenticed himself for two years to Barthélemy de Pierre, a French goldsmith resident in the city. Giacomo was to serve him without pay and without his keep unless Barthélemy went to do work outside the city. In return he was to be taught the goldsmith's art. In the case of children the apprentice sometimes (though this is rare) promised to pay the master for instruction. In 1310, a master engaged to teach an apprentice 'the art of stone and woodwork' for three years in return for £25 (about 9 florins), paid in three instalments at the end of each year. Often the master would pay nothing and receive nothing. On other occasions the master promised the boy either a small wage, or food, accommodation and clothing, or both. In 1303, for instance, a goldsmith promised to pay a boy a salary of £15 a year; in 1324 a painter gave his apprentice £18; in 1331, £23. Whether the master paid or received payment for the apprenticeship was apparently unrelated to his own status; all the contracts which survive for this period concern minor and little-known masters. Presumably where the parents gave money, the boy received more formal instruction and was excused the more menial tasks about the workshop.

Generally the notaries recorded the promise of the apprentice to work 'faithfully and studiously' at the 'learning and exercise' (theory and practice) of his art, and not to steal anything or run away. The master in his turn promised to teach him 'well and lawfully'. Less frigidly, some Sienese documents note his declaration that he would act 'as a good father towards his good son and as a perfect master towards his disciple'. In Lapo Mazzei's letter to his wealthy friend, Francesco Datini, written in January 1408, he tells how his son, Bruno, has just begun on his career as an artist: 'Bruno's at the goldsmiths, and he's got such an accomplished head for design that your figures by Niccolò [Gerini—executed in the Datini palace] will come to seem made of chestnut. And he's very obedient to me, and if he lives another year you'll remember what I'm writing to you now, for he's already highly praised in his art.'[8] Not all parents were like this. At Genoa in May 1347, Master Matteo, 'painter of saints', asked the consuls of law to fine Pietro da Saviro from the Val d' Aosta, the father of an apprentice he had taken on. He claimed that Pietro had stopped his son coming to work, especially on public holidays, and had failed to provide him with adequate clothing or even food, so that from very pity he had fed the boy himself 'lest he die of hunger'.[9]

There are some brief pictures of the artist's existence in the stories of Franco Sacchetti, written in the 1380s. He writes of the apprentice being roused at dawn to catch the first light of morning, and of the Florentine goldsmith at Porta Santa Maria, working, 'as they all do', inside the house, but with the shutter raised open to the road. In one story, a painter is working in the piazza at Perugia on an open-air fresco, sheltering behind a mat screen 'as is customary', and continually being irritated by passers-by calling out such things as: 'Oy, master, aren't you ever going to be finished?' or 'When are we going to see our saint?'. In another story, Orcagna, Taddeo Gaddi, and other masters dine with the abbot of San Miniato al Monte after working in the church, and there debate the question: who were the best painters after Giotto? The conclusion is 'the ladies of Florence', since they decorate their faces so well that they improve even upon God's handiwork. There is even here at times a suggestion of the *vie de Bohème*. A painter's wife complains: 'Anyone who marries a painter must have a hard time of it; you're all fantastic and lunatic, and always getting drunk, and not ashamed of it.' But the lady has been surprised in embarrassing circumstances, and should not be taken too literally. More convincing, perhaps, is Sacchetti's remark (*Novella* clx) that 'it's always been true that among painters you find some weird people'.

A fuller revelation of the spirit of the artist's workshop is found in Cennino Cennini's *Libro dell' arte*. The work has a deeply religious sentiment. As aid to his hand Cennino invoked: 'first the high omnipotent God, that is to say, the Father, Son, and Holy Spirit; second, that most delightful advocate of all sinners, the Virgin Mary and St. Luke the Evangelist, the first Christian painter, and generally all the saints, male and female, of Paradise'. This religious feeling is probably typical of most artists of the age, for, despite the gradual secularisation of art during the fourteenth century, they still often thought of themselves as having a primarily religious function. The statutes of the Sienese guild of painters, drawn up in 1355, for instance, open with a declaration that: 'we, by the grace of God, make manifest to gross men who cannot read the wondrous works performed by virtue and in virtue of the holy faith'.

As seen in the previous chapter, however, there is more in Cennino than this simple religious faith. It is a work written with a deep sense of the dignity of the painter's art, and it opens with the praise of painting. It is because of the high character of the painter's work, Cennino tells us, that 'he, a small fellow, working in the art of painting', had decided to give the benefit of all that his master Agnolo had taught him, and of all the little knowledge that God had given him, to those who might wish to learn of the methods of painters. There are some, he says, who follow the arts through poverty and necessity, but others, moved by the love of nature, are excited to it by the stimulus of a noble mind. The apprentice, working in this spirit, should eat and drink in moderation, and not, at the most, more than twice a day. Of course, he should avoid anything, such as throwing stones or iron bars, which might damage his hand or cause it to shake. There is also, he adds, with rather heavy humour, something else to be avoided: the over-much frequenting of the company of women 'which will make your hand so unsteady that it will oscillate and tremble more than a leaf in the wind.'

Most of Cennino's book is concerned with the workaday know-ledge that the apprentice would have to acquire during his training. Seven years, at least, he believed, were necessary for gaining the foundations of the art. 'You must begin by drawing', he says. He explains how to make panels for drawing, how to prime them, to execute work with silverpoint, and to make tracing paper. He explains how to draw with lead or pen on parchment, with brush on tinted paper, and with charcoal or in water-colours. In drawing one should always copy the best subjects of the great masters, but it is most sensible to choose one particular master and use his manner in case 'the different style of each master unsettles your mind, and your own style becomes fantastic'. Yet the most perfect guide, he adds, somewhat inconsequentially, is still to draw from nature. Glue your sheets of paper together on a hardboard, and go off alone or with like-minded companions, to churches or chapels to draw.

After drawing one should learn how colours, either bought from the apothecary or taken from the soil, should be ground and prepared. Then one must study the painting of frescoes, and how to represent figures, draperies, and buildings. Cennino also explains the new technique of painting in oil, 'which is much', he says, 'practised by the Germans'. Then he goes on to describe panel painting, working in relief, gilding, the use of mordants, and how to take plaster casts of faces and bodies.

He is tolerant before the whims of patrons. 'You will find some who ask for a picture and then want it varnished. I tell you that it's not the custom and that with the green-earth colour you don't need it. However, people will please themselves. You should adopt this method . . .' He urges the artist towards lavishness: always use fine gold ('in which flowers all the works of our art') and good colours, especially ultramarine blue ('a noble colour, beautiful, more perfect beyond all colours') 'particularly in a figure of Our Lady'.

'If you say you cannot afford it, I answer that if you work well, and give sufficient time to your work, and good colours, you'll get so much fame that from a poor person you'll become a rich one, and your name will stand so high for using good colours, that if one master gets a ducat for a figure, you'll certainly get two, and so you'll gain your end. As the old saying has it, "good work, good pay", and even if you're not well paid, God and Our Lady will reward your soul and body for it.'

Much of what Cennino wrote was to be superseded during his own lifetime by the rise of a more scientific ideal of art. His anatomy, for instance, is crude and surprising. He gives details of male proportions, but omits those of women, 'because there is not one of them perfectly proportioned', though he does give such curious hints as that 'a man has on his left side one rib less than a woman', 'men should be dark, women fair', etc. Irrational animals, he believed, had no certain proportions, though he then went on, illogically enough, to advise: 'draw them as frequently as you can from nature and you will discover them for yourself.' This seems a long way from the world of Ghiberti and Brunelleschi. Moreover the whole work, despite its ritualistic obeisance to 'science', still presents the artist primarily as craftsman. Cennino's level of culture, as his occasional botched citations of Latin show, was not very high. In all this, however, he seems typical of the majority of artists in the fourteenth century. They could all probably read and write, but few could have known much Latin. Ghiberti wrote of Ambrogio Lorenzetti as being 'learned like none of the others', meaning 'learned in his craft'. Vasari in the sixteenth century took this phrase up and portrayed Ambrogio as 'devoting himself to humanistic studies in his youth'. But the unlikelihood of this is brought out by a Sienese account book of 1335. One entry in this shows Ambrogio's elder brother Pietro being paid for a picture of S. Savino. The very next entry records the payment of a pound to 'Cecco, master of Grammar, who translated the story of Saint Savino into the vulgar tongue, so that it might be portrayed on the panel'.[10] With the end of the fourteenth and the beginning of the fifteenth century the artist appears as intellectual. This is how Ghiberti, speaking of his youth, tells of his education: 'I feel great and infinite gratitude to my parents, who, following the laws of the Athenians, took care to have me instructed in arts, in which one can achieve nothing without the discipline of letters and a grasp of all principles. So through the care of my parents and the teaching of my instructors, I have grown in knowledge of [Latin] letters, and the discipline of philology and technics, and I delight in the commentaries on these. . . .'[11]

Had he lived on to read these words, Cennino, one suspects, would have considered them rather pretentious. He and his apprentices came from a more workaday world, and in this they are typical, not only of the fourteenth century, but probably of most artists during the next hundred years.

The Guild

On completion of his apprenticeship, two courses were open to the young artist. In the first place he could work for hire by the year, month or day in the service of some master of his craft. In 1339, for instance, Jacopo di Donato, in Florence, contracted to work for a year in a shop which produced chests with painted scenes on them; his annual salary was the (small) sum of £38.5.0 (about 12 florins) paid monthly. Alternatively, by setting up his own shop a young man could become a master himself. In these circumstances he would normally take a lease of one of those *botteghe*, or shops, built into the lower part of a house, such as can be seen in Ambrogio Lorenzetti's painting of the town of Siena. In Siena itself, for example, Nicoluccio di Segna took out a two-year lease on a shop from the Brothers of the Town Hospital, at a rent of two florins every six months. At Florence the rents paid by painters for *botteghe* seem to have varied from 7 to 15 florins a year. These contracts sometimes gave rise to disputes. At Siena, in 1328, the painter Guido di Ghezzo renounced the lease he had taken on a shop from Petra, widow of the painter Cosone. He complained that Petra had not restored the property as she promised she would, and that, accordingly, 'on account of rain-water and other incidents . . . he has not been able, is not able, and will not be able to exercise his art there'.[12]

In other circumstances the apprentice might seek a more limited independence by forming a company with other men, sometimes as many as six others at a time, with whom he would share expenses and profits. Alternatively he might enter one of those 'half-produce' contracts which were in very common use in the financing of such trades as smithing, sword-making, and shoe-making in all Italian towns. An example from Siena will show how this form of agreement worked. Here Fede di Nalduccio, himself a painter, formed a partnership for a year with the painter Lando Stefani. Fede was to provide the shop and equipment (chests, panels, and paint) and some cash in hand, which all together were valued at 100 gold florins. Lando was to do the actual painting and selling. At the end of the year the cost of the materials used was to be deducted from the total takings, and returned to Fede. The profits were then equally divided between both parties. An interesting feature of this document is that it suggests the capital sum, 100 florins, which was required for setting up a workshop. Another indication is an inventory of the goods in the workshop of two Florentine painters in 1341, where the 'movables' were assessed at a total value of 58 gold florins, 33 shillings.

Once established independently, the artist became a master, was formally matriculated in his guild, and swore obedience to its officials and statutes. The position of the various guilds in which artists might be enrolled differed from town to town within Italy. In Florence they occupied a very subordinate place within the trade and commercial hierarchy. Here, the painters' *arte* (first recorded in 1295), was by 1316 a junior branch of the greater guild of the *Medici e Speciali* (formed from doctors, purveyors of drugs, and retail traders). The goldsmiths were a minor element in the *Arte Por S. Maria* (the guild of the great silk merchants). Members of these lesser guilds had no autonomy, and no rights against the rich upper bourgeoisie who controlled the major organisation. During the fourteenth century the painters' guild included among its members such tradesmen as mattress-makers, box-makers, glass and wax workers, house and sign painters, and colour grinders. The main guild, the *Medici e Speciali*, forbade them to meet independently until 1339. In that year they formed a confraternity called 'the Company of St Luke', with the main aim of promoting religious devotion. The company was open to the wives and daughters of the painters; members engaged to go to confession and communion together once each year, and to say every day five 'Our Fathers' and five 'Hail Marys'. Jacopo da Casentino, who, along with Bernardo Daddi, was one of the first four 'councillors' of the company, painted a picture of the members at prayer before the Virgin, the men on one side, the women on the other.

In other towns in Italy, although the artists' guilds had little political or economic importance, they generally had a freer right of association. The guild statutes, drawn up by the masters themselves, had to be approved by the commune or Lord, but, once accepted, were held to be binding in law on all the masters, and on their workmen and apprentices, who were compelled to swear obedience to them before obtaining employment. The organisation of the *arte* of painters at Siena, in the second half of the fourteenth century, can be taken here as typical. In this guild some 30 to 100 masters elected every six months a rector (who received a nominal 20 shillings for his time in the office), a chamberlain or treasurer who kept the account books (paid 15 shillings), and three councillors. These officials were assisted by a messenger, presumably drawn from the apprentices, who received five shillings for his six months tenure, and in addition twopence for every message taken to a member of the *arte* and fourpence for messages to those outside it. The rector was able to impose fines upon those infringing guild statutes. No one, say the statutes, was to ignore his message, and no one (though here the frequent repetition of the decree suggests at the same time its ineffectiveness) was to use foul words against him. At the beginning of his office he secretly appointed a 'guard' who reported infringements of the statutes to him.

Any non-Sienese painter coming to the town had to join the guild, to pay an entrance fee of a florin, and to give security of up to £S25 that he would obey its statutes. Refusal to pay fines or to obey the guild was met by boycott and social ostracism. Much of the business of the guild was concerned with conditions of work. The guild statutes decreed that no one was to work on feast days (of which no less than 57 are listed) without the permission of the rector, or unless working for the commune. No one was to take away work given to another master or lure away another's workman. To provide against theft, no master was to buy materials from another's workpeople, and so on. At the same time, the statutes attempted to maintain standards. No one was to use inferior materials, where better have been promised; the statutes instance the substitution of 'half-gold' for fine gold, of lead for silver, of German blue for ultramarine, or indigo for sky-blue. Here, of course, the guild was merely reinforcing that informal policing of others' work which mutual jealousy is likely to inspire in any body of men engaged in the same craft. There survives, for instance, a note, probably written in 1414, in which one Turino denounces to the Lords of Siena his fellow goldsmith, Pietro di

Cristofano. The commune had commissioned this man to make a leopard of fine silver, but Turino asserts that the feet and tail were made of other material. 'What's more—and this is worse—you think that the leopard is gilded. In fact, it's done with sulphur and saffron ... ask someone who knows and you'll see that I'm telling you the truth.'[13]

But the guild had a social and religious function too. Its statutes, opening with an invocation of the Trinity, go on, 'since spiritual are prior to temporal matters', to describe 'how we celebrate the feast of St Luke, who was not only [according to a persistent medieval tradition] the painter of the body and form of the glorious Virgin Mary, but was the writer of her most holy life'. On his feast day, each painter, whether master or worker, was to go to the church of S. Maria della Scala with a candle bought at his own expense, and there in union with other members of the guild, to hear Mass. When any member of the guild, or even any close relative, was buried, one or two men from each shop were to attend the funeral. It was, more-over, the duty of the rector to make peace between members in any mutual ill-will or controversy. The guilds too could give insurance to their members: the statutes of the Perugian painters in 1366 allowed the rector to pay out up to £10 a day to any member who was sick or had been imprisoned, without previously convening the guild to obtain its consent. The guild of Sienese goldsmiths provided a forge in its house, where members could, for a small fee, refine work and manufacture bronze.

It has been claimed that the guild system was a burden upon the individual artist, that it stifled initiative, that it had a levelling effect on originality.[14] Brunelleschi's refusal to pay dues to the Florentine guild of stone and woodworkers in 1434 (which possibly arose from a demarcation dispute between rival guilds) has been seen as a victory for art 'of supra personal importance', inasmuch as it established 'the right of a free man to look after himself and act as his conscience dictated'. Yet it seems a difficult thesis to maintain, at least as far as Italy is concerned. Were Giotto's and Donatello's originality stifled by the guilds? In what way did they menace Brunelleschi? Any restriction of initiative, supposing it existed, might more fairly be

ascribed to society as a whole, rather than to this one part of it. No
guild, for instance, as has been claimed, prescribed the use of specified
materials or colours: all that it was likely to do was to order that
when certain ingredients had been contracted for, the artist must use
them. Nor were there in Italy any rigid entry terms, or, as existed in
Northern Europe, any prohibitions of entry to those who did not
already belong to guild families. When a wealthy businessman refused to honour his contract with an artist, as when the merchant
Datini of Prato dismissed Bartolomeo Bertozzi without payment in
1391, it was in the guild court that the injured man could obtain
redress. A more balanced consideration will see the guild system as
an impressive material and emotional support to the Italian artist; as
a focus of fraternity in work, shielding him from what was often a
precarious world.

Certainly the guild system did not inhibit any artist who sought
to gain his living by an itinerant or semi-itinerant life. Taddeo di
Bartolo of Siena journeyed from his native town to paint at Pisa, at
Genoa (for at least a year), at Perugia and at Volterra, without any
protest from local guild members. Indeed, complete foreigners were
welcomed by the guilds: Mark of Constantinople (working in Genoa
in 1313), the Catalan Ferrer Bassa (who was painting in Urbino in the
late 1330s), the Fleming, Alexander of Bruges (in Genoa in 1408),
and the many German masters who worked in the cathedral *opera*.
Many Italian artists in this period followed a peripatetic existence.
Typical of them is Simone Martini. He was born about 1284, not
improbably of Sienese parents resident in France. By 1315, the date
on the *Maestà* executed in the Palazzo Comunale, he had taken up
residence in what was to be his home town, Siena. From 1316 to 1317
he was at Naples in the service of King Robert. In 1318 to 1319 he
had moved to Pisa, where he was working for the Dominicans. It
was presumably at their recommendation that he was commissioned
to execute a polyptych for the Dominicans of Orvieto in 1320. In
1321 he returned to Siena, was married there in 1324, and does not
seem to have left until 1333. At some time, possibly between 1334 and
1339, he painted the frescoes of St Martin at Assisi. From 1339 to his
death in 1344 he was working at Avignon.

In this semi-wandering existence of Simone and his fellows it is difficult to see any evidence of real hardship; indeed it could probably be matched by the lives of many academics today. On the other hand, some artists of great fame, such as Ghiberti, were able to pass almost all their lives in their native city. Artists with less talent or ambition could also make a modest living without travel.

The 'Architect'

Although Vitruvius' *De architectura* had a certain circulation in the middle ages, the word 'architect' was not commonly employed as it is today. In the thirteenth-century dictionary of John of Garland an *architectus* was defined as a 'master carpenter'. In a different sense the term was preserved in a text from the New Testament (I Cor. iii, 10): 'According to the grace of God which is given unto me, as a wise master builder [Vulgate—*architectus*] I have laid the foundation, and another buildeth thereon.' Side by side with these uses, however, St Thomas Aquinas had taken over the term from the Latin translations of Aristotle, and employed it in his philosophic discussions. In considering, for instance, how power deriving from one source flows to 'secondary principles', he remarked that: 'the plan of those things done in government descends by the king's order to lower officials, and in buildings too, the plan of the building descends from the architect [*architectore*] to lower artisans who work with their hands'.[15] Accordingly the word came to have a wider currency in the fourteenth century, and some builders, especially builders for the Dominican order, to which St Thomas belonged, came occasionally to be called 'architects'. But it was only from 1418, when Cencio Rustici discovered and popularised a manuscript of Vitruvius, that the term came to have a certain vogue, and it was only by the mid-fifteenth century that its use became customary in Italy.

Does this absence of the word indicate a general absence of the man it describes? There are some who see our modern architect as already existing in the middle ages. It could be argued, however, that in Italy in this period one does not normally find the man who designs but does not build, the man whose plans and drawings dictate the structure of a building even after his death. In other words such questions as 'who was the architect of Milan Cathedral?' are anachronistic. Some sketches survive from these years, such as the ground layout of the proposed new cathedral of Siena, and Maitani's drawing for the façade of the Duomo of Orvieto, and models were often made before building. But it is very doubtful whether craftsmen built or had learnt to build from plans. A comparison of the Campanile at Florence with Giotto's 'design' for it shows that this had an almost symbolic character and was intended merely to give the patron some rough idea of what the finished building might look like. Nor were there any specialists who could be considered as being purely 'builders'. Of the men associated with building in this period, Giotto, for instance, was a painter, Andrea Pisano and Lando di Pietro were goldsmiths, and Giovanni Pisano, Giovanni d' Agostino, and Orcagna were sculptors.

In these circumstances the responsibility for the erection of a new building was, in Tuscany, normally divided between the *operaio* or master of the works, who might or might not be a professional artist or craftsman, and the *capomaestro* or foreman-supervisor. One or both of these men would put forward general ideas for the building, and these would be discussed and modified by informal councils of craftsmen called together from time to time by the *operaio*. In Lombardy the role of the *operaio* and *capomaestro* was taken over by men called 'engineers'. In the building of the Charterhouse of Pavia it seems that six men were concerned with the design. For the building of Milan cathedral no less then 14 'engineers' sat down to discuss details of design in 1391, while between 1387 and 1420 over 30 men at the Cathedral were described as 'engineers'. Architecture was directed by committees whose membership was continually fluctuating. Any one building was likely to be constructed over a long period of time, with previously unplanned additions being made over the years (See Palazzo Pubblico of Siena, pp. 77–9, plate 11). These conditions did not make for architecture as we understand it.

Sometimes, within the committees of the *opera*, there might be one man whose acknowledged expertise would enable him to domi-

22 Milan Cathedral (1735)

23 Milan Cathedral today

24 Manuscript of the Divine Comedy (fourteenth century)

nate the proceedings and ensure that his own vision of what was required would prevail. As such, his fame would grow and he would be given credit for the building which the *opera* had made. One of the earliest examples was Arnolfo di Cambio. On 1 April 1299, the priors of the *arti* in Florence decreed that he should be free from all taxation and other civic burdens. They justified this on the grounds that: 'he is a famous master, more skilled in the building of churches than any other known in these parts. The commune and people of Florence augur from the visible magnificence of the work begun by Master Arnolfo upon the cathedral, the creation of a temple, which through his industry, experience, and intellect, will be more beautiful than any other in Tuscany'.[16] Men like this, who by force of personality could stand above the committee system, were rare. Yet it was recognised that there were considerable advantages in having single minds who were capable of controlling a whole building enterprise in this way. On 12 April 1334, the commune of Florence appointed Giotto as 'governor' of the *opera* of the cathedral and of the commune, with a retainer of 100 florins a year, in the hope that he might be just such a man. Their object, the priors explain, is:

> that the works, present and projected, in the city of Florence on behalf of the commune should proceed honourably and decorously. This will not be possible at all unless some skilled and famous man is appointed to govern, control, and supervise these works. It is said that in the whole world no one can be found who is more capable in these and other things than Master Giotto di Bondone, painter of Florence. He should have cause for agreeing to a continued domicile within it. With this many will profit from his knowledge and learning [*scientia et doctrina*] so that no little beauty will come to the city.... [Accordingly, we] elect and appoint Master Giotto as Master and Governor to the Works of the church of Santa Reparata [i.e., the Cathedral], to the construction and completion of the walls and fortifications of the city, and to the other works of the said commune.[17]

Giotto here is made not only 'Governor' of the cathedral but also Town Planner to the commune. He is not, however, appointed as architect, but primarily as an administrator. What the commune seems to be seeking is a man whose reputation and ability will allow him to dominate and give general direction to all the individual masters working upon communal projects. One suspects that a principal element in the *scientia et doctrina* which the commune required was ability as a committee man.

Towards the end of the century the role of certain individuals in building became more pronounced. In Lombardy Bernardo da Venezia seems to have gained something of the fame which Arnolfo di Cambio had enjoyed in Tuscany. Antonio di Vicenzo (*c.* 1340–1401 or 1402) took a very large personal part in the design of San Petronio at Bologna. Like Bernardo da Venezia, Antonio was described as an 'engineer'. This word was used in a double sense. In the first place it meant a craftsman with some supervisory capacity in building work. Bernardo himself, for example, was by trade a wood carver, Giovannino de' Grassi and Giacomo da Campione, 'engineers' of Milan, were respectively a miniature painter and a sculptor. At the same time, however, in Emilia, noticeably at Ravenna and Bologna, the word was also used quite frequently to mean 'someone skilled in engineering', referring particularly to men who had expertise in irrigation works. Such men were likely enough to be called upon to supervise the building projects of the commune.

Antonio di Vicenzo[18] is one example of this. In 1382 he was concerned with building the castle and improving the walls of Bologna. In 1384 he was working in the *Loggia della Mercanzia* and the Notarial Palace; in 1385 and 1386 he was involved in castle-building, and in the construction of the *Podestà*'s palace. In 1387 he was working on the dam across the Reno; in 1396 building mills at Castelbolognese. He has very much the appearance of an 'engineer of the commune'. By this time the *opera* of San Petronio had already commissioned from him a scale model of his plans for the church. Antonio represents the first union of the proto-engineer with the proto-architect.

It is noticeable that when, in June 1390, he was first appointed as *capomaestro* to San Petronio, Vicenzo's salary was quite low. He received only 10 shillings *bolognesi* for each day's work. This unimpressive fee (an occasional day labourer could earn 7 shillings *bolognesi*) was raised in 1391 to £B17 a month, and in the following year to £B30 a month. This last sum gave an annual salary which was less than that of a doctor of medicine to a man with a lifetime's experience of building, one moreover on whom the whole commune depended for the fulfilment of their deepest aspirations. Why should this be? It is possible, of course, that men were willing to work for little in return for the opportunity of taking part in so significant an activity in the life of the community. It is equally possible that the *capomaestro* was expected to supplement his official income by negotiating rake-offs from contractors. The final possibility, and the one which is perhaps the most likely, is that the unique role of the architect, the concept of an individual's sole, personal responsibility for the final form of a building, still did not exist. One thing, however, is certain: that Antonio enjoyed considerable status. In 1390 he was sent as an ambassador to Florence, and in 1400 held important office as one of the 'Reformers of the State of Liberty' in the city.

The appearance of the engineer in building projects did not imply, however, the presence in Italy of any corpus of scientific or theoretical knowledge of building. All architecture was brought into being by a combination of traditional practice and empirical response to specific situations. This is brought out even in Brunelleschi's plans for the dome of the cathedral of Florence, reported to the *Opera* in 1419–20. Here he writes: 'Above the height of about 60 feet let it be built in the way that shall be advised and resolved upon by the masters who shall then be in charge of it, for in building, practice teaches what is to be done'.[19]

'*Nel murare la pratica insegna quello che si ha da seguire*: these words might serve as motto for all the building of the age. The spirit behind them is most clearly seen in the early work upon Milan cathderal.[20] The native engineers who embarked upon the project took as their pattern the traditional simple Lombard-Gothic idiom characteristic of the period. However, they planned to build, not as was customary, in the usual unfaced red-brick, but in granite, and, above all, they planned to build on a much larger scale. For this work they started out only with their traditional skills, and with no conception, beyond these, of the engineering involved in what they were doing, or indeed of what their final engineering purpose was. Between 1386 and 1401 no one knew how the vaulting was to be constructed, or at what height. In the words of Ackermann, every part of the cathedral was designed 'before its structural purpose had been determined . . . buttresses and piers rose towards an unknown objective.'

From time to time their courage faltered, and they called in foreign experts to give their verdict on what was being done: Nicholas Bonaventure (1389–90), Hans of Fernach (1390–1), Heinrich Paler of Gmünd (1391–May 1392), Ulrich of Essingen (October 1394–March 1395), Jean Mignot of Paris and Cône of Bruges (April 1399–October 1401). These men profoundly misunderstood their task. They had been hired at considerable expense. They all professed, as was characteristic of northern builders, a *scientia* of building knowledge, and they believed, naturally enough, that they had been employed to put this knowledge at the service of the Lombard craftsmen. They were deeply horrified by what they saw. The thin buttresses and piles, the flat terrace roofs, the search for stability through the use of iron stays rather than by sound calculation of the equilibrium of vault transepts, was unlike anything that their science had taught them. They remonstrated, were met first with extraordinary theoretical arguments (as that 'pointed arches do not exert a thrust upon the buttress'), and were then told that their 'science' was useless: 'the science of geometry should have no place in these matters since science is one thing, art is another'.

They had failed to realise that they had been hired, not to criticise, but to confirm the intuitive feeling of the Milanesi builders that what they were doing was sound. Science (or theory) was supposed to have told art (or craft) that it was on the right lines. Not understanding this, they had floundered in a sea of incomprehension, were dismissed with a flurry of abuse: 'Ill has he served the *Fabbrica*, yes! he has through his misdeeds done great harm and damage to it' (Heinrich of Gmünd); 'Dismissed for his failure, ignorance, and malice' (Jean Mignot); and they departed, prophesying imminent disaster and the collapse of the building. The cathedral, of course, still stands. Through the sixteenth- and seventeenth-century accretions one can still see an essentially traditional, low-set, Lombard church, resting upon the thin buttresses of the original planners. Like all Italian architecture of the time, Milan is a triumph of building practice which cares nothing about theory. The neglect of that *scientia*, without which, as the northern architects claimed, 'art was nothing', was justified. It was not a science of architecture as it would be understood today, but merely the formalisation and ossification of the hallowed rules of Gothic tradition.

thirteen

The Artist in Society
III.   The Art Market

Supply and Demand

There was a vast expansion in the amount of art produced in Italy between the years 1250 and 1420. Governments and government agencies had become the principal patrons of art in their commissions for buildings, sculptures, and paintings, 'to lighten and delight the hearts and eyes of the citizens'. Ecclesiastics and churches, though less wealthy, could still afford to demand works of high quality. Two other major developments affected the market, the export of works outside Italy and an ever increasing demand for art from the bourgeoisie.

This demand was stimulated both by the desire for a luxurious environment and the needs of private religious devotion. Writing at the beginning of the fifteenth century on the religious education of children, Fra Giovanni Dominici observed that:

The first thing is to have paintings in the house of holy little boys or of tiny young virgins . . . and what I say of paintings goes for sculpture too. The Virgin Mary goes well with the child in her arm and the little bird or the pomegranate in his fist. Or good figures would be Jesus taking suck, Jesus sleeping at his mother's breast, Jesus standing courteously before her, the Mother sewing his garment. And one could show the holy Baptist, clothed in camel skin, as a little boy, entering the desert, joking with the birds, sucking the honeyed leaves, sleeping on the ground. There's no harm in seeing Jesus and the Baptist portrayed; Jesus and the Evangelist as little ones embracing together; the slaughter of the innocents (so that they shall grow fearful of arms and armed men). . . .

The list continues with the images to become traditional in Italian childhood, such as the 11,000 virgins, Agnesa with her fat lamb, Cecilia crowned with roses, Catherine and her wheel. Then comes the traditional ecclesiastical justification of art:

> For it should be known that the painting of angels and saints is permitted and ordained for the intellectual capacity of the lowest. These things are the books of the men in the street, and looked at and understood, they give guidance of the highest good. The revealed scriptures, on the other hand, are principally for the more able, for in them one finds all truth, created and uncreated, in so far as the mind is capable of appreciating it.[1]

It was in part to meet this sort of middle-class need that the artist's workshop came to take on more and more the appearance of a commercial organisation. Men like Giotto and Bernardo Daddi (whose shop specialised in small devotional pictures) in Florence, Duccio's cousin, Segna di Bonaventura(*fl.* 1298) in Siena, and Sano d' Agnelli of Siena who in 1384 owned no less than seven workshops in Genoa,[2] began to establish *botteghe* which catered commercially for the new mass market. One sign of what was happening is the appearance from the third quarter of the fourteenth century of the first surviving 'model books': pattern books giving suggestions of how to treat basic themes likely to be in demand. Another is the increasing difficulty in making attributions of works to individual artists. By the beginning of the fourteenth century works were coming increasingly to be sold under the name of a master when they had been executed by his assistants. John White has suggested that the three extant works which bear Giotto's signature (the St Francis receiving the *Stigmata* in the Louvre, the altarpiece at Bologna, and the *Coronation of the Virgin* in the Baroncelli chapel, S.Croce) were signed by him precisely because he had not painted them. 'These were the works that were in need of the protection of a signature to prove their provenance. In the panels that he carried out himself his brushwork was its own endorsement.' Paradoxically, perhaps, just at this moment when the personality of the individual artist was coming into greater prominence, the personal character of his work was more and more likely to be diluted. Accordingly, many artists might spend their days merely painting details in works which were sold under the name of another.

This development, it should be added, was not only the fruit of commercial demand. It arose too from the new cooperative techniques of mural painting. Work in fresco had to be carefully phased. First the master would make a charcoal sketch of the painting in great detail on an initial layer of plaster (the *arricio*). He would go over it in red earth with a brush to form the *sinopia* or working design. The picture was then divided up into smaller sections known as *giornate* or 'day's work'. At the beginning of each day a *giornata* was plastered, and the master and his assistants, working at great speed before the plaster dried, would paint in that part of the wall. Finally, other colours, such as blue and some reds and greens, were painted in when the surface was dry (*a secco*). Working in this way, painting largely from memory of what lay behind the still wet plaster, demanded organisation and assistants who had been trained in implicit obedience to the master's direction. One effect of this system was to allow wall paintings a much greater element of unified design; Giotto's own achievements owed much to this technique. In addition, for the artist himself, it meant a much stronger division of function between the ordinary master who executed other's conceptions, and the *protomagister* (as Giotto is called in a Neapolitan document) who was directing their work. The *protomagister* had to train and discipline his assistants, and had become a director of a great cooperative enterprise.[3]

Turning to the humbler productions of the workshops, more and more art objects were produced on speculation, that is to say, without being specifically commissioned. These works probably formed the largest part of what was exported. Not only painters, but goldsmiths and sculptors too, were engaged in production for this trade. Some painted stucco figures, produced in Italy in this period, were sent as far north as Amsterdam. In this business foreign buyers, such as 'Antonio de Gorenna' (Antoine de Guienne in France?) who bought 'painted pictures to the value of 80 florins' at Siena in 1348,[4] sometimes came themselves to examine the market. More often it was native merchants who arranged for the pictures to be painted and delivered. In March 1373, the merchant, Francesco di Marco Datini, wrote from Avignon to his partners at Florence with the following order:

Two painted panels, with pedestal, in fine gold, with two figures, with two doors, with pinnacles, at a price of $3\frac{1}{2}$ florins each;

Two smaller painted panels of the same type at 2 to $2\frac{1}{2}$ florins each;

Four square panels of the size of *mezzana* of paper [about 2 × $1\frac{1}{2}$ feet], with good figures, cheap.

In the following September he ordered:

A panel of Our Lady with gold background, with two doors and pedestal, with decorations and leaves, finely and well-worked in the frame, imposing, with beautiful and fine figures of the best master who lives there [Florence]; with lots of figures. In the middle there should be either Our Lord on the Cross, or Our Lady, according to what you find. It really must be fine with beautiful and large figures, the most beautiful you can get costing between $5\frac{1}{2}$ and 6 florins, not more. One panel of Our Lady in fine gold, as above, but somewhat smaller, costing from $3\frac{1}{2}$ to 5 florins and no more.

These two panels should have beautiful figures. I want them for people who are asking fine work. I'm in no hurry. Look well everywhere for them and if you find something cheap and likely to be profitable, take it. If you don't find anything, wait until you get something which seems really good. These are things which one sells only from time to time and I advise you to buy them cheaply according to the prices over there [in Florence].

Two panels of Our Lady, of medium size, with fine gold, of the quality and type of the two that you sent with the four bales a short time ago, for which you paid $4\frac{3}{4}$ florins altogether. If you get them in the same style and manner but more beautiful and with better figures, it doesn't matter if they cost three florins each, if you think there's advantage in it.

Datini, the hero of one of the most depressing rags-to-riches stories of the fourteenth century, was insensitive to any claims of art, and lived in a fool's paradise in thinking that he could get works of real quality at these prices. Yet in looking for bargains, he was at one with his partners who had a clear knowledge of what the French market would take. In March 1387, when he had returned to Florence, an associate wrote to him from Avignon on the character of the trade:

> You say you can't find panels at the price we want, because there aren't any at such low prices. Well, we say this to you: if you don't find good works which are cheap, leave them. They're not much in demand here. You should only buy them when the master's hard up. Do this, for we've no need to take these things on. They aren't things which one sells every day or for which there are many buyers. So, if you're looking around and find a master who's in need of money, then come to terms.
>
> Of the five panels which Andrea bought, we've sold three. We took ten florins gold each, making a very good profit on it. If the master he got them from should have any fine, good panels costing four, five, or six florins—if they are fine and cheap—you could take one or two and no more. Or one more if there is a better master. For those with good figures do sell well; ugly things don't go here.

There were no merchants in this period who confined themselves exclusively to marketing pictures, though there were some among them who seem to have stood out as picture-dealers. One such was Domenico di Cambio, a partner in the Datini firm, whose letters to Datini himself reveal something of his activities. In December 1390 he wrote:

> I've had two pieces, one for Boninsegna [di Matteo, a merchant at Avignon]. The first has each part folio size, and I've had painted there on the first side Our Lord on the Cross, and Our Lady and St John, and on the second, Our Lady holding the Child, all set in fine gold. The other is a third less each way with the same figures and gold. It cost me $3\frac{1}{2}$ florins. There was a painter here who asked six florins and there were some for $5\frac{1}{2}$, and some for five.

In February of the following year he wrote of 'a good master who did a large picture for me at Avignon which cost 12 florins. I'm getting another master to do a smaller one costing 5½ florins.'

When a member of a religious order from the provinces made a visit to one of the centres of art with the purpose of obtaining a painting for his church, it was to men like Cambio that they were likely to turn. It was he, for instance, who acted as agent for Fra Bonifazio, from a Franciscan house in Corsica, on the four occasions (1398, 1401, 1402, and 1403) when the friar visited Florence to buy pictures for his convent. Doubtless it was through some such intermediary that Abbot Thomas of St Alban's (1349–96) was able to bring back from Italy a large panel painting for the high altar of his monastery.[5]

In meeting demands from import clients, men like Cambio and Datini were seeking above all to obtain small works as cheaply as possible. But quite reputable painters like Jacopo di Cione, the brother of Orcagna, could be involved, while others, such as Giovanni Fei, turned out some large panels for the foreign market, especially for Avignon. Occasionally quite highly priced *objets d'art* were despatched to other centres on speculation. In June 1378, for instance, a Florentine businessman recommended that two jewel-boxes, 'pictured with stories of King Priam', and valued at 60 florins, should be sent to a branch of his firm at Rome.

At the same time, there was a limited outlet to the north of works of really high quality for cultivated and wealthy patrons. Typical products here were the panels executed by Tommaso da Modena, which were sent for the Emperor Charles IV to the chapel of St Catherine at Karlstejn in Bohemia; or the Florentine tapestries, north Italian manuscripts, richly worked reliquaries, cameos, coins, and medals, provided by Italian merchants for that great patron, Jean, Duc de Berry (1340–1416), son of King John II of France. This new international trade in art, seen also in Italy with the import of French ivories, enamels, and tapestries, and English alabasters, was important in breaking down provincial styles and in quickening the rhythm of stylistic change throughout Europe. Its first fruit was to be the 'International Gothic' style.

A 'Patron' of Artists

Within the home market it is clear that during the fourteenth century social pressures were already forcing the successful entrepreneur to spend money on art. There were men like Lorenzo Trenta, the silk merchant of Lucca, trading in Bruges and Paris, for whom Jacopo della Quercia carved the Trenta altar in the church of San Frediano within his native town. Another example is the Milanese money-lender and merchant, Marcuolo Carelli, dealing from Venice in cloths, malmsey, cattle, and slaves, who, on his death in 1394, left rights and possessions valued at 35,000 ducats towards the building of Milan cathedral. His tomb, carved by Fillippino da Modena, is still there. How did men such as these view the artists who worked for them, and what esteem did they give to art?

Obviously no general answer is likely to emerge from questions which should properly only be asked of individuals. Yet one notice-able individual, Francesco di Marco Datini of Prato, provides some evidence about this. In January 1383 Datini returned from Avignon to his native Prato, aged about 48. Starting from nothing, he had built up a business which now extended over much of Europe. He was extremely wealthy and his wealth was increasing. He dealt in everything: wool, cloth, silk, jewels, luxury goods, slaves, armour—the list seems unending. In middle age he presented the standard pat-tern of the man who by his own efforts has become rich through unceasing hard work: febrile activity was still necessary to him, not for more riches, but for its own sake. His friends realised his position even if he could only dimly appreciate it, and, in their letters, whose frankness was tempered only by Latin humanity, they tried to draw him from the exclusive preoccupations of his early life. 'I tell you', Niccolò di Buono wrote to him: 'you shouldn't go on killing your-self for a hundred florins more or less. No, you should pass some of the day in enjoying yourself, and go to church in the morning for mass. Cut yourself off from the church, you cut yourself off from God. And I know, and you know, how your work has cut you off.' This message, repeated by many different men, had little effect. The habits of a lifetime could not be broken. Yet the homilies of his acquaintances were not wholly wasted. Datini was persuaded now and then to turn from his commercial preoccupations. He devoted some time to the building of a palace (at a cost of 6,000 florins) at Prato, and a villa on the Calvana hills, and he incurred some heavy expenses in furnishing them. In his chamber, for instance, the canopy of his bed was of silver cloth, with his arms and those of his wife painted upon it; there was a picture of the Madonna there, and a shrine with Christ inside. In the linen room there was a *cassone* (or wedding-chest) with a picture of the Virgin, and a shrine to the Virgin. Among other precious objects were two old jewel-cases painted by a certain Donovelle of Avignon, and a small jewel-case worked by the same artist in black and white. Other occasional purchases were made for the house. In January 1383 he asked a partner of his firm resident at Pisa to buy him there a slave girl and 'a little panel of our Lady in two parts'. (The slave was unobtainable, but the picture was picked up for a mere 3 florins.) Some months later he seems to have thought of commissioning wooden carvings of the Virgin and St John from 'some great master'. A letter to him on this survives from the Florentine painter, Agnolo Gaddi:

> Francesco. Your Agnolo salutes you. You send by Berto to say that you want two figures made, St Mary and St John. I answer that among the others here there's a grave master who would do good work for you. For making them three *braccia* [5 feet 9 inches] high the least he'd want is 25 florins. You could try at Pistoia. There's a man there called Francesco the Saddler who can't stay at Florence. You could try him. Also there's a Giovanni the Painter who cuts figures. Again you could look him up and find out how it goes. I think that you'd do better for everything here. I recommend you to God. Yours.

Whether anything came of this is not known. But in June 1391 Datini got an unknown painter from Montepulciano to paint a garden shrine.

The spirit in which this work was commissioned is illustrated by a series of letters sent to Datini by Domenico di Cambio. On 22 December 1390 Domenico wrote:

You say that you want me to get one of those little panels of Our Lord painted for you, but not whether you want it on a cross or how you want it. And you tell me to see about it with the master of Sant' Apollinare. He's not in Florence at the moment so I can't find out from him. . . .

However he promised to consult someone else. A week later he reported a conversation with an unnamed master.

He suggests a *Pietà*, that is Our Lord coming from the tomb. For putting fine gold in the background he asks five pounds. I suggest he should do it for a gold florin. I'll have a talk with some other masters about it when the holiday's over, and I'll see what they think about the painting and what they want, and I'll tell you what they say so that you can give your opinion.

On 20 January he wrote again:

About your picture, I've got the point of what you've said. It should be painted with devout and compassionate [*pietose*] figures, so that the soul of the man seeing them may turn sooner to devotion towards God. It's true that men who're hard of heart towards God and wrapped up in worldly things need these compassionate scenes, and since it seems to me you are one of these yourself, I'll make every effort to see that you get good service.

Cambio's frankness doesn't seem to have been taken amiss. On the 16 February the work had been commissioned: 'I'm pressing for your picture as hard as possible; I've given it to a good master who did a large one for me at Avignon which cost 12 florins.' A month later, however, difficulties had begun to appear. On 17 March he wrote:

I've already explained how I've commissioned one side of your little panel, and arranged to have the *Pietà* there, that is to say our Lord half out of the tomb with our Lady on one side and St John on the other. I thought it would be painted by now. However it's only got so far as being chalked in, and he [the master] said that the figures will have to be very small. But he's not being truthful about this. It's because he's had a lot of business with a panel he's getting me to send to Avignon and with other things, that he hasn't done yours. They're all liars, and big ones too.

Domenico however went on to suggest that the scene be changed to a crucifixion with Our Lady and St John, and asked Datini to say what figures he wanted on the other part of the panel.

At this Datini's patience broke, and he seems to have replied by asking Domenico to stop the negotiations. But his friend was not so easily to give up the chance of bestowing the religious benefits expected from a 'compassionate' painting. On the 21 March he wrote:

> You say I'm not to touch your little panel again unless you write to me, because the painter can't find a devout subject. It strikes me that either you haven't been able to read my letter or I haven't been able to write it properly. I told you about getting the *Pietà* made—which is a very devout subject. The master, though, said that the figures would be small, and that he hasn't done it because of this. But he's not telling the truth about this. He's leaving it because something more profitable has come into his hands. So think if you want other saints and I'll get them done and let you know.

On the 18 April he was enquiring again: 'What saints do you want in the other part? Tell me if you want me to get them hinged together. In my opinion it's better. Then I'll have a sheath of cured leather made so that you can take it anywhere without damage.'

Domenico remained indifferent to further complaints from Datini. Four days later he wrote:

> You say I haven't taken much advice from the masters. I tell you there's no good master in Florence I haven't talked to, and the opinion is that this is the most devout subject. . . . You say you want me to get painted on the other part of the panel St John with St Francis and St Catherine, St Margaret, St Peter, and St Mary Magdalene. The painter says it seems you want a procession. We'll put there those that best go, and I'll have it all set in fine gold so that, with God's grace, you should like it. Of course, it's quite

right that you should want a lot of advocates for yourself to plead for you before God, but if they were to cost as much as the advocates at Florence you might have less to do with them and do your own pleading for your soul. But they tell me you've become a sort of hermit who never goes out. You'd do well to visit the church and commend yourself to God, that he'll give you grace here in this life and in the next.

This is obviously a long way from enthusiasm for art. The name of the artist does not appear and apparently has not in any way aroused Datini's interest. The only demand that the merchant made of the painter was that he should be 'a grave master', by which, presumably, he meant a sober craftsman who would do the job assigned to him without fuss. He did not bother to leave Prato to consider in person the merits of the different painters of Florence. All this was left to Domenico di Cambio. Datini's patronage of art was nothing more than an attempt, at the heavy prompting of his friends, to perform a religious duty, to find 'compassionate' subjects which might turn his mind to spiritual matters, and to secure at cheap rates 'advocates' who might plead his case before God.

Side by side with this there went too a concern for what might be called the interior decoration of his palace. Between 1389 and 1390, Paganino di Ugolino, Dino di Puccio, and Jacopo di Puccio were painting inside the building and its loggia. Here too it is extremely doubtful whether for this work, in which the coats of arms of Datini and his wife seem to have played an extravagant part, there was anything but the most rudimentary concern on his part for aesthetic satisfaction. At the end of 1391 the task was resumed by Niccolò Gerini, Arrigo di Niccolò, Bartolomeo Bertozzi, and Agnolo Gaddi. But their employment led only to disputes; those instincts with which Datini had amassed his fortune were over-sharply attuned to anything by which it might be frittered away. The painters arrived at Prato in the middle of September, and, so Datini said, took so much time off for visits back to Florence that the work had proceeded with extreme slowness. By 21 December, he claimed, they had spent half of the three months in which they had been employed merely in putting up scaffolding, grinding colours, and painting beams and joists. At this he dismissed the three men without any immediate payment for what work they had done. When the bills came in, the painters asked for a florin a day each (counting in that their expenses). Datini was outraged: 'I don't think when Giotto was alive he did better business . . . these people, because they find the soil soft, want to thrust their spade in right up to the hilt.' In return he offered eight to ten shillings. But he himself was treading on dangerous ground here, and Domenico advised him to pay: 'You know what one gives for a painter's arm, and you know what they're asking.'

This was wise counsel, but it was ignored. In the end Bartolomeo Bertozzi took out a suit against him in the court of the Doctor's Guild, of which the painters of Florence formed a part, and was awarded 50 florins. To complete Datini's discomfiture it came out in the course of proceedings that he had traded in medicinal drugs, and the court therefore commanded that he should pay the entrance fee to the guild. At this he fell for a time into a deep *malinchonia del capo*, and his judgments on painters from then on were tinged with strong animosity: 'They always seem to be dying of hunger. . . .' or (on Niccolò Pieri): 'May God deliver me from his hands and those of his peers, for they're all made the same way. I'll never have anything else painted.'

But this was easier said than done. In 1401, in memory of a business associate, he and his partners gave ten florins, and the firm of Ambrogio di Meo, five florins, for a small panel painting to be executed by Giovanni Fei for the church of the Franciscan friars at Bonifacio in Corsica. In 1403 Fei was commissioned by Domenico di Cambio to do another work, for which Datini paid 50 florins, probably designed to be hung in the Franciscan church at Prato. This church was a major object of his concern. In 1384 he had commissioned Tommaso del Mozza to paint a fresco there. In 1392 he obtained a veil and silk cloth for the tabernacle, and commissioned new altars, lamps, and candelabra. In 1395 Niccolò Gerini (whom he had dismissed only four years before) and Lorenzo di Niccolò painted a Crucifixion and a panel of the Virgin, and perhaps also painted the chapter house there, at Datini's expense. In 1408 he bought the friars a chalice worth 50 florins. In the same year Arrigo di Niccolò painted a shrine in Datini's villa and produced two pictures in San Francesco of the merchant on his knees before St Francis. In addition, before the end of his life, Datini gave stained-glass windows to many of the churches of Florence and Prato.

His death in 1410 also brought employment to the artists he had reviled. His palace, then turned into an asylum for the poor, was decorated by six painters with sixteen scenes from the story of his life. His will provided for two panel paintings at altars in his parish church, for 12 silver lamps there, and for the frescoing of the refectory of the convent of San Niccolò. His tombstone was carved by the Florentine sculptor, Niccolò Lamberti. So, in death as in life, he had art thrust upon him.

Datini was a mean-souled man (which was the secret of his financial success) and his patronage of art reflected his character. Through Domenico di Cambio he shopped around for bargains, though without any understanding of what a bargain might be. The results were unhappy: a grudging, loveless dispensation of money on the second rate and a feeling of bitterness against those who had produced it. But money from people like Datini helped the workshops along the Arno to keep going, gave the artist the promise of a relatively secure existence, and formed part of the background for the new humanist approach to art.

The Profits of the Artist

It is obvious that in the attitude of a man like Datini to the artists he employed, there is a stark contradiction of the views of his humanist contemporaries. Faced with this contrast, setting aside theoretical formulations of the position of artists, it should be asked what status they enjoyed in practice. It is generally assumed that their social rank was inevitably low, and that they were poorly rewarded for their work. 'Very few of them,' writes one scholar, 'could ever manage to acquire a house or landed property. The greater majority lived with their families in a state of permanent financial dependency.' In fact, this conventional view should be considerably modified. It is true that artists of the lower and middle ranks were fairly poor, that most of their work was directed to artisan-type tasks, and that for this work they were paid and esteemed as artisans. Yet, for the artists who attained the greatest reputation of their day and who were considered to be the leading painters or sculptors of the age, a rather different picture emerges. It is this élite which is to be considered in the present section.

It is not easy to estimate how much the greatest artists could be expected to earn. Artists were paid in various ways. They could receive a lump sum, previously agreed upon. Alternatively, the payment for their work might be assessed by independent valuers when it had been completed (in which circumstances the upper and lower limits of what it might be valued at were normally specified in advance). They might obtain a day-wage for every working day that they filled at a specific task, or be given a monthly or yearly salary, in which case money was normally deducted for each day they did not work, whether through illness, unsuitable weather conditions, or because it was a feast day of the church. Outside the contract system, artists were occasionally taken into signorial households and received gifts of money from time to time at their master's whim. But any arrangement or contract for work was temporary and for a limited period. And there is no artist in this period whose working life is fully and continuously documented. Consequently generalisation is difficult; the very fact that an artist left behind documentary traces in certain periods may mean that these were times of remarkably good fortune, which were exceptional precisely because he was able to secure contracts. These contracts, too, are often insufficiently detailed. They often fail to show, for instance, how long the artist was at work, or whether his assistants, paints, gilding, and other materials, were to be paid out of his own pocket.

None the less it is possible to gain a limited insight. (See, for comparison here, the 'Preliminary note upon money', pp. 3–4, at the front of this book.) In 1308 Duccio, at the height of his powers, was earning about 120 florins a year. At the beginning of the same year, King Charles II of Naples was paying almost the same amount (30 gold *uncie* of the Regno) as the annual fee of Pietro Cavallini for his frescoes in S. Maria Donna Regina. This payment was increased in December by his son, King Robert, by a further two *uncie* (about eight florins). Nine years later, Simone Martini was granted 50 *uncie* (about 200 florins) by the same king.[6] At the beginning of the fif-teenth century, Taddeo di Bartolo and Spinello Aretino were receiving salaries in the order of 150 and 140 florins.[7]

Goldsmiths could receive higher rewards. In the 20 years between 1405 and 1424 Ghiberti received an average of 200 florins a year. Stone sculptors were likely to receive somewhat less. Pietro di Giovanni 'of Brabant' probably earned something like 300 florins for his work on the façade of Florence cathedral between 1387 and 1389. At the beginning of the fifteenth century the young Donatello was probably earning about 100 florins a year.[8] In addition, one of the most remunerative positions which an artist could occupy was that of *capomaestro* of a cathedral works. This might involve acting as master builder or as resident sculptor. In such a post a high pre-mium was placed upon all-round ability. When Andrea Orcagna agreed to act as *capomaestro* of Orvieto in 1358, his duties included, according to his contract, 'the building of walls and making of statues, painting with a brush, making mosaic, and burnishing marble figures'. For this he was offered no less than 300 florins a year, plus a grant to his brother, who was also to be employed, of 96 florins a year. (It is significant that he was sufficiently well off to cancel the contract in 1360 and returned to the post which he had previously held as *capomaestro* of Or San Michele at Florence.) Between 1407 and 1425 Sano di Matteo held the same position at Orvieto in return for 20 florins a month and the lease of a furnished house.[9] On the other hand, as has been seen, Antonio di Vicenzo, as 'engineer' of S. Petronio in Bologna, was not really well paid, considering his responsibilities.

These sums were not in any way comparable to those received by great lawyers, doctors, or capitalists. They do not in any way ap-proach the rewards of Raphael in the sixteenth century. It should be emphasised that they are what only a minority achieved: those who worked for the communes or the greater guilds of Florence, not those who spent their lives in commissions offered by local reli-gious confraternities. Still this minority could and did attain to a certain measure of bourgeois prosperity.

This general impression of prosperity is confirmed in considering other evidence on their economic status. It is true that the dowries of their wives were not high, a reflection perhaps of what the ordinary artist might be expected to earn, yet they were not negligible. In 1310 the wife of Agostino di Giovanni, one of the sculptors of the Tarlati monument in Arezzo, brought him a dowry of £112 *senesi* (about 40 florins), half a house, and two pieces of land valued at £80. The wives of Donato Martini, Bartolo di Fredo, and Fede di Nalduccio, all brought 100 florins. Often they possessed substantial houses, and were landlords in a modest way. By 1339 Agostino di Giovanni had come to own land, a house, and a barn in the *contado*, valued at 200 florins; lands in the city of Siena valued at about £850 *senesi* (about 260 florins); and a house with courtyard, well, orchard, and *loggia*. Simone Martini, in his will of 1314, left his wife a house and furnishings, valued at 60 florins, four vineyards let out on lease, another house, and 220 florins to be used for the dowry of his niece. Income tax returns drawn up at Florence in 1363 show that the painter Ristoro d'Andrea rented a house in the city for ten florins a year, and possessed 'a little broken-down house' with orchard, vineyard, and land, valued at 220 florins in the *contado* at Signa. This property was leased out to a share-cropper who paid an annual food rent of grain, oats, and wine. At the same time Giovanni da Milano had a revenue of six florins a year from three pieces of land at Ripoli, valued at 150 florins, and Michele di Maso a house in which he dwelt in via Nuova, valued at 120 florins. Since these declarations were made by the men themselves to the assessors of taxation it may be assumed that, if anything, they understated the value of what they owned.[10]

Many painters were *rentiers*: they had shares in the funded communal debt at Florence. Between 1326 and 1343 only about 8,000 people in Florence were wealthy enough to take out or be forced to take out these shares; their average individual holding was about seven florins. Since in 1345 Taddeo Gaddi had shares to the value of 21 florins, and Donato di Giotto and Lappo Guccio both had shares of over 24 florins, it can be assumed that these men were reasonably prosperous. Bernardo Daddi with seven florins and Lando Falcone with ten florins must have enjoyed an average or more than average prosperity. And later, in 1391, the Florentine painter and miniaturist, Cenni di Francesco, lent no less than 300 florins to the commune.[11]

In 1403 the descendants of Taddeo Gaddi and Neri Fioravanti were among the 600 most wealthy families of Florence.[12] Such men, like Giotto, seem to have been able to dispose of a sufficient surplus to speculate in the business activities of the great companies in which large fortunes were to be made. It is difficult to see the economic position of the well-established artist in the fourteenth century as in any way necessarily depressed. Vasari wrote, though his information here is particularly questionable, that the painter, Starnina, was in some way implicated with the *Ciompi* or lower-class revolt of 1378, and certainly a goldsmith was executed in 1393 for his partisanship of the lesser guilds against the Florentine ruling class. Yet it is not necessary to deduce from this that these men were characteristic of artists of the period, or that they had, through the pressure of economic exploitation, aligned themselves with the proletariat against the Florentine ruling class. Artists sometimes went through temporary or permanent financial crises. The goods of Ambrogio Lorenzetti were seized, ostensibly for debt, at Florence in 1321. Maso di Banco's goods were sequestrated there in 1341. According to Vasari again, Giovanni del Ponte died in 1365, having wasted his earnings, with hardly enough money left behind for a decent burial. The painter, Bartolomeo di Michele (d. 1408) was executed for theft.[13] But it would be wrong to generalise from such individual incidents to a whole group.

Freedom and Constraint

Although some artists earned a lot of money, was this, as has been generally asserted, in poor or humiliating conditions of work? It has been claimed that the painter and sculptor were crushed under the burden of the guild system, that this system stifled individuality and had a levelling effect on originality. It has been said that art in this period was so much the product of cooperative work that it eliminated that individuality which distinguishes the artist from the artisan. Finally it has been claimed that the contract system of patronage reduced the artist to a humiliating dependence upon his employer.

Something has already been written in the previous chapter on the first of these claims, which can be dismissed as untrue. It seems unlikely that the originality of Giotto, Orcagna, or Ghiberti, was stifled by their membership of a guild. Turning to the second point, cooperative work was frequent both in painters' workshops and in the employment of sculptors. There is an impression of the collective character which a sculptured work might possess in a relief, probably executed by Andreolo de' Bianchi around 1392, in the attic to the southern porch of S. Maria Maggiore at Bergamo (see plate xx). This shows a *scultoretus* sitting at a desk drawing with a compass and directing three assistants whose names are obscure but whose functions are clear enough. A figure entitled *grechus* roughly blocks out a capital from stone; a man called *aristatius* holds the capital inverted before him, and carves it roughly with hammer and chisel; finally a *paschomastius* makes the finishing touches to it when put into position. In other words, four men were involved in the carving of the one capital.

A recent study of the making of the reliefs in the façade of Orvieto has shown how some men were organised to square off the blocks which had arrived from the quarries, how others sketched the designs, others punched in the final form, and yet others smoothed and polished the completed stones. Then certain men would concentrate on certain features; some specialising in wings, some in architectural aspects, some on drapery, some on hair, and so on.[14] At first sight, this certainly reduces the individual character of the artist's work. And this development was matched in painting by the rise of the new fresco technique. Yet just as the personality of the *protomagister* in works in fresco grew as a result, so in sculpture a much greater freedom and power rested in the hands of the *capomaestro* who actually organised the work. As seen in the career of Giovanni Pisano (pp. 272–274), the individual character of an artist's work was coming more and more to be recognised. In Ghiberti's contract with the Cloth Guild for the north doors of the Florentine Baptistery in 1407, the guild insisted that it should be he personally who worked 'on those parts which require the greatest perfection'.

In other words the growth of collective work in art meant not simply a loss of individuality, but rather that a number of men sub-merged their own personalities in the vision of one leading artist. And the man who was most likely to achieve success was one who combined a wide and versatile knowledge of the arts with the ability to organise and direct the work of others It was natural that the highest salaries and the most secure positions were given to *capo-maestri*, for it was precisely in these positions that men of organising talents were required.

The contractual system was the largest restrictive element in the artist's pursuit of his freedom. Most work which artists produced was normally done under contract. They did not, as most do today, simply paint or sculpt in the hope that what they were doing might possibly be sold in the future. Almost all the greater works of art were made *ad hoc*, in response to a specific demand. Each picture or sculpture was generally made for one particular place; painting as well as sculpture had an intimate relation with architecture. Often the contract laid down precisely the measurements of the painting and the figures which should be present in it. This example from 1372 shows a contract for panel painting (for notes on some other contracts, see the appendix to this chapter, pp. 335–48):

In the name of God, Amen. In the year from the incarnation of our Lord, one thousand, three hundred and seventy two, in the tenth indiction, on the twelfth day of the month of April. Drawn up in the *contado* of Florence, in the monastery of San Michele di Passignano, in the presence of these witnesses: Jacopo di fu Vanni and Francesco di fu Corso, servants of the said monastery, the lord Pietro di Giovanni, prior of the canonry of San Bartolomeo di Scampato etc.

Let it be clear to all that Jacopo di fu Mino, painter, of the parish of Sant' Antonio, from the district of Camollia in the city of Siena, has promised the reverend father and lord in Christ, the lord Martino, by the grace of God and the apostolic see, Abbot of the monastery of San Michele di Passignano, of the Vallambrosian order, in the diocese of Fiesole, in the *contado* of Florence, that he shall make or cause to be made a panel of wood with a predella and two columns, suitable for an altar, with a length in all of 4¼ *braccia* [7 feet 9 inches], and of a height in all of five *braccia* [9 feet 2 inches], with three divisions and with all the pinnacles which are required for the panel, and that he will paint with his own hands upon it the figures and stories written below. He has promised and agreed to give, bear, and carry or cause to be given, borne, or carried this panel to the said monastery of Passignano, painted, placed, and installed on the altar of the said monastery over which the said lord abbot Martino aforesaid deputes that it shall be placed or established, at the entire and single charge and expense of the same Jacopo, save for the carriage costs; this within the seven months now to come.

In this panel the same Jacopo, the aforesaid painter, has promised and agreed to make and to paint the below-mentioned figures, set in good and lawful gold, with good ultramarine silver, and with other good, suitable, and appropriate colours: that is, in the middle section to make and paint the story of the Holy Spirit as he descended on the Apostles; for the other sections, in one the figure of St Catherine with the figure of a monk kneeling at her feet, and in the other the figure of St Anthony Abbot; and in the parts above the said sections, in the middle one, the figure of God the Father sending the Holy Spirit upon the apostles with various angels, in the others, the figure of holy Mary ever Virgin and the Annunciation from the angel. In the lower predella of the said panel [he has promised] to make and paint four stories of Holy Catherine as she received her martyrdom; at the top of the said predella, two half figures, that is to say the figure of St Mary Magdalene, and of St Agnes; and in each of the said columns to make and paint three figures, that is to say the figure of St Pancras with a banner raised in his hand with a red cross painted therein, the figure of St Gregory as pope, St Laurence the Martyr, St Benedict the Abbot clothed in black, St Brigid, and the figure of St Nicholas.

He has promised and agreed with the same lord abbot guaranteeing and contracting as above to make and with his own hands paint in the said panel all the aforesaid figures beautifully and showing respect, and to bring and bear or cause to be brought and borne the panel to the said monastery of Passignano within the said time and term of the seven months now to come. And for his part the said lord Abbot Martino aforesaid has promised to the same aforesaid Jacopo, painter, to release and pay for his labour and reward for the said panel 80 good and lawful florins of the right weight and coin of Florence, making payment of the said florins at the end of the said seven months in the said monastery of Passignano or in the said city of Siena.

I, Bindo di fu Cardo da Balbiano, notary, intervened in each and every of the aforesaid transactions, and having drawn up the instrument for them, have written and published it.[15]

As is characteristic of these agreements, there are three main items contracted for here by the abbot: the panel, the paints, and the painting. The panels of this age are often works of art in their own right, and could be very expensive. The cost of the gilding too, when gold was used, and of the other colours, noticeably of the imported ultramarine azure, was high. When in 1385 Spinello Aretino painted an altarpiece at Chiusuri he received 100 florins for his work. Simone Cani who carved the panel (measuring 5 feet 9 inches by 7 feet 8 inches) was given 50 florins, and Gabriello Saraceni who did the gilding was also paid 100 florins.

For the painting itself the figures to be present and their arrangement are very precisely determined. This is characteristic of many contracts, though often they are as likely to refer to some supplementary *schema* which has been or is to be provided by the patron and which the artist is to follow. In July 1408 the council of Siena 'decided that *maestro* Spinello, painter, should illustrate the story of the battle of the Venetians with the Emperor Frederick by sea, as appears on that paper which Betto di Benedetto suggested'. Such conditions were equally likely to be imposed upon goldsmiths and still more upon sculptors, whose forms were often, curiously enough by our standards, dictated by painter's designs. The figures of the apostles worked by Pietro di Giovanni 'of Brabant' on the Talenti façade of Florence cathedral, for instance, were executed according to designs drawn up by Lorenzo Bicci, Agnolo Gaddi, and Spinello Aretino.[16]

Occasionally contracts expressly gave the artist a wider discretion. In August 1406, for instance, Taddeo di Bartolo was commissioned to paint in the chapel of the Nine in the Palazzo Pubblico of Siena frescoes of the life of the Virgin 'with those figures, ornaments, and gold, and in that manner and form as shall seem appropriate to him for the adornment of the said chapel and the honour of our commune.' But such stipulations were very rare; in this case the commune was looking for a particularly speedy completion of the work in expectation of a visit by Pope Gregory XII. More often the artist was controlled by the patron's whims. Naturally, even the most carefully drawn contract left some discretion to the artist in the narrative scenes. This was recognised by Bishop Durand in his work on the symbolism of churches, where he wrote that 'The diverse histories of the Old and New Testament may be represented after the fancy of the painter. For:

Pictoribus atque poetis
Quod libet addendi semper fuit aequa potestas.

('painters and poets have always had an equal licence in adding what they please').

This slightly garbled version of *Ars poetica*, 9–10 (what Horace in fact wrote was *quodlibet audendi*, that is, 'an equal licence in daring invention') seems to have been in common currency in ecclesiastical circles in the fourteenth century, and had passed from them to artists. Cennino Cennini quotes it in his treatise. None the less it is obvious that the contract of the patron was by our standards a seriously limiting factor in the artist's freedom of expression.

Moreover, the contractual system gave the patron a considerable measure of control over the artist's conditions of work. From the contracts referred to in the appendix it may be seen that a patron could reject a completed work if it were held to be below standard and that he could insist on an exact accounting of materials used. Above all, patrons expected from the artist continuous and regular application and the uninterrupted performance of his task. In 1407, for instance, the Cloth Guild of Florence expected Ghiberti to work on the Baptistery Doors 'every working day all day long, with his hands, like any other journeyman', and every interruption to this work was to be noted in a special book kept for the purpose. There still survives the work record of Taddeo di Bartolo, kept by the officials of the *Opera*, when he was painting six Old Testament figures in Florence Cathedral between mid-June and mid-August 1407. They show that, apart from not working on Sundays, he generally had Saturday afternoon off, that occasionally he would have a long weekend by not working on Monday either, and that in addition there were eight days when he did not come in to work at all, and three weekdays when he came in for only half a day.[17] Presumably some of these non-working days were feast days of the church, and others were periods when the wall was being prepared for fresco. Even allowing for this it does not suggest an atmosphere of great pressure. On the other hand, the record of attendances was very carefully kept.

Moreover, the question of completion by an agreed time was something which often exercised patrons. In 10 November 1407 Taddeo di Bartolo was being threatened by the commune of Siena with a fine of 25 florins if he had not finished the frescoes he had begun in the palace of Siena within a month. Six days later, the council lost patience again, and the officials commanded that Taddeo should be sent for and told not to leave the Palace until the work was finished (though they cannily added that this did not mean that they would be held responsible for paying for his meals in the Palace during that time). Nine years later, in April 1415, Donatello was being threatened with a fine of 25 florins if he failed to complete a statue by the end of May.[18]

It might seem from this that the artist was treated as an artisan. Certainly these were conditions which artists of the time were seeking to escape. In September 1390, for instance, Luca di Giovanni, *capomaestro* of Orvieto cathedral, petitioned that he should have 'freedom of work as *capomaestro* of the building ... that if it should happen that I come one night and do a figure or anything else, that I shall be able to do what I like'. In addition he asked that no money should be taken off him for days on which he did not work. In their reply the commune agreed, with some reservations, to these requests.[19]

None the less, to make too much of the constrictions of the artist is in a sense anachronistic. In the first place, the limitations of artistic freedom arose in large part out of the very sophisticated character of fourteenth century art. In the fourteenth century only men of excellent education were likely to understand the full meaning of such elaborate allegories as Lorenzetti's frescoes in the Communal Palace at Siena. To plan such works demanded a learning which the artist was unlikely to possess. Consequently, the subject matter, and to a certain extent the way in which it was to be treated, was dictated to the artist from outside, by those who commissioned the work.

Moreover, in any field of social life or work during the century, the idea of contract was supreme. For example, the terms of employment of university professors of law, men who were in this period without doubt among the social, political, and intellectual élite, show the same types of restrictive conditions and regulations as those of artists.[20] They were fined if they started a lecture five minutes late, and if they went on for five minutes over the hour. They were fined if they failed to cover difficult passages in the text on which they were lecturing, and if they failed to cover the whole text in a term. If they got married they were allowed to absent themselves from their teaching for 24 hours only, and so on. It was not only artists who were strictly regulated by contract in the way they worked. Italians of the fourteenth century sought to define precisely people's duties and rights in all ranks of society. Artists were not being singled out for this treatment; the fact that they were bound by contract does not mean either that they were necessarily regarded as mere artisans, or that they were considered to be of low status.

That this is indeed so can be seen from many of their careers. Too much importance should not be attributed to the fact that Giotto was admitted into the household of King Robert of Naples, for this was an administrative expedient rather than a social grading. Similarly, when in another document from Naples Simone Martini was described as a knight, the word *eques* had the same imprecision as 'esquire' today, and was likely to be used as casually. Yet certainly one Sienese goldsmith attained high office under the Angevins. This was Pietro di Simone who, after cutting coins for the mint of Charles II of Naples, followed the fortunes of Carlo Roberto, Angevin King of Hungary, and ended his days as a viscount and as castellan of Zips.[21] Obviously there was a world of difference between being a viscount at Zips and being one at Bari, and it is likely that Pietro no longer carried on his old trade. Still, nearer home, many artists managed to acquire positions of quiet dignity in their communes. Though at Florence the tight circle of the upper bourgeoisie was too close ever to receive them, in other communes many artists participated in civic office. At Pistoia, the painters Martino Boncetti (*fl.* 1391) and Giovanni Cristani (*fl.* 1374, the son of a tailor) served as *anziani*, while Francesco da Volterra (*fl.* 1352), who settled in Pisa, was enrolled there as a member of the Great Council. At Siena, Andrea Vanni went frequently as ambassador of the commune to Avignon, Florence, and Naples, and served in numerous positions within the government. Taddeo di Bartolo, in his 60s, was frequently a member of the council and held the post of Captain of the People in his district of San Salvatore. Other artists, Lippo Vanni, Luca di Tommè, Niccolò Tegliacci, Paolo di Giovanni Fei, all held similar positions.

The number of men, who like Giotto, Taddeo Gaddi, or Ghiberti, made a great deal of money from art and attained great social esteem, must have been small. In the fourteenth century the majority of artists struggled on in a limited world which their more talented companions had left behind. Many of these are to be found in the Florentine tax records, living in the slum areas of S. Spirito and S. Croce, and judged too poor even to pay the sums that were wrenched from their fellow workers. Others, more prosperous, appear in the stories of Boccaccio and Sacchetti about the three painters, Calandrino, Bruno, and Buffalmacco. These men are still not rich. Calandrino, for instance (in *Decameron* viii, 3) owns only a house and a little farm near Florence which came to him as his wife's dowry. Faced with the possibility of wealth, he is exultant: 'we can get money quickly without having to scribble on walls all day like snails'. Yet if the stories of him and his fellows are anything to go by, these are not men who seem to be discontented with their lot. Indeed, Sacchetti perhaps reproves the importance we assign to the whole question of status when he tells a story about a learned but rather stupid doctor who, seeing them, is surprised 'that they took less regard for the world than others', and cannot understand 'how they, being poor men, can live with such gaiety'. Above all, one presumes these men, like their greater contemporaries, found a form of happiness in their work. In the words of the guild of Sienese painters in 1355 it was work which, 'however slight it is, can have neither beginning nor end without these three things: that is to say, without power, and without knowledge, and without that will which comes from love.'

Appendix

Some Notes on Contracts and Payments to Artists

The object of these notes is to give some impressions, directly from original sources, of the working conditions and payments of artists.

A   PANEL PAINTINGS

1   15 April 1285, the Company of S. Maria, who had their chapel in the church of S. Maria Novella at Florence, contracted with Duccio di Buoninsegna. He was to make a large panel of the Virgin, her Son, and other figures 'at the will and pleasure of the said contractors' in return for £150 *flor. parv.* (about 85 florins). He was to meet the expenses of the painting himself. If the panel was not beautiful or not according to the wish of the contractors, they would not pay, and Duccio himself would keep it. This is probably the Rucellai Madonna now in the Uffizi. (Milanesi, *Documenti, cit.* i, 158–160.)

2   October 1308. Duccio di Buoninsegna was commissioned by the master of works of the cathedral of Siena to paint a *Maestà* for the high altar. Duccio was to be paid 16 shillings a day for each day that he worked on the picture and a proportion of this sum for each part of a day that he worked at it. The cathedral was to provide all the paints and materials needed, so that he himself was to provide 'nothing save his own person and labour'. Duccio promised not to accept any other commission until the work was finished and to paint 'as best he can and knows and as the Lord shall bestow on him, and to work continuously on the said painting at those times he is able to until the said painting is finished and completed'. Under this agreement Duccio probably worked for about 16 months, and possibly made a profit of about 150 florins. Then in a later contract, for which only a preliminary memorandum has survived, he engaged to paint the back of the panel with 34 stories from the life of Christ for a total payment of 95 florins. Here again the master of works was to provide the paints. (C. Brandi, *Duccio, cit.*, pp. 71–84.)

3   17 April 1320. Pietro Lorenzetti contracted to paint a panel of 6 × 5 *braccia* (approximately 11 feet 6 inches × 9 feet 7 inches) for the Bishop of Arezzo in return for £160 *pisani* (about 55 florins). The painting was to consist of the Virgin Mary and Child, with four figures at the side, and prophets and saints 'as shall be decided by the Lord Bishop'. The area between the figures was to be gilded with the best gold, 'counting a florin for each 100 leaves'. The other ornaments were to be of silver; the blues to be of best quality ultramarine. The bishop was to provide the panel, the painter the colours. Pietro was not to take on other commissions until this had been finished. (Borghesi and Banchi, *Nuovi documenti, cit.*, pp. 10–11.)

4   26 October 1329. The Carmelite friars of Siena contracted with Pietro Lorenzetti. He should paint for the high altar of their church a panel containing figures of the Virgin, St Nicholas, with apostles, martyrs, confessors, and virgins, in return for 150 florins. This painting is now in the Pinacoteca of Siena. (Milanesi, *Documenti, cit.*, i, 193–4.)

5   1380. 'In the name of God, amen. Let it be noted by whoever shall see this writing that master Cecco del Guiccha, worker in wood, arbiter on behalf of the master of works of [the cathedral of] Santa Maria [of Siena] has been appointed to value the panel done by master Francesco del Tonghio and his son Jacomo, together with Stefano di maestro Fantozzo, arbiter on behalf of master Francesco. And that we value the said painting in all at 22 gold florins. And I Stefano di maestro Fantozzo have written this with my own hand.

And I master Cecco di Guiccha consent to the said writing.'
(Milanesi, *Documenti, cit.*, i, 288–9.)

6   9 May 1382. Bartolo di Fredo agreed with the Company of St Peter
at Montalcino to paint a picture for the chapel of the Annunciation
in the church of San Francesco at Montalcino. It was to be completed
within a year of the painter's arrival at Montalcino. The painter was
to provide fine gold, silver, and varnish, and was to receive 170 florins
in three instalments. (Milanesi, *Documenti, cit.*, pp. 292–3.)

7   1385. Spinello Aretino agreed with the General of the Congregation
of Monteoliveto to paint an altarpiece for the church of Monteoliveto
Maggiore, Chiusuri. The painting 'with an infinite number of figures'
and 5 feet 9 inches × 7 feet 8 inches in size, was to be completed
within eight months. Spinello was to receive 100 florins. In addition
Simone Cini was to receive 50 florins for six months work in carving
the frame with ornament in half-relief, and Gabriello Saracini 100
florins for gilding. Part of this work is probably now in the Accademia
in Florence. (Vasari, *cit.*, ed. Milanesi, i, 688 n. 1.)

8   11 December 1393. It was agreed that Bartolo di Fredo, Cristofano
Bindocci, and Meo di Petro should receive four florins from the commune of Siena for restoring the Mappamondo (which had been executed by Ambrogio Lorenzetti). For the paints used in the restoration
they were to receive £12 *senesi*. (about 3 florins). (Milanesi, *Documenti,
cit.*, ii, 37.)

9   August 1401. Giovanni Fei was to paint at Florence a small panel for
the church of San Francesco at Bonifacio in Corsica. He would receive
12 florins for his work, and 3 florins for the panel. The paints were
to be provided by Fei; no gold was to be used, but silver gilt instead.
The money was provided by Francesco Datini and another business
man. The contract stipulated completion by November 1402. Fei was
busy at this period and it was not delivered until the end of January
1403. (Piattoli, *Rivista d' arte*, xi, 239–40, 251–2.)

10   1402. Giovanni Fei had completed a panel picture, 7 feet 8 inches ×
3 feet 10 inches, for Domenico di Cambio. He was probably negotiating on behalf of Francesco Datini who intended it for the church of
San Francesco at Prato. For this and another work, Giovanni received
50 florins. The payment was made after three valuers had assessed the
work at 40, 50, and 60 florins, respectively. (Mazzei, *Lettere, cit.*, ii,
415–7).

11   25 January 1402. Simone di fu Pucci, silk merchant, acting as pro-
curator for the friars of San Marco in Florence, commissioned Lorenzo
di Niccolò to deliver a picture on a panel, which had been made by

Marco di Buoninsegna de' Cari, for the high altar of S.Marco. The prior was to order the figures. Lorenzo was to pay for the colours and to deliver the picture within two years. Simone was then to say how much he was to receive for it. The picture is at present in the church of the Dominican friars at Cortona. (Milanesi, *Nuovi documenti, cit.*, p. 70.)

12   27 April 1402. The Ospedale of Santa Chiara at Pisa commissioned Giovanni di Piero of Naples and Martino di Bartolomeo of Siena to paint a panel for the church of Santa Chiara at Pisa. It was to contain the following scenes:

top	Virgin	Trinity	Angel
middle	St Augustine and St John the Baptist	Virgin Mary holding the child in her arms	St John the Evangelist and St Clare

predella Seraphim 4 Prophets 12 Apostles 4 Prophets Seraphim.

The predella has disappeared, but from the rest of the picture which survives, it can be seen that for the Virgin and Angel originally ordered, the figures of St Mark and St Luke have been substituted. The work was to be completed in eight months. The painters were to receive 95 florins payable in three instalments: 15 at the beginning of the work; 30 when they began gilding; and the remainder when the work was on the altar. Giovanni was to paint the figures. The rest of the work was to be divided between them. They were to meet the cost of colours, gold, and panel. The first payment was made in 5 May 1402; the second on 23 August 1402. (Milanesi, *Documenti, cit.*, ii, 8–12.)

13   5 April 1407. Francesco da Siena at Genoa contracted to paint a *Maestà* for Manfredina de' Carli in return for 100 florins. (Alizeri, *Notizie*, i, 214.)

14   20 April 1412. The canons of the cathedral of S. Florido in Città di Castello contracted with Giorgio di Andrea Bartoli of Siena and Jacopo di Ser Michele of Città di Castello. They were to produce a panel for the high altar of the church which should show the Virgin Mary with Child, to the right the blessed Florido, to the left S. Amantii. It was to be finished by mid-August. The painters were to receive 35 florins and a *salma* of wine. (Milanesi, *Nuovi doc., cit.*, pp. 74–5.)

B   PAINTINGS IN FRESCO

I   1347. Alessio d' Andrea and Bonaccorso di Cino painted the chapel of
S. Jacopo in the cathedral of Pistoia with scenes from the life of St
James. They began in January and the work was finished in September. The two masters were paid 12s. a day, and were given wine
valued at 7d. a day. (This probably worked out at four florins a month
each for the nine months.) Their assistants, Duccio Nutini and Niccolò
Ghini, painters of Florence, and Jacopo and Tommaso di Lazzero,
painters of Pistoia, were paid 7s to 8s. a day with wine (about 2½
florins a month, plus wine.) Giovanni di Pistoia and Lorenzo Cambini,
who were occasionally employed to grind colours, received 2s. and
4s. a day, respectively. These frescoes were destroyed in 1786. (Ciampi,
*Notizie inedite, della sagrestia pistoiese, de' belli arredi del Campo Santo
pisano e di altre opere di disegno*, Florence, 1810, pp. 145–50.)

2   30 June 1352. Lippo Vanni was paid £85 16s. 8d *senesi* (about 25
florins) for painting a Coronation of the Virgin in the office of the
Biccherna within the palace of the commune of Siena. (Milanesi,
Documenti, cit., i, 27 n. 1.)

3   1369. In this year, from July, many artists were employed at Rome
during the short stay of Urban v in the Vatican palace. In July,
Giovanni da Milano, Guarnerio da Venezia, Niccolò da Roma,
Stefano da Perugia, and Nicholas the German, were employed for
11 days at ten shillings a day. In the same month, Antonio da Monte-
rano, Antonio Ipolito, Jacobello Jacchetti, Rainaldo da Cesano,
Giuliano di maestro Giovanni, Domenico di 'Mirandie', Lorenzo da
Roma, received 8s. a day. Also present were Giovanni dell' Ora of
Florence and Giovanni di Taddeo of Florence. Giottino of Florence
received 16s. a day from 23 July to 31 August, working 24 days in all
for a total of £19 4s. From 1 September he began to serve for seven
florins a month. In this document 1 florin = 47 shillings. (E. Müntz,
Les Archives des Arts, Paris, 1890, pp. 1–11.)

4   1370–1371. Between August 1370 and June 1371, Cecco di Pietro was
working at the Campo Santo of Pisa for 18s. *pisani* a day (= about
six florins a month), and Neruccio di Federigo for 20s. a day (= about
seven florins a month.) (Ciampi, *Notizie inedite, cit.*, p. 46.)

5   27 June 1385. Francesco di Michele agreed to paint a tabernacle at
Colonnata for the Ospedale of S. Matteo. On the inside there was to
be a nativity of Christ, a coronation of the Virgin, and a Last Judgment, with the four Evangelists in the vault. On the outer façade
there was to be an Annunciation with two angels. The work was to

be assessed by two masters. If they considered it to have been well done, Francesco was to be paid 24 florins. In addition he was to be given food and drink, and lime and sand. The work was to be finished by mid-August. (Milanesi, *Nuovi doc., cit.*, no. 84.)

6   1386–8. Between December 1384 and March 1386 Antonio Veneziano was painting three 'stories' from the life of S. Ranier, for which he was paid 70 florins each. (Ciampi, *Notizie inedite, cit.*, pp. 151–2.)

7   *Spinello di Luca Aretino* (cf. A no. 7)

(a)   1390. Spinello was called to Pisa by the cathedral *opera*. In March 1391 he completed three frescoes of S. Ephesus and three of S. Potitus in the Campo Santo, for which he received 150 and 130 florins respectively. (Ciampi, *Notizie inedite, cit.*, p. 152.)

(b)   1 October 1404. Spinello, with his son Parri, began a year's employment with the *opera* of the cathedral of Siena in return for 140 florins a year. All expenses of colours, etc. were to be paid for by the *opera*. (Milanesi, *Documenti, cit.*, ii, 18.)

(c)   18 June 1407. It was agreed that Spinello and Parri were to paint frescoes illustrating the life of the Sienese pope, Alexander III, on the walls of the Sala di Balìa in the Palazzo Pubblico of Siena. The work was to begin on March 1408. He and his son were to receive their morning and evening meals at the expense of the commune, and 15 florins a month. The commune was to meet all the expenses of paints, scaffolding, etc.

At the same time it was agreed that Martino di Bartolomeo was to paint the four vaults down to the cornice in the Sala di Balìa. The mortar and scaffolding were to be provided at the expense of the commune, though Martino was to pay for the colours. However, no gold was to be used. He promised to do the work within the following February. For this he was to receive 404 florins *sen*. (Milanesi, *Documenti, cit.*, ii, 32–3.)

8   *Taddeo di Bartolo*

(a)   4 February 1401. Taddeo di Bartolo was to paint a Last Judgement in the chapel of Saint Anthony in the cathedral, with those figures and motifs which he and the *operaio* should agree together. The *operaio* was to pay for colours, scaffolding, and all other expenses. Taddeo should work every day, save on those days forbidden by the Church. He should receive 150 florins in the coming year, paid monthly. On 10 June 1401 this contract was cancelled, and it was agreed that instead Taddeo should paint six stories from the

Old Testament in the sacristy. This was to take two months. He was to receive 12½ florins a month. The master of works was to be responsible for the scaffolding, for putting the first layer of plaster on the wall, for preparing the lime for the second coat, and for paying for all colours, 'so that it is to be understood that master Taddeo shall put into the said work only his own person and brushes.' (Milanesi, *Documenti, cit.*, ii, 5–7.)

(b) May 1404. Taddeo was to work for a year in painting the walls around the chapels of the cathedral of Siena. He was to receive 12½ florins a month, and the *operaio* was to meet all expenses. In two months of the year to be decided by the *operaio*, he was allowed to absent himself for his own work. He was not to work during bad weather, when good work is spoilt, but in that time he was not to be paid. (Milanesi, *Documenti, cit.*, ii, 15–16.)

9   1408. Gherardo Starnina contracted with the Annunciation Brotherhood of Empoli to paint scenes from the life of Mary in the chapel of the church of San Stefano at Empoli. He was to receive 85 florins. The work, already begun, was to be completed in four months. Gherardo promised to use silver and ultramarine blue costing one florin an ounce; for the robe of the Virgin he promised a blue costing two florins an ounce. (Lerner-Lehmkuhl, 18, citing *Rivista d' arte*, iii, 1905, pp. 19ff.)

10   7 April 1411. Benedetto di Biondo received 40 florins from the commune of Siena for his repainting of the figure of the Virgin on the Camollia Gate. (Borghesi e Banchi, pp. 76–7.)

C   MINOR COMMISSIONS TO PAINTERS

These examples are all drawn from Sienese documents printed in Milanesi, *Documenti, cit.*, All payments are in pounds, shillings, and pence *senesi*.

1   Jacomo Bindo, 1329, was paid 10 shillings by the commune for painting the covers of 15 books of the syndics, and 23s. 4d. for painting 40 little shields on the books of the *podestà*.

2   Biagio Fori, 1369, was paid £1 by the *opera* of the cathedral for placing 100 pieces of fine gold in the picture of the Madonna before the cathedral door. The gold cost £4 14s.

3   Giacomo Mini, 1369, was paid 8s. 10d. by the commune of Siena for painting the cover of an exchequer account book.

4   Francesco Neri and his son, 1370, received £5 10s. (about 1½ florins) for plastering a wall in the cathedral of Siena in preparation for a fresco.

5 Galgano Minuccio, 1375, was paid £27 16s. (about 7½ florins) for painting pennants of trumpets and the flag of the cathedral, and £22 (about 6 florins) for painting the pennants of trumpets and the kettledrums of the commune.

6 Francesco Pieri, 1380, was paid two florins by the *opera* of the cathedral for painting the tabernacle of St Daniel, though not the shutters upon it.

7 Meo Pieri, 1383, received £1 16s. for restoring a Madonna at the door of the cathedral. This work had to be done again after 12 years (see no. 9 below).

8 Meo Pieri and Cristofano Bindocci, 1393, received 20 florins from the commune for painting the arms of the Duke of Milan on the Camollia gate. The commune paid for the paint.

9 Cristofano Bindoccio, 1395, was paid £1 10s. by the cathedral *opera* for restoring the Madonna at the door of the cathedral.

10 Antonio di Niccolò, 1398, was paid £5 12s. (about 1½ florins) for grinding colours for *maestro* Andrea, painter.

11 Piero Jacomi, 1418, received £4 19s. from the commune for painting shields and the arms of the commune and people, and a small pair of angels. He worked for six days (14–20 July) and was paid at a rate of 16s. 6d. a day.

D STONE SCULPTURE

1 5 October 1266. The master of works of Siena cathedral contracted with Nicola Pisano for the sculpting of a pulpit. Nicola was promised eight shillings a day for each working day (which possibly meant about 80 florins a year) while his assistants, Arnolfo di Cambio and Lapo, were to have six shillings a day each (perhaps 60 florins a year), and his son, Giovanni, were he to come, four shillings a day (about 40 florins). (Milanesi, *Documenti, cit.*, i, 145–153).

2 January 1314. The master of works of S. Maria Novella in Florence entrusted Lapo di Ricevuto with a monument for the nobles of the house of Manelli in the cloister. Lapo was to provide all the marble, and to receive £170 (about 58 florins). (Davidsohn, *Forschungen, cit.*, iv, 481–2.)

3 July 1314. Tino di Camaino received £400 *pisani* (about 136 florins) for making the tomb of Henry VII at Pisa. (Ciampi, *Notizie inedite, cit.*, p. 126.)

4 1342. The officials responsible for the building of the walls of Florence commissioned from one Paolo and his son Giovanni six figures for the San Gallo gate. In the centre were to be the standing figures of

Christ crowning his mother, both figures to be almost 4 *braccia* (7 feet 8 inches) high. At the sides were to be the standing figures of St John the Baptist, St Reperata, St Peter, and St Lawrence, also about 4 *braccia* high. In addition they were to build the pillars and frame upon which the statues were to be placed. They were to provide the lead and lime, and to arrange for the statues to be painted afterwards. For this the two men were to receive 160 florins. (Milanesi, *Nuovi documenti, cit.*, pp. 39–42.)

5   1354. Niccolò del Mercia was paid 24 shillings *flor. parv.* a day (perhaps 90 florins a year) and his apprentice eight shillings a day, for working on the marble pulpit of the chapel of the Holy Girdle in the Duomo of Prato. (Milanesi, *Nuovi documenti, cit.*, pp. 54–6.)

6   31 July 1377. Bartolomeo di Tommè and Mariano d' Agnolo, goldsmiths of Siena, contracted with the master of the works of the Chapel of the Campo of Siena. They were to carve the marble statue of an apostle. They were to be paid for this a sum between 40 and 60 florins as should be decided by valuers when the work was completed. In the following year the two men were asked to provide a further eight statues for each of which they were to be paid in the same way. The *opera* was to provide the marble and the colours necessary for painting the statues when finished. (Milanesi, *Documenti, cit.*, i, 277–8, 279–80.)

7.   *Pietro di Giovanni of Brabant*

(a)   1387–9. Pietro worked 14 figures of apostles and saints, for the façade of the cathedral at Florence, 13 at 22 florins, one at 20. In all for this period he must have earned at least 306 florins. These statues were afterwards gilded and painted by Lorenzo Bicci, Agnolo Gaddi, Jacopo di Cione, and Lapo di Corso. Four of the apostles that he executed were done on the designs of Lorenzo Bicci, Agnolo Gaddi, and Spinello Aretino.

(b)   August–November 1395. Pietro was paid 18 florins for a marble shepherd.

(c)   To Pietro di Giovanni and Niccolò di Piero Lamberti, August 1395, were confided the execution of four great saints of the church, to be executed on the designs of Agnolo Gaddi. In December they went to Carrara to choose the marble. Pietro's St Jerome was valued, 20 March 1398, by a goldsmith and two painters, at 140 florins. His St Ambrose was valued, 1 April 1398, at 140 florins. Agnolo Gaddi received six florins for the design. These four saints have been transformed by the clumsy superimposition of new heads into the 'laureate poets' which now stand in the

Viale di Poggio Imperiale. (Poggi, *Il duomo di Firenze, cit.*, pp. xxiv–xxvii, 19.)

6   *The Four Evangelists of Florence Cathedral*

For the Four Evangelists which now stand within the cathedral, the *opera* of the cathedral sent two men to Carrara in 1405 to select the marble. Their travelling expenses were assessed at 10 florins. The four blocks they selected cost 19 florins each. Two of them were transported to Florence by a professional marble dealer and carrier at a cost of 110 florins. 16s. 6d. *flor. parv.* were paid to the man who measured them. The two other blocks were despatched for about 118 florins. Taking into account all these expenses, each of the blocks cost on average about 77 florins. In December 1408, Niccolò Lamberti, Donatello, and Nanni di Banco, were each assigned one of the blocks (though they did not arrive in Florence until over a year and a half later). Their payment was to be determined after valuation, and they were promised that the one who produced the best statue would be commissioned to do the fourth figure. (This promise was not kept; Bernardo Ciuffagni was given the fourth block in May 1410). Eventually Lamberti's figure was valued at 137 florins; Ciuffagni's at 137 florins, and Donatello's (October 1415), at 160 florins: that is to say at just below to just above double the cost of the materials. Donatello's *St John* was not completed without friction. In April 1415 the supervisors of the *opera* were threatening a fine of 25 florins if Donatello were unable to complete the work by the end of May. (H. W. Janson, *The Sculpture of Donatello*, Princeton, 1957, 12–16; Lerner-Lehmkuhl, *cit.*, pp. 42–3.)

E   GOLDSMITH'S WORK

1   *Altar Panels for San Jacopo at Pistoia*

In 1357 the custodians of the church of S. Jacopo at Pistoia commissioned Pero of Florence to produce a panel to cover one side of the altar, promising in return a fee of 300 florins to cover both his labour and the cost of silver and gilt used. When Pero delivered the panel, however, the patrons declared it to be of no merit, and refused payment. As a result Ugolino di Vieri, the most famous goldsmith of the day, the maker of the reliquary of Orvieto cathedral, was chosen to arbitrate between the two parties, and, after inspection, found against his fellow craftsman. 'The work was neither beautiful nor adorned as Pero had promised to do it.' Accordingly the contract was cancelled, and Pero was himself forced to meet Ugolino's arbitration fee of 13 florins.

In June 1360 the custodians re-assigned the panel to Francesco Niccolai of Florence; but their troubles were not yet ended. They had stipulated that the completed frame, with its nine panels, should be delivered by November 1361. In fact it was only finished two years later, and at once a new difficulty arose. The contract had declared that the total weight of silver in the completed work should be 28 lbs, and that the goldsmith should be paid £5 *flor. parv.* for each ounce of silver which he had worked. On assay, however, it was discovered that the panels weighed a little over 31 lbs. At this the goldsmith claimed that he should be paid for the extra 3 lbs at the rate of £5 the ounce. The *opera*, for their part, were willing to pay only the cost of the unworked silver, calculated at £2 7s. the ounce. The question was decided finally by the Consuls of the Arte di Por' Santa Maria, to which the goldsmiths guild was subordinate: half of the additional silver was to be paid for at £5 the ounce, half at £2 7s. Warned by this experience, in commissioning a companion panel for the other side of the altar in December 1367 the master of works drew up a much more carefully drafted document. The artist here was Leonardo di Giovanni of Florence, who was to execute the altar-panels for the Florentine Baptistery. The work was to consist of nine panels on the life of St James, completed, says the master of works, 'according to that form which I shall give to him in each panel'. As soon as it was completed each individual panel was to be sent to Pistoia from the workshop of Florence for approval. The whole frame was not to weigh more than 32 lbs 'and rather less than more'. Leonardo was to receive 100 florins on the drawing up of the contract, and then four six-monthly instalments of 100 florins; the work was to be delivered on 1 January 1371. With this contract the *opera* were more successful; on the feast of St James in 1371 the completed work was exhibited for the first time at Pistoia. Communal records of the same date showing payments for the provision of wafers and malmsey suggest almost the atmosphere of a modern 'first viewing'. (Pèleo Bacci, *Documenti toscani per la storia dell' arte*, Florence, 1910, pp. 109–12.)

2 *Lorenzo Ghiberti*

Ghiberti was certainly the most prosperous of goldsmiths of the period. It was as a young man of 20 that he won the competition for the design and casting of the north door of the Baptistery of Florence. When the officials of the *Calimala* guild, to whom the supervision of the doors had been given, came to draw up the first agreement for the work in November 1403 they were faced with the embarrassment of finding that their chosen master was as yet not old enough to have matriculated in the goldsmiths' guild. Accordingly they made out their contract to him jointly with his (presumptive) father. The materials (bronze, charcoal, wax, sand, and clay), the building of the casting furnace, and the wages of assistants, were all to be paid by the *Calimala*. The final price given for Ghiberti's work was to be settled when it was completed. In the meanwhile the two men were given an annual joint salary of 200 florins. Three panels out of the 28 envisaged were to be completed each year. Between 1403 and 1407, 11 assistants (including Donatello and Giuliano Andrea) were also paid for by the guild, though none was employed on average for more than 12 months at a time.

By June 1407 the work was behindhand, and Ghiberti had failed to finish the three panels each year as promised. Accordingly a new agreement was drawn up, this time with Ghiberti alone. It was stipulated that he was 'to work every working day, all day long, with his hands, like any journeyman' and that every interruption of his work was to be recorded in a book kept for that purpose. He was forbidden to accept any other contract without the permission of the officials of the *Calimala*. He was to work 'with his own hand in wax and bronze [i.e., in executing casts, and in chasing them] . . . particularly on those parts which require the greatest perfection such as hair, nudes, and similar parts.' But his pay was raised. This time he himself was given 200 florins a year while his father was paid as an assistant. The materials were still provided by the *Calimala*, who also paid Ghiberti's assistants, chosen by himself. By 1424 when the work was completed, the total cost of the gates had mounted to 16,204 florins. Of this about 4,000 florins, minus deductions for employment on other work, was accounted for as Ghiberti's payment for his 20 years of work. Between 1407 and 1415, 22 assistants and three apprentices worked with him, mostly for a year or less, though in two cases for about four years. The salaries of these men ranged from 75 florins a year, paid to the most important workmen, to the five, six, or nine florins given to the apprentices.

During this period the *Calimala* allowed Ghiberti to take other commissions. Between 1412 and 1416, he cast the bronze St John the Baptist for the *Calimala* guild, and between 1419 and 1422, the bronze St Matthew for the *Cambio*, both of which works were destined for Or San Michele. For the first he received, with his assistants, about

526 florins. For the second he was given another 200 florins a year. With this type of regular payment, Ghiberti, at the age of 40, was already well on the road to becoming a man of real substance among his fellow artists. (From Richard Krautheimer [with Trude Krautheimer-Hess], Lorenzo Ghiberti, Princeton, 1956.)

F EMPLOYMENT AS CAPOMAESTRO – ORVIETO

As *capomaestro* of Orvieto, Lorenzo Maitani, on his first appointment in 1310, received a retaining fee of 12 florins a year, a grant of a house and 15 years' immunity from taxation. In addition he took payment for each specific job done. At his death in 1330 his position was taken over jointly by his two sons, and by Meo di Nuto. The demand for skilled artists, despite the financial inducements offered, is suggested here by the fact that the document appointing them to the post remarks casually that Meo had been condemned and banished by the commune 'on the occasion of a certain homicide enacted by him', but that this condemnation was to be suspended for ten years. In fact he held the position continually until his death in 1348.

In 1358, Andrea Orcagna was offered 300 florins a year in the post. Later, Paolo di Antonio received 18 shillings *cortona* for each working day (i.e., about 6½ florins a month) with the use of a furnished house for him and his family. By the beginning of the fifteenth century, perhaps through the competition for talent with Florence, the value of the post had doubled. In 1405 Sano di Matteo was receiving 20 florins a month and a furnished house. With some intervals he seems to have held the office at that salary from 1407 to 1425. (Milanesi, *Documenti, cit.*, i, 172–3, 197–200, 261–2, 272–3; ii, 22–5, 189–91; *idem*, 'Documenti dei lavori fatti da Andrea Orcagna nel duomo d' Orvieto', *Giornale storico degli archivi toscani*, iii, 1859, pp. 100–10.)

G WOODWORK

1 May 1371. Piero di Lando of Siena was commissioned to make the choir stalls of the cathedral of Fiesole. All the wood, which was to be walnut, was to be bought at his own expense. He was to be paid 5½ florins for each seat and to be given his meals by the cathedral authorities. The total cost of the work is unknown, but by April 1373, he had received 144 florins. (Milanesi, *Nuovi documenti, cit.*, pp. 60–2.)

2 From 1380 Francesco di Tonghio, for himself, his three sons, and three other workers from his shop, received 400 florins a year for the carving of the wooden choir stalls of Siena cathedral. Part of

this sum was to compensate him for having received so little in the years 1362–9. (Milanesi, *Documenti, cit.*, i, 351–6.)

3 In 1408 Barna di Turino received from the commune of Siena five florins *senesi* for a chest to hold consistory documents, and was promised one florin *senese* for each *braccio* in area of seats he was to make in the Sala di Balìa (these were completed in April 1410). (Borghesi and Banchi, *cit.*, 50.)

H STAINED GLASS

Clerics were frequently employed in the making of glass. The late fourteenth century treatise on glass making by Antonio da Pisa assumes that the manufacturer will also be the designer of the glass, but often the scheme was drawn by some other artist (Ghiberti and, probably, Duccio designed windows).

1 1369. The cathedral of Siena paid Giacomo di Castello for a glass window above the high altar, measuring 35 square feet at a rate of $1\frac{1}{2}$ florins a square foot (52 florins, 34 shillings *senesi* in all). The same rate of payment was taken by him in 1370 and 1372 when it was agreed that the master of works should provide the scaffolding for erecting the windows. (Milanesi, *Documenti, cit.*, ii, 20–2.)

2 November 1388. The Vallambrosian monk, Leonardo da Simone, was to be paid $3\frac{1}{4}$ florins a *braccio* for the two windows he was to execute in the façade of Florence cathedral. The cathedral was to provide the scaffolding. December 1395. Antonio da Pisa (author of the treatise mentioned above) will receive 4 florins a square *braccio* for the windows in Florence cathedral. But 30 shillings *flor. parv.* will be deducted from each of the 4 florins for Agnolo Gaddi who had done the design. (Poggi, *Il duomo, cit.*, lxxviii–lxxix.)

3 28 February 1394. The Dominican, Francesco Naddozzi, agreed with the Vallambrosian monastery of San Pancrazio at Florence to make a glass 'eye' and a window for the church of the monastery, for the sum of 28 florins and 30 shillings. Within the 'eye' was to be 'the whole figure of S. Pancrazio'. (Milanesi, *Nuovi documenti, cit.*, 66.)

Conclusion

Secularisation is the leading theme in the story of official or 'high' culture in this period. The century which began with the 'sacred poem' of Dante ended with the glorification of the pagan Roman Republic by the Florentine humanists. A primarily religious art was transformed into an art which, though still religious, was inspired by the classical world.

It would be misleading to think of earlier centuries as possessing a culture which was exclusively dominated by transcendentalism and otherworldliness. Moreover, in this period the movement away from an ecclesiastical formation of literature and art was obviously neither continuous nor uniform. To consider the intellectual life of even the fifteenth century simply in the terms of von Martin[1] as 'materialistic, rational, and secular' is grossly distorting. The overwhelming majority of the works which Ghiberti, Donatello, Masaccio, and Brunelleschi executed were on religious themes, and, though commissioned by governments, were destined to take their place in ecclesiastical settings. Much of what was written by the leading authors of the time, such as Sacchetti and Salutati, has the characteristic tone of the lay-preacher. None the less it is obvious that throughout this period there was a growing division between culture and religion.

This appears plainly in the way in which the creator of art and literature was considered. The artist who in the 1290s was held to be merely the executive agent of the priest-patron had come by the beginning of the fifteenth century to be seen in a new and more independent role. So too with the writer, though the change here is less pronounced. Dante, the *Dantes theologicus* of the early *Trecento*, was revered by the end of the century as a poet who had earned a secular immortality. In December 1396, the Florentine government commanded that the master of works of the cathedral should, within six years, obtain the bones of the jurist, Accursius, and of Dante, Petrarch, and Zanobi da Strada, 'poets', and that for these remains 'magnificent sculptures' should be constructed within the church. The project was not achieved. Yet the words in which the decree stressed that 'although they have gone from this world, none the less they can be thought, through the glory and fame of their quality, to live still',[2] express an idea of justification through literature which is pagan rather than Christian in origin.

In this climate a contemporary history of culture came into existence for the first time. It is seen in the new attempt at periodisation: the ideal of 'letters and arts restored to life', found in Boccaccio and Petrarch. It is made explicit in Boccaccio's life of Dante, and those biographies of famous Florentine poets and painters written by Filippo Villani. In Villani's biographical collection, moreover, there is an enhanced interest in the individual which will be a characteristic of Italian *quattrocento* culture. A self-conscious individualism, a new passion in the expression of personal opinions and feelings, a new respect for one's own subjectivity, already appear both in Petrarch's letters and in the *ricordanze* or diaries of Florentine merchants in the period. The originality of this development should not be over-emphasised: in earlier centuries works like Abelard's letters and auto-biography or Joinville's *Life of St Louis* had shown a deep interest in individual psychology. Yet such writings were rare, and there were very few sustained attempts in the early middle ages to capture the essential flavour of personality; even such men as Frederick II and Boniface VIII, who clearly were of great interest as personalities, can only be known partially and externally. It is in the *Trecento* that this situation begins to change. At the same time individual portraiture, with its representations of the great, of civic worthies, and of donors, made its first appearance.

For these phenomena various explanations have been given. One is the diffusion of nominalist philosophy with its emphasis upon the uniqueness of each individual thing. More recently the new interests have been associated with a presumed change in the character of the family.[3] Following this thesis, thirteenth-century Italy was the home of the 'extended family'. In this period family bonds were extremely tight and all members of a family tended to live and work together in unison. During the following hundred years this system broke down and gave way in the fifteenth century to the dominance of the 'nuclear family' whose centre of interest lay merely in the husband–wife, parent–child relationships. With this change there came a much greater scope for the individual, and women too began to enjoy a larger, freer role in society. Released from the tyranny of the extended family, individuals could feel, as never before, their uniqueness. This is an interesting hypothesis, but the evidence does not really support the idea of the thirteenth-century family as 'extended'. Indeed, from the beginnings of the economic revolution in the eleventh century, from, that is, the time of large-scale emigration from the villages of the countryside into the town, one would expect the extended family to be weakened. At the same time studies in the structure of present-day families reveal the unreliability of drawing too sharp distinctions between 'nuclear' and 'extended' groupings. The two types in fact constantly blend into each other in a variety of social circumstances.

More probably this is a question of style rather than substance. Men of earlier ages, doubtless, had as much interest in individuality and as much self awareness (something indeed which the Christian examination of conscience imposed upon them) as in the fourteenth century. Certainly they produced very strongly individualised characters. What was lacking was merely the convention of expressing this individuality. With the renewed and intenser interest of the humanists in classical literature, in Cicero's letters and Plutarch's *Lives*, new models were found for writing in this vein. But this sympathy and acuter understanding of the Roman world was itself a product of changes in society, the appeal of one secular culture to another, and accordingly the question of individuality is to be seen as yet another aspect of the process of secularisation.

There are those who seek to explain this process by stressing the importance of certain periods of crisis. Hans Baron has gone so far as to narrow the crucial era to the years 1390 to 1402. It was, he argues, in that period, under the stress of the Florentine–Visconti war, that a 'medieval' concern with the contemplative life gave way to a 'modern' interest in the active life in society, a change bringing a profound reappraisal of ethical values. George Holmes, on the other hand, has laid emphasis on the relations between Florence and the Papacy in the years after 1375 in producing what he sees as 'a movement of rather extreme and sudden secularisation of ideas'. The War of the Eight Saints (1375–8) between Florence and the Church, he claims, brought a violent wave of anti-clericalism to Florence which impelled the Florentine humanists to exalt the national and classical glories of Italy against the 'French' papacy of Avignon. During the Schism, in the generation which followed, the weakness of the Papacy allowed them by contrast to regard it with detachment, in a spirit of friendly if condescending superiority. In these circumstances they were easily able, without any direct quarrel with Christianity, and without any fear of ecclesiastical censure, to formulate their own values independently of traditional teaching.[4]

Though one must not suggest that humanism as such was specifically anti-ecclesiastical, it need not be doubted that both the Visconti–Florentine war and Florentine–papal relations played their part in the development of secularisation of thought in Florence. Yet it would be unwise to give overdue weight to the importance of what are essentially incidents. The rhythms of cultural development move slowly and the causes of change are complex and long-term; ultimately it is more profitable to see them in broad perspective, than to consider them as peripeteia. Looking at secularisation in these terms the most common suggestion is that the culture of the fourteenth century was the inevitable concomitant of the creation of a bourgeois civilisation by the economic revolution: that 'Renaissance' culture was the culture of merchants.

This again seems a large oversimplification. It is very true that the patronage of culture in the *Trecento* demanded a mature economic base. Oviously too the needs of early capitalist society produced, for the first time, the need for an educated laity. Since the eleventh century Italy had prospered in the economic revolution; the twelfth and thirteenth centuries were the period of its greatest economic growth. Yet the prosperity of that time had not been matched by any comparable cultural triumphs. Genoa provides an instructive example. In these years it stood at the centre of a vast merchant empire. 'On land and sea', wrote Jacopo d' Oria, 'she shone out before the other cities of Italy in honour, power, and riches.' Here were all the 'rational' elements of a capitalist society, the merchants, the wealth. But the culture of the age passed the city by almost completely. What art and literature it produced was deeply conservative. Its finest painter was a Bartolomeo da Camogli, its finest author was Fra Jacopo da Voragine, thirteenth-century compiler of a compendium of saint's lives. It had only three visiting artists of any note: Giovanni Pisano at the beginning of the fourteenth century, Barnaba da Modena in the middle years, and Taddeo di Bartolo at the end. How can one explain this indifference to those currents of literature and art which affected the life of the other commercial centres of the peninsula?

The likeliest answer is that the political environment of a society is as important as its economic structure in providing the background for its culture. The weakness of Genoese culture in this period can best be explained by the extreme weakness of Genoa as an independent political entity. Weak states can produce strong cultural activity. The dying empire of the Paleologi in the fourteenth and fifteenth centuries, shrunk then within its narrowest limits, saw one of the finest eras in Byzantine culture. But it was a civilisation which could not survive conquest by the Ottoman Turks. And at Genoa, at a time when governments were at the centre of patronage, it was the fall of the city to external powers, to the Visconti, and then to France, which worked against the development of its culture.

It is in the story of the Genoese failure that we find the central explanation for the secularisation of culture in this period. The principal moving force behind the art and literature of the age was not the Church nor the merchant as individual patron, but secular government. The new culture of the *Trecento* is to be seen as part of the great story of early modern Europe: the emergence of the state. It was only at the end of the thirteenth century that Italian civilisation came to predominate in Europe, because only then had the Italian communes fully thrown off the political claims of the German Emperors and emerged as separate, independent entities. During the fourteenth century the power of the Italian communes was constantly increasing; their claims upon and pressure against the citizen were ever growing their more sophisticated institutions, such as the Public Debts, were binding more and more citizens to the interests of the ruling classes.

As part of this expansion of power, governments intervened decisively in the patronage of culture and became the major patrons of art and humanism. And the practical spirit of these governments was carried over into the patronage they awarded. They required the representation of specific individuals, towns, and landscapes. They demanded glorification, not of the Church, but of themselves. Already by the end of the thirteenth century they had begun to identify themselves with ancient Rome. The very cathedrals that they built were raised as monuments of civic glory and of the spirit of their community. Culture was secularised in this period because it was patronised by the rulers of the towns, because the nascent states provided a context in which secular men could discover themselves as citizens of this world. Nor curiously enough was it the secular powers alone which worked in this spirit. The Church too was a government. It waged war, both against infidels and Christians; it collected taxes, and possessed a sophisticated administrative system. It was obsessed by financial and economic problems. Accordingly, it too was an instrument of rationalisation and secularisation.

It was the number and variety of governments in Italy which partly explain the variety and profusion of Italian culture in the period. Was there in fact any significant difference between the patronage offered by commune and *signoria*? Already contemporaries had begun to discuss this problem. In his *Discussion on the Preferable Way of Life* (1404) Giovanni Conversino of Ravenna argued for the superiority of the *signoria* as patron.[5] Pointing to the aid given to the arts by such men as Robert of Naples, Francesco II da Carrara, and

Giangaleazzo Visconti, he claimed that only princes could ensure an harmonious society in which the artist and intellectual could be esteemed. Republics, he complained (without realising that this indeed was their particular strength, especially in the field of architecture) worked so slowly; and here, moreover, men were only interested in profit. Against this thesis men like Villani, Salutati, and Bruni were already, at least by implication, suggesting that it was republican government which was responsible for the cultural triumphs of Florence.

But more important than this is the distinction to be drawn in the second half of our period between the large regional powers and the intimate world of the city-states. The rise of the larger territorial unit had already done something by the end of the fourteenth century to break down that spirit of community which had previously existed in the towns and in which much of the culture of the age was rooted. Together with the narrowing of the oligarchies controlling government, which is a feature of the *Trecento*, this was to lead to a culture in the fifteenth century which was much more dependent on the patronage of individuals than on the community as a whole, which was in fact aimed at the interests of an élite.

In our period this development was only beginning. For most men in this 130 years, Charles Martel's question to Dante: 'Would it not be worse for man on earth, if he were not a citizen?' evoked an instant response. These words provide the key to a culture which is essentially civic and related to the whole community. Its writers were moved by the thought 'that the noblest part of all sciences in governing a city is rhetoric'; its musicians were employed 'for the delight and joy of the citizens'. Its architecture was the fruit of the wish 'that the commune may be protected from harm and held in honour in perpetuity'; its paintings were borne to their setting 'by all the officials of the commune and all the people ... while the bells sounded a *gloria* with reverence for so noble a painting as was this'. Only the rootless Petrarch stood out from this sense of participating in the world of communal endeavour, and he, more than any other in this age, looks forward to the cultural patterns of the future.

Selective Bibliographies
and Notes

The bibliographies here are confined to those works which were most helpful in the preparation of the book, and make no claim to be exhaustive. The occasional notes are given either for the purpose of acknowledging my most direct borrowings or because they are of particular interest to students in the field.

Abbreviations

Annales *Annales: Economies, sociétés, civilisations*
ASI *Archivio storico italiano*
BSSP *Bullettino senese di storia patria*
GSLI *Giornale storico della letteratura italiana*
JWCI Journal of the Warburg and Courtauld Institutes
RIS *Rerum Italicarum Scriptores*
    1. ed. L. A. Muratori, 1723–51
    2. ed. G. Carducci and V. Fiorini, 1900 ff.

Preliminary note upon money
1 R. de Roover, *Rise and Decline of the Medici Bank*, Cambridge, Mass., 1963, pp. 44–5, 232; L. Martines, *Lawyers and Statecraft in Renaissance Florence*, Princeton, 1968, pp. 100–6

Part I The Age of Dante and Giotto

Ch. 1 *Cultural change, 1290–1340*
The fullest general studies of the arts over the whole period, 1290–1420, are to be found in the volumes of A. Venturi, *Storia dell' arte italiana*, Milan,

1940-1; of R. van Marle, *The Development of the Italian Schools of Painting*, The Hague, 1923-38; and more concisely in P. Toesca, *Storia dell' arte italiana*, vol. 2, *Il Trecento*, Turin, 1951; John White, *Art and Architecture in Italy 1250-1400*, Harmondsworth, 1966; and R. Oertel, *Die Frühzeit der italienischen Malerei*, Stuttgart, 1966 (now in English translation by Lily Cooper, London, 1968).

The only extensive attempt to relate art and society in the years 1290–1340 is the stimulating but erratic exercise in neo-Marxist exegesis of F. Antal, *Florentine Painting and its social background*, London, 1947. A noticeable defect in this book is that it draws upon a now outmoded view of the role of the various classes within Florentine government. For these years I have found Eve Borsook, *The Mural Painters of Tuscany*, London, 1960, and Georg Weise, *L'Italia e il mondo gotico* (revised Italian translation of the German original of 1939), Florence, 1956, particularly helpful.

For literature 1290–1420, see the three volumes of the *Storia letteraria d' Italia*: G. Bertoni, *Il Duecento*, 3rd ed., Milan, 1954; N. Sapegno, *Il Trecento*, 3rd ed., Milan, 1949; and V. Rossi, *Il Quattrocento*, ed. A. Vallone, 6th ed. Milan, 1956. See also Sapegno's *Storia letteraria del Trecento*, Milan-Naples, 1963, and the first three volumes of the new *Storia della letteratura italiana*, under the general editorship of E. Cecchi and N. Sapegno, Milan, 1965 ff. For the growth of an Italian literary language, see P. O. Kristeller, 'The origin and development of the language of Italian prose' in his *Renaissance Thought II. Papers on Humanism and the Arts*, New York, 1965, pp. 119–41.

On French cultural predominance before 1250, see P. Kristeller, *Renaissance Thought: The Classic, Scholastic and Humanist Strains*, New York, 1961, pp. 93–4.

Ch. 2   Italy, 1290–1340

The two most recent surveys of Italian history in the later middle ages are: N. Valeri, *L'Italia nell' età dei principati dal 1343 al 1516*, Verona, 1950, and L. Simeoni, *Le signorie 1313–1559*, Milan, 1950. But the writing of a unitary Italian history in this period is beset with great difficulties (see chapter three of Denys Hay, *The Italian Renaissance in its Historical Background*, Cambridge, 1961) and neither of these studies has escaped criticism. Italian history is essentially the history of its various regions, and the bibliography of local studies is so vast that one cannot include even the briefest summary here. Three recent surveys which discuss the material are: F. Chabod, 'Gli studi di storia del Rinascimento' in *Cinquant' anni di vita intelletuale italiana: Scritti in onore di B. Croce*, Naples, 1950, I, 127–207; E. Dupre-Theseider, 'Literaturbericht über italienische Geschichte des Mittelalters;

Veröffentlichungen 1945 bis 1958' in *Historische Zeitschrift*, 1962, Sonderheft I, 613–725; and N. Rubinstein, 'Studies on the political history of the age of Dante', *Atti del congresso internazionale di studi danteschi*, Florence, 1965, Relazioni, I, 225–47. Since however there are many works in English which misrepresent the period 1250–1340 in Florentine history, one should refer here to three important studies: N. Ottokar, *Il comune di Firenze alla fine del dugento*, Florence, 1926; E. Fiumi, 'Fioritura e decadenza dell' economia fiorentina' in the volumes of the *ASI* for 1957–9; and Berthold Stahl, *Adel und Volk im Florentiner Dugento*, Cologne, 1965.

In economic and social history good introductions are provided in articles and bibliographies by P. J. Jones in vol. 1 (new ed., 1966), by R. S. Lopez and E. Carus Wilson in vol. 2 (1952), and by R. de Roover, E. B. Fryde, and M. M. Fryde in vol. 3 (1963) of *The Cambridge Economic History of Europe*. Two other particularly important works may be mentioned here, G. Luzzatto, *Storia economica di Venezia dall' XI al XVI secolo*, Venice, 1961; and A. Sapori, *Studi di storia economica (Secoli xiii–xiv–xv)*, 3rd ed. Florence, 1956. K. Beloch, *Bevölkerungsgeschichte Italiens*, 3 vols., Berlin, 1939–61, rests on rather unstable foundations for our period which explains the caution with which I have treated demographic figures.

For Italian merchants and missionaries in the East, see R. S. Lopez, 'European merchants in the medieval Indies: the evidence of commercial documents', *Journal of Economic History*, 1943; L. Olschki, *L' Asia di Marco Polo*, Rome, 1957; G. Soulier, *Les influences orientales dans la peinture toscane*, Paris, 1924; and L. Olschki, 'Asiatic exoticism in Italian art of the Early Renaissance', *Art Bulletin*, 1944.

1 See D. Herlihy, *Medieval and Renaissance Pistoia*, London, 1967, pp. 1–3

2 Compare the views of Sapori, 'La funzione economica della nobiltà' in his *Studi di storia economica, cit.*, 1, 577–95, with those of Fiumi, 'Fioritura e decadenza', *cit., ASI*, 1957, pp. 437–9

3 Galvano Fiamma, *Opusculum de rebus gestis ab Azone, Luchino et Iohanne Vicecomitibus (1328–1342)*, RIS, xii, 4, ed. C. Castiglioni, p. 16

4 R. S. Lopez, 'Hard times and investment in culture', in E. K. Dannenfeldt, *The Renaissance: Medieval or Modern?*, Boston, 1959, pp. 50–61

5 See *Codice diplomatico dantesco*, ed. R. Piattoli, Florence, 1950, nos. 7, 8, 11, 12, 14, 18, 19, 30, 47; and Fiumi, '*Fioritura e decedenza*', *cit., ASI*, 1957, pp. 399–401

Ch. 3 Intellectual and Religious Life
On philosophy in this age there are valuable introductions in E. Gilson, *La philosophie au moyen âge des origines patristiques à la fin du XIVe siècle*, 2nd

ed., Paris, 1952, and D. Knowles, *The Evolution of Medieval Thought*, London, 1962. For more detailed studies of Italian developments the principal guides are the works of Bruno Nardi, among which, particularly, *Saggi sul aristotelismo padovano dal secolo XIV al XVI*, Florence, 1956; E. Gilson, *Dante et la Philosophie*, Paris, 1939 (see the review by Nardi, 'Dante e la filosofia' in his *Dante e la cultura medievale*, Bari, 1942, pp. 207–45); and P. O. Kristeller, *Le Thomisme et la pensée italienne de la Renaissance*, Montreal-Paris, 1967.

On the physical sciences see Lynn Thorndike, *A History of Magic and Experimental Science*, New York, 1923–58, vols. 3 and 4; A. C. Crombie, *Augustine to Galileo*, London, 1952; P. Duhem, *Le système du monde*, Paris, 1954 ff.; C. H. Haskins, *Studies in the History of Medieval Science*, Cambridge, Mass., 1926 (especially pp. 242 ff. for Frederick II); the volumes of Annaliese Maier, *Studien zur Naturphilosophie des Spätscholastik*, Rome, 1949 ff.; and J. H. Randall, *The School of Padua and the emergence of Modern Science*, Padua 1961. Three important aspects are treated respectively in Charles Singer, 'The Confluence of Humanism, Anatomy and Art' in *Fritz Saxl 1890–1948*, ed. D. J. Gordon, London, 1957, pp. 261–9; Otto Pächt, 'Early Italian nature studies and the early calendar landscape', *JWCI*, 13, 1950; and G. F. Vescovini, *Studi sulla prospettiva medievale*, Turin, 1965.

Fundamental for the understanding of the general lines of European intellectual-sentimental development is W. Goetz, 'Die Entwicklung des Wirklichkeitssinnes vom 12. zum 14. Jahrhundert', *Archiv für Kulturgeschichte*, xxvii, 1937.

These is no general study of Italian religious life in this period. For Florence however, see R. Davidsohn, *Geschichte von Florenz*, Berlin, 1896–1927, iv. pt. 3, chs. 1 and 2, and on heresy, G. Volpe, *Movimenti religiosi e sette ereticali nella società medievale italiana*, 2nd ed., Florence, 1961. On iconography there is G. Kaftal, *Iconography of the Saints in Tuscan Painting*, Florence, 1952, and *Iconography of the Saints in central and south Italian Painting*, Florence, 1965; on religious sentiment, E. Delaruelle, 'La spiritualité aux xive et xve siècles, *Cahiers d'histoire mondiale*, 5, 1959; and *Il movimento dei disciplinati nel settimo centenario dal suo inizio*, Perugia, 1960.

On the new hagiography see Antal, *Florentine Painting*, cit., pt. 2, 3B. As examples, see Jacopo da Voragine, *The Golden Legend or Lives of the Saints. As Englished by William Caxton*, ed. F. S. Ellis, London, 1900; *The Meditations on the Life of Christ. An illustrated Manuscript of the fourteenth century*, translated by I. Ragusa, Princeton, 1961; and the three works on St Francis, *The Life* by St Bonaventura (c. 1260), the *Mirror of Perfection* (c. 1318), and the *Fioretti* (after 1322), which have been gathered together and translated by T. Okey, *The Little Flowers of St Francis with the 'Mirror of Perfection'*, London, 1910.

On religious aesthetic, the texts of Albert, Ulrich, and St Thomas are translated in Amanda K. Coomaraswamy, 'Medieval Aesthetic', *Art Bulletin*, 1935, pp. 31–47, and 1938, pp. 66–77. I quote Gullielmus Durandus, *Rationale Divinorum Officiorum*, Rome, 1473 (and many other editions) in the translation of the first book by J. M. Neale and B. Webb, *The Symbolism of Churches and Church Ornament*, Leeds, 1843.

On patronage by religious bodies see, for the papacy: F. Gregorovius, *History of the City of Rome in the Middle Ages*, trans. A. Hamilton, London, 1894–1902, v, pt. 2, pp. 631 ff., vi, pt. 2, pp. 679 ff.; T. S. R. Boase, *Boniface VIII*, London, 1933, pp. 239–43; V. Golzio and G. Zander, *Le chiese di Roma dall' XI al XVI secolo*, Bologna, 1963; E. Hutton, *The Cosmati*, London, 1950; C. Mitchell, 'The Lateran Fresco of Boniface VIII', *JWCI*, xiv, 1951; Walter Oakeshott, *The Mosaics of Rome*, London, 1967, ch. 7. On the patronage of the friars there is: L. Gillet, *Histoire artistique des ordres mendiants: l'art religieux du XIIIᵉ au XVIIIᵉ s.*, Paris, 1939; G. Meersseman, 'L'architecture dominicaine au XIIIᵉ siècle, législation et pratique', *Archivium Fratrum Praedicatorum*, xvi, 1946; Vincenzo Marchesi, *Memorie di più insigni artefici domenicani*, Florence, 1845–6. On the celebrated thesis of H. Thode, *Franz von Assisi und die Anfänge der Renaissance in Italien*, Berlin, 1885 (French translation of the 2nd edition of 1904 by G. Lefèvre, Paris, 1909) and on the personal role of St Francis in religious and artistic developments, see A. Jullian, 'Le Franciscanisme et l'art italien', *Phoebus*, i, 1946; P. Francastel, 'L'art italien et le rôle personnel de Saint François', *Annales*, xi, 1956.

On the laudesi and religious confraternities, see G. M. Monti, *Le confraternitate medievali dell' alta e media Italia*, Venice, 1927; L. Passerini, *Storia degli stabilmenti di beneficenza e di istruzione elementare gratuita della città di Firenze*, Florence, 1853; G. Poggi, 'La compagnia del Bigallo', *Rivista d'arte*, ii, 1904, and his *Or San Michele*, Florence, 1895.

On the patronage of the laudesi, see Davidsohn, *Geschichte von Florenz*, *cit.*, iv, pt. 3, pp. 98–103, 298–9; A. Cellesi, 'Il lirismo musicale religioso in Siena nel trecento e quello profano nel cinquecento', *BSSP*, 1933; G. Rondoni, 'Laudi drammatiche dei disciplinati di Siena', *GSLI*, ii, 1883; R. Renier, 'Un codice antico de' flagellanti nella biblioteca di Cortona', *GSLI*, xi, 1888; A. d'Ancona, *Origini del teatro italiano*, 2nd ed., Turin, 1891; and A. Lazzarini, 'Il codice Vitt. Em. 528 e il teatro musicale del trecento', *ASI*, 1955.

1   Thorndike, *cit.*, ii, 540, 535

2   V. Cian, 'Vivaldo Belcalzer e l' enciclopedismo italiano delle origini', *GSLI*, supp. v, 1902, p. 145

3   G. Gaye, *Carteggio inedito d' artisti dei secoli xiv–xvi*, Florence, 1839–40, i, 61–2

4   'Rime genovese della fine del secolo xiii e del principio del xiv', ed. N. Lagomaggiore and E. Parodi, *Archivio glottologico italiano*, ii, 1876, pp. 161–312; x, 1886–8, pp. 109–40

5   M. Meiss, '"Highlands" in the Lowlands', *Gazette des Beaux Arts*, 1961, p. 274

6   G. Francastel, 'Une peinture anti-hérétique a Venise?', *Annales*, 201, 1966, pp. 1–17

7   Davidsohn, *Geschichte von Florenz, cit.*, iv, pt. 3, 214–5

8   Dante Alighieri, *Epistolae*, ed. and trans. P. Toynbee, Oxford, 1920, p. 199. Cf. *Il convivio*, ed. G. Busnelli and G. Vandelli, Florence, 1953, ii, 2, xii. For Boccaccio see Charles G. Osgood, *Boccaccio on Poetry*, Princeton, 1930, p. 18

9   E. Panofsky, *Early Netherlandish Painting*, Cambridge, Mass., 1953, i, 24; Millard Meiss, *French Painting in the Time of Jean de Berry. The Late Fourteenth Century and the Patronage of the Duke*, London, 1967, pp. 23–7. But see E. Castelnuovo, *Un pittore italiano alla corte di Avignone*, Turin, 1962, pp. 139 ff.

10   *Catalogus Archiepiscoporum Mediolanensium*, ed. W. Wattenbach, *Monumenta Germaniae Historica*: Scriptores, 8, p. 109

11   For this order, P. Lugano, 'Di Fra Giovanni da Verona, maestro d' intaglio e di tarsia e della sua scuola', *BSSP*, xii, 1905, pp. 135–239

12   Some notable Dominican churches of this time are:

Città di Castello	(S. Domenico, from 1295)
Siena	(S. Domenico, 1226–1465)
Venice	(SS. Giovanni e Paolo, from 1333)
Verona	(S. Anastagio, 1261–1422)
Treviso	(S. Niccolo, 1304–52)
Vicenza	(S. Corona, façade *c.* 1300)
Florence	(S. Maria Novella, 1278–1349)
Rome	(S. Maria sopra Minerva, reconstructed from 1280)
Pisa	(S. Caterina, 13th–14th c.)

Naples   (S. Domenico, from 1283)

Some principal Franciscan churches are:

Verona	(S. Fermo, from 1312)
Pistoia	(S. Francesco, from 1294)
Florence	(S. Croce, from 1294)
Naples	(S. Chiara, 1310–28,
	S. Lorenzo Maggiore, 1280–1324)
Padua	(S. Antonio, 1231–1307)
Venice	(S. Maria Gloriosa dei Frari, 1330–1430s)
Treviso	(S. Francesco, from 1306)
Todi	(S. Fortunato, E. half, 1292–1328)
Pisa	(S. Francesco, 13th–14th c.)
Piacenza	(S. Francesco, after 1278)
Siena	(S. Francesco, from 1326)

There are many more examples. The various churches of the orders, it should be added, present no uniform style

13   V. Mariani, *Il Petrarca e gli Agostiniani*, 2nd ed. Rome, 1959; B. Smalley, *English Friars and Antiquity in the Early Fourteenth Century*, Oxford, 1960, pp. 265–72

14   R. Davidsohn, *Forschungen zur Geschichte von Florenz*, Berlin, 1896–1908, iv, 481–2; G. Milanesi, *Nuovi documenti per la storia dell' arte toscana*, Rome, 1893, p. 32

15   B. M. Nelson, 'The Usurer and the Merchant Prince, Italian Business-men and the ecclesiastical law of restitution', *Journal of Ecclesiastical History*, vii, *Suppl.*, 1947, pp. 104–22

Ch. 4   Government and Patronage I

On commune and signoria two recent and sophisticated surveys are: P. J. Jones, 'Communes and Despots: The city State in late-medieval Italy', in *Transactions of the Royal Historical Society*, 1965, and D. Bueno de Mesquita, 'The place of despotism in Italian politics' in *Europe in the Late Middle Ages*, ed. J. R. Hale, J. R. L. Highfield, B. Smalley, London, 1965. On 'the State' see too L. Minio-Paluello, 'Remigio Girolami's *De bono communi*', *Italian Studies*, 1956; M. B. Becker, 'Dante and his literary contemporaries as political men', *Speculum*, 1966; N. Rubinstein, 'Marsilius of Padua and Italian political thought of his time' in *Europe in the Late Middle Ages, cit.*

On communal patronage I am particularly indebted to the excellent article of Helene Wieruszowski, 'Art and the commune in the time of

Dante', *Speculum*, 1944. For Siena, much of the source material I have consulted is printed in G. Milanesi, *Documenti per la storia dell' arte senese*, Siena, 1854; and S. Borghesi and L. Banchi, *Documenti per la storia dell' arte senese*, Siena 1898. For Tuscany in general there is G. Milanesi, *Nuovi documenti per la storia dell' arte toscana*, Rome, 1893; and for Florence, 'Regesta florentina internam reipublicae historiam spectantia' in G. Gaye, *Carteggio inedito d' artisti dei sec. xiv–xvi*, 1839–40, i, 413–547. On the role of the guilds in Florentine communal patronage see A. Doren, *Studien aus der Florentiner Wirtschaftsgeschichte*, vol. 2, *Das Florentiner Zunftwesen*, Stuttgart and Berlin, 1908, ch. 10, and 'Aus den Statuten . . . der Arte di Calimala' in G. Vasari, *Le Vite*, ed. K. Frey, pt. I, vol. i, 1911, pp. 320–4. On ecclesiastical patronage by the commune see C. E. Norton, *Historical Studies of Church-building in the Middle Ages*, London, 1881. For Siena: E. Cecchini, 'L' archivio dell' Opera del Duomo e il suo riordinamento', *BSSP*, 1953; V. Lusini, *Duomo di Siena*, vol. I, Siena, 1911; *idem*, *Il San Giovanni di Siena*. For Florence there is A. Grote, *Das Dombauamt in Florenz 1285–1370*, Munich, n.d. (1960?); C. Guasti, *Santa Maria del Fiore*, Florence, 1887; Giovanni Poggi, *Il duomo di Firenze*, Berlin, 1909; id, *Or San Michele*, Florence, 1895. The architectural history of each Florentine church, together with accounts of the artistic monuments within them, is given in W. and E. Paatz, *Die Kirchen von Florenz*, Frankfurt am Main, 1940–54. Still useful too are the ten learned volumes of G. Richa, *Notizie istoriche delle chiese fiorentine*, Florence, 1754–62. On the difficult questions concerned with the building of the cathedral of Florence, M. Weinberger, 'The first façade of the cathedral of Florence', *JWCI*, iv, 1940–1; G. Kiesow, 'Zur Baugeschichte des Florentiner Domes', *Mitteilungen des Kunsthistorischen Institutes im Florenz*, x, 1961–3; H. Saalman, 'Santa Maria del Fiore, 1294–1418', *Art Bulletin*, 1964.

For Orvieto, see E. Carli, *Il duomo di Orvieto*, Rome, 1965; and (documents) L. Fumi, *Il duomo di Orvieto e i suoi ristauri*, Rome, 1891. For Pistoia and Pisa, S. Ciampi, *Notizie inedite della sagrestia pistoiese, de' belli arredi del Campo Santo pisano e di altre opere di disegno dal secolo xii al xv*, Florence, 1810. For Pisa some indications are given in L. Tanfani, *Della chiesa di S. Maria del Pontenovo*, Pisa, 1871

On secular patronage by the communes see N. Rodolico and G. Marchini, *I palazzi del popolo nei comuni italiani del medio evo*, Milan, 1962. For Siena there is F. Donati, 'Il palazzo del comune di Siena' in the vol. *Arte antica senese* (vol. xi of the *BSSP*), Siena, 1904, i, pp. 311–54, and A. Cairola and E. Carli, *Il palazzo pubblico di Siena*, Rome, 1963. For individual paintings and artists consult particularly G. Paccagnini, *Simone Martini*, Milan, 1955; G. Rowley, *Ambrogio Lorenzetti*, Princeton, 1958;

E. Carli, *Le tavolette di Biccherna*, Florence, 1950; A. Lisini, *Le tavolette di Biccherna e di Gabella del R. Archivio di stato in Siena*, Siena, 1901; and W. Heywood, *A Pictorial Chronicle of Siena*, Siena, 1902. For Florence, see K. Frey, *Die Loggia dei Lanzi*, Berlin, 1885 (Piazza della Signoria, pp. 180–250; the Loggia, pp. 251–310).

On town planning Pierre Lavedan, *Histoire de l'urbanisme*, vol. 2, Paris, 1941, offers little relevant to Italy for our period, and my principal guide has been Wolfgang Braunfels, *Mittelalterliche Stadtbaukunst in der Toskana*, 3rd ed., Berlin, 1966. For Florence there is source material in R. Davidsohn, *Forschungen zur Geschichte von Florenz*, Berlin, 1896–1908, 4, 521–9; *Carteggio, cit.*, and Frey, *Die Loggia, cit.*, See also M. Barbi 'Dante e i lavori di via San Procolo', *Studi danteschi*, 3, 1921. For Lucca, see *Statuti urbanistici medievali di Lucca*, ed. D. Corsi, Venice, 1960. For Siena, see V. Lusini, 'Note storiche sulla topografia di Siena nel secolo XIII' in *Dante e Siena*, vol. 28 of *BSSP*; L. Zdekauer, 'Le spese di selciatura e di riparazione della via di Malcucinato', *BSSP*, 3, 1896; F. Bargagli Petrucci, *Le fonti di Siena e i loro acquedotti*, Siena, 1906; Anne C. Hanson, *Jacopo della Quercia's Fonte Gaia*, Oxford, 1965.

1   Milanesi, *Documenti, cit.*, i, 186–9

2   *Ibid*, i, 166–9

3   V. Lusini, 'La Basilica di San Francesco in Siena' in *San Francesco e Siena*, ed. P. Misciatelli and A. Lusini, Siena, 1927; V. Lusini, 'San Domenico in Camporeggio', *BSSP*, xiii, 1906; Milanesi, *Documenti, cit.*, 1, 193; Borghesi and Banchi, *Nuovi documenti, cit.*, pp. 28–30

4   *Epistolae, cit.*, 6, 4

5   *Chronache senesi*, ed. A. Lisini and F. Iacometti, *RIS*, xv, pt. 6, p. 428

6   Particularly N. Rubinstein, 'Political ideas in Sienese art: the frescoes of Ambrogio Lorenzetti and Taddeo di Bartolo in the Palazzo Pubblico', *JWCI*, 1958, pp. 179–207

7   Giovanni Villani, *Cronica*, ed. F. Dragomanni, Florence, 1846, ix, 256–7; x, 129, 216; Milanesi, *Nuovi documenti, cit.*, pp. 39–43; Marchionne di Coppo Stefani, *Cronica fiorentina*, ed. N. Rodolico, *RIS*, xxx, pt. 1, p. 173

8   Borghesi and Banchi, *Nuovi documenti, cit.*, pp. 31–6

9   Guasti, *Santa Maria del Fiore, cit.*, pp. 51 ff.; Braunfels, *Mittelalterliche Stadtbaukunst, cit.*, p. 252

10   Gaye, *Carteggio, cit.*, i, 72

11   Borghesi and Banchi, *Nuovi documenti, cit.*, p. 1. See A. Canistrelli,

'L'architettura medievale senese', *BSSP*, ix, 1904; V. de Vecchi, 'L'architettura gotica civile senese', *BSSP*, 1949

12   Borghesi and Banchi, *Nuovi documenti, cit.*, pp. 75–6

13   See L. Thorndike, 'Sanitation, baths, and street-cleaning in the Middle Ages and Renaissance', *Speculum*, 1928

14   Borghesi and Banchi, *Nuovi documenti, cit.*, p. 76 (Braunfels, *Mittelalterliche Studtbaukunst, cit.*, p. 254, corrects the date). On the Rialto, see *I capitolari delle arti veneziane*, ed. G. Monticolo, Rome, 1896–1914, i, 259

15   Lewis Mumford, *The City in History. Its origins, its transformations and its prospects*, New York, 1961, p. 423. On property investment, see A. Sapori, 'Case e botteghe a Firenze nel Trecento' in *Studi di storia economica, cit.*, i, 305–52

Ch. 5   Government and Patronage II

For patronage of the arts by the Visconti, see *Arte lombarda dai Visconti agli Sforza* (introduction by R. Longhi), Milan, 1958; C. Magenta, *I Visconti e gli Sforza nel castello di Pavia*, Naples, 1883; L. Beltrami, *Il castello di Milano*, Milan, 1894 and *La Certosa di Pavia*, Milan, 1895; C. Romussi, *Milano ne' suoi monumenti*, Milan, 3rd ed., 1912–3; the articles by A. Viscardi, A. M. Romanini, C. Baroni, M. Salmi in vol. 5, and by E. Garin, A. Romanini, C. Baroni, and M. Salmi in vol. 6 of the *Storia di Milano* of the Fondazione Treccani degli Alfieri, Milan, 1955; P. Toesca, *La pittura e la miniatura lombarda*, Milan, 1912.

For the Bonacolsi and Gonzaga of Mantua see the articles in *Mantova: La storia*, vol. I, ed. G. Coniglio, Mantua, 1958; *Mantova: Le lettere*, vol. I, ed. E. Faccioli, Mantua, 1959; *Mantova: Le arti*, vol. I, ed. G. Paccagnini, Mantua, 1960.

On Sicily see Stefano Bottari, *La cultura figurativa in Sicilia*, Messina, 1954; S. Tramontana, *Michele da Piazza e il potere baronale in Sicilia*, Messina, 1963, pp. 136–8.

For the Kingdom of Naples see E. G. Léonard, *Les Angevins de Naples*, Paris, 1954; W. Goetz, *König Robert von Naples*, Tubingen, 1910; H. W. Schulz, *Denkmäler der Kunst des Mittelalters in Unteritalien*, ed. F. von Quast, Dresden, 1860; O. Morisani, *Pittura del Trecento in Napoli*, Naples, 1947; A. de Rinaldis, *Naples angevine*, Paris, 1927, and *Santa Chiara*, Naples, 1920; E. Bertaux, *Santa Maria di Donna Regina e l' arte senese a Napoli nel secolo XIV*, Naples, 1899; W. R. Valentiner, *Tino di Camaino: a Sienese Sculptor of the fourteenth century*, Paris, 1935.

1   Galvano Fiamma, *Opusculum de rebus gestis, cit.*, pp. 15–16, 35

2   *Statuta Faventiae*, ed. G. Rossini, vol. I, *RIS*, xxviii, pt. 5, Bk. 7; *Annales Arretinorum Minores*, ed. A. Bini and G. Grazzini, *RIS*, xxiv, pt. I, pp. 16–17; *Mantova: Le arti, cit.*, i, 31, 146–8

3   A. Colombo, 'Le mura di Milano comunale e la pretesa cerchia di Azzone Visconti', *Archivio storico lombardo*, 1923, pp. 277–334; Pietro Azario, *Liber gestorum in Lombardia*, *RIS*, xvi, pt. 4, ed. F. Cognasso, p. 33; Galvano Fiamma, *Opusculum de rebus gestis, cit.*, pp. 20, 22–3, 26; *Annali della Fabbrica del Duomo di Milano*, Milan, 1877–85, i, 50, 73

4   Azario, *Liber gestorum, cit.*, p. 152

5   Azario, *Liber gestorum, cit.*, pp. 133–4; Fiamma, *Opusculum de rebus gestis, cit.*, pp. 16–17

6   *Storia di Milano, cit.*, vi, p. 522

7   Milanesi, *Documenti, cit.*, i, 217. In considering the effects of Government patronage, I must acknowledge here again my particular debt to the article of H. Wieruszowski, 'Art and the commune', *cit.*

8   For these citations, see Milanesi, *Documenti, cit.*, i, 180–1; *idem, Nuovi documenti, cit.*, p. 19; Antonio Pucci, 'Centiloquio' in *Delizie degli eruditi toscani*, ed. I. di San Luigi, Florence, 1772–5, iv, 180; G. Villani, *Cronica, cit.*, x, 174

9   Milanesi, *Documenti, cit.*, ii, 11–12

10   *Le prediche volgari di San Bernardino da Siena detta nella piazza del campo l'anno 1427*, ed. L. Bianchi, Siena, 1880–8, iii, 373

11   G. Boccaccio, *Genealogie deorum gentilium libri*, ed. V. Romano, Bari, 1951, xiv, 9 (vol. iii, 708–9)

12   Translated by W. A. Pantin in *The English Church in the Fourteenth Century*, Cambridge, 1953, from *Snappe's Formulary*, ed. H. E. Salter (Oxford Historical Society, lxxx) 1923, p. 304. Cf. Dante, *Paradiso*, viii, 145–7

Part II   The Age of Orcagna and Petrarch.

The Environment of Literature

Ch. 6   *Italy in Crisis, 1340–80*

On plague in the period, see: E. Carpentier, 'La peste noire: famines et épédémies dans l'histoire du xive siècle', *Annales*, xvii, 1962, and her *Une ville devant la Peste: Orvieto et la peste noire de 1348*, Paris, 1962; Anna Campbell, *The Black Death and Men of Learning*, New York, 1931; Lynn Thorndike, 'The blight of pestilence in early modern civilisation', *Ameri-*

can Historical Review, xxxii, 1927; Yves Renouard, 'Conséquences et intérêt démographique de la Peste noire de 1348', *Population*, iii, 1948. On famine there have been no modern studies, but G. Corradi, *Annali delle epidemie occorse in Italia*, vol. i, Bologna, 1863, assembles some information.

On particular aspects of demographic, economic, and social change, see: G. A. Brucker, *Florentine Politics and Society, 1343–1378*, Princeton, 1962; E. Fiumi, 'La demografia fiorentina nelle pagine di Giovanni Villani', *ASI*, 1950; A. Frugoni, 'G. Villani, "Chronica", xi, 94', *Bullettino dell' Istituto storico italiano per il medio evo*, 1965; A. Sapori, *La crisi delle compagnie mercantili dei Bardi e dei Peruzzi*, Florence, 1926; W. Bowsky, 'The impact of the Black Death upon Sienese government and society', *Speculum*, 1964; J. Day, *Les douanes de Gênes, 1376–77*, Paris, 1963; D. Herlihy, 'Population, plague and social change in rural Pistoia, 1201–1430', *Economic History Review*, 1965, and *Medieval and Renaissance Pistoia*, London, 1967; *Storia di Milano*, cit., vi, 519–20.

My principal source for the understanding of spiritual change and Tuscan art in this chapter has been the brilliant study of Millard Meiss, *Painting in Florence and Siena after the Black Death*, Princeton, 1951.

On communal and signorial patronage in this era, see the works already cited in the notes to chs. 4 and 5. For Venice, C. Boito, *La Basilica di San Marco*, Venice, 1888; and W. F. Volbach *et alii*, *La Pala d' Oro*, Florence, 1965.

On papal patronage in this period, see: Y. Renouard, *Les relations des papes d'Avignon et des compagnies commerciales et bancaires de 1316 à 1378*, Paris, 1941, pp. 185–6, 344; F. Gregorovius, *History of Rome*, cit., vi, pt. 2, pp. 679 ff.; E. Castelnuovo, *Un pittore italiano alla corte di Avignone*, Turin, 1962.

On the beginnings of humanism, see especially the works of Kristeller cited in the notes to ch. 1; R. Weiss, *The Dawn of Humanism in Italy*, London, 1947; and Giuseppe Billanovich, *I primi umanisti e le tradizioni dei classici italiani*, Freiburg, 1953. On classics in the early Italian universities, see E. Rand, 'The classics in the thirteenth century', *Speculum*, 1929; and H. Wieruszowski, 'Arezzo as a centre of learning and letters in the thirteenth century', *Traditio*, 1953.

1   J. H. Randall, 'The development of scientific method in the school of Padua', *Journal of the History of Ideas*, 1940, p. 177

2   See T. E. Mommsen, 'Petrarch's concept of the Dark Ages', *Speculum*, 1942. On the 'Renaissance idea', see W. K. Ferguson, *The Renaissance in Historical Thought*, Cambridge, Mass., 1948. The most intelligent discussion of this concept is that of A. Sapori, 'Medioevo e rinascimento: spunti

per una diversa periodizzazione', *ASI*, 1957, reprinted with additional matter in vol. 3 of his *Studi di storia economica, cit.*

3 V. Branca, *Boccaccio medievale*, Florence, 1956, pp. 209–13

4 Matteo Villani, *Cronica*, ed. F. Dragomanni, Florence, 1846, Bk. 1, Introduction and chs. 1–4, and cf. Giovanni Villani, *Cronica, cit.*, Bk. 1, ch. i. (M. B. Becker, *Florence in Transition*, vol. 1, *The Decline of the Commune*, Baltimore, 1967, p. 39, n. 59, points out however that Matteo Villani assumes a more optimistic tone from 1358). For other references to plague in the text, see Gentile da Foligno, 'Tractatus de pestilentia et causis eius et remediis', *Archiv für Geschichte der Medizin*, 1912, p. 84; Michele da Piazza in R. Gregorio, *Bibliotheca scriptorum qui res in Sicilia gestas retulere*, Palermo, 1791–2, i, 562 ff.; *Cronache senesi, cit.*, p. 555; Antonio Pucci, *La pestilenza del 1348*, Florence, 1884

5 F. Petrarca, *Rerum senilium liber xiii. Ad magnificum Franciscum De Carraria Padue dominum Epistola I*, ed. V. Ussani, Padua, 1922

6 P. Azario, *Liber gestorum in Lombardia, cit.*, pp. 133–4; idem, *Chronicon placentinum, cit.*, col. 544–5

7 F. Petrarca, *Epistolae Seniles*, v, 1. as translated in J. H. Robinson and H. W. Rolfe, *Petrarch: The First Modern Scholar and Man of Letters*, London, 1898, pp. 320 ff.

8 *Documenti diplomatici tratti dagli Archivj milanesi*, ed. L. Osio, Milan, 1864–72, i, 212; Carlo Magenta, *I Visconti e gli Sforza nel castello di Pavia*, Milan, 1883, ii, 27. On the Dondi, see, G. Dondi dall' Orologio, *Il 'Tractatus Astrarii'*, ed. A. Petrucci *et al.*, Vatican, 1960, and H. Alan, *Some Outstanding Clocks over Seven Hundred Years 1250–1950*, London, 1958, pp. 9–24

9 *Epistolario di Coluccio Salutati*, ed. F. Novati, Rome, 1891–1905, i, 80–4

10 Rowley, *Ambrogio Lorenzetti, cit.*, i, 64–6

11 See M. Becker and G. Brucker, 'The *Arti Minori* in Florentine Politics, 1342–1378', *Mediaeval Studies*, 1956

12 G. Boccaccio, *Opere latine minori*, ed. A. F. Massera, Bari, 1928. I follow Branca, however, in dating this to 1372

13 R. Ramat, 'Indicazioni per una lettura del *Decamerone*', in *Scritti su Giovanni Boccaccio*, Florence, 1964, pp. 7–19

14 See R. Weiss, *The Dawn of Humanism, cit.*, pp. 11, 14; and F. Saxl, 'Petrarch in Venice' in his *Lectures*, London, 1957, pp. 144–5

15 Dante, *Epistolae, cit.*, viii, 10, p. 137; F. Petrarch, *Le familiari*, ed. V. Rossi, vi, 2 (vol. ii, 58)

16   *Mantova: Le lettere, cit.*, vol. 1, pt. 1, ch. 1; Davidsohn, *Geschichte von Florenz, cit.*, iv, pt. 3, pp. 126–7

17   L. Ghiberti, *I commentari*, ed. O. Morisani, Naples, 1947, iii, 3, p. 56; Cairola and Carli, *Il palazzo, cit.*, p. 49

Ch 7   Literature and Music

On oral and visual culture, see Walter J. Ong, 'System, space and intellect in Renaissance symbolism', *Bibliothèque d'Humanisme et Renaissance*, 18, 1956. On this theme H. J. Chaytor, *From Script to Print*, Cambridge, 1945, is interesting, though concerned primarily with twelfth and thirteenth century France; E. P. Goldschmidt, *Medieval Texts and their first appearance in print*, Oxford, 1943, gives some assistance, though much of what he says could only with difficulty be applied to Italy in this period. Some of the conclusions of Istvan Hajnal, *L'enseignement de l'écriture aux universités médiévales*, 2nd ed., Budapest, 1959, suffer from his exclusive concentration on academic milieux. Marshall McLuhan, *The Gutenberg Galaxy*, London, 1962, forms the materials of these works into the shape demanded by his thesis.

On spectacles and script see E. Rosen, 'The invention of eyeglasses', *Journal of the history of medicine and allied sciences*, xi, 1956; B. L. Ullmann, *The Origin and Development of Humanist Script*, Rome, 1960, chs. 1 and 2; O. Pächt, 'Notes and observations on the origin of humanistic book-decoration' in *Fritz Saxl. A volume of Memorial Essays*, ed. D. J. Gordon, London, 1957.

On the audience for literature see, for popularity of Dante, C. Grayson, 'Dante and the Renaissance' in *Italian Studies presented to E. R. Vincent*, Cambridge, 1962. For provenance of Boccaccio manuscripts, V. Branca, 'Prima diffusione del Decameron', *Studi di filologia italiana*, vol. 8, Florence, 1950. For chivalric literature, E. G. Gardner, *The Arthurian Legend in Italian Literature*, London, 1930; and F. Saxl, 'The Troy Romance in French and Italian art', in his *Lectures, cit.*, pp. 125–38.

On music in society see *Ars Nova and the Renaissance 1300–1540*, ed. A. Hughes and G. Abraham (New Oxford History of Music, vol. 3), chs. 2 and 5; Luigia Cellisi, 'Documenti per la storia musicale da Firenze', *Rivista musicale italiana*, 24, 1927; 25, 1928; Francesco Landini, *The Works*, ed. L. Ellinwood, Cambridge, Mass., 1939. P. O. Kristeller, 'Music and learning in the early Italian Renaissance' in his *Renaissance Thought II, cit.*, pp. 142–62; J. Wolf, 'Italian Trecento Music', *Proceedings of the Musical Association*, lviii, 1931–2; and Davidsohn, *Geschichte von Florenz, cit.*, iv, pt. 3, 299–305; *L'Ars Nova*, ed. Suzanne Clercx (vol. 2 of *Les Colloques de*

Wégimont), Paris, 1959, gives some indication of the difficulties attendant upon a study of Italian music in this period.

On minstrels and 'men of the court' see Davidsohn, *Geschichte von Florenz*, iv, pt. 3, 305–13; E. Levi, 'Antonio e Niccolò da Ferrara, poeti e uomini di corte di Trecento', *Atti e memorie della deputazione ferrarese di storia patria*, xix, 1908; K. Speight, '*Vox Populi* in Antonio Pucci' in *Italian Studies presented to E. R. Vincent, cit.*; A. Viscardi, 'La cultura milanese nel secolo xiv' in *Storia di Milano, cit.*, v, pt. 2, ch. 4; E. Levi, 'L'ultimo re dei giullari', *Studi medievali*, 1928.

1 'Rime genovesi', *cit.*; Boccaccio, *Espozioni sopra la Commedia di Dante*, ed. G. Padoan, 1965, p. 166; P. J. Jones, 'Florentine families and Florentine diaries in the fourteenth century', *Papers of the British School at Rome*, 1956

2 Paolo di Pace di Certaldo, *Libro di buoni costumi*, ed. S. Morpurgo, Florence, 1921, no. 282, p. 126; Davidsohn, *Geschichte von Florenz, cit.*, iv, pt. 3, pp. 26–7; Boccaccio, *Genealogie deorum gentilium libri, cit.*, xv, 6 (vol. 2, 763)

3 *Epistola metricae*, 1, 6, in the translation of E. H. Wilkins, *Petrarch at Vaucluse*, Chicago, 1958, p. 9

4 F. Villani, *Liber de civitate Florentiae*, ed. G. C. Galletti, preface. See too B. L. Ullmann, 'The dedication copy of Giovanni Dominici's *Lucula Noctis*—a landmark in the history of the Italian Renaissance', *Medievalia et Humanistica*, i, 1943; and Salutati's letter to Vergerio of 1402 in his *Epistolario, cit.*, iv, 85 (giving less probable date of 1405)

5 *De vulgari eloquentia*, ed. A. Marigo, 3rd ed. of P. G. Ricci, Florence, 1957, ii, IV, 2, p. 188 (see too, ii, VIII, 5, p. 236). For this reading see A. Schiaffini, 'Dante, Retorica, Medioevo' in *Atti del congresso internazionale di studi danteschi, cit.*, ii, 162–3

6 T. E. Mommsen, *Medieval and Renaissance Studies*, New York, 1959, p. 88

7 *Le familiari, cit.*, xxi, 15 (iv, 94–100) in the translation of J. H. Robinson and H. W. Rolfe, *Petrarch: The First Modern Scholar, cit.*, pp. 178–90

8 *Annali della fabbrica del duomo di Milano*, Milan, 1877–85, i, 105, 68

9 *Documenti diplomatici tratti dagli archivi milanesi, cit.*, i, 180

10 J. K. Hyde, *Padua in the age of Dante*, Manchester, 1966, pp. 298–9

11 N. C. Carpenter, *Music in the Medieval and Renaissance Universities*, Oklohoma, 1958, pp. 32–46

12   Davidsohn, *Forschungen, cit.*, iv, 432, 479; idem, *Geschichte von Florenz, cit.*, iv, pt. 3, 99–103

13   *Annali della fabbrica del duomo di Milano, cit.*, i, 146, 148–50, 154, 168, 177, 210, 252, 270, 281

14   Davidsohn, *Geschichte von Florenz, cit.*, iv, pt. 3

15   Borghesi e Banchi, *Nuovi documenti, cit.*, p. 65

16   G. Bertoni, *I trovatori d' Italia*, Modena, 1915, pp. 245–6; *Annales Caesenates, RIS*, xiv, 1141

17   *Epistolae seniles*, v. 3, as translated in Robinson and Rolfe, *Petrarch: The First Modern Scholar, cit.*, pp. 197–204

18   Cellisi, 'Documenti', *cit.*, 1927, p. 597

19   C. Foligno, 'Epistolae inedite di Lovato de' Lovati e d'altri a lui', *Studi medievali*, ii, 1906, p. 49

Ch. 8   The Environment of Literature: Books, Libraries, Education
On booksellers I am particularly indebted to the Ph.D thesis of Albinia C. de la Mare, *Vespasiano da Bisticci, Historian and Bookseller*, 1965. See also A. Kirchhoff, *Die Handschrifthändler des Mittelalters*, Osnabruck, 1966 (reprint of 2nd ed., Leipzig, 1843) and G. H. Putnam, *Books and their Makers during the Middle Ages*, New York, 1896–7. On university stationers, H. Denifle, 'Die Statuten der Juristen-Universität Bologna vom J. 1314–17 und deren Verhältniss zu jenem Paduas, Perugias, Florenz', *Archiv für Litteratur und Kirchengeschichte des Mittelalters*, iii, idem, 'Die Statuten der Juristen-Universität Padua vom J. 1331', *ibid.*, vi, 1892; J. Destrez, *La pecia dans les manuscrits universitaires du xiiie et du xive siècle*, Paris, 1935.
    On libraries see J. W. Thompson (with Dr. Robathan), *The Medieval Library*, Chicago, 1939; F. Milkau and G. Leyh (eds.) *Geschichte der Bibliotheken* (vol. 3 of *Handbuch de Bibliothekwissenschaft*), 2nd ed. Wiesbaden, 1955, chs. 5 and 6; Theodor Gottlieb, *Ueber Mittelalterliche Bibliotheken*, Leipzig, 1890; Paul Kibré, 'Intellectual interests reflected in the libraries of the fourteenth and fifteenth centuries', *Journal of the History of Ideas*, 1946.
    For additional material on ecclesiastical libraries, see F. Ehrle, 'Zur Geschichte des Schatzes der Bibliothek und der Archivs der Päpste im vierzehnten Jahrhundert', *Archiv für Literatur- und Kirchengeschichte des Mittelalters*, i, 1885; A. Caravita, *I codici e le arti a Montecassino*, Montecassino, 1869–70, ii, 261–90; A. C. Quintavalle, *Miniatura a Piacenza: I codici dell' archivio capitolare*, Venice, 1963. For the libraries of the orders, K. W. Humphreys, *The Book Provisions of Medieval Friars*, Amsterdam,

1964, and *The Library of the Carmelites at Florence*, also Amsterdam, 1964; M.-H. Laurent, *Fabio Virgili et les bibliothèques de Bologne*, Vatican, 1943; C. T. Davis, 'The early collection of books of S. Croce in Florence', *Proceedings of the American Philosophical Society*, 1963.

On signorial libraries see A. Cappelli, 'La biblioteca estense nella prima metà del secolo xv', *GSLI*, xiv, 1889; P. Rajna, 'Ricordo di codici francesi posseduti dagli estensi nel secolo xv', *Romania*, ii, 1873; G. Paris, W. Braghirolli, and P. Meyer, 'Inventaire des manuscripts en langue française possedés par Francesco Gonzaga i', *Romania*, ix, 1880; F. Novati, 'I codici francesi de' Gonzaga secondo nuovi documenti', *Romania*, xix, 1890; P. Girolla, 'La biblioteca di Francesco Gonzaga secondo l'inventario del 1407', *Accademia virgiliana: Atti e memorie*, xiv–xvi, 1921–3; C. Santorno, 'La biblioteca dei Gonzaga e cinque suoi libri nella Trivulziana di Milano', *Arte, pensiero e cultura a Mantova nel primo rinascimento*, Florence, 1965; (G. d' Adda, under pseud. 'Bibliofilo'), *Indagini storiche artistiche e bibliografiche sulla libreria visconteo—sforzesca del castello di Pavia*, Milan, 1875–9; E. Pellegrin, *La bibliothèque des Sforzas, ducs de Milan au xve siècle*, Paris, 1955.

On private libraries see G. Fiocco, 'La biblioteca di Palla Strozzi', *Studi di bibliografia e di storia in onore di Tammaro de Marinis*, Verona, 1964, ii, 289–310; R. Blum, *Biblioteca della Badia fiorentina e i codici di Antonio Corbinelli*, Vatican, 1951; W. Bombe, 'Hausinventar und Bibliothek Ugolinos da Montecatini', *Archiv für Geschichte der Medizin*, v, 1912; B. L. Ullman, *The Humanism of Coluccio Salutati*, Padua, 1963, ch. 9; A. Mercati, 'La biblioteca privata e gli arredi di cappella di Gregorio xii', *Miscellenea Francesco Ehrle*, Rome, 1924, v, 128–65; V. Lazzarini, 'I libri, gli argenti, le vesti di Giovanni Dondi dall' Orologio', *Bollettino del Museo Civico di Padua*, 1925; C. Garibotto, 'Una libreria veronese del secolo xv', *Antiquarium*, 1922.

On education see Davidsohn, *Geschichte von Florenz, cit.*, iv, pt. 3, ch. 3; C. T. Davis, 'Education in Dante's Florence', *Speculum*, 1965; A. Fanfani, 'La préparation intellectuelle et professionelle à l'activité économique en Italie, du xive au xvie siècle', *Le moyen âge*, 1951; A. Sapori, 'La cultura del mercante medievale italiano', *Studi di storia economica, cit.*, i, 53–93; P. Boskoff, 'Quintillian in the later middle ages', *Speculum*, 1952; G. Manacorda, *Storia della scuola in Italia*, Milan-Palermo-Naples, 1913, i, pt. 2.

On university education see H. Rashdall, *The Universities of Europe in the Middle Ages*, new ed. of F. M. Powicke and A. B. Emden, Oxford, 1936; G. Zaccagnini, *La vita dei maestri e degli scolari nello studio di Bologna nei secoli xiii e xiv*, Florence, 1926; G. Prunai, 'Lo studio senese dalle origini alla "Migratio" bolognese' and 'Lo studio senese dalla "Migratio' bolognese alla fondazione della "Domus Sapientiae"', *BSSP*, 1949 and 1950;

G. Ermini, *Storia della università di Perugia*, Bologna, 1947; G. M. Monti, 'L' età angoina' in *Storia della università di Napoli*, Naples, 1924; P. Vaccari, *Storia della università di Pavia*, Pavia, 1948.

On the origins of humanist education see W. H. Woodward, *Vittorino da Feltre and other Humanist Educators*, Cambridge, 1905; idem, *Studies in Education during the Age of the Renaissance*, Cambridge, 1906; Remigio Sabbadini, *Guariniana*, ed. M. Sancipriano, Turin, 1964 (contains his *Vita di Guarino Veronese*, Genoa, 1891 and *La scuola e gli studi di Guarino*, Catania, 1896); E. Garin (ed.), *Il pensiero pedagogico dell' umanesimo*, Florence, 1958. Two modern editions of educational texts from the period are: Pier Paolo Vergerio, 'De ingenuis moribus', ed. A. Gnesotto, *Atti e memorie della R. Acc. di Scienze, Lettere ed Arti in Padova*, 34, 1918; and 'De studiis et litteris liber', in Leonardo Bruni, *Humanistisch-Philosophische Schriften*, ed. H. Baron, Leipzig-Berlin, 1928, pp. 5–19.

1   Richard de Bury, *Philobiblion*, ed. A. Altamura, Naples, 1954, ch. 8, p. 103; M. Levi d' Ancona, *Miniature e miniatori a Firenze dal xiv al xvi secolo*, Florence, 1962, p. 81; Putnam, *cit.*, i, ch. 4

2   F. Ehrle, 'Zur Geschichte des Schatzes der Bibliothek', *cit.*, pp. 308–16

3   Kirchoff, *Die Handschrifthändler*, *cit.*, p. 144

4   Levi d' Ancona, *Miniature e miniatori*, *cit.*, pp. 212, 182–3, 239; *De arte illuminandi: The Technique of Manuscript Illumination*, transl. D. V. Thompson and G. H. Hamilton, New Haven, 1933

5   See G. Padoan, 'Dante di fronte all' umanesimo letterario' in *Atti del congresso internazionale di studi danteschi*, *cit.*, ii, pp. 377–400; cf. P. Renucci, *Dante, disciple et juge du monde gréco-latin*, Paris, 1954

6   T. E. Mommsen, *Medieval and Renaissance Studies*, *cit.*, pp. 230–2

7   *Mantova: Le lettere*, *cit.*, i, 488–9

8   Sapori, 'Un bilancio domestico a Firenze alla fine del dugento', *Studi di storia economica*, i, 355; M. E. V. Rossi, 'Maestri e scuole a Venezia' *cit.*, p. 767

9   See E. Curtius, *European Literature and the Latin Middle Ages* (transl. W. Trask), London, 1952; A. Schiaffini, 'Dante, retorica, Medioevo' in *Atti del congresso internazionale di studi danteschi*, *cit.*, ii, 155–86

Ch. 9   Authorship

For the influence of the notary and administrator among authors see: *Il notariato nella civiltà italiana*, ed. Consiglio nazionale del notariato, Milan,

1961; E. Motta, 'Notai milanesi del trecento', *Archivio storico lombardo*, xxii, 1895; D. Marzi, *La cancelleria della republica fiorentina*, Rocca S. Casciano, 1910; and L. Lazzarini, *Paolo di Bernardo e i primordi dell' umanesimo in Venezia*, Geneva, 1930.

On the social position of the Italian humanist, see J. K. Hyde, *Padua in the age of Dante*, Manchester, 1966, ch. 10, and Lauro Martines, *The Social World of the Florentine Humanists 1390–1460*, London, 1963.

The life and writings of Dante present an inexhaustible source for conflict among scholars. To some of the *cruces* a good introduction is U. Cosmo *A Handbook to Dante Studies*, translated by D. Moore, Oxford, 1950. The earliest biographies have been reprinted in A. Solerti, *Le vite di Dante, Petrarca e Boccaccio scritte fino al secolo XVI*, Milan, 1904; and in translation by Philip H. Wicksteed, *The Early Lives of Dante*, London, 1904. All documents referring to the poet and his family are drawn together in *Codice diplomatico dantesco*, ed. R. Piattoli, Florence, 1950. A major source, of course, are the poet's own writings. From this material the latest biography is that of S. A. Chimenez in *Dizionario biografico degli italiani*, vol. ii, Rome, 1960, pp. 385–451.

On Dante at Ravenna I follow A. Torre, *I Polentani fino al tempo di Dante*, Florence, 1966, pp. 215–29.

On Boccaccio's life the only wholly satisfactory study is V. Branca's 'Profilo biografico', pp. 2–302, which prefaces vol. 1 of his *Tutte le opere di Giovanni Boccaccio*, Verona, 1967. In addition E. G. Léonard has written an interesting defence of Acciaiuoli in his relations with Boccaccio in his *Boccace et Naples*, Paris, 1944.

On Petrarch's life reference need only be made to the numerous studies of E. H. Wilkins, particularly *The Making of the 'Canzoniere' and other Petrarchian Studies*, Rome, 1951; *Studies in the Life and Works of Petrarch, Petrarch's Eight Years at Milan, Petrarch's Later Years*, all published at Cambridge, Mass., 1955, 1958, and 1959, respectively, and his summary, *Life of Petrarch*, Chicago, 1961.

1 *Familiares*, xiii, 7, as translated in J. H. Robinson and H. W. Rolfe, *Petrarch: The first modern scholar and man of letters*, cit., pp. 162–9

2 Cf. this passage in *De vulgari eloquentia*, I, xvii, 5, with the thesis of E. P. Goldschmidt, *Mediaeval Texts and their first appearance in Print*, Oxford, 1943, pp. 88–116

3 On which see H. Wieruszowski, '*Ars dictaminis* in the time of Dante', *Mediaevalia et humanistica*, i, 1943, pp. 95–108

Part III   Italian Culture and Society in Transition
(*c.* 1380–*c.* 1420)

The Environment of Art

Ch. 10   Social and Cultural Change, 1380–1420

For art in this period there are, in addition to the more general works already cited, valuable studies by L. Castelfranchi Vegas, *International Gothic Art in Italy*, translated by B. D. Phillips, revised by D. Talbot Rice, Leipzig, 1966, and Charles Seymour Jr., *Sculpture in Italy 1400–1500*, Harmondsworth, 1966. Among numerous works on individual artists, one should particularly mention Richard Krautheimer (with T. Krautheimer-Hess), *Lorenzo Ghiberti*, Princeton, 1956, and H. W. Janson, *The Sculpture of Donatello*, Princeton, 1957. On Italian literature the studies of Sapegno and Rossi, cited in the bibliography to chapter 1, give an adequate introduction.

For the debate on the economy in this period see C. M. Cipolla, 'The trends in Italian economic history in the later Middle Ages', *Economic History Review*, 1949; R. S. Lopez and H. A. Mismikin, 'The economic depression of the Renaissance', *ibid.*, 1962; C. M. Cipolla, 'Economic depression of the Renaissance?', *ibid.*, 1964; E. A. Kosminsky, 'Peut-on considérer le xive et le xve siècles comme l' époque de la décadence de l'économie européene?' in *Studi di onore di A. Sapori, cit.*, i, 553–69; F. C. Lane, 'The Cambridge Economic History; The Medieval Period', *The Journal of Economic History*, 1963; and the articles in *Città, mercanti, dottrine: Saggi in memoria di Gino Luzzato*, ed. A. Fanfani, Milan, 1964.

Evidence of 'depression' is stressed particularly in E. Fiumi, 'Fioritura e decadenza dell' economia fiorentina', *ASI*, 1957–9, and J. Heers, *Gênes au XVe siècle*, Paris, 1961. These claims are to be contrasted with C. M. Cipolla, 'I precedenti economici' in *Storia di Milano*, viii, Milan, 1957, pt. 3; D. F. Dowd, 'The economic expansion of Lombardy 1300–1500', *The Journal of Economic History*, 1961; G. Miani, 'L'économie lombarde aux xive et xve siècles: un exception à la règle?', *Annales*, xix, 1964; F. Melis, 'La vita economica di Firenze al tempo di Dante', *Atti del congresso internazionale di studi danteschi, cit.*, ii, 99–128. For the arguments from the fluctuations in gold–silver exchange rates see C. M. Cipolla, *Studi di storia della moneta, I movimenti dei cambi in Italia dal secolo xiii al xv* Pavia, 1948. R. A. Goldthwaite's *Private Wealth in Renaissance Florence*, Princeton, 1968, suggests that there is no withdrawal from investment in commerce by the Florentine upper-class.

On the Church in the great schism the fullest and most recent account is E. Delaruelle, E. R. Labande, and P. Ouliac, *L'Eglise au temps du Grand Schisme et de la Crise Conciliaire* (Histoire de l'Eglise, ed. A. Fliche and V. Martin, vol. 14), Paris, 1963. For the war between Florence and Milan see D. M. Bueno de Mesquita, *Giangaleazzo Visconti*, Cambridge, 1941. A different interpretation is to be found in H. Baron, 'A struggle for liberty in the Renaissance', *American Historical Review*, 58, 1953. In this and his other works Baron argues for an idealistic Florentine foreign policy and accepts the truth of Bruni's claims about the character of the Florentine constitution.

On Humanism see E. Garin, *L' umanesimo italiano*, Bari, 1958 (and in English translation, Oxford, 1965), and the writings of Hans Baron, summarised in his *The Crisis of the Early Italian Renaissance*, Princeton, 1955 (and revised one volume edition, 1966). Baron's most learned interpretation of humanism in this period has powerfully influenced scholarly thought, and all students of the period will acknowledge their debt to him. But the general outlines of his theories have not escaped criticism. See particularly: G. Sasso, 'Florentina libertas e Rinascimento italiano nell' opera di Hans Baron', *Rivista storica italiana*, 1957; P. O. Kristeller, 'Studies in Renaissance Humanism during the last twenty years', *Studies on the Renaissance*, ix, 1962; J. E. Seigel, '"Civic Humanism" or Ciceronian rhetoric? The culture of Petrarch and Bruni', *Past and Present*, July, 1966; and the review by P. J. Jones in *History*, 1968, pp. 410–13. Baron has replied to his critics in: 'Leonardo Bruni', *Past and Present*, 36, 1967; and *From Petrarch to Leonardo Bruni*, Chicago, 1968, chs. 3, 4, and 5. George Holmes, *The Florentine Enlightenment 1400–50*, London, 1969, gives a well-balanced account of both humanism and art in the period, On Milanese humanism, see E. Garin, 'La cultura milanese nella prima metà del xv secolo', *Storia di Milano, cit.*, vi, pt. 4, chs. 1–3.

On Greek studies see K. M. Setton, 'The Byzantine background to the Italian Renaissance', *Proceedings of the American Philosophical Society*, 100, 1956; and R. Weiss, 'The Greek culture of South Italy in the Later Middle Ages', *Proceedings of the British Academy*, xxxvii, 1951. On the influence of humanism on art and literature see E. H. Gombrich, 'From the revival of letters to the reform of the Arts', *Essays in the History of Art presented to Rudolf Wittkower*, London, 1967, and C. Grayson, 'Dante and the Renaissance', *cit.*

On patronage see, for the Gonzaga, *Mantova: Le arti*, ed. G. Paccagnini, *cit.*, i; on Bologna, F. Gatti, *La basilica petroniana*, Bologna, 1913; on Siena, Florence, Venice, and the Visconti, the works cited in the bibliographies to chapters 4, 5, and 6.

On Milan cathedral the documents of the *Veneranda Fabbrica* for this period have been (sometimes arbitrarily and inaccurately) registered and in part published in *Annali della Fabbrica del Duomo di Milano*, Milan, 1877–85, vols. I and 2, and *Appendice*, vols. I and 2. See also A. Nava, *Memorie e documenti storici intorno all' origine* . . . *del Duomo di Milano*, Milan, 1854; Romussi, *Milano ne' suoi monumenti, cit.*, ii, chs. 22–7; P. Mezzanotte, 'Il duomo' in *Storia di Milano, cit.*, vi, 856–931; G. Bascapè and P. Mezzanotte, *Il duomo di Milano*, Milan, 1965; and E. Bishop, 'How a cathedral was built in the fourteenth century', *Downside Review*, July 1899 (reprinted in his *Liturgica Historica*, Oxford, 1918, pp. 411–21).

1 cf. H. Baron, 'A sociological explanation of the early Renaissance in Florence', *South Atlantic Quarterly*, 28, 1939; and F. Antal, *Florentine Painting, cit.*, pp. 25–31; 55–8, 86–8, 105–9

2 Krautheimer, *Ghiberti, cit.*, pp. 77–8

3 Garin, 'La cultura milanese', *cit.*, p. 547

4 M. Meiss, *French Painting in the time of Jean de Berry; The Late Fourteenth Century and the Patronage of the Duke*, London, 1967, pp. 53–8

5 On which see Rubinstein, 'Political ideas in Sienese art', *cit.;* and S. Symeonides, *Taddeo di Bartolo*, Siena, 1965, pp. 40–153

6 F. Gatti, *La basilica petroniana, cit.*, p. 291

7 Milanesi, *Documenti, cit.*, ii, 39

8 C. Magenta, *I Visconti e gli Sforza nel Castello di Pavia, cit.*, ii, 65

9 *Annali della Fabbrica, cit.*, i, 49

10 *Idem, Appendici*, i, 49

Ch. 11   The Artist in Society—I   The Idea of the Artist
For fuller references to the material in this chapter, see my 'The Artist and the Intellectuals in Fourteenth Century Italy', *History*, 1969. On the artist in early medieval Europe see F. Bologna, '"Operis causa non fervor devotionis"; Spunti di critica d' arte medioevale', *Paragone-Arte*, xii, no. 137, 1961; Johannes Jahn, 'Die Stellung des Künstlers im Mittelalter', *Festgabe für Friedrich Bülow*, ed. O. Stammer and K. C. Thalheim, Berlin, 1966; George Henderson, *Gothic*, Harmondsworth, 1967, ch. 1. In addition the second Italian edition of J. von Schlosser's *La letteratura artistica*, Florence 1956, with bibliographical additions by O. Kurz, gives some good general guidance.

On the liberal and mechanical arts see E. Bonnaffé, *Arts liberaux et Arts serviles*, Paris, 1895; R. Wittkower, *The Artist and the Liberal Arts*, London,

1952; P. O. Kristeller, 'The modern system of the arts', *Journal of the History of Ideas*, 12, 1951; 13, 1952. For this chapter the writings on art criticism in the fourteenth century provide much information; see Lionello Venturi, 'La critica d'arte in Italia durante i secoli xiv e xv', *L' arte*, xx, 1917; *idem*, 'La critica d' arte alla fine del trecento (Filippo Villani e Cennino Cennini)', *L' arte*, xxviii, 1925; R. Krautheimer, 'Die Anfänge der Kunstgeschichtschreibung in Italien', *Repertorium für Kunstwissenschaft*, 1929; R. Assunto, *La critica d' arte nel pensiero medievale*, Milan, 1964. For Petrarch and Boccaccio on art see L. Venturi, 'La critica d' arte e Francesco Petrarca', *L' arte*, xxv, 1922; Prince d'Essling and E. Müntz, *Pétrarque: ses études d' art*, Paris, 1902; L. Chiovenda, 'Die Zechnungen Petrarcas', *Archivium Romanicum*, xvii, 1933; A. Prandi, 'L' attesa dell' arte nuova dal Boccaccio al Cennino' in *L' attesa dell' età nuova nella spiritualità della fine del Medioevo*, Todi, 1962, pp. 336–69.

On Giovanni Pisano, see John White, *Art and Architecture in Italy, cit.*, pp. 68–89; H. Keller, *Giovanni Pisano*, Vienna, 1924; A. Venturi, *Giovanni Pisano*, Paris, 1928. On Giotto, I. B. Supino, *Giotto*, Florence, 1920, i, 315–20; Peter Murray, 'Notes on some early Giotto sources', *JWCI*, xvi, 1953.

1 For this and the following passages, 'De remediis utriusque fortunae' in Francesco Petrarca, *Opera Omnia*, Basle, 1581, Lib. i, Dial. xl, xli, pp. 39–41

2 *L' ottimo commento della Divina Commedia*, ed. A. Torri, Pisa, 1827–9, ii, 186–8; Benvenuto da Imola, *Comentum super Dantis Aldigherii Comoediam*, Florence, 1887, iii, 310

3 C. Guasti, *S. Maria del Fiore, cit.*, p. 43. Cf. W. Paatz, 'Die Gestalt Giottos im Spiegel einer zeitgenössischen Urkunde' in *Eine Gabe der Freunde für Carl George Heise*, ed. E. Meyer, Berlin, 1950, pp. 85–102

4 Cennino d' Andrea Cennini, *Il libro dell' arte*, ed. D. V. Thompson (text and translation into English), New Haven, 1932. Schlosser-Magnino, *La letterature artistica, cit.*, p. 77, dates this work to 1390. Thompson believes it unlikely to have been composed before 1396

5 The text of Filippo Villani's *Liber de origine civitatis Florentiae et eiusdem famosis civibus* has been printed in J. von Schlosser, *Quellenbuch zur Kunstgeschichte des Abendländischen Mittelalters*, Vienna, 1896. I have compared this passage with Villani's manuscript draft of the book in the Laurentian Library at Florence (Laurenziana-Ashburnhamiani, 942 (873), f. 36r) which was marginally annotated by Salutati. For the date see Novati's note in *L'epistolario di Coluccio Salutati*, Rome, 1891–1911, ii, 47. The passage is reproduced again in the Vatican manuscript of the work (Biblioteca

Apostolica Vaticana, Fondo barberiniano latino, 2610 (xxxiii, 130), written in 1395-7 (for which date see A. F. Massèra, 'Le più antiche biografie di Boccaccio', *Zeitschrift für Romanische Philologie*, 27, 1903, pp. 298-338). The old translation into Italian: F. Villani, *Le vite d' uomini illustri fiorentini*, ed. G. Mazzucchelli, Florence, 1847, p. 47, omits much of importance in the original

6   Pier Paolo Vergerio, 'De ingenuis moribus', *cit.*, pp. 122-3

7   See M. Baxandall, 'Guarino, Pisanello, and Manuel Chrysoloras', *JWCI*, 1965

Ch. 12   The Artist in Society—II   Workshop and Guild
There has been little written on the social history of the *trecento* artist. F. Antal, *Florentine painting and its social background*, *cit.*, is, on balance, misleading. Much the same is true of the incidental remarks on our period found in Arnold Hauser, *The Social History of Art*, London, 1951; and G. G. Coulton, *Art and the Reformation*, Cambridge, 1953. But, as ever, John White's *Art and Architecture*, *cit.*, is useful, and Andrew Martindale, 'The changing status of the craftsman', in *The Flowering of the Middle Ages*, ed. Joan Evans, London, 1966, gives an interesting survey of the European position. Both Martin Wackernagel, *Der Lebensraum des Künstler in der florentinischen Renaissance*, Leipzig, 1938; and U. Procacci, 'Di Jacopo di Antonio e delle compagnie di pittori del Corso degli Adimari nel xv secolo', *Rivista d' arte*, xxxv, 1961, deal with the period after 1420, though some of their information has relevance to previous years. Hans Huth, *Künstler und Werkstatt der Spätgotik*, Augsburg, 1932, confines itself almost wholly to German experience. Giorgio Vasari's famous *Le vite di più eccelenti pittori, scultori ed architettori* is unreliable on the *Trecento*, but can be read with profit in the editions of G. Milanesi (vols. 1 and 2, Florence, 1878) and K. Frey (of which only pt. i, vol. 1 was published, Munich, 1911). Much of value can be gleaned from D. E. Colnaghi, *A Dictionary of Florentine Painters from the 13th to the 17th centuries*, ed. P. G. Konody and S. Brinton, London, 1928. There are also some portrayals of artists in the contemporary stories of Boccaccio's *Decameron* and Franco Sacchetti's *Il trecentonovelle*. But most of my information here is taken from the collections of documents made by Milanesi, Gaye, Borghesi and Banchi, etc.

For the guilds, see, for Siena, Milanesi, *Documenti*, *cit.*, i, 1-104; V. Lusini, 'Dell' arte del legname innanzi al suo statuto del 1426' in *Arte antica senese*, *cit.*, i, 183-246; for Perugia, L. Manzoni, *Statuti e matricoli dell' arte dei pittori del secolo XIV*, Rome, 1904, pp. 29-50; for Venice, *I capitolari delle arti veneziane*, ed. G. Monticolo, Rome, 1896-1914, ii, 363-

89 (painters, 1271, with additions to 1311); i, 115–34, 257–63 (goldsmiths, 1233, with additions to 1324); ii, 283–305 (masons, 1271, with additions to 1325). For Florence, see 'Statuto del membro dei pittori del 1315' in *Statuti dell' arte dei medici e speziali*, ed. R. Ciasca, Florence, 1922; and R. Ciasca, *L' arte dei medici e speziali*, Florence, 1927, pp. 37–9, 65–9, 98 131–6. Both Gaye (who published their statutes, *Carteggio*, ii, 32–43) and Manzoni, *cit.*, confused 'the Company of St Luke' with a guild proper; see C. Fiorilli, 'I dipintori a Firenze nell' arte dei medici, speziali e merciai', *ASI*, 78, 1920, vol. 2. On the company of St Luke see, too, R. G. Mather, 'Il primo registro della compagnia di S. Luca', *L' arte*, xl, 1938.

On the architect see N. Pevsner, 'The term "Architect" in the Middle Ages', *Speculum*, 1942; and Braunfels, *Mittelalterliche Stadtbaukunst, cit.*, ch. 6. I should warn the reader that most art historians give a much more personal role to the builder's work in this period, and see someone much more like the modern architect at work, than I do; compare, for instance, W. Paatz, *Werden und Wesen der Trecento Architektur in Toskana*, Burg, 1938; and John Harvey, 'The Mason's skill; the development of architecture', in *The Flowering of the Middle Ages, cit.*

1   'Note e documenti per la vita e le opere di Simone e Donato Martino, di Lippo e Tederigo Memmi', in his *Fonti e commenti per la storia dell' arte senese*, Siena, 1954, ch. ii

2   On Lando di Pietro and Memmi, Gaye, *Carteggio, cit.*, i, 103; Milanesi, *Documenti, cit.*, i, 228–31; 103

3   R. Piattoli, 'Un mercante del trecento', *cit.*, xi, 1929, pp. 397–403

4   On numbers of artists, see Davidsohn, *Forschungen, cit.*, ii, 309; P. Bacci, *Fonti e commenti, cit.*, pp. 97–107; Ciasca, *L' arte dei medici e speziali, cit.*, pp. 696, 701; Davidsohn, *Geschichte von Florenz, cit.*, iv, pt. 2, pp. 16, 19, 29–31; Colnaghi, *cit., passim;* for Arezzo goldsmiths, Milanesi, *Nuovi documenti, cit.*, pp. 53–4

5   For this and the following passage, Lorenzo Ghiberti, *I Commentari, cit.*, p. 32 (cf. Ernst Kris, *Psychoanalytic Explorations in Art*, London, 1953, pp. 64–84); *Commento alla Divina Commedia d' Anonimo Fiorentino del secolo XIV*, ed. P. Fanfani, Bologna, 1866–74, ii, 187–8

6   Antonia di Tuccio Manetti, *Filippo Brunelleschi*, ed. H. Holzinger, Stuttgart, 1887, pp. 6–7 (cf. C. von Fabriczy, *Filippo Brunelleschi*, Stuttgart, 1892, pp. 1–3)

7   For contracts of apprenticeship: Milanesi, *Nuovi documenti, cit.*, pp. 10–15, 18, 23, 27, 30, 35, *idem, Documenti, cit.*, i, 174–5; ii, 65–7; Davidsohn,

Forschungen, iii, 224–6; V. Ottokar, 'Pittori e contratti d' apprendimento presso pittori a Firenze alla fine del dugento', *Rivista d' arte*, xix, 1937

8   Lapo Mazzei, *Lettere di un notaro a un mercante del secolo xiv*, ed. C. Guasti, Florence, 1880, ii, 96

9   Federigo Alizeri, *Notizie dei professori del disegno in Liguria dalle origini al secolo xvi*, Genoa, 1870–80, i, 404–5

10   Milanesi, *Documenti, cit.*, i, 194

11   Ghiberti, *Commentari, cit.*, p. 41

12   For the contracts in this and the following paragraph: Milanesi, *Documenti, cit.*, i, 307–9; Borghesi and Banchi, *Nouvi documenti, cit.*, 12–13; Milanesi, *Nuovi documenti, cit.*, pp. 36, 134–5

13   Milanesi, *Documenti, cit.*, ii, 67–8

14   R. and M. Wittkower, *Born under Saturn*, London, 1963, p. 10

15   St Thomas Aquinas, *Summa theologiae*, vol. 28, *Law and Political Theory*, ed. T. Gilbey, London, 1963, ia2ae, 93, 3, p. 58. I must thank my colleague Dr M. T. Clanchy for this reference

16   Gaye, *Carteggio, cit.*, i, 445–6

17   See note 3 to chapter 11

18   On whom, A. Gatti, *La basilica petroniana*, Bologna, 1913, ch. 1

19   A. Doren, 'Zum Bau der Florentiner Domkuppel', *Repertorium für Kunstwissenschaft*, xxi, pt. 4, 1898, p. 13. See too, White, *Art and Architecture, cit.*, pp. 166–7, on the limitations of Maitani's building technique at Orvieto

20   See J. S. Ackermann, 'Ars sine scientia nihil est, Gothic theory of architecture at the cathedral of Milan', *Art Bulletin*, 1949; and the discussion in P. Frankl, *The Gothic: Literary Sources and Interpretations through eight Centuries*, Princeton, 1960

Ch. 13   The Artist in Society—III   The Art Market

Obviously many of the works referred to in the bibliographies to the previous chapters are relevant here. Some information is also to be found, for the end of our period, in Hannah Lerner-Lehmkuhl, *Zur Struktur und Geschichte der florentinischen Kunstmarktes im 15. Jahrhundert*, Wattenscheid, 1936, and Charles Seymour Jr., *Sculpture in Italy 1400–1500*, Harmondsworth, 1966, pp. 10 ff.

See too, on the trade in art, R. Brun, 'Notes sur le commerce des objets d' art en France et principalement à Avignon à la fin du xivᵉ siècle', *Bibliothèque des écoles des chartres*, xcv, 1934; R. Piattoli, 'Un mercante del trecento e gli artisti del tempo suo', *Rivista d' arte*, xi, 1929, 227–52; Ruth Grönwoldt, 'Florentiner Stickereien in dem Inventaren des Herzogs von Berry und der Herzöge von Burgund', *Mitteilungen des Kunsthistorischen Instituts in Florenz*, x, 1961–3. On pattern books, R. W. Scheller, *A Survey of Medieval Model Books*, Haarlem, 1963.

On Francesco di Marco Datini as patron, see Iris Origo, *The Merchant of Prato*, rev. ed., Harmondsworth, 1963; and, for a less enthusiastic assessment of the man, A. Sapori, 'Cambiamento di mentalità del grande operatore economico tra la seconda metà del trecento e i primi del quattrocento' in his *Studi di storia economica, cit.*, iii, 457–85. Important material on Datini is also found in R. Piattoli, 'Un mercante del trecento' *cit.*, above, xi, 396–437, 536–79; xii, 97–150; Lapo Mazzei, *Lettere, cit.*, especially, ii, 383–443; I. B. Supino, 'Una ricordanza inedita di Francesco Datini', *Rivista d' arte*, v, 1907; G. Livi, *Dall' archivio di Francesco Datini, mercante pratese*, Florence, 1910; F. Melis, *Aspetti della vita economica medievale*, Florence, 1962, i, 58–9.

On the market for domestic art, see A. Schiaparelli, *La casa fiorentina e i suoi arredi nei secoli xiv e xv*, vol. 1, Florence, 1928, and M. Praz, *An Illustrated History of Interior Decoration*, London, 1964.

1 Giovanni Dominici, *Regola del governo di cura familiare*, ed. D. Salvi, Florence, 1860, pp. 131–2

2 Alizeri, *Notizie, cit.*, i, 156–7

3 On fresco technique, see Eve Borsook's introduction to her *The Mural Painters of Tuscany*, London, 1960, and Oertel, *Die Frühzeit der italienischen Malerei, cit.*, pp. 76–9, 101–2. On Giotto as 'protomagister', see Morisani, *Pittura del Trecento in Napoli, cit.*, p. 141

4 Milanesi, *Documenti, cit.*, i, 50

5 Thomas Walsingham, *Gesta Abbatum Monasterii S. Albani*, ed. T. H. Riley, London, 1869, iii, 381

6 See for Duccio, *Appendix*, A.2. For the Neapolitan payments, H. W. Schulz, *Denkmäler der Kunst des Mittelalters in Unteritalien*, ed. F. von Quast, Dresden, 1860, iv, 127 (Cavallini), iii, 165 (Martini)

7 See *Appendix*, A7, B7, B8

8 See *Appendix*, D6

9 See *Appendix*, F

10 Borghesi and Banchi, *Nuovi documenti, cit.*, 17–19, 27–8, 49; Milanesi, *Documenti, cit.*, i, 243–4; idem, *Nuovi documenti, cit.*, pp. 57–8

11   M. B. Becker, 'Notes on the Monte holdings of Florentine Trecento painters', *Art Bulletin*, xlvi, 1964; M. Levi d'Ancona, *Miniature e miniatori a Firenze dal xiv al xvi secolo*, Florence, 1962, p. 77

12   Martines, *Social World, cit.*, pp. 356 (no. 16), 357 (no. 50)

13   See Colnaghi, *Dictionary, cit.*, under names

14   White, *Art and Architecture, cit.*, pp. 294–7

15   Milanesi, *Documenti, cit.*, i, 269–71

16   Milanesi, *Documenti, cit.*, ii, 33; Poggi, *Il duomo, cit.*, pp. 24–7

17   S. Symeonides, *Taddeo di Bartolo, cit.*, pp. 125–6

18   Milanesi, *Documenti, cit.*, ii, 28

19   Fumi, *Il duomo di Orvieto, cit.*, p. 326

20   See H. Denifle, 'Die Statuten der Juristen-Universität Bologna vom J. 1317–1347', *Archiv für Litteratur und Kirchengeschichte des Mittelalters*, iii, 1887 (for Padua, *idem*, v, 1892)

21   A. Lisini, 'Notizie di orafi e di oggetti di oreficeria senesi', *Arte antica senese, cit.*, ii, 659

Conclusion

1   A. von Martin, *The Sociology of the Renaissance*, Oxford, 1944

2   Gaye, *Carteggio inedito, cit.*, i, 124–5

3   For which see A. R. Goldthwaite, *Private Wealth in Renaissance Florence*, Princeton, 1968, especially pp. 251 ff.

4   George Holmes, *The Florentine Enlightenment 1400–1500*, London, 1969

5   See Baron, *Crisis*, 1966 ed., *cit.*, pp. 134–45

Index